Succession Law
in Ireland

SUCCESSION LAW IN IRELAND

Dr Albert Keating
BCL, LLB, LLM, BL, DLitt

CLARUS PRESS

Published by
Clarus Press Ltd,
Griffith Campus,
South Circular Road,
Dublin 8.
www.claruspress.ie

Typeset by
Gough Typesetting Services,
Dublin

Printed by
CPI Antony Rowe,
Chippenham,
Wiltshire

ISBN
978-1-905536-72-6

A catalogue record for this book is available from the British Library

To my Mother, Maureen

FOREWORD

At the present time it is probably a comfort to legal practitioners that succession is not as susceptible to "boom and bust" as other areas of the law. While the value of estates may be less than it was in 2006 and 2007, I would assume that succession and administration of estates is generating as much business for legal practitioners as usual.

What may be a source of discomfort to legal practitioners practising in the area of the law of succession is that the law gets more complicated year by year, with the enactment of new legislation, for example, relatively recently the enactment of the Civil Partnership and Certain Rights and Obligations of Cohabitants Act 2010. The law of succession is also the source of much litigation at every level in the court system. At High Court level and above, it tends to give rise to a not inconsiderable amount of case law with which legal practitioners should be familiar.

The essential tool of the trade of a legal practitioner practising in any area of law is an up-to-date legal text which informs him or her of the current state of the law. I might add *en passant* that judges also need, and value, such legal texts.

Having considered the content of Dr. Keating's book on *Succession Law in Ireland*, I believe that it fills the needs of the legal practitioner practising in the area of succession law admirably. The chapter headings and the summary of the contents of the chapters bear that out. Chapters 2 to 6 deal with the execution of wills, testamentary capacity, revocation and revival of wills and various matters which the legal practitioner should be aware of at the stage of drafting a will for a client. Chapter 7 deals with intestate succession. Chapters 8, 9 and 10 deal with statutory rights which members of the family of a testator can enforce, for example, the legal right of a spouse under the Succession Act 1965, the legal right of a civil partner under the Civil Partnership and Certain Rights and Obligations of Cohabitants Act 2010, and the moral duty of testators to children under s. 117 of the Succession Act 1965.

Notwithstanding that the law on succession was codified just a half century ago in the Succession Act 1965, the common law and equitable principles still impact on the law of succession. Chapter 11 deals with *donationes mortis causa* (one of the few Latin "tags" which remains in the area of chancery, property and succession law!), joint bank accounts and suchlike. Chapter 12 deals with equitable property rights such as proprietary estoppel. In order to properly advise a client, the legal practitioner practising in this area must understand the relevant legal and equitable principles.

At a practical level, Dr. Keating deals in succeeding chapters with the intricacies of applications for grants of probate and administration. He also deals with the practicalities of the administration and distribution of the estate of a deceased person.

As regards the involvement of the courts, various types of litigation are dealt with in succeeding chapters. For example, fairly frequent applications, probate motions and applications under s. 27(4) of the Succession Act 1965, are dealt with in Chapter 20. Costs of probate and administration actions are dealt with in Chapter 21.

Of particular importance to legal practitioners who are involved in the drafting of wills, which probably includes every solicitor at some time in his or her career, is to understand the principles governing the construction of wills, which is dealt with in Chapter 22. Perhaps of even more importance from the practitioner's perspective is to be fully *au fait* with and understand the application of statutory limitation provisions to succession claims, which is discussed in Chapter 23.

The next four chapters of the book will be of particular assistance to legal practitioners. They contain wills precedents, probate precedents and administration precedents. The final chapter contains Succession Act precedents. It contains useful templates for notices as diverse as giving a surviving spouse notice of his or her right of appropriation of the dwelling and household chattels under s. 56 of the Succession Act 1965 and a statutory notice to creditors under s. 49 of the same Act.

I have outlined the contents of Dr. Keating's very focused publication to illustrate that it is an essential item in the toolkit of legal practitioners who practise in the area of succession law. They owe a debt of gratitude to Dr. Keating for making their working life easier. In saying that, I am not overlooking the benefit which academics, students and judges will derive from it.

Mary Laffoy
The Supreme Court
May 2015

PREFACE

Succession law is that branch of the law which provides the rules for the creation of testate and intestate succession rights to property on the death of a person. Testate succession rights are created by will in the form devises, legacies and bequests that take effect from the date of death of the testator. Intestate succession rights accrue when a person dies without making a will, or where a will made by him or her is invalid or ineffective, and are governed by the rules of intestacy which in turn are based on the degree of relationship to the deceased by means of affinity or consanguinity. Succession rights may also be made subject to other rights like the statutory legal right of a surviving spouse or civil partner. Since the enactment of the Succession Act 1965 (the 1965 Act), where a spouse dies leaving a will, a surviving spouse will have an automatic legal right share in the estate of the deceased spouse, and since the Civil Partnership and Certain Rights and Obligations of Cohabitants Act 2010 (the 2010 Act) so also will a surviving civil partner. The legal right of a surviving spouse or civil partner will have priority over devises, legacies and bequests, and shares on intestacy. Also, under s.117 of the 1965 Act, where the court is of opinion that a testator has failed in his or her moral duty to make proper provision for his or her child the court may order that such provision be made for the child out of the estate. Since the 2010 Act, qualified cohabitants within the meaning of the Act may apply to the courts for adequate provision to be made for them out of estate of a deceased qualified cohabitant. Property rights in the form of *donationes mortis causa* may become effective on the date of death of a person or may arise out of the application of an equitable doctrine like proprietary estoppel, and where such rights are established they may impinge on or even supplant succession rights created by wills or arising out of intestacies.

Even though testate and intestate succession rights to property are effective from the date of death they do not immediately vest in beneficiaries. This is because s.10 of the 1965 Act provides that that the real and personal estate of a deceased person devolve on and vest in his personal representatives and they hold the estate as trustees for the persons entitled to it by law. However, before the personal representatives can proceed to administer and distribute the estate they must first obtain a grant of representation to the estate. Where a will exists and executors are appointed by it and willing to act as such they may, having completed the essential proofs, apply to the Probate Office or a District Probate Registry for a grant of probate. Where there is a will but the executors have either predeceased the testator or have renounced their entitlement to apply for a grant of probate, the person entitled under Order 79 of the Rules of the Superior Courts 1986 may, having completed the essential proofs, apply to the Probate Office or a District Probate Registry for a grant of letters of administration with the will annexed. But where there the deceased has died intestate then the person entitled under Order 79 of the Rules of the Superior Courts 1986 may, having completed the essential proofs, apply to the Probate Office or a District Probate Registry for a grant of letters of administration intestate. After the issuing of the relevant grant the personal representatives may then proceed to administer the estate of the deceased person, first, by paying debts owing and due by the estate and discharging liabilities, and secondly, by distributing the estate among the beneficiaries in accordance with the provisions of the will or the rules of intestacy. Also, as the real and personal estate of a deceased person vests in his or her personal representatives under s.10 of the 1965 Act when distributing the estate they must first divest themselves of it by their assent in writing to the vesting of the testamentary gifts or shares on intestacy in the beneficiaries, especially where land is concerned. During the administration of the estate the beneficiaries will have an immediate and beneficial equitable interest in the estate subject however to the administrative and distributive rights of the personal representatives.

Testamentary gifts may fail to take effect where, for instance, it is discovered that the property forming the subject matter of a gift has been disposed of by the testator during his or her lifetime, and, if so, the gift will be adeemed under the probate doctrine of ademption, or that a beneficiary has pre-deceased the testator, and, if so, the gift will lapse and become part of the residuary estate.

Disputes may arise surrounding the issuing of grants to particular applicants, or relating to the rights of beneficiaries, or even relating to the validity of a will, and where such is the case the appropriate proceedings must be instituted, and wherever there is litigation the issue of costs will follow. A defendant may also argue that succession rights to the deceased's estate have become statute-barred by the provisions of the 1965 Act, the Statute of Limitations 1957 or the Civil Liability Act 1961, and where this occurs the onus of proof rests on the defendant to establish that the limitation period for the particular action has expired.

All of the foregoing matters are, inter alia, dealt with in the book from an Irish perspective.

The author wishes to express his sincere gratitude to The Hon. Ms Justice Mary Laffoy, Judge of the Supreme Court, for taking time out of her busy schedule to write a Foreword for the book.

The author is extremely grateful to David McCartney of Clarus Press Ltd and members of his staff for their assistance, great efficiency and encouragement during the course of writing the book.

Albert Keating,
May 2015

SHORT TABLE OF CONTENTS

DETAILED TABLE OF CONTENTS

TABLE OF CASES

TABLE OF LEGISLATION

ACTS OF PARLIAMENT PRE 1922

ACTS OF THE OIREACHTAS

STATUTORY INSTRUMENTS

UNITED KINGDOM

NORTHERN IRELAND

Chapter 1

SUCCESSION RIGHTS

Introduction

Succession rights primarily consist of testate and intestate rights. Testate succession rights are created by a validly executed will by a person who is at least eighteen years old and is of sound disposing mind.[1] Testate succession rights will be determined by the nature and extent of a gift in the will in the form of a devise, legacy or bequest. A validly executed will may also give rise to equitable succession rights where a will also creates a trust in compliance with the rules for creating valid trusts.[2] Where a will is used to create a trust, not only must the will be validly executed, but the creation of the trust must also comply with the rules for creating trusts. These may be called testamentary trusts.[3] Intestate rights of succession are those governed by the rules of distribution on intestacy and are based on relationships by affinity — for instance, a spouse or civil partner — or by consanguinity, for instance, issue or children, to the deceased person who dies without making a will. The quantitative value of the intestate share in the estate will also be governed by the relationship to the deceased person. Testate and intestate rights of succession rights take effect from the date of death of a deceased person. **1–01**

---

1 See s.77(1) of the Succession Act 1965; s.31(1) of the Family Law Act 1995 (marital age is now 18 years); Albert Keating, *Probate Law and Practice* (Dublin: Round Hall, 1999) Chapter 3; Chapter 2 – The Execution of Wills; Chapter 3 – Testamentary Capacity; Albert Keating, *Keating on Probate* (4th ed) (Dublin: Thomson Round Hall, 2011); Albert Keating, *First Supplement to the Fourth Edition of Keating on Probate* (Dublin: Thomson Round Hall, 2013).

2 See Chapter 5 – Testamentary Gifts and Trusts; Albert Keating, *Equitable Succession Rights* (Dublin: Thomson Round Hall, 2005).

3 See Chapter 5 – Testamentary Gifts and Trusts; Albert Keating, *Keating on Probate* (4th ed) (Dublin: Thomson Round Hall, 2011); Albert Keating, *First Supplement to the Fourth Edition of Keating on Probate* (Dublin: Thomson Round Hall, 2013); Albert Keating, *Equitable Succession Rights* (Dublin: Thomson Round Hall, 2005).

1–02 The beneficiaries of testate or intestate succession rights to property of a deceased person do not become immediately entitled to gifts in a will or shares on intestacy. This is because s.10(1) of the Succession Act 1965 (the "1965 Act") provides that the real and personal estate of a deceased person will on his or her death, "notwithstanding any testamentary disposition, devolve on and vest in his personal representatives". Section 10(2) of the 1965 Act provides that:

> "The personal representatives for the time being of a deceased person are deemed in law his heirs and assigns within the meaning of all trusts and powers."

Section 10(3) of the 1965 Act provides that:

> "The personal representatives shall be the representatives of the deceased in regard to his real and personal estate and shall hold the estate as trustees for the persons entitled thereto."

In *O'Hagan v Grogan*[4] Macken J. stated that, under s.10 of the 1965 Act,

> "the whole of the intestate estate vests in the personal representative, who nevertheless does not hold the estate on his own behalf, but (under s.10(3)) as a trustee for the persons in law who are entitled to it, and he must act accordingly".

She added that beneficiaries "have an immediate beneficial equitable interest in the estate by way of trust", subject to the rights of the personal representatives.

1–03 Legal rights also come into existence where a deceased person made a will and is survived by a spouse or civil partner.[5] The legal right is therefore based on the status of spouse or civil partner and on the existence of a will. The quantitative value of the legal right will depend on the existence of children of the marriage or civil partnership. Legal rights are absolute rights and effective from the date of death of the testator spouse or civil partner.

1–04 The children of deceased testator parents may apply to the courts under s.117 of the 1965 Act to have proper provision made for them out of the estate. Section 117(1) provides that:

> "Where, on application by or on behalf of a child of a testator, the court is of opinion that the testator has failed in his moral duty to make proper provision for the child in accordance with his means, whether by his will or otherwise, the court may order that such provision shall be made for the child out of the estate as the court thinks just."

1–05 Two hurdles must be surmounted in such applications to the courts, first,

---

4 [2012] I.E.S.C. 8.

5 See Chapter 8 – The Legal Right of Spouses and Civil Partners and Applications by Qualified Cohabitants.

that the parent testator did not fulfil his or her moral duty towards the child, and secondly, that he or she did not make proper provision for the child in the will. The definition of children encompasses all children of the deceased testator parent including any non-marital children since the enactment of the Status of Children Act 1987.[6] The children of deceased intestate civil partners may apply to the courts to have their intestate share in the estate increased and:

> "the court may, on the application by or on behalf of a child of an intestate who dies leaving a civil partner and one or more children, order that provision be made for that child out of the intestate's estate only if the court is of the opinion that it would be unjust not to make the order".[7]

Qualified cohabitants under s.194 of the Civil Partnership and Certain Rights and Obligations of Cohabitants Act 2010 (the "2010 Act") may also apply to the court for adequate provision to be made for them out of the estate or "net estate" of a deceased cohabitant.[8]

There are also certain property rights which take effect on the date of death of a deceased person,distinguishable from succession rights and the legal rights of surviving spouses and civil partners which take effect from the date of death of a deceased person. *Donationes mortis causa* are an example of such property rights. Once the prerequisites for creating such gifts are satisfied, they become effective on the date of death of the donor. In the case of joint bank accounts: on the death of a joint holder, the survivor becomes the sole owner of the account. Also, an equitable doctrine may give rise to equitable property rights, for instance, where such rights are acquired under the equitable doctrine of proprietary estoppel. Property rights established by way of *donationes mortis causa* or proprietary estoppel may also impinge on the succession rights of beneficiaries where the same property forms the subject matter of gifts in a will or shares on intestacy. **1–06**

Succession Rights

The testate and intestate succession rights of beneficiaries to property, while effective from the date of death of the deceased person, do not immediately vest in them. The estate of a deceased person from the date of his or her death devolves on and vests in his personal representatives.[9] The ultimate intestate and intestate succession rights of beneficiaries are therefore subject to the intermediary rights of personal representatives to the estate **1–07**

---

6 See Chapter 9 – The Moral Duty of Testators.

7 s.73 of the Civil Partnership and Certain Rights and Obligations of Cohabitants Act 2010 amended s.67 of the 1965 Act by inserting a new s.67(A)(3); see Chapter 7 – Intestate Succession.

8 See Chapter 8 – The Legal Right of Spouses and Civil Partners and Applications by Qualified Cohabitants.

9 s.10 of the 1965 Act; see Chapter 19 – The Administration and Distribution of Estates.

of a deceased person, and these intermediary rights are confirmed by the issuing to them of a grant of probate,[10] or letters of administration,[11] for the purposes of administering and distributing the estate. However, that does not necessarily mean that the beneficiaries during the administration of an estate by the personal representatives are devoid of all interest in the estate; beneficiaries "have an immediate beneficial equitable interest in the estate by way of trust", but such interest is subject to the rights of the personal representatives whose powers to deal with the property commence from the date of the issuing of a grant.[12] The property forming the subject matter of succession rights will become vested in the beneficiaries when the personal representatives have divested themselves of the property by assenting to the vesting of it in the beneficiaries.

1–08 The rights of personal representatives consist of duties and powers to administer and distribute the estate of the deceased person.[13] The personal representatives when performing their administrative and distributive duties may exercise such powers as are given to them in the will or by the provisions of the 1965 Act.[14] They may sell or convert the whole or any part of the estate, not only for the payment of debts to creditors, but also for the purpose of distributing the estate among the beneficiaries.[15] They also have powers of appropriation over the whole estate. Under s.55 of the 1965 Act, executors may, for instance, appropriate any part of the estate in or towards the satisfaction of any share in the estate. By virtue of s.56 of the same Act, the executors may be required by the surviving spouse to appropriate the dwelling and household chattels in or towards the satisfaction of that spouse's share in the estate. Under s.57, executors will also be trustees where none is appointed for a minor who is entitled to a share in the estate of a deceased person, and they will have trustee powers for this purpose under s.58. The executors may lease such land and premises as may be reasonably necessary for the due administration of the estate or the trust.[16] In carrying out their duties, they may raise money by way of mortgage or charge for the payment of expenses, debts and liabilities. They may also compromise or settle any debt, account or claim relating to the estate.[17] The executors may also be given additional powers by the testator. Executors may, for instance, be empowered to exercise the power of appropriation under s.55

---

[10] See Chapter 13 – Applications for Grants of Probate.

[11] See Chapter 14 – Applications for Grants of Letters of Administration with Will Annexed; Chapter 15 – Applications for Grants of Letters of Administration Intestate.

[12] *O'Hagan v Grogan* [2012] I.E.S.C. 8.

[13] See Chapter 19 – The Administration and Distribution of Estates; Albert Keating, *Keating on Probate* (4th ed) (Dublin: Thomson Round Hall, 2011); Albert Keating, *First Supplement to the Fourth Edition of Keating on Probate* (Dublin: Thomson Round Hall, 2013); Albert Keating, *The Law and Practice of Personal Representatives* (Dublin: Thomson Round Hall, 2004).

[14] See Chapter 19 – The Administration and Distribution of Estates.

[15] s.50(1) of the 1965 Act.

[16] s.60(1)(a) of the 1965 Act.

[17] s.60(8) of the 1965 Act.

without serving notices or obtaining consents required by the section. They may also be given the power to invest and to change investments freely and to invest in unsecured interest-free loans or other non-income-producing assets, including property for occupation or use by a beneficiary. They may even be allowed by a testator to buy an asset of the estate.

The Nature of Intestate Interests in Estates

In *Gleeson v Feehan*[18] Keane J. (as he then was), when considering the nature of intestate interests during the administration of an estate, stated that, as the whole estate vested in the personal representatives, a beneficiary had no right to claim any part of the estate, and he or she could only insist on the due administration of the estate by the personal representatives. He also stated that, as the whole right of property in the estate vested in the personal representative, there was no need to distinguish between legal and equitable interests in an attempt to show that an equitable interest vested in beneficiaries. He referred to *Commissioner of Stamp Duties (Queensland) v Livingston*[19] and *Sudeley (Lord) v Attorney General*[20] and stated that it cannot be now plausibly contended that the 1965 Act "brought about a wholly different result in Ireland from that identified by the English decisions in *Sudeley's* case, *Barnardo* and *Livingston*". As a result of the decision in *Gleeson v Feehan,* a beneficiary's right to receive a share or interest in a deceased's estate cannot be enforced while the estate is still under administration by the personal representative. The personal representative does not, however, hold the property for his own benefit. He may be properly regarded as a trustee who must perform the duties of his office in the interests of those who are ultimately entitled to the deceased's property, i.e., the beneficiaries. While an estate is still under administration, the beneficiaries will have no legal or equitable interest until the residue is ascertained, but they will have a right to ensure that the estate is being properly administered by the personal representatives. **1–09**

In *O'Hagan v Grogan,*[21] Macken J. looked afresh at the nature of interests in estates during the administration of an estate. In her judgment, she referred to s.10 of the 1965 Act, and stated that, while the whole of an intestate estate vests in personal representatives, they do not hold the estate on their own behalf, but as trustees for the persons in law who are entitled to it. She also stated that, under s.10 of the 1965 Act, **1–10**

> "the whole of the intestate estate vests in the personal representative, who

[18] [1997] 1 I.L.R.M. 522; see Albert Keating, "The Interest of a Creditor and Beneficiary in an Estate under Administration" (2004) 9(3) C.P.L.J. 50.

[19] [1964] 3 All E.R 692.

[20] [1897] A.C. 11.

[21] [2012] I.E.S.C. 8.

> nevertheless does not hold the estate on his own behalf, but (under s.10(3)) as a trustee for the persons in law who are entitled to it, and he must act accordingly".

1–11 She added, however, that beneficiaries "have an immediate beneficial equitable interest in the estate by way of trust", subject to the rights of the personal representatives. Macken J. also considered issues similar to those discussed by Keane J. in *Gleeson v Feehan*, including that of the nature of intestate interests in estates of deceased persons during the administration of estates. It will be remembered that Keane J. based his judgment on former decisions of the English courts, and concluded that, while an estate is being administered, the beneficiaries will have no legal or equitable interest until the residue is ascertained, although they have a right to ensure that the estate is being properly administered by the personal representatives. Macken J. based her judgment on a close interpretation of s.10(1) and s.10(3) of the Act of 1965. She stated that:

> "Under the provisions of s.10(1) of the Act of 1965 the whole of the intestate estate vests in the personal representative, who nevertheless does not hold the estate on his own behalf, but (under s.10(3)) as a trustee for the persons in law who are entitled to it, and he must act accordingly. Those persons have an immediate beneficial equitable interest in the estate by way of trust, which is nevertheless, subject to rights of the administrator, who has certain powers, including, for example, those for the purposes of disposition. The power to deal with the property of an intestate dates only from the date of grant, however, (as opposed to the position of an executor of a person who dies testate where the property vests on death)."

1–12 The judgments of Keane J. in *Gleeson v Feehan* and Macken J. in *O'Hagan v Grogan* share the same view by regarding a personal representative as trustee of the persons who are entitled by law to an estate under administration. Keane J. stated that a personal representative:

> "is properly regarded as a trustee who must perform the duties of his office, not in his own interest, but in the interests of those who are ultimately entitled to the deceased's property, whether as beneficiaries or as creditors."

Macken J. stated that:

> "under the provisions of s.10(1) of the Act of 1965 the whole of the intestate estate vests in the personal representative, who nevertheless does not hold the estate on his own behalf, but (under s.10(3)) as a trustee for the persons in law who are entitled to it, and he must act accordingly".

1–13 But they held divergent views when it came to identifying the nature of the interests of persons entitled to the estate. Keane J. thought that it was contrary to elementary legal principles to treat the persons entitled to a share in the intestate estate of a deceased person as being the owners in equity of specific items forming part of the estate until the balance is ascertained after the payment of expenses, debts and liabilities. Macken J. preferred the view that persons with interests in estates:

> "have an immediate beneficial equitable interest in the estate by way of trust, which is nevertheless, subject to rights of the administrator, who has certain powers, including, for example, those for the purposes of disposition".

It appears now, as a result the decision of the Supreme Court in *O'Hagan v Grogan*, that persons entitled to intestate shares in an estate of a deceased person have an immediate beneficial equitable interest in the estate by way of trust, though subject to the rights of the personal representative whose powers to deal with the property of an intestate commence from the date of a grant of letters of administration intestate.[22] **1–14**

Legal Rights of Spouses and Civil Partners

The legal right is based on the status of spouse or civil partner and the existence of a will, and takes effect on the death of a deceased testator spouse or civil partner. It is an absolute statutory right given by s.111 of the 1965 Act as amended by the 2010 Act and will take priority over all gifts in a will.[23] Its quantitative value will depend on whether or not there also children of a marriage or civil partnership. In *O'Dwyer v Keegan*[24] Barron J. stated that the legal right has the same quality as an interest arising under a will or a share arising on intestacy. **1–15**

Section 111 of the 1965 Act provides that:

> "(1) If the testator leaves a spouse and no children, the spouse shall have a right to one-half of the estate.
>
> (2) If the testator leaves a spouse and children, the spouse shall have a right to one-third of the estate."

Section 80 of the 2010 Act amends the 1965 Act by inserting the following section after s.111 of 1965 Act:

> "111A (1) If the testator leaves a civil partner and no children, the civil partner shall have a right to one-half of the estate. (2) Subject to section 117(3A), if the testator leaves a civil partner and children, the civil partner shall have a right to one-third of the estate."

Section 56 of the 1965 Act as amended by the 2010 Act also gives the surviving spouse or civil partner a right to have the dwelling and household chattels appropriated in or towards the satisfaction of the legal right share.

---

22 See Albert Keating, "The Nature of Intestate and Residuary Interests in Estates in the Course of Administration" (2013) 18(2) C.P.L.J. 26.

23 See Chapter 8 – The Legal Right of Spouses and Civil Partners and Applications by Qualified Cohabitants.

24 [1997] 2 I.L.R.M. 401.

Court Applications by Children and Qualified Cohabitants

1–16 An application may be made to the courts under s.117 of the 1965 Act as amended by the 2010 Act by the children of a deceased parent-testator for proper provision to be made for them out of his or her estate. Section 117(1) of the 1965 Act as amended by the 2010 Act provides that:

> "Where, on application by or on behalf of a child of a testator, the court is of opinion that the testator has failed in his moral duty to make proper provision for the child in accordance with his means, whether by his will or otherwise, the court may order that such provision shall be made for the child out of the estate as the court thinks just."[25]

1–17 The definition of children includes all children of the deceased testator-parent, including a non-marital child since the enactment of the Status of Children Act 1987.[26] In *A v C & Anor*[27] Laffoy J. stated that "the court's function in adjudicating on an application under s.117 of the 1965 Act is a two-stage process". The first stage is to decide whether the testator has failed in his moral duty to make proper provision for the applicant child and that decision is made by reference to the circumstances which prevailed at the date of death of the testator.

1–18 Under the 2010 Act, the children of deceased civil partners may apply to the courts for further provision to be made for them out of the estate of a deceased intestate civil partner.[28] The definition of children includes all children of a deceased intestate civil partner, including a non-marital or non-civil partnership child since the enactment of the Status of Children Act 1987. Section 73 of the 2010 Act amended s.67 of the 1965 by inserting a new s.67(A) and s.67(B). Section 67A(3) provides that the court may, on the application by or on behalf of a child of an intestate who dies leaving a civil partner and one or more children, order that provision be made for that child out of the intestate's estate only if the court is of the opinion that it would be unjust not to make the order.

1–19 Section 67A(1) of the 1965 Act now provides that:

> (1) If an intestate dies leaving a civil partner and no issue, the civil partner shall take the whole estate.
> (2) If an intestate dies leaving a civil partner and issue—
>   (a) subject to subsections (3) to (7), the civil partner shall take two-thirds of the estate; and
>   (b) the remainder shall be distributed among the issue in accordance with section 67B(2).
> (3) The court may, on the application by or on behalf of a child of an intestate

---

[25] See Chapter 9 – The Moral Duty of Testators.
[26] *ibid.*
[27] [2007] I.E.H.C. 120.
[28] See Chapter 7 – Intestate Succession.

who dies leaving a civil partner and one or more children, order that provision be made for that child out of the intestate's estate only if the court is of the opinion that it would be unjust not to make the order, after considering all the circumstances, including—

(a) the extent to which the intestate made provision for that child during the intestate's lifetime,
(b) the age and reasonable financial requirements of that child,
(c) the intestate's financial situation, and
(d) the intestate's obligations to the civil partner.

(4) The court, in ordering provision of an amount under subsection (3), shall ensure that—

(a) the amount to which any issue of the intestate is entitled shall not be less than that to which he or she would have been entitled had no such order been made, and
(b) the amount provided shall not be greater than the amount to which the applicant would have been entitled had the intestate died leaving neither spouse nor civil partner.[29]

The new status of qualified cohabitant introduced by the 2010 Act does not give rise to legal rights similar to spouses and civil partners. Under s.194 of the 2010 Act, however, surviving qualified cohabitants may apply to the court for provision to be made for them out of the estate or "net estate" of a deceased cohabitant.[30] The "net estate" of a deceased cohabitant means the estate that remains after the payment of debts, funeral and testamentary expenses, and the discharge of the legal rights and intestate succession rights of spouses or civil partners.[31] The court, when considering an application by a surviving cohabitant under s.194 of the 2010 Act, may also take into account other court orders made during the lifetime of cohabitants under ss. 174, 175, 187 of the 2010 Act, and the provisions of any cohabitants' agreement.[32] 1–20

Property Rights Effective on Death

A *donatio mortis causa* is an *inter vivos* gift of property effective on the death of the donor. For a valid *donatio mortis causa* to come into existence and receive the recognition of the courts, it must be made in contemplation of the death of the donor. The property forming the subject matter of the *donatio* must be delivered to the donee at the time of its creation. The delivery of the property may be performed by the donor handing it over to the donee. Once these requirements are satisfied, the property forming the subject matter of the *donatio* will become the property of the donee on the death of the donor.[33] But where the existence of a *donatio mortis causa* is 1–21

[29] *ibid.*
[30] See Chapter 8 – The Legal Right of Spouses and Civil Partners and Applications by Qualified Cohabitants.
[31] s.194(11) of the 2010 Act.
[32] See s.202 of the 2010 Act.
[33] See Chapter 11 – *Donationes Mortis Causa*, Joint Bank Accounts and Advancements; Albert Keating, "*Donationes Mortis Causa* in Irish Law" (2005) 10(3) C.P.L.J. 62;

challenged, the onus of proof rests on the donee to show that the conditions for its creation existed at the time the *donatio* was made.[34] The opening of a joint bank account is a form of contract between the joint holders that gives a surviving account holder a legal interest in the monies on deposit. Since the decision of the Supreme Court in *Lynch v Burke*[35] the opening of a joint bank account no longer gives rise to a presumption of a resulting trust, but instead is viewed as a contract between the joint account holders and the bank, giving a surviving account holder a legal interest in the monies on deposit based on the contract.[36]

Equitable Property Rights

1–22 Equitable property rights may be acquired by a person who satisfies the prerequisites of the equitable doctrine of proprietary estoppel.[37] In *Thorner v Major*[38] Lord Walker stated that the concept of proprietary estoppel is based on three fundamental elements:

> "a representation or assurance made to the claimant; reliance on it by the claimant; and detriment to the claimant in consequence of his (reasonable) reliance".[39]

Lord Walker also stated that a claim based on the existence of a proprietary estoppel requires the claimant to prove a promise or assurance that he will acquire a proprietary interest in specified property. In *Naylor v Maher*[40] O'Keeffe J. referred with approval to the decision in *Thorner v Major* and the three fundamental elements for establishing a proprietary estoppel, and also the judgment of Murphy J. in *McCarron v McCarron.*[41] When commenting on the nature of detriment, Murphy J. stated that in

> "a suitable case it may well be argued that a plaintiff suffers as severe a loss or detriment by providing his own labours or services in relation to the lands of another and accordingly should equally qualify for recognition in equity".

The onus of proof rests on the claimant to show that all of the elements necessary for establishing a proprietary estoppel have been satisfied.

Albert Keating, *Keating on Probate* (4th ed) (Dublin: Thomson Round Hall, 2011); Albert Keating, *First Supplement to the Fourth Edition of Keating on Probate* (Dublin: Thomson Round Hall, 2013).

34 *Bentham v Potterton*, Unreported, High Court, Barr J., 28 May 1998.

35 [1996] I.L.R.M. 114.

36 See Chapter 11 – *Donationes Mortis Causa*, Joint Bank Accounts and Advancements.

37 See Chapter 12 – Equitable Property Rights.

38 [2009] U.K.H.L. 18.

39 See also *Snell's Principles of Equity* (28th ed), (London: Sweet & Maxwell, 1982) referred to by Blayney J. in *Haughan v Rutledge* [1988] I.R. 295 at 300 and O'Sullivan J. in *McDonagh v Denton*, Unreported, High Court, 15 April 2005.

40 [2012] I.E.H.C. 408.

41 Unreported, Supreme Court, 13 February 1997.

CHAPTER 2

THE EXECUTION OF WILLS

INTRODUCTION

The execution of wills is governed by s.78 of the Succession Act 1965 (the "1965 Act"). Section 78(1) of the 1965 Act provides that a will, in order to be valid, must be in writing and must be signed "at the foot or end thereof" by the testator "or by some person in his presence and by his direction". Section 78(2) of the 1965 Act provides that the testator's signature must be made "or acknowledged" in the presence of two witnesses present at the same time when he signs his name or acknowledges his signature. It is important to remember when selecting witnesses that, where a beneficiary or his or her spouse or civil partner witnesses a will, any gift to him or her will be nullified.[1] A testator may also sign his will by using initials or by making a mark. Where a testator signs his will in the absence of the witnesses, he may later acknowledge the signature, or the initials or the mark made by him when both witnesses are present. A testator may acknowledge his signature, initials or mark by indicating to the witnesses that the signature, initials or mark was made by him.[2] Each witness must attest by his or her signature "the signature of the testator in the presence of the testator".[3] It is not necessary for the witnesses to sign in the presence of each other, though **2–01**

1 s.82 of the 1965 Act as amended by s.77 of the Civil Partnership and Certain Rights and Obligations of Cohabitants Act 2010; see Chapter 10 – The Cessation of Succession and Legal Rights.

2 *Kavanagh v Fegan* [1932] I.R. 566; see Albert Keating, "The Concept of a Will" (2010) 15(3) C.P.L.J. 46.

3 s.78(2) of the 1965 Act; Albert Keating, *Keating on Probate* (4th ed) (Dublin: Thomson Round Hall, 2011); Albert Keating, *First Supplement to the Fourth Edition of Keating on Probate* (Dublin: Thomson Round Hall, 2013); Albert Keating, *Probate Causes and Related Matters* (Dublin: Round Hall *Sweet & Maxwell*, 2000); Albert Keating, *Keating on Probate – The Complete Works*, CD-ROM (Dublin: Thomson Round Hall, 2004).

the wise course is to have them do so. As regards the position of the testator's signature, s.78(3) of the 1965 Act provides that:

> "it is sufficient if the signature is so placed at or after, or following, or under, or beside, or opposite to the end of the will that it is apparent on the face of the will that the testator intended to give effect by the signature to the writing signed as his will."

2–02 The rules regarding the execution of wills are equally applicable to codicils.[4] It is important to ensure that the attestation clause in a will or codicil is drafted in a way that reflects the rules of execution prescribed by s.78 of the 1965 Act.[5] A testator is free to alter his will, but for an alteration to be valid, it must be made before the execution of the will. If made after the execution of the will, it must done in compliance with s.86 of the 1965 Act. A testator may incorporate executed or unexecuted documents by reference to them in his or her will, but for the incorporation to be effective, the documents referred to must be in existence and identified by the testator at the time of execution. A testator must also be given the opportunity of reading his will, or having it read over to him by another. After he has read it or had it read over to him and indicates his approval of its contents, the will may then be executed. The solicitor who prepares the will owes a duty of care to intended beneficiaries:

> "to draft the will with such reasonable care and skill as to ensure that the wishes of the testator are not frustrated and the expediency of the legatee defeated through lack of considerable care and skill on the part of the solicitor."[6]

The Testator's Signature, Initials or Mark

2–03 While s.78 of the 1965 Act provides that a will must be signed by a testator, it does not specify what constitutes a valid signature for that purpose, although it is now settled law that a testator may sign a will by using his name or initials, or by making a mark in the shape of a cross: thus, X will suffice.[7] A mark may be accepted as a valid signing even though there is no proof that a testator is unable to write. Indeed, a mark will be acceptable even though a testator is able to write. Even where a testator signs in a way different to that specified in the attestation clause, it will still be a valid signing. For instance, a declaration in the attestation clause that the testator made his mark in the presence of the witnesses will not invalidate the will if he uses his initials instead. In *In the Goods of Emerson*[8] the testator affixed a seal

---

4 See Chapter 24 – Wills Precedents.

5 *ibid.*

6 *Wall v Hegarty and Callanan* [1980] I.L.R.M. 124; see *Ross v Caunters* [1980] Ch. 297.

7 See *In the Goods of Blewitt* (1880) L.R. 5 P.D. 116; *In the Estate of Cloney*, Unreported, High Court, Kearns J., 8 October 2001.

8 (1882) 9 L.R. Ir. 443.

stamped with his initials to a will handwritten by himself and placed his finger on the seal saying: "This is my hand and seal." Warren J. held that the testator by touching the seal with his finger when saying "This is my hand and seal" intended the seal to be used as a signature. Although he added that "a seal, *qua* seal, is not sufficient". A will may therefore be signed by a testator using his signature or initials, or by making a mark (X), or by affixing a seal stamped with his initials intending it to be used as his signature.

A testator may also sign under an assumed name, or by using descriptive words of himself, or by making a mark other than by using an X once he does so *animus testandi*. In *In the Goods of Kieran*[9] the testator attempted to initial his will but was only able to make two indecipherable scrawls. But as the scrawls were made "as a personal act or acknowledged as such by him, *animo testandi*, to verify the making of the will as his own act," the will was held to be validly signed. In that case, the will was drawn up by the testator's solicitor in accordance with his instructions. The testator, having first read the will and having expressed satisfaction with it, commenced to sign it. However, as he was suffering from a debilitating illness, he was unable to make his usual signature. He finally only managed to make two indecipherable scrawls. In a grounding affidavit by his solicitor supporting a motion to have the will admitted to probate, the solicitor deposed that the two scrawls were the result of the testator's attempt to write his initials "E" and "K". The solicitor added the words "his" before the "E" and "mark" after the letter "K". He also amended the text of the attestation clause by adding the words: "The testator made his mark being unable to write owing to physical debility". The solicitor and the testator's nurse witnessed the will. The court had to decide on the sufficiency of the testator's mark as a valid substitute for a signature. Hanna J., even though he considered it as settled law that a testator may sign by name, initials or mark, was satisfied: **2–04**

> "the evidence here that not only did the testator commence to make his signature *animo testandi* but continued in the same state of mind until the termination of the execution of his will,"

Accordingly, he admitted the will to probate.

A testator who is incapable of signing or initialling or make a mark in compliance with the settled law on the matter may direct another person to sign on his behalf.[10] A testator may resort to this alternative method of signing a will if, through illness or otherwise, he or she is incapable of signing the will himself or herself. By doing so, he or she will also remove any doubt regarding the adequacy or sufficiency of a signature should he or she insist on signing the will himself or herself, and negate the possibility of a costly application to the court to resolve the issue. In *Fulton v Kee*[11] the testator **2–05**

---

[9] [1933] I.R. 222.
[10] See s.78(1) of the 1965 Act.
[11] [1961] N.I. 1.

was suffering from disseminated sclerosis which made any movement of his hands extremely difficult. One of the witnesses guided the testator's hand in making a mark. It was argued in that case that, if a testator allowed a passive contact to continue, when able to break it if he so desired, there would be a sufficient participation on his part in the signing to make the signature his own. However, Lord MacDermott L.C.J. could not accede to this submission. He said that something positive and discernible was required of the testator and, having regard to the all the circumstances of a case, the testator had not executed his will.

2–06 The testator may also validly execute his will by acknowledging the signature already made by him in the presence of the two witnesses.[12] In such an event, however, he must first inform the witnesses that he intends to acknowledge the signature before they begin to subscribe their own names as witnesses. He may do this by indicating that the signature already made is his, or he may use words:

> "that will adequately convey the idea, if the signature be proved to have been then existent; no particular form of expression is required either by the word acknowledge or by the exigency of the act to be done".

In *Hudson v Parker*[13] Dr Lushington stated that:

> "It would be quite sufficient to say 'that is my will', the signing being there and seen at the time, for such words do import an owning thereof; indeed, it may be done by any other words which naturally include within their true meaning acknowledgment and approbation."

2–07 The witnesses must actually see the testator's signature, or at least have the opportunity of seeing it. Where a testator remains silent, or is unable to speak, a request by one witness to another to attest the will already signed by the testator within the hearing of the testator may be a sufficient acknowledgment.[14]

The Position of the Testator's Signature

2–08 In a professionally drafted will a space is usually left under the testimonium clause and above the attestation in the will for the testator to sign his name.[15] A great deal of latitude is given to the position of the testator's signature by s.78, s.78(3) and s.78(4) of the 1965 Act. Rule 3 provides so far as concerns the position of the signature of the testator or of the person signing for him under Rule 1, that it is sufficient if the signature is so placed at or after, or following, or under, or beside, or opposite to the end of the will that it is

12 See s.78(2) of the 1965 Act; *Hudson v Parker* (1844) 1 Rob. Ecc. 14 at 15.

13 (1844) 1 Rob.Ecc.14 at 25.

14 *Kavanagh v Fegan* [1932] I.R. 566.

15 See Chapter 24 – Wills Precedents.

for a variety of purposes concerning the contents of a will, for instance, appointing new executors or increasing or decreasing the value of gifts to legatees.[22] They may revoke a former will by express reference to it.[23] They may also be used to revive an earlier will made by the testator.[24] Whatever their purpose, they must be duly executed in the same way as a will, and the same rules which are applicable to the testator's and witnesses' signatures and presence at the time of execution are similarly applicable to codicils.

Where codicils are used, it is important to ensure that correct references are made to the provisions that are intended by the testator to be altered or revoked. While codicils are useful devices, their overuse may, however, increase the likelihood of mistaken references, especially where they are used to revive former wills. Where a testator intends to revive a former will, perhaps the safer course is to have it re-executed instead of using a codicil. All testamentary documents duly executed by the testator, no matter what the number, will held together as forming his last will: a testator does not die leaving two wills. Any codicils will be viewed as an extension of the testator's intentions contained in his will and will be interpreted accordingly. The probate will consist of the whole of a testator's testamentary papers, including codicils. It is important when preparing a first codicil that it should not be referred to as the first codicil on its face as the implication will be that it is the first of two or even more codicils. The date of the codicil will be sufficient to indicate that it was the first in time to any subsequent codicils.[25] **2–15**

Alterations

Testators are also free to make alterations to their wills, but their validity will depend on whether they were made before or after the execution of the will. Where it is shown that they were made before execution of the will, they are valid, but where they are made after execution, they will be invalid unless executed in the same manner as a will.[26] Section 86 of the 1965 Act provides that the will, **2–16**

> "with such alteration as part thereof, shall be deemed duly executed if the signature of the testator and the signature of each witness is made in the margin or on some other part of the will opposite or near the alteration or at the foot or end of or opposite to a memorandum referring to such alteration, and written at the end of some other part of the will."

Order 79, r.10 of the Rules of the Superior Courts 1986 also provides that interlineations and alterations appearing in a will are invalid unless they existed prior to its execution or, if made afterwards, unless they were **2–17**

22 See Chapter 24 – Wills Precedents.
23 See Chapter 4 – The Revocation and Revival of Wills.
24 *ibid.*
25 See Chapter 24 – Wills Precedents.
26 s.86 of the 1965 Act.

executed and attested in the mode required by law, or unless they were made valid by the re-execution of the will or by a subsequent codicil to the will. Where alterations or interlineations are not duly executed, or cited or identified in the attestation clause, an affidavit in proof of their having existed in the will prior to its execution must be filed, except for alterations of small importance where the initials of the attesting witnesses will suffice.[27] Order 79, r.12 goes on to provide that alterations in the nature of erasures and obliterations will not be valid unless they are shown to have existed in the will prior to its execution, or unless they were rendered valid by the re-execution of the will or by the subsequent execution of a codicil. If no satisfactory evidence can be adduced as to the time when erasures or obliterations were made, and the words erased or obliterated are not entirely effaced, and can be ascertained by a physical inspection of the paper — for instance, by a magnifying glass — they may form part of the probate.

2–18 The court when considering the matter may also place reliance on the internal evidence furnished by the fabric of the will. In *In the Goods of Benn*[28] two lines in the will were completely obliterated by using a blue copying pencil and adhesive stamp paper, leaving the underlying words indecipherable. There was also an interlineation in the principal disposition of the testatrix's property. Hanna J. found that, having regard to the internal evidence of the will and the opinion of a handwriting expert, the interlineations were inserted before execution, even though there was no direct evidence of any kind as to the time when the interlineations were made. On the question of character or weight of evidence to be adduced, it was said by Warren J. in *In the Goods of Duffy*[29] that:

> "the presumption that alterations were made after the execution only exists in the absence of all evidence to the contrary, and that very slight affirmative evidence is sufficient to rebut the presumption, and sustain the alterations as made before execution, and therefore, valid."

2–19 As to whether interlineations or alterations were made before the execution, Warren J. in *Moore v Moore*[30] said that the Court:

> "is not confined to any species of evidence, but may act upon any evidence which, having regard to all the circumstances, reasonably leads the judgment to the conclusion that the alterations were made before execution".

[27] Ord. 79, r.11 of the Rules of the Superior Courts 1986.
[28] [1938] I.R. 313.
[29] (1871) I.R. 5 Eq. 506.
[30] (1872) L.R. 6 Eq. 166.

Incorporation of Documents

Testators are free to incorporate executed and unexecuted documents by reference to them in their wills. Order 79, r.13 of the Rules of the Superior Courts 1986 provides that: **2–20**

> "If a will contains a reference to any deed, paper, memorandum, or other document, of such a nature as to raise a question whether it ought, or ought not, to form a constituent part of the will, such deed, paper, memorandum, or other document shall be produced, with a view to ascertaining whether it be entitled to probate; if not produced, its non-production shall be accounted for."

Order 79, r.14 goes on to provide that:

> "No deed, paper, memorandum, or other document shall be admitted to probate as part of a will, unless it was in existence at the time the will was executed, and is therein referred to."

Therefore, where documents are referred to in a will, or indeed a codicil, they will be properly incorporated by the will and will be admitted to probate with the will, if they exist and are clearly identified by the testator at the date of execution of the will.[31]

Knowledge and Approval

A testator must be given the opportunity of reading the will or having it read over to him or her and indicate approval of it before signing it.[32] A testator must know and approve of the contents of the will and this may be done by a testator reading the will himself or herself, or by having it read over to him or her by another, so as to afford him or her the opportunity of confirming that this will truly reflects his or her wishes, or of having certain matters arising out of the will explained to him or her more clearly. Apparently, where this has been done at the instructions stage, it need not be repeated at the date of execution provided it is further established that he or she knew that he or she was executing a will. Order 79, r.62 of the Rules of the Superior Courts 1986 specifically requires that, in the case of a blind and illiterate testator, the probate officer will not be allowed to issue a grant of probate or letters of administration with the will annexed unless he or she is satisfied by affidavit evidence that the will was read over to the testator before its execution, or that the testator had knowledge of its contents at such time.[33] **2–21**

---

31 See *Woodroofe v Creed* [1894] 1 I.R. 508.

32 See Albert Keating, "The Principle of Knowledge and Approval: A Judicial Term of Art" (2005) 10(2) C.P.L.J. 30.

33 See Albert Keating, "A Plea of Want of Knowledge and Approval as an Alternative to Undue Influence" (2008) 13(1) C.P.L.J. 10.

Presumption of Due Execution

2–22 Where a will is signed and witnessed, it will be presumed that it was executed in compliance with s.78 of the 1965 Act. This useful presumption will continue to apply notwithstanding the subsequent death of a witness, or that a witness cannot be traced, or that a witness is unable to recall the circumstances surrounding the execution. Where, however, the testator's signature is called in question and there is some doubt regarding its authenticity, the court may refuse to apply the presumption. The Supreme Court considered the application of the presumption in *In the Estate of Early.*[34] In that case, the deceased was an elderly man. He died in the house of a distant relative who had cared for him during his last years. His only assets consisted of a farm. Nearly two years after his death, this distant relative produced a document purporting to be the will of the deceased leaving his farm to her. The document, although signed by the deceased and two witnesses, contained no attestation clause. The two witnesses were dead when the document was produced. The signature of one of the witnesses, who was a friend of the deceased, was identified by his widow. There was no evidence, however, verifying the signature of the deceased. The Court was asked to apply the maxim *Omnia praesumuntur rite et solemniter esse acta* to the circumstances surrounding the execution of the document. O'Higgins C.J. in his judgment thought that it was asking too much of the Court to apply the presumption to the circumstances of the case. It was essential that evidence be adduced to show that the will was actually signed by the deceased. Applying the presumption to the facts of the case, O'Higgins C.J., was of the view that two conditions must be observed:

> "In the first place an intention to do some formal act must be established. In the second place there must be an absence of credible evidence that due formality was not observed. Here it can be said that the second condition is established. But what of the first? While the document has a testamentary flavour, it is established that it is not a holograph. In the absence of any evidence that it was signed by the deceased, there is no evidence of an intention on his part to enter into the formality of making a will."

The evidence was insufficient to justify the making of a grant.

A Solicitor's Duty of Care to Intended Beneficiaries

2–23 Solicitors owe a duty of care, not only to testators, but also to intended beneficiaries to ensure that a will is properly prepared and executed. Liability may arise in this instance where an intended beneficiary is deprived of a gift because the will was not duly executed or, though duly executed, an intended beneficiary was excluded.[35] Sir Robert Megarry, when faced with the issue

---

[34] [1980] I.R. 223.

[35] *Wall v Hegarty and Callanan*[1980] I.L.R.M. 124; see Albert Keating, "A Solicitor's

of liability in *Ross v Caunters*,[36] thought that the remedy consisted of an ordinary action in tortious negligence: a solicitor must know that, if he fails in his professional duty to draft and execute a will properly, a beneficiary will suffer loss. In that case, the testator left part of his residuary estate to the plaintiff. Two years later he sent instructions to his solicitor to alter the provisions of the will. During the course of correspondence, the testator asked his solicitor whether beneficiaries in a will might also be witnesses. The solicitor made no reply to this question. The solicitor, however, sent the will in draft form to the testator with instructions to have it witnessed by two independent witnesses. The will was duly executed and returned to the solicitor. It transpired that one of the witnesses was the husband of the plaintiff and, as a result, she lost her legacy. Sir Robert Megarry held that the plaintiff was entitled to recover the amount of the lost legacy from the solicitor who owed her a duty of care and was accordingly liable for any loss caused to her by his negligence. His judgment may be summarised as follows: (1) a solicitor may be liable both to his client and to others for the tort of negligence; (2) the basis of the solicitor's liability to others is either an extension of the *Hedley Byrne & Co. Ltd. v Heller & Partners Ltd.*[37] principle or, more probably, a direct application of the principle of *Donoghue v Stevenson*[38]; (3) a solicitor who is instructed by his or her client to carry out a transaction that will confer a benefit on an identified third party owes a duty of care towards that third party in carrying out that transaction; (4) the mere fact that the loss to such a third party caused by the negligence is purely financial, and is no way a physical injury to person or property, is no bar to the claim against the solicitor; and (5) in such circumstances, there are "no considerations which suffer to negative or limit the scope of the solicitor's duty to the beneficiary". Although the will was executed properly in *Ross v Caunters,* the failure of the solicitor to advise of the repercussions of a spouse of a beneficiary witnessing the will was a sufficient ground for negligence.

The question of a solicitor's duty of care to an intended beneficiary also **2–24**
arose in *Wall v Hegarty and Callanan*[39] where the will was not duly executed in compliance with s.78 of the 1965 Act. As a result of the will being condemned, the plaintiff lost a legacy of £15,000. The plaintiff also happened to be the executor of the will. He sued the firm of solicitors retained by the testator for breach of duty of care which he alleged was owing to him as legatee to ensure that the will was properly drafted in accordance with the testator's instructions, and executed and attested in accordance with s.78 of the Succession Act. He sought to recover damages for the loss of the legacy and further for the expenses he had incurred in attempting to

Duty of Care to Intended Beneficiaries and Personal Representatives" (2004) 9(2) C.P.L.J. 30.

36 [1980] Ch. 297.

37 [1963] 2 All E.R. 575.

38 [1932] A.C. 562.

39 [1980] I.L.R.M. 124.

establish the will. The defendant solicitors admitted that the signature of one of the witnesses was later added to the will in their offices. Barrington J. approved of the judgment of Sir Robert Megarry in *Ross v Caunters* where it was held that the solicitor owes a duty of care to an intended beneficiary. Barrington J. went on to say that:

> "a solicitor does owe a duty to a legatee named in a draft will, to draft the will with such reasonable care and skill as to ensure that the wishes of the testator are not frustrated and the expediency of the legatee defeated through lack of considerable care and skill on the part of the solicitor".

2–25 As the solicitor had failed to show the appropriate care and skill and as the plaintiff had lost the legacy as a result, he was entitled to recover the value of the legacy from the solicitor. However, in assessing damages, the court may also take other matters into account, such as the solvency or insolvency of the testator's estate and the likelihood of a legatee receiving nothing at all in the case of insolvency, or that the will might be found invalid on some other ground in respect of which the solicitor bore no responsibility.

2–26 In *Wall v Hegarty and Callanan,* the testator's estate had sufficient funds to meet the payment of the legacy and he was accordingly entitled to receive the value of it. The plaintiff had also sustained loss in seeking admission of the will to probate. As regards this, it appeared to Barrington J. that a solicitor who drafts a will in which an executor is named must foresee that that executor will eventually seek the admission of the will to probate. Therefore it followed that the costs incurred by the plaintiff as executor in having the will admitted to probate flowed naturally from the solicitor's lack of care and were recoverable by him. Barrington J. was of the opinion, based on the principles in *Donoghue v Stevenson* and *Hedley Byrne & Co. Ltd. v Heller and Partners Ltd.*, that the costs were recoverable because of the circumstances surrounding the sending of a copy of the will to the plaintiff without drawing his attention to the fact that the will was not validly executed. He also recognised the plaintiff's entitlement to recover damages for loss of interest on his legacy. As a result of *Wall v Hegarty and Callanan,* a solicitor owes a duty to exercise "considerable" care and skill in drafting and executing a will and may be liable in damages to intended beneficiaries for loss of legacies where he has failed to exercise such care and skill, and for any other attendant loss flowing naturally from the solicitor's lack of care.

Chapter 3

TESTAMENTARY CAPACITY

Introduction

Section 77 of the Succession Act 1965 (the "1965 Act") is the relevant statutory provision dealing with testamentary capacity. It provides that, for a person to make a valid will, he or she must have attained the age of eighteen years and be of sound disposing mind.[1] The two statutory prerequisites of age and sound disposing mind must be satisfied for a testator to make a valid will. It may be noted that, while s.77 prescribes a minimum age for a testator to make a valid will, there is no maximum age so that a valid will may be made by a person of any age over eighteen years. The statutory prerequisite of sound disposing mind is, however, more problematical and, where it is raised as an issue impugning a will, a testator's intellectual or mental capacity will become the focus of attention. It may be alleged, for instance, that a testator lacked the necessary capacity because of the degree of deterioration of his or her intellectual powers owing to physical illness and/or old age. Or it may be alleged that a testator lacked capacity because of mental illness. Whether or not such factors deprive a testator of testamentary capacity will depend on the evidence adduced at a trial, and the onus of proof will rest on the party who alleges incapacity. Where it is alleged that old age or physical illness had deprived the testator of capacity, the evidence adduced must establish that such factors had affected the testator's mind so much that he could not possibly have a sound mind, memory and understanding. In such a case, while medical evidence will be **3–01**

1 See s.77(1) of the Succession Act 1965; s.31(1) of the Family Law Act 1995 (martial age is now 18 years); s.7(3) of the Civil Partnetship and Certain Rights and Obligations of Cohabitants Act 2010 (civil partnership age is 18 years); Albert Keating, *Probate Law and Practice* (Dublin: Round Hall Sweet and Maxwell, 1999) Chapter 3; Albert Keating, "Testamentary Capacity" (2011) 16(3) C.P.L.J. 46; Albert Keating, *Keating on Probate* (4th ed) (Dublin: Thomson Round Hall, 2011); Albert Keating, *First Supplement to the Fourth Edition of Keating on Probate* (Dublin: Thomson Round Hall, 2013); Albert Keating, *Probate Causes and Related Matters* (Dublin: Round Hall Sweet & Maxwell, 2000); Albert Keating, *Keating on Probate – The Complete Works*, CD - ROM (Dublin: Thomson Round Hall, 2004).

of importance, more weight may be given to the evidence of the testator's family or those who knew him well, and to that of the legal practitioner who attended him and took instructions for the will subsequently executed by him.[2] Where mental illness is raised as an impugning factor, the question of whether it deprived the testator of testamentary capacity will depend on the severity of the illness and, in this instance, it appears that more weight will be given to medical evidence. The location where instructions are taken for the making of a will may make testamentary capacity an issue. Where, for instance, instructions are taken in a nursing home for the elderly or a mental hospital, the question of capacity comes to the fore. It is prudent in such cases to adopt certain procedures when deciding whether or not a testator is capable of making a will.

THE *BANKS V GOODFELLOW* TEST

3–02 A person must have a sound disposing mind when it comes to the disposition of his or her property by will. In *Boughton v Knight*[3] Sir J. Hannen stated that:

> "The testator's mind must be sound to be capable of forming the testamentary intentions embodied in the will; his memory must be sound to recall the several persons who ought to be considered as his possible beneficiaries; his understanding must be sound so that he may comprehend their various ties with him by blood or friendship, and their claims on these or other grounds upon his testamentary bounty."

3–03 In *Scally v Rhatigan*[4] Laffoy J. stated the Court must be satisfied on the balance of probabilities that a testator had testamentary capacity by reference to the *Banks v Goodfellow* test. The *Banks v Goodfellow*[5] test is composed of three questions:

- (i) Did the testator understand the nature of the act of making a will and its effect?
- (ii) Did the testator understand the extent of the property of which he was disposing?
- (iii) Did the testator comprehend and appreciate the claims to which he ought to give effect?

Laffoy J. stated that:

> "it is a question of fact, which is to be determined having regard to all of the evidence and by applying the evidential standard of the balance of probabilities, whether a testator was of sound disposing mind when the testamentary document which is being propounded was executed".

---

2 See *Duffy v Kearney and Duffy*, Unreported, High Court, O'Hanlon J., 10 August 1994.

3 (1873) L.R. 3 P. & D. 64 at 65.

4 [2011] 1 I.R. 639.

5 (1870) L.R. 5 Q.B.D. 549.

The evidence adduced at the hearing fell into the following four categories:

(a) Evidence of family members of the deceased;
(b) Evidence of the circumstances in which the will was made;
(c) Medical evidence as to the deceased's physical and mental condition;
(d) Evidence of appropriate practice on the part of a solicitor in addressing the issue of capacity of a person to make a will.

Laffoy J., while having regard to all of the evidence, stated that the main focus of her judgment was on the evidence referred to at (b) and (c) above.

Applying the threefold *Banks v Goodfellow* test with regard to the evidence, Laffoy J. concluded that: **3–04**

(i) The testator understood that, in executing his will, he was executing a document that would take effect on his death and would determine the manner in which assets which he owned which were in his name would be distributed on his death;
(ii) The testator understood the extent of the property of which he was disposing. On the evidence, she was quite sure that he did;
(iii) In taking an overview of what the evidence disclosed in relation to the provision he made within and outside the terms of the will for those to whom he owed a legal or moral duty, there was no evidence of any insane delusion that influenced the will in disposing of his property and brought about a disposal of it which, if his mind had been sound, would not have been made. Nor was there any evidence of a disorder of the mind that poisoned his affections, perverted his sense of right or prevented the exercise of his natural faculties.

She was satisfied that, despite his severe physical disability and the cognitive limitations, the testator did have testamentary capacity when he executed his will.

In *Re Key*[6] Briggs J. referred to the shifting of the burden of proof during the course of a trial. He said that: **3–05**

(i) While the burden starts with the person who propounds the will to establish capacity, where the will is duly executed and appears rational on its face, then the court will presume capacity;
(ii) In such a case the evidential burden then shifts to the objector to raise a real doubt about capacity;
(iii) If a real doubt is raised, the evidential burden shifts back to the person who propounds the will to establish capacity.

Therefore, where a testator's will is challenged on the grounds of testamentary capacity, it is a question of fact which is to be determined having regard to all of the evidence and by applying the evidential standard of the balance

[6] [2010] 1 W.L.R. 2020.

of probabilities, whether the testator was of sound disposing mind when the testamentary document which is being propounded was executed.

Mental Ill Health

3–06 When a will is challenged on the grounds of the mental ill-health of the testator, the onus of proof rests on the party making the allegation to establish that the testator's mind was so affected by the illness that he was incapable of making a valid will. When deciding whether a testator lacked the necessary testamentary capacity, the court will not only take into account a testator's mental state at the time when the will was executed, but it may also take into consideration any history of mental ill health suffered by the testator during the course of his life. In *Mudway v Croft*[7] Sir H.J. Fust stated that:

> "It is absolutely and essentially necessary to look to the peculiar circumstances of each individual case; and to judge the whole character of the person whose mental capacity is the subject of enquiry, what was the state and condition of mind of that individual; not only with respect to the immediate times at which a will is executed, but at the intermediate states of his life."

3–07 The nature of the illness may be so obvious that the court may have no difficulty in finding that a testator lacked capacity, or it may be of a nature which may become evident only over a period of time, thus making it more difficult for the court to determine the precise moment that a testator began to lose the capacity to make a will.[8] Where, however, a person is diagnosed as suffering from a particular form of mental illness as a result of which his mind cannot be said to be sound, he will not have the required capacity to make a will.[9] A person who is diagnosed as suffering from insane delusions would fall into this category.[10]

3–08 While a person will normally be presumed to be sane, this presumption may be rebutted where a testator is undergoing treatment for a mental illness.[11] An exception may, however, be made in the case of a testator whose mental illness can be effectively controlled by medication. Such was the case in *O'Donnell v O'Donnell*[12] where the evidence showed that the negative elements of paranoid schizophrenia were capable of being controlled by medication, and as they were not even apparent to the testator's solicitor or to those who knew him and had dealings with him, and as no such elements were present when he executed his will, he was deemed capable of making a valid will.

---

7 *Mudway v Croft* (1843) 3 Curt. 671 at 676.

8 *Boyse v Rossborough* (1857) 6 H.L.C. 2 at 45.

9 See *Banks v Goodfellow* (1870) L.R. 5 Q.B.D. 549 at 559 *per* Cockburn C.J.; *Sharp & Anor. v Adam & Others* [2006] EWCA Civ 449 (28 April 2006).

10 *Banks v Goodfellow* (1870) L.R. 5 Q.B.D. 549.

11 *Bannatyne v Bannatyne* (1867) 2 Rob.472 at 501.

12 Unreported, High Court, Kelly J., 24 March 1999.

Physical Ill Health

Physical ill-health may also affect a person's mental capacity to make a will. The effect of physical ill-health on a testator's mental capacity to make a will was considered by McCarthy J. in *Glynn v Glynn*.[13] The facts of *Glynn* were that the testator died on 14 February 1982, at the age of 77. He suffered a stroke on 5 October 1981, and was thereafter confined to hospital. He executed his will on 20 October. On that day, without obtaining any medical advice, the witnesses concluded that the testator knew what he was doing and was capable of making a will. One of the witnesses drew up the will in accordance with the deceased's instructions. The deceased left all his property to a second cousin with whom he had no connection, other than that they both shared the same family name, and excluded his elder sister who was unmarried and who had lived all her life with him on the family farm. Neither of the witnesses was a beneficiary in the will. The testator's doctor, however, was of the opinion that the testator was "disorientated" on the day he executed the will. He also concluded that the testator's level of consciousness was such that he was unable to communicate any of his own ideas and that some method of communication would first have to be devised for him, "some code whereby he understood and agreed that the ideas that were being communicated to him coincided with his own ideas". Another doctor was of the same opinion. The question was whether his state of ill-health deprived him of testamentary capacity. McCarthy J. held that the deceased in this case was merely confirming instructions already taken, and he was told truthfully that the document signed by him represented his expressed testamentary wishes, and as the two witnesses were quite satisfied that he knew what he was doing, the will was a valid one. **3–09**

The decision in *Duffy v Kearney and Duffy*[14] is a good example of the approach taken by the Court to evidence involving testamentary capacity. In that case, the testator was a bachelor who lived alone on a farm in close proximity to his brother, the plaintiff, who also farmed in the same locality. The defendants were a sister and brother of the deceased who had left Ireland and gone to live in the United States many years before the death of the deceased and who made only occasional visits to Ireland prior to his death. The testator left his farm to the plaintiff. At the time of making his will, however, he was extremely ill in hospital and that caused the defendants to have doubts about his capacity to make a will. As a result of such doubts, they entered a caveat that eventually led to a full probate action challenging the validity of the will made by the deceased. O'Hanlon J. considered the evidence given by a medical expert and the solicitor who prepared the deceased's will regarding the mental capacity of the deceased at the date of execution of the will. Although he stated that the evidence of the medical expert had to be treated with respect, he nevertheless thought that **3–10**

13 [1990] 2 I.R. 326; see also *In the Estate of Blackall*, Unreported, Supreme Court, 1 April 1998.

14 Unreported, High Court, O'Hanlon J., 10 August 1994.

> "what he had to say about the general effect of the human intellect and perception of personal relationships and affairs of administration of drugs of the type which were administered to the deceased during his last illness up to and including December 27, 1988, was not, in my opinion, sufficient to dislodge the very comprehensive evidence given by Mr O'Carroll, Solicitor, and by the other witnesses who visited and conversed with the deceased on December 27, and the period immediately preceding that date.""'

3–11 The solicitor knew the deceased and had acted for the deceased's family for a long period before the will was made. The evidence of the deceased's solicitor as to the general physical and mental state of the deceased was strongly supported by the evidence of the other witnesses who visited him in hospital around the time of execution of the will and the general conclusions of another medical practitioner about the capacity of the deceased. O'Hanlon J. said he had no difficulty in declaring in favour of the will and finding that the deceased testator was of sound disposing mind.

Issues of Testamentary Capacity When Taking Instructions

3–12 When taking a client's instructions, a practitioner will also be in a position to ascertain the testator's capacity to make a will. Where he or she has any doubt regarding the testamentary capacity of the testator because of old age and/or illness, medical opinion may be required to clarify the issue of capacity by recourse to the testator's own medical practitioner. The place where instructions are taken may also suggest the necessity for medical opinion to determine the question of capacity. Where, for instance, a practitioner is called to attend a client who is a patient in a mental hospital, medical opinion may well be required to determine a client's capacity to make a will. Where a practitioner is called to attend a client at his or her home or a nursing home, because the client is too elderly or too ill to attend his or her offices, medical opinion may be necessary here also to determine the client's capacity to make a will. It is also prudent to have a clear set of procedures when taking instructions in hospitals or nursing homes and for the purposes of recording medical opinion on the question of testamentary capacity where that is necessary.

3–13 When taking instructions in hospitals or nursing homes, it is important to ensure that:

1. The testator is capable of giving instructions, and medical opinion supports this as an affidavit of medical practitioner may be necessary;
2. The testator reads the will, or it is read over to him;
3. The testator understands and approves of the contents;
4. The attestation clause reflects the manner of signing by the testator (e.g. by signature or mark);

5. The will is witnessed by two independent witnesses (preferably, at least one medical witness);
6. Attendance regarding the taking of instructions is prepared;
7. Attendance regarding the execution of the will is prepared;
8. Under no circumstances send a will for execution by post.

According to a Probate Office update issued on 6 July 2012: **3–14**

> "Where there is an issue as to the testamentary capacity of a proposed testator at the time of taking instructions inquiries should be made of the proposed testator's general medical practitioner as to whether or not the individual in question has the requisite testamentary capacity to execute such a document.
>
> Where the medical practitioner is satisfied that such person is of sound disposing mind, it would be best practice for the solicitor to obtain an affidavit of testamentary capacity from such practitioner.
>
> Once the will is executed, the affidavit of testamentary capacity and original will should be maintained together in the solicitor's offices until such time as it is necessary to prove the will.
>
> Practitioners should note that where a proposed testator is already a ward of court, it is necessary to obtain an order from the President of the High Court before a will may be executed by the ward in question.
>
> When the testator dies and application is made to the Probate Office to prove will.
>
> Within a Probate Office context, questions of testamentary capacity do not arise until a testator has died. When an application is made to the Probate Office to prove a deceased person's will and to issue a grant of probate in the deceased's estate, the will in question will be regarded by the Probate Office as having been made by a person of sound disposing mind unless there are indicators which would raise a concern as to the testamentary capacity of the testator.
>
> Such indicators are as follows:
>
> 1. Testator died in a psychiatric institution.
> 2. Testator died a ward of court.
> 3. The death certificate of testator indicates any one of the following causes of death either as a main cause of death or a co-existing condition: alzheimers, dementia, cognitive impairment.
>
> As a general principle, where such indicators manifest, an affidavit of testamentary capacity may be required by the Probate Office."

The Law Reform Commission in its report dealing with Vulnerable Adults and the Law[15] considered that it: **3–15**

> "would be desirable for the Law Society to produce guidelines for solicitors in this area which would recommend that solicitors take the precaution of obtaining a certificate of capacity in cases where capacity is in doubt or a future challenge to testamentary capacity is likely, for example, because the will is made during a lucid interval by a person with dementia or the testator is resident in a psychiatric facility".

---

15 LRC 83 – 2006 at p. 89 *et seq.*; see also Law Reform Commission's *Consultation Paper on Law and the Elderly*, LRC – CP 23 – 2003.

3–16 The Commission also considered that the taking of contemporaneous notes of a consultation between solicitor and client in relation to the execution of a will would be of assistance in the event of any challenge to the testator's capacity to make a will. The Commission went on to recommend that the Law Society and the Medical Council produce guidelines on the assessment of testamentary capacity for the benefit of their members. The guidelines should also stress the importance of taking contemporaneous notes when assessing the testamentary capacity of the testator.

3–17 There is no statutory provision in Ireland similar to s.96 of the U.K. Mental Health Act 1983 which empowers the Court of Protection to order the execution of a will for an adult patient who is mentally disordered if the court has reason to believe that the patient is incapable of making a will for himself.[16] The Law Reform Commission, having considered the matter in its report dealing with Vulnerable Adults and the Law,[17] recommended that:

> "in exceptional circumstances, the High Court should be given the discretionary power to order the alteration of a will of an adult who lacks testamentary capacity. The court, acting on its initiative or on an application being made to it by any third party including the proposed Guardianship Board,[18] would exercise these powers in exceptional circumstances where the justice of the case demands".

3–18 It will be noted that the Law Reform Commission recommended that the High Court should be given the discretionary power to order the alteration of an existing will, but not "to intervene where no will is in existence". Chapter 3,(4), paragraphs 3.61 *et seq.* of the same report deals with the application of the doctrine of ademption where property forming the subject matter of a specific devise is sold to fund care arrangements for the testator. It recommends that:

> "if land owned by a person who is the subject of a guardianship order is sold to fund their long-term care, the persons who would otherwise have been entitled to the land on the death of the original owner will be deemed to have the same proportionate interest in any surplus monies from the proceeds of sale which remain after the relevant care needs have been provided for."[19]

3–19 The Commission also recommended that the discretion given to the courts under the proposed statutory will procedure should be capable of accommodating ademption in appropriate circumstances.

3–20 Section 108(1) of the Assisted Decision-Making (Capacity) Bill 2013 provides that, subject to the provisions of (2), nothing shall be construed

---

16 See *Re D (J)* [1982] 2 All E.R. 37; also U.K. Mental Health Capacity Act 2005, s.16; Terrell, *Wills for Person Without Capacity* (2004) 154 (7314) N.L.J. 968.

17 See Law Reform Commission's *Consultation Paper on Law and the Elderly*, LRC – CP 23 – 2003, p. 92.

18 *ibid*, Ch. 6.

19 *ibid*, Ch. 11.

as altering or amending the law relating to the capacity of a person to make a will. Section 108(2) proposes that:

> "Where a person who has made a will loses testamentary capacity, the High Court may, acting on its own motion or on application to it by the Public Guardian, alter the will where it is satisfied that exceptional circumstances have arisen since the loss of testamentary capacity and the interests of justice so demand, and a will so altered shall have the same force and effect as if the alteration had been made by that testator in the manner required by the Act of 1965."

CHAPTER 4

THE REVOCATION AND REVIVAL OF WILLS

INTRODUCTION

A testator is free to revoke his will at any time during his lifetime because of the ambulatory nature of a will which is effective on death. Where a testator decides to revoke his will, he must do so by one of the methods prescribed by s.85 of the Succession Act 1965 (the "1965 Act") as amended by the Civil Partnership and Certain Rights and Obligations of Cohabitants Act 2010 (the 2010 Act). Section 85 provides that a will may be revoked by the subsequent marriage or civil partnership of the testator, except a will made in contemplation of that marriage or civil partnership, or by a testamentary instrument (including "some writing" executed in testamentary form), or by a testator destroying his will *animo revocandi,* i.e. with the intention of revoking it. **4–01**

Section 85(1) provides that: **4–02**

> "A will shall be revoked by the subsequent marriage of the testator, except a will made in contemplation of that marriage, whether so expressed in the will or not."

Section 85(1) of the 1965 Act is now amended by s.79 of the 2010 Act. The amended s.85 now provides that:

> "A will shall be revoked by the subsequent marriage or entry into a civil partnership of the testator, except a will made in contemplation of that marriage or entry into a civil partnership, whether so expressed in the will or not."

Section 85(2) goes on to set out the other methods by which a will may be revoked and it provides that:

> "no will, or any part thereof, shall be revoked except by another will or codicil duly executed, or by some writing declaring an intention to revoke it and executed in the manner in which a will is required to be executed, or by the burning, tearing, or destruction of it by the testator, or by some person in his presence and by his direction, with the intention of revoking it".

4–03 As a result of s.85(1) of the 1965 Act, where a testator marries or enters into a civil partnership, any prior will made by him or her will be revoked, except where it was made in contemplation of that marriage or civil partnership.[1] Under s.85(2) of the 1965 Act, a testator may revoke a former will and any codicils made by him or her by making a new will containing a suitably-worded revocation clause. A revocation clause usually appears after the name and address of the testator in a professionally drafted will.[2] Also, by virtue of s.85(2), a will may be revoked "by some writing" in the form of a letter, note or memorandum duly executed by the testator in compliance with s.78 of the 1965 Act declaring an intention to revoke his or her will. While a will may be revoked under s.85(2) by destruction by burning it or tearing it up, the testator must intend to revoke his will by using this method of revocation. The act of destruction must be accompanied by the requisite intention to revoke, *viz. animus revocandi*.[3] Therefore, the destruction of a will by accident will not result in a revocation because of the absence of the requisite intention of revoking.

4–04 A revocation must also be absolute to be effective, and thus, where a revocation is made dependent or conditional on the making of a new will, the revocation of a former will by the testator may not be absolute, and therefore ineffective, by the judicial doctrine of dependent relative revocation. Where a testator revokes a will or codicil with the intention of making a new but dies without doing so, that intention alone will not reinstate the revoked will or codicil. But the courts by applying the doctrine of dependent relative revocation may deem the revocation a conditional one if the act of revocation is connected with some other act or event. The doctrine of dependent relative revocation is a judicial invention and may be applied where it is shown that the testator revoked his will or codicil as a first step towards accomplishing his intention to make a new will. The doctrine will also be applied if a will or codicil is destroyed with the same intention. As Kenny J. stated in *In the Goods of Irvine*[4] the matter is altogether a question of intention,

---

1 See Albert Keating, "Wills Made in Contemplation of Marriage or Civil Partnership" (2012) 17(3) C.P.L.J. 49; Albert Keating, *Keating on Probate* (4th ed) (Dublin: Thomson Round Hall, 2011); Albert Keating, *First Supplement to the Fourth Edition of Keating on Probate* (Dublin: Thomson Round Hall, 2013); Albert Keating, *Probate Causes and Related Matters* (Dublin: Round Hall *Sweet & Maxwell*, 2000); Albert Keating, *Keating on Probate – The Complete Works*, CD-ROM (Dublin: Thomson Round Hall, 2004).

2 See Chapter 24 – Wills Precedents.

3 *Cheese v Lovejoy* (1877) 2 P.D. 251 at 263 *per* James L.J.

4 [1919] 2 I.R. 485.

> "and if, as part of the act of making a fresh will, there will be a revocation of a previous will, that revocation will be absolute provided the fresh will be made,"

If the new will is not made, it would defeat the testator's intention to hold the revocation to be absolute.

Two testators may decide to make mutual will in furtherance of an agreement to do so and, if such is the case, equity may preclude a surviving testator from revoking the mutual will on the grounds that a constructive trust was established by virtue of the testators' pre-testamentary agreement to make the mutual wills. **4–05**

Section 87 of the 1965 Act prescribes two methods for the revival of former wills. The first method is by re-execution of the will intended to be revived; the second is by codicil showing an intention to revive a former will. The requisite intention is that of revival, i.e. *animo vivendi* **4–06**

Revocation by Subsequent Marriage or Civil Partnership

Once the marriage or civil partnership of the testator is duly solemnised or entered into, any former will or codicil made by him or her will be revoked. The subsequent marriage or civil partnership will automatically revoke the will without the necessity of showing an intention to revoke. The marriage or civil partnership must, however, be a valid one, and if, owing to the presence of a vitiating element, it is rendered void, it will not revoke a former will. Where the marriage or civil partnership is shown to be a voidable one owing to the presence of a vitiating element, the marriage or civil partnership will continue to subsist, and will not have the effect of revoking a former will, unless the marriage or civil partnership is subsequently annulled by the courts. In *In the Estate of Fleming*[5] the testator, during the course of his life, married several times. His fourth marriage took place in Nevada, USA, in 1967, and this marriage was annulled in 1968 by the Nevada courts. He made a will in 1971, and in 1977, he married his fourth wife for a second time. This marriage was dissolved in 1980. The deceased returned to Ireland where he remained until his death in 1983. The deceased's sister applied to the courts for a grant of letters of administration intestate under s.27(4) of the 1965 Act on the grounds that the deceased's will of 1977 was revoked by his second marriage to his fourth wife in 1977. However, a question arose relating to the validity of his marriage in 1977. Gannon J., applying the law of this country and on a review of the evidence before him, held that the 1967 marriage was not validly dissolved in 1968, and as a result the deceased was not free to marry again in 1977, and that the purported **4–07**

[5] [1987] I.L.R.M. 638; see also *Warter v Warter* (1890) 15 P.D. 152; *Mette v Mette* (1859) 1 Sw. & Tr. 416.

marriage in 1977 was in effect a nullity, and consequently, the will of 1971 was not revoked under s.85(1) of the 1965 Act.

4–08 Section 85(1) of the 1965 Act further provides that a will made in contemplation of a subsequent marriage, whether so expressed in the will or not, will not be revoked by that marriage. Where a will is made prior to the testator's marriage, but is made in contemplation of that marriage, the subsequent marriage will not revoke the will, even though there is no express mention of the testator's forthcoming marriage in the will. Obviously, where there is no mention of a marriage in the will, sufficient evidence will have to be adduced proving that the will was made in contemplation of it. In *In the Estate of Baker*[6] Gannon J. stated that:

> "There is nothing in the evidence on this application which would enable a court to draw an inference of probability that the will was made in contemplation of any particular marriage. Had the will been made in contemplation of some marriage, it is probable that the person taking the instructions for the making of the will would have received some intimation of that nature and could give evidence to that effect."

4–09 In *In the Estate of O'Brien*[7] O'Neill J., when considering the nature of the evidence that must be adduced to show that a testator had in fact made his or her will in contemplation of marriage, stated that it is sufficient:

> "if the evidence establishes that when the will was made, the testator actually had or must have had in contemplation a marriage to a particular person. To require an intention that the will continues to have effect after the marriage in question exceeds what the language of the section expresses and would, in effect, involve an addition to the section. Section 85(1) does not expressly say that 'contemplation' in the context of the section means an intention that the will would continue to have effect after the marriage. Neither can it be said that such a construction of the section is warranted as a necessary or obvious implication from the language used in the section. It is noteworthy that the language used in the section does not mention the word 'intention' at all, let alone any specific intention. The section adopts the much broader concept of 'contemplation' which persuades me that the legislative intent was that a testator would merely bear in mind or have regard to a particular forthcoming marriage."

4–10 In *Pilot v Gainfort*[8] the testator was married to a woman who had left him a number of years before he made his will and who was not seen or heard of for more than seven years, thus allowing for the presumption of death to be applied. He bequeathed the whole of his estate to a woman with whom he was living and whom he described as his "wife" in his will. Shortly after he made his will, he married this woman. The Court ruled that he had made his will in contemplation of marriage to her and that the will was a valid one. Lord Merrivale said that:

---

6 [1985] I.R. 101.

7 [2011] I.E.H.C. 327.

8 [1931] P. 103.

> "Under the circumstances I do not think that it can be doubted that the will was in contemplation of the subsequent marriage and practically expresses that contemplation and is good."[9]

Revocation by Implication

A later will may be revoked expressly by a clause to that effect appearing in a later will or may occur by implication. A will was held to be revoked by implication in *In the Goods of Martin.*[10] In that case, the testatrix, a widow, died leaving two wills. The later of the two contained no revocation clause and consisted of a legacy of "all my money" and a bequest of personal belongings. The estate of the testatrix comprised stocks and shares, monies in deposit and current accounts in two banks, and monies in Irish and English Post Office Savings Banks. An application was made for a grant of letters of administration with the later will annexed, or alternatively, with the two wills annexed. O'Keeffe P. considered it well-settled that the meaning of the word "money" may cover much more than the primary meaning of the word so that a gift in a will of "all my money" may be equivalent to "all my personal estate".[11] He concluded that the words "all my money" in the later will covered the entire personal estate of the deceased other than personal belongings, and that the earlier will was revoked by implication. A later executed document, though not necessarily a formal will, may also revoke a prior will, regardless of the fact that it contains no revocation clause. In *In the Goods of Brennan*[12] a will was held to be revoked by a later instruction sheet duly executed by the testatrix. In that case, the testatrix gave instructions to her solicitor for the preparation of a new will. The instructions were recorded on a sheet of paper that also contained notes made by her solicitor. She signed the instructions sheet in the presence of her solicitor and a typist. The instructions sheet, however, contained no revocation clause. The testatrix never returned to the solicitor's office to execute a formal will. The executors named in the instructions sheet applied for a grant of probate. Hanna J. stated that it was the function of the court exercising probate jurisdiction to decide what document or documents the testatrix intended to be her last will. He held that the testatrix intended, when she signed the instructions sheet, to revoke her prior will and to substitute the executed instructions until a more formal document was drawn up. **4–11**

Where, however, two existing wills bear the same date and contain revocation clauses, intestacy may ensue unless the order of execution can **4–12**

---

9 *Pilot v Gainfort* [1931] P. 103at 104; see also *Sallis v Jones* [1935] P. 43; *In the Estate of Gray* [1963] 107 S.J. 156.

10 [1968] I.R. 1.

11 See also *Caldeck v Stafford and Lindemere* [1930] I.R. 196; *Perrin v Morgan* [1943] A.C. 399; [1943] 1 All E.R. 187.

12 [1976] I.R. 633; see also *In the Goods of Bryan* [1907] P. 125; *O'Leary v Douglass* 3 L.R. Ir. 323 at 330.

be established. In *In the Goods of Millar*[13] two wills of the same date were executed. Each will had a revocation clause. There was no evidence to establish the order of execution. They also contained inconsistent provisions. As a result, Hanna J. held that the Court could not construct a will by selecting parts of two inconsistent testamentary documents so as to make a consistent whole. Where it is alleged that the will propounded by the plaintiff was revoked by a subsequent will but that will is not produced at the trial, the Court will not accept it as a valid revoking instrument unless there is clear and satisfactory evidence of its contents.[14] A codicil revoking a former will does not necessarily revoke a prior codicil, although there may be an implied revocation of all prior or intermediate codicils. Because of its supplementary nature, a codicil will be construed as interfering as little as possible with a will.[15]

4–13 The revoking instrument need not take the form of a testamentary instrument, nor does it have to dispose of property. It will be sufficient if it consists of some written declaration made by the testator revoking a former will, although such writing must be duly executed like a will. It may take the form of a letter, although such a letter will differ from an ordinary letter in the sense that it must be executed like a will. In *In the Goods of Eyre*[16] a letter sent by the testatrix to her daughter which was duly signed and attested and which directed her daughter to destroy her will was held to be a valid instrument of revocation.

Revocation by Destruction

4–14 Section 85(2) of the 1965 Act provides that a will may be revoked:

> "by the burning, tearing, or destruction of it by the testator, or by some person in his presence and by his direction, with the intention of revoking it".

4–15 To constitute a valid revocation by destruction of a will, the physical act of destruction by the testator must be accompanied by an intention to revoke the will. It was aptly said by one judge that

> "all the destroying in the world without intention will not revoke a will, nor all the intention in the world without destroying; there must be the two".[17]

It is also important to emphasise that, where a testator directs another person to destroy a will it, must be done in the testator's presence. A telephone or postal direction by a testator to another to destroy a will is not a sufficient revocation, even though the requisite intention exists. Section 85(2) of the

---

13 [1931] I.R. 364.
14 *In the Goods of Miller* [1940] I.R. 456.
15 See *Re Stoodley* [1916] 1 Ch. 242.
16 [1905] 2 I.R. 540.
17 *Cheese v Lovejoy* (1877) 2 P.D. 251 at 263 *per* James L.J.

1965 Act provides that the physical act of destruction may take the form of burning, tearing or otherwise destroying. Any of these forms of destruction may be used to revoke a will, either totally or partially. In the latter event, where a testator intends to destroy part of his will only, the remainder in its mutilated form may be admitted to probate. In addition to burning or tearing, other acts of destruction which undermine the essence of the will, namely, the writing, will also be acceptable, and it will be the writing which will be subject-matter for debate by the courts, and not the material on which a will is made. In reality, both the writing and the material are usually destroyed by the same act of destruction, for instance by the testator completely erasing a will written in pencil. Other instances involved the scratching out or severing by the testator of his signature from his will, or where he erases the signatures of the attesting witnesses.

The intention to revoke is essential to an effective revocation. The act without the intent will not suffice. Further, if there is some doubt about the mental capacity of the testator to form the necessary intention, it must be shown to the satisfaction of the court that he was capable of forming the necessary intention, and the same kind of evidence required to show the testamentary capacity of a testator will be required here also. A testator, who destroys his will while being of unsound mind, will not revoke his will.[18] A will which is destroyed by mistake will also not be a valid revocation, as it is not done with the intention of revoking it — for instance, where a testator destroys his will because he believes it to be useless,[19] or where he thought that "he was merely disposing of rubbish".[20] The testator must not only intend to destroy his will, but he must also intend to revoke it. **4–16**

The Presumption of Revocation by Destruction of Lost Wills

Where it is known that a person has made a will in compliance with the rules of execution but it cannot be found after his death, it will be presumed that he destroyed the will with the intention of revoking it.[21] In *In the Goods of Coster*[22] Kenny J. stated that, where it is shown that a person has executed a will **4–17**

> "and retains the original or subsequently comes into possession of it and it cannot be found after her death and there is no evidence to show what has become of it, there is a presumption that she destroyed it with the intention of revoking it".

18 *In the Goods of Hine* [1893] P. 282.

19 See *Stamford v White* [1901] P. 46.

20 *Re Jones* [1976] Ch. 200 at 205.

21 See Albert Keating, "Rebutting the Presumption of Revocation by Destruction of Lost Wills" (2010) 28 I.L.T. 128.

22 Unreported, Supreme Court, 19 January 1978, citing the judgment of Parke B. in *Welch v Phillips* (1836) 1 Moore P.C. 299.

4–18 He went to say that it is "a presumption only and not an absolute rule so that it may be rebutted". But where the court applies the presumption of revocation by destruction, the result will be intestacy. In *Coster,* the applicant party sought a declaration that the deceased died intestate based on the presumption of revocation by destruction of the will by the testatrix. In that case, the deceased took possession of her original will from her solicitors and brought it home. She also purchased a printed form will and that will was found among her papers after her death but it had nothing written on it. The original will was not found among her papers. Advertisements placed in newspapers and gazettes also proved unsuccessful in discovering its whereabouts. The Court, however, refused to make an order declaring that the deceased had died intestate. But on appeal the Supreme Court applied the presumption and declared that the deceased died intestate, and the applicant was given liberty to apply for a grant of letters of administration intestate to her estate.

4–19 Another instance where the court applied the presumption of revocation by destruction may be found in *In the Goods of Paget.*[23] In that case, the testator made his will and placed in a drawer and, some years later, he asked his daughter to get it from the drawer to see that it was properly executed. On that occasion, he expressed satisfaction with the terms of his will. No other member of the testator's family ever saw the will again. On his death, all his papers were found in good order, though the will was not among them. The Court presumed that the testator had destroyed his will with the intention of revoking it. The fact that a will was last traced to the testator's possession and cannot be found after his death after a diligent search for it will be sufficient to raise the presumption. There can be no such presumption of revocation where it is shown that the will was destroyed by mistake, as there can be no revocation without the intention to revoke, although the same evidence regarding due execution and evidence of contents for rebutting the presumption in the case of lost wills is also necessary in seeking the admission to probate of the contents of a will unintentionally destroyed.[24]

4–20 The first step in rebutting the presumption is for the propounding party to show that the testator duly executed the lost will. The evidence of the attesting witnesses and the solicitor who supervised the execution of the will may establish that the will was duly executed. Where the propounding party succeeds in proving the due execution of the lost will, he or she must then produce secondary evidence of its contents. The evidence of contents must, however, be clear, precise and satisfactory. An affidavit deposing to the contents of the will and exhibiting a copy or draft of the will by the testator's solicitors may be sufficient proof of contents.[25] It must also be shown that the will was not found after a diligent search for it was conducted, including

[23] (1913) 47 I.L.T.R. 284.

[24] See *In the Goods of Gilliland* [1940] N.I. 125.

[25] See *In the Goods of O'Hare* (1908) 42 I.L.T.R. 75.

the placing of advertisements seeking its whereabouts.[26] In *In the Goods of Mulvany*[27] the original will of the testator disappeared in a solicitor's office and, while a copy of the will was found, the original remained undiscovered following a diligent search, including the placing of advertisements. The Court in that case gave liberty to the propounding party to apply for a grant of letters of administration with the copy will annexed.

Where no copy or draft is available, the court may still be able reconstruct the will from the evidence of contents provided by the grounding affidavit or affidavits. The latter task may be a difficult one, but if statements are forthcoming from members of the testator's family who had knowledge of the contents of the will, the court may admit to probate a reconstructed version of the will, although such persons may be required to give oral evidence of due execution of the will and the means by which they acquired knowledge of the will's contents. In *In the Goods of Regan*[28] it was held that, where no contemporary copy or instructions of the lost will were forthcoming, the court may still grant probate of a typed copy of a reconstructed will made from statements of the testator's next of kin, though the court may require them to give oral evidence of the contents of the will and the circumstances surrounding its execution. Verbal declarations and statements made by a testator around the time of the execution of his will may also be accepted as evidence of contents of the lost will. In *In the Goods of Ball*[29] the Court affirmed that it was settled law that declarations made before the execution of a will were always admissible to prove the contents of lost wills, and further, in principle, that there should be no distinction between declarations made before, and declarations made after, the execution of a will in relation to contents. **4–21**

Where it is established that the will was mistakenly destroyed, evidence of due execution and contents must be adduced. In *In the Goods of Gilliland*[30] the testatrix's will was prepared by an experienced solicitor and was afterwards mistakenly destroyed. The solicitor who succeeded to the practice was able to prove that the will bore the signature of the testatrix and the signatures of two witnesses. This was the only evidence of due execution. On the day on which the testatrix made the will, she wrote a letter to the sole beneficiary informing the beneficiary that she had made a will, and that she had left all she possessed to that beneficiary. This letter was the only evidence of the contents of the will. Andrews L.C.J. held that the evidence was sufficient to justify a finding of due execution of the will, and that the letter written by the testatrix was admissible in evidence to prove the contents of the will mistakenly destroyed. **4–22**

26 *In the Goods of Mulvany* (1902) 36 I.L.T.R. 152.
27 (1902) 36 I.L.T.R. 152.
28 [1964] Ir. Jur.Rep. 56.
29 (1890) 25 L.R. Ir. 556.
30 [1940] N.I. 125.

The Doctrine of Dependent Relative Revocation

4–23 Section 85(2) of the 1965 Act provides that a will or any part of it may be revoked:

> "by another will or codicil duly executed, or by some writing declaring an intention to revoke it and executed in the manner in which a will is required to be executed, or by the burning, tearing, or destruction of it by the testator, or by some person in his presence and by his direction, with the intention of revoking it".

4–24 The revocation of a will or codicil will therefore be absolute

> "if the act of revocation, whether by another will duly executed or by the destruction of the existing will, be without reference to any other act or event".[31]

But the revocation of a will or codicil may be conditional "if the act (of revocation) be so connected with some other act or event," and the courts by applying the doctrine of dependent relative revocation may deem the revocation as conditional only.[32] The intention of the testator is of crucial importance to the application by the courts of the doctrine of dependent relative revocation when deciding that a testator's destruction of his will was conditional, because the act of revocation was connected with some other act or event. As was stated by Kenny J. in *In the Goods of Irvine*[33]:

> "It is altogether a question of intention, and if, as part of the act of making a fresh will, there will be a revocation of a previous will, that revocation will be absolute provided the fresh will be made."[34]

4–25 However, if the new will is not made, it may defeat the testator's intention to hold the revocation to be absolute.[35] Where a testator destroys his will with the intention of making a new one but fails to do so, the revocation may, by applying the doctrine of dependent relative revocation, be viewed as a conditional revocation only.[36] The doctrine of dependent relative revocation may also be applied to render a revocation by destruction conditional where a current will is destroyed with the intention of reviving an earlier will already revoked by the testator's current will, because the testator's intention was to revive the former will and not revoke the current one.[37]

---

31 *In the Goods of Irvine* [1919] 2 I.R. 485 at 489.

32 *ibid.*

33 [1919] 2 I.R. 485 at 489-490.

34 See *Attorney General v Lloyd* (1747) 1 Ves. Sen. 32 at 34; *Re O'Toole*, Unreported, High Court, Barrington J., 26 June 1980; *Curtin v O'Mahony* [1991] 2 I.R. 562 at 573.

35 *In the Goods of Hogan* [1980] I.L.R.M. 24; see *In the Goods of Irvine* [1919] 2 I.R. 485 at 489.

36 *In the Goods of Irvine* [1919] 2 I.R. 485 at 489; *West v West* [1921] 2 I.R. 34; *In the Goods of Hogan* [1980] I.L.R.M. 24.

37 *In the Goods of Hogan* [1980] I.L.R.M. 24.

Where the doctrine of dependent relative revocation is applied to an alleged conditional revocation by a will or codicil, extrinsic evidence of the testator's intention may be admitted under s.90 of the 1965 Act where it tends "to show the intention of the testator and to assist in the construction of, or to explain any contradiction in the will".[38] The facts surrounding the act of destruction will also be of primary importance in ascertaining the intention of the testator.[39] In *In the Estate of McMullan*[40] the Court had to consider the admissibility of written declarations made by the testatrix contemporaneously with the destruction of her will. In that case Sheil J. stated: **4–26**

> "Therefore, a statement by a testator that he has altered his mind as to the disposition of his property, and that he has therefore destroyed his will, although it may not be evidence of the fact of destruction of the will, is evidence of intention from which the fact of destruction may be inferred, there being other circumstances leading to the same conclusion."

Where a will is totally revoked by a later will or by codicil, or by some writing duly executed, the revocation will be absolute. But where a revocation is made conditional on making a new will, and where no such will is made, the revocation may not be viewed as an absolute one. By applying the doctrine of dependent relative revocation, the revocation may be looked on as the first step towards accomplishing the testator's intention to make a new will. The doctrine of dependent relative revocation was described by Kenny J. in *In the Goods of Irvine*.[41] He said that: **4–27**

> "If the act of revocation, whether by another will duly executed or by the destruction of the existing will, be without reference to any other act or event, the revocation may be an absolute one; but if the act be connected with some other act or event that its efficacy is meant to be dependent on the other act or event, it will fail as a revocation. If that other act be efficacious, the revocation will operate; otherwise it will not. It is altogether a question of intention, and if, as part of the act of making a fresh will, there will be a revocation of a previous will, that revocation will be absolute provided the fresh will be made."

In *In the Goods of Irvine,* the testator executed a will and a codicil. He subsequently executed another will in printed form containing blanks that were filled in after the execution had taken place. It was admitted by the applicant for a grant of probate that the blank spaces were filled in after execution, but he sought to have so much of that will, as revoked all former wills, admitted to probate, in other words, the revocation clause only. The **4–28**

38 See *Rowe v Law* [1978] I.R. 55 at 72; see also *O'Connell v Bank of Ireland* [1998] 2 I.R. 596; *Corrigan v Corrigan & Anor* [2007] I.E.H.C. 367; see *Keating on Probate* (4th ed) (Dublin: Round Hall, 2011).

39 See *Dixon v Solicitor to the Treasury* [1905] P. 42; *Reeves v Reeves* [1909] 2 I.R. 521; *In the Goods of Hogan* [1980] I.L.R.M. 24.

40 [1964] Ir. Jur.Rep. 33.

41 [1919] 2 I.R. 485 at 489-490; see also *Onions v Tyrer* (1716) 1 P. Wms. 343; *Ex parte The Earl of Ilchester* (1803) 7 Ves. 348.

question for the Court was whether, in the circumstances, the revocation clause contained in the will executed by the deceased was an absolute or conditional revocation. Kenny J. had no doubt that the doctrine of dependent relative revocation was applicable. From the evidence, he drew the following conclusions of fact: one, that the attempted revocation was merely the first step towards accomplishing the design of the testator to make a new will; two, that it was dependent and conditional on a will being actually made; and three, that no will was made, and consequently that the intention failed in execution.

4–29 In *West v West*[42] the testator made a will in February 1913. He died in September 1919. After his death, the will of February 1913 could not be found. An envelope was found among his papers bearing the message "My will made Jan 26, 1918, one made February, 1913, destroyed". The envelope contained a signed but unattested testamentary writing dated 26 January 1918, which was found to be based on the will made by the testator in February 1913. A copy of that will was produced by the testator's solicitors, and was put in evidence as constituting the contents of the destroyed will of February 1913. Probate in solemn form was sought of that will. The Court held that the destruction of the will of February 1913 was conditional on the testator's belief that the testamentary writing dated 26 January 1918 would be effective as a will and, as that instrument failed as a will, the doctrine of dependent relative revocation was applicable. Accordingly, the will of February 1913 should be admitted to probate as the last will of the testator. Moore J. having cited with approval the judgment of Kenny J. in *In the Goods of Irvine*[43] describing the doctrine of dependent relative revocation, went on to say:

> "In my opinion, therefore, on the best judgment I can form, there is evidence on which I should hold that the revocation of the earlier will was conditional on the testator's belief that the revocatory clause in the later will would be effective; and once it transpired that this belief was unfounded, the doctrine of dependent relative revocation applies, and the earlier will is set up, notwithstanding its revocation."[44]

4–30 The doctrine of dependent relative revocation may also be applied to a gift in a will. Where, for instance, a testator in a former will leaves legacies to named legatees, and makes a new will leaving the same legacies to other legatees in the mistaken belief that the legatees mentioned in the former will have died, and he makes a statement to that effect in his new will, by applying the doctrine of dependent relative revocation, the legacies in the new will may be deemed conditional on the death of the legatees named in

---

[42] [1921] 2 I.R. 34.

[43] [1919] 2 I.R. 485 at 489-490; see also *Onions v Tyrer* (1716) 1 P. Wms. 343; *Ex parte The Earl of Ilchester* (1803) 7 Ves. 348.

[44] *West v West* [1921] 2 I.R. 34 at 37.

the former will, and, as they were still alive, they are entitled by virtue of the doctrine to the legacies left to them in the former will.[45]

When considering whether or not to apply the doctrine of dependent relative revocation in the case of a will, codicil or some writing duly executed, the court will construe the relevant testamentary disposition in an attempt to ascertain the testator's intention.[46] In *West v West*,[47] Moore J. stated that the testator's intention must be established as a matter of evidence. Any declarations or statements made by the testator surrounding the making of a conditional revocation by testamentary instrument will only be admissible if they should prove to be of assistance to the court when interpreting the revoking instrument.[48] Extrinsic evidence of intention may also be admitted under s.90 of the 1965 Act where it tends "to show the intention of the testator and to assist in the construction of, or to explain any contradiction in the will".[49] **4–31**

Where a testator destroys an existing will *animo revocandi* there will be an absolute and unconditional revocation of the prior will. Where a testator destroys a will with the intention of making a new but dies without doing so, that intention alone will not reinstate the destroyed will. It was stated by Haugh J. in *In the Goods of Walsh*[50] that: **4–32**

> "It has often happened that a person destroying a will with the intention of making another, dies without having made it but I could not hold that because an intention was expressed and not carried out, the will destroyed should therefore be set up."[51]

Where a will is destroyed *animo revocandi* accompanied by a mere general intention to make a new will, the revocation will not be deemed conditional on the making of a new will. Furthermore, the discovery of an unexecuted will found among the papers of a deceased after his death will not be sufficient evidence of a conditional revocation of a will by destruction.[52] **4–33**

Therefore,

> "If the act of revocation, whether by another will duly executed or by the

---

45 See *Campbell v French* (1797) 3 Ves. 321; *In the Goods of Hope* [1942] P. 136.

46 *Re O'Toole*, Unreported, High Court, Barrington J., 26 June 1980; *Curtin v O'Mahony* [1991] 2 I.R. 562 at 573; see also Albert Keating, *The Construction of Wills* (Dublin: Round Hall *Sweet & Maxwell*, 2001).

47 [1921] 2 I.R. 34 at 37.

48 *In the Estate of McMullan* [1964] Ir. Jur.Rep. 33.

49 See *Rowe v Law* [1978] I.R. 55 at 72; see also *O'Connell v Bank of Ireland* [1998] 2 I.R. 596; *Corrigan v Corrigan & Anor* [2007] I.E.H.C. 367; see Albert Keating, *Keating on Probate* (4th ed) (Dublin: Round Hall, 2011).

50 [1947] Ir. Jur.Rep. 44.

51 See also *Re Jones* [1976] 1 All E.R. 593 at 603.

52 See *In the Goods of Coster*, Unreported, Supreme Court, 19 January 1978.

> destruction of the existing will, be without reference to any other act or event, the revocation may be an absolute one."[53]

4–34 But if the act of revocation by the destruction of the existing will is so connected with some other act or event, the revocation may be a conditional one.[54] A testator may, for instance, destroy his will in the belief that an earlier one made by him will be revived.[55] In *Powell v Powell*[56] the testator destroyed his will with the expressed intention of validating an earlier one and substituting it for the destroyed will. However, such an act could not accomplish the intention, as such a process could only be achieved by reviving the earlier instrument. It was held by Sir J.P. Wilde that such conditional destruction did not operate as a revocation, owing to the absence of the *animus revocandi*.[57] The application of the doctrine of dependent relative revocation was also considered by Gannon J. in *In the Goods of Hogan*.[58] In that case, the testatrix made her first will in 1977. She made another will in 1979. She later destroyed the will of 1979 in the belief that the will of 1977 would thereby be revived. The evidence showed that the testatrix destroyed her will of 1979 in the mistaken belief as to the legal consequences, "namely, the effective disposition by the 1977 will, would ensue". The question therefore which the court had to determine was whether the revocation of the 1979 will was an absolute or a conditional revocation. Gannon J. adopted the description of the doctrine of dependent relative revocation by Kenny J. in *In the Goods of Irvine*,[59] and accepted the view of Meredith M.R. in *In Re Faris*[60] where he stated that:

> "a revocation grounded on an assumption of fact which is false takes effect unless, as a matter of construction, the truth of the fact is the condition of the revocation, or in other words, unless the revocation is contingent upon the fact being true".

4–35 Gannon J. found that the function of the Court was not to give:

> "effect to the intentions of the deceased as they might appear to be but to consider whether or not the formal acts undertaken by the deceased in purported conformity with the requirements of the Succession Act have been performed in the manner prescribed by statute".

4–36 The question of whether or not there was an effective revocation depended on the truth of the facts believed by the deceased to exist at the time of the purported revocation and, if the facts did not reflect the belief, the will

---

[53] *In the Goods of Irvine* [1919] 2 I.R. 485 at 489.
[54] *ibid.*
[55] *In the Goods of Hogan* [1980] I.L.R.M. 24.
[56] (1866) L.R. 1 P. & D. 209.
[57] See *Dancer v Crabb* (1873) L.R. 3 P. & D. 98; *Dixon v The Solicitor to the Treasury* [1905] P. 42.
[58] [1980] I.L.R.M. 24; see *Powell v Powell* (1866) L.R. 1 P. & D. 209.
[59] [1919] 2 I.R. 485 at 489-490; see also *Onions v Tyrer* (1716) 1 P. Wms. 343; *Ex parte The Earl of Ilchester* (1803) 7 Ves. 348.
[60] [1911] 1 I.R. 469 at 472.

purportedly revoked remained unrevoked. He held that there was no doubt that the will of 1977 was revoked but, as the purported revocation of the 1979 will was dependent on the truth of facts mistakenly believed by the testatrix, it had no effect, and consequently, the 1979 will remained unrevoked and stood as the last will of the testatrix.

Where the doctrine of dependent relative revocation is raised in relation to a revocation by an act of destruction, the facts surrounding the act of destruction will be of primary importance in ascertaining the intention of the testator.[61] Where, for instance, it is shown that a testator destroyed his will believing that his wife will become entitled to his entire estate on an intestacy, the revocation of his will by destruction will be viewed as conditional and the destroyed will reinstated.[62] All declarations or statements made by the testator at the time of the destruction of the will are admissible to establish the intention of the testator.[63] **4–37**

When considering the absolute or conditional nature of a revocation by a will or codicil, the courts may allow the admission of extrinsic evidence of the testator's intention in accordance with s.90 of the 1965 Act, and such evidence may take the form of declarations or statements made by the testator at the time of the revocation. When considering the absolute or conditional nature of a revocation by destruction, the court may admit any declarations and statements made by the testator at the time of destruction to establish his true intention. **4–38**

Revocability and Mutual Wills

It may happen that two testators may make mutual wills benefiting each other in furtherance of a pre-testamentary agreement to do so. If, on the death of one testator, the other purports to revoke the will made by him in accordance with the agreement and make a new one, equity may preclude him from doing so if he is in breach of the terms of the pre-testamentary agreement on the grounds that a constructive trust was established against changing the provisions of the mutual wills on the death of one of them. The reason for equity's intervention in this way is: **4–39**

> "he that dies first, does by his death carry the agreement on his part into execution. If the other refuses, he is guilty of fraud, can never unbind himself, and become a trustee of course. For no man shall deceive another to his prejudice. By engaging to do something that is in his power, he is made a trustee for the performance, and transmit that trust to those that claim under him".[64]

---

61 See *Dixon v Solicitor to the Treasury* [1905] P. 42.
62 *In the Estate of Southerden* [1925] P. 177.
63 See *Powell v Powell* (1866) L.R. 1 P. & D. 209; *West v West* [1921] 2 I.R. 34.
64 *Dufour v Pereira* (1769) 1 Dick. 419; see *Re Hagger* [1930] All E.R. 620; see Albert Keating, *Equitable Succession Rights* (Dublin: Thomson Round Hall, 2005).

4–40 In other words, on the death of one of the testators, the terms of the pre-testamentary agreement will take effect in the guise of a constructive trust and will be enforced accordingly. The death of one of the testators activates the trust founded on the pre-testamentary agreement. The survivor who becomes entitled to take a benefit under the will is thereafter bound by it and, as such, forfeits his right to revoke his will.

4–41 Mutual wills, like all other wills, must be executed in accordance with s.78 of the 1965 Act, but unlike other wills, they cease to be revocable on the death of one of the testators because of the existence of a pre-testamentary agreement. Although the right to revoke continues to exist during the lifetime of the testators, and the exercise of the right to revoke during that time causes the demise of the potential equity created by the pre-testamentary agreement, the death of one of the testators will close the door against a later revocation by the surviving testator. The surviving testator is not precluded from making a new will *per se*, but he is precluded from making a new will which revokes the terms of the mutual will made by him and the deceased testator. The mutual will continues to remain irrevocable. Moreover, it appears that, even should a surviving testator disclaim a beneficial interest under the mutual will, he will continue to be bound by the equity created by the pre-testamentary agreement which becomes operative on the death of the first testator.[65]

4–42 In *Re Hagger*[66] Clauson J. stated that:

> "*Dufour v Pereira* (1769) 1 Dick. 419; 21 E.R. 332 decides that where there is a joint will such as this, on the death of the testator who first dies the position as regards that part of the property which belongs to the survivor is that the survivor will be treated in this court as holding the property on trust to apply it so as to carry into effect the provisions of the joint will."

4–43 In *Re Hagger,* a husband and wife made a joint will by which they both agreed that neither of them would revoke the will without the other's consent. The wife was the first to die. During the lifetime of the husband, one of the remaindermen named in the will died. A question arose as to whether the deceased remainderman became entitled to a vested interest on the death of the wife. Clauson J. felt that he was bound to hold:

> "from the death of the wife the husband held the property, according to the tenor of the will, subject to the trusts thereby imposed upon it, at all events if he took advantage of the provisions of the will".

4–44 So far as the husband's interest in the property was concerned, the will operated as a trust from the date of the wife's death. There was accordingly no lapse by reason of the remainderman's death in the husband's lifetime,

---

[65] See Albert Keating, "The Effect of Pre-Testamentary Agreements to Make Mutual Wills and Secret Trusts on the Legal Right" (2007) 12(1) C.P.L.J. 13.

[66] [1930] All E.R. 620.

but after the wife's death. It may be noted that the fact that testators make contemporaneous and similar wills does not necessarily mean that they had entered into an agreement not to revoke them. Evidence may have to be adduced from the surrounding circumstances to show that they intended their wills to be irrevocable but, once the intention is established, the constructive trust will be found to exist by operation of law.

Revival of Wills

An earlier will made by a testator may be revived by re-execution or by codicil in accordance with s.87 of the 1965 Act. Revival by re-execution occurs where the whole or part of a revoked will is executed afresh by the testator in compliance with the s.78 of the Succession Act 1965. The only real difference between the revival of a former revoked will by re-execution and the making of a new will is one of intention: in the former, the intention to revive a revoked will must be present at the date of execution of the reviving instrument, while in the latter, the intention is to make a new will.[67] It is important to remember that revocation by destruction of a current will does not automatically revive an earlier will.[68] If a former revoked instrument is intended by the testator to be revived, he must use one of the methods for revival under s.87 of the Succession Act. Perhaps the more prudent approach would be to make a new will incorporating the provisions of the will intended to be revived. For a will to be revived by a codicil, an intention to revive must be expressed in the codicil.[69] The reviving codicil, to be an effective reviving instrument, must also accurately identify the will to be revived, as the courts will be slow to correct any mistaken references.[70] **4–45**

[67] See *In the Goods of Steele* (1868) L.R. 1 P. & D. 575; *In the Goods of Reade* [1902] P. 75; *Re Hall* [1943] Ir. Jur. Rep. 25.

[68] *In the Goods of Hogan* [1980] I.L.R.M. 24.

[69] *In the Goods of Davis* [1952] P. 279.

[70] *In the Goods of Mulock* [1933] I.R. 171.

CHAPTER 5

TESTAMENTARY GIFTS AND TRUSTS

INTRODUCTION

The type of estate which a testator wishes to dispose of will determine the nature of the testamentary gift as a devise, a legacy or bequest. Where a gift in a will consists of real estate, then the gift will be a devise of land, and the land comprised in the devise will pass to the devisee with whatever estate the testator had had in the land in the form of freehold or leasehold, and whether registered or unregistered land. It is also important to note that s.11(1) of the Land and Conveyancing Reform Act 2009 (the "2009 Act") provides that the only legal estates which may be created or disposed of are the freehold and leasehold estates specified in s.11(2) of the Act. Where a gift in a will consists of personal estate, then the gift will be a legacy or bequest, and the legacy or bequest will pass to the legatee whatever form of personal estate is comprised in the legacy or bequest, and this includes pecuniary legacies. Devises, legacies and bequests form part of the vocabulary of wills, and gifts of real and personal estate must be described as such when drafting wills.[1] A testator may also create a gift subject to a power of appointment. The effect of a power will depend on whether it is a general or special power. A general power will allow the donee to exercise it in favour of anyone, including himself. The exercise of a special power is limited to the objects designated in the instrument creating the power. A testator may also create a class gift in favour of a designated group of persons, for instance, the children of X. Where such a gift is created, it must comply with certain class-closing rules that determine the beneficiaries of the class entitled to a share in the gift. A devise may create a joint tenancy or a tenancy in **5–01**

1 See Chapter 24 – Wills Precedents; Albert Keating, *Keating on Probate* (4th ed) (Dublin: Thomson Round Hall, 2011); Albert Keating, *First Supplement to the Fourth Edition of Keating on Probate* (Dublin: Thomson Round Hall, 2013).

common. The essential differences between a joint tenancy and a tenancy in common is that, in the case of the former, there is a right of survivorship which means that a surviving joint tenant will automatically succeed to the share of a deceased joint tenant. In the case of the a tenancy in common, there is no right of survivorship and a share of a deceased tenant in common will form part of his or her estate.

5–02 Where a testator intends to create a testamentary trust, not only must the will be duly executed in compliance with s.78 of the Succession Act 1965 (the "1965 Act"), but also the trust must comply with the rules for creating trusts.[2] Where a trust of land is created, it will be governed by Part 4 of the 2009 Act.[3] The term "trust of land" covers every kind of settlement (whether or not the instrument creating it creates an express trust), holding trusts and trusts for sale whereby land is to be held for persons in succession to each other, and any other situation where land is subject to a trust, including a constructive or resulting trust declared by a court. A testator may also create a discretionary or a protective trust. A discretionary trust is one that empowers the trustees to pay or apply any part or parts of the capital and income of the trust fund to "all or any one or more" of the beneficiaries, but without giving a beneficiary a right to any part of the capital or income of the trust fund. A protective trust is one that becomes determinable on an event occurring, like the bankruptcy of a beneficiary or an attempted alienation of trust property by a beneficiary. On the occurrence of that event, the trust is transformed into a discretionary trust and will take effect accordingly. It must be emphasised, however, that the bankruptcy of a beneficiary or an attempted alienation of the trust property by him does not result in the determination of the trust, but rather in the transformation of it into a discretionary trust, and one where the discretionary powers of the trustees will play a prominent role in the administration of the trust. A protective trust may be created by a testator to ensure that the trust funds or property will not be frittered away by a profligate or spendthrift beneficiary or by extravagant claims made by creditors against trust funds or property. Where a testator wishes to create a charitable gift or trust, it must be for a charitable purpose recognised by the law of charities.[4] A testator may also intend a secret or half-secret trust. A secret trust is one that arises out of a will, although there is no mention of the trust in the will. A half-secret trust in a will is one that discloses the existence of a trust, though not the actual trust itself or the beneficiaries of the trust. Where an express trust fails to take effect, the property comprised in the trust may revert to the estate by way of a resulting trust.

5–03 As brief note on current inheritance tax thresholds, s.109 of the Finance Act 2012 amends Schedule 2 of the Capital Acquisition Tax Consolidation Act

[2] See Albert Keating, *Equitable Succession Rights* (Dublin: Thomson Round Hall, 2005); see Chapter 24 – Wills Precedents.

[3] See s.18 of the 2009 Act.

[4] See Albert Keating, *Equitable Succession Rights* (Dublin: Thomson Round Hall, 2005).

2003 and applies to gifts taken on or after 7 December 2011. It introduces new group thresholds as follows: Group A— son/daughter—€225,000, Group B—parent/brother/sister/niece/nephew/grandchild—€30,150, Group C—relationships other than Group A or B – €15,075.

Devises

A devise is a gift of land and the beneficiary of a devise is called a devisee. **5–04**
A devise may create a life estate or a fee simple estate. It may also create a life estate followed by a remainder in fee simple and, on the death of the life tenant, the remainder in fee simple will take effect. Where a devise of land is made to a devisee but, in the event of his dying without issue, the land passes to another person, the devisee will be divested of the gift where he or she leaves no issue, and the devise in default will take effect instead.[5] A devise may be made by a parent to a child and, in the event of that child's predecease, then in trust for his or her children in equal shares or jointly.[6] A brother or sister may create a devise in favour of another brother or sister and, in the event of that brother or sister predeceasing the testator, then to the children of that brother or sister in equal shares or jointly.[7] A parent may leave all of his or her real estate to a child and, in the event of that child's predecease, then to his or her children in equal shares or jointly.[8] A brother or sister may leave all of his real estate to another brother or sister and, in the event of that brother or sister predeceasing him or her, then to the children of that brother or sister in equal shares or jointly.[9] A testator may create a residuary devise which consists of all of a testator's real estate which is not disposed of by the will.[10] The devisee in this instance is called the residuary devisee. Devises may also be made subject to a condition.[11] There are two main types of condition: a condition precedent and a condition subsequent. Where the condition purports to suspend the vesting of a gift until the terms specified in the condition have been satisfied, the condition will be classified as a condition precedent. Where, on the other hand, it purports to divest a beneficiary of the gift where he fails to satisfy the terms of the condition, the condition will be classified as a condition subsequent.[12]

Section 3(1) of the 1965 Act provides that "real estate" has the meaning **5–05**
assigned to it by s.4 of that Act, and s.4(a) provides that "real estate" includes chattels real, and land in possession, remainder or reversion, and every estate or interest in or over land. Section 14 of the 1965 Act provides

[5] See Chapter 22 – The Construction of Wills; Albert Keating, *Irish Wills Precedents Service* (Dublin: Round Hall, 2009.
[6] See Albert Keating, *Irish Wills Precedents Service* (Dublin: Round Hall, 2009).
[7] *ibid.*
[8] *ibid.*
[9] *ibid.*
[10] See Chapter 24 – Wills Precedents.
[11] See Chapter 22 – The Construction of Wills.
[12] *ibid.*

that the estate of a deceased person includes references to both his real and personal estate. As real estate includes freeholds and leaseholds, it is important to point out that the meaning of freehold and leasehold estates is now subject to the provisions of the 2009 Act. The 2009 Act also contains provisions dealing with future interests in land, and abolishes a significant number of long-established rules. Section 9(1) of the 2009 Act provides that ownership of land comprises the estates specified in Part 2 of that Act only. The concept of an estate in land is, however, retained by the Act.[13] Section 11(1) of the 2009 Act provides that the only legal estates which may be created or disposed of are the freehold and leasehold estates specified in s.11(2) of the Act. Section 11(2) provides that:

> A freehold estate means a fee simple in possession and includes:
> (a) a determinable fee,
> (b) a fee simple subject to a right of entry,
> (c) a fee simple subject only to a power of revocation, an annuity or other payment of capital or income for the advancement, maintenance or other benefit of any person, or a right of residence which is not an exclusive right over the whole land.[14]
>
> A leasehold estate means the estate which arises when a tenancy is created for any period of time or any recurring period and irrespective whether or not the estate:
> (a) takes effect in immediate possession, or
> (b) is subject to another legal estate or interest, or
> (c) is for a term which is uncertain or liable to termination by notice, re-entry or operation of law or by virtue of a provision for cessor on redemption or for any other reason.

5–06 Section 12(1) of the 2009 Act prohibits the creation of a fee farm grant at law or in equity. Under s.12(2), any instrument, including a will, purporting to create a fee farm grant vests a legal fee simple in the grantee or devisee, or an equitable fee simple where appropriate. Section 13(1) of the 2009 Act provides that the creation of a fee tail of any kind at law or in equity is prohibited. Under s.13(2), any instrument, including a will, executed after the commencement of the 2009 Act purporting to create a fee tail in favour of any person vests in that person a legal fee simple or, where appropriate, an equitable fee simple. Section 14 prohibits the creation of leases for lives. Section 15(1) of the 2009 Act, which deals with the operation of future interests in land, provides that all future interests in land, whether vested or contingent, exist in equity only. Where a testator intends to create a future interest in land, the executors may also be appointed trustees for the purposes of the 2009 Act. Section 16 of the 2009 Act abolishes the rule against perpetuities, the rule against accumulations, the common law contingent remainder rules, the rule in *Purefoy v Rogers*[15] and the rule in *Whitby v Mitchell*.[16]

---

[13] s.10(1) of the 2009 Act.
[14] s.11(2) of the 2009 Act.
[15] (1671) 2 Wm. Saund. 380.
[16] (1890) 44 Ch. 85.

Legacies and Bequests

A legacy or bequest is a gift of personal estate, including a pecuniary legacy. A legacy or bequest may be classified as a specific legacy, a general legacy, or a demonstrative legacy. A specific legacy is a gift of specified personal estate.[17] A general legacy is also a gift of personal estate, but one that payable out of a testator's general estate.[18] A demonstrative legacy, although in the nature of a general legacy, is one to be paid out of a particularly designated fund, for instance, where a testator gives and bequeaths a sum of money out of a named bank account.[19] Although specific, general and demonstrative legacies may be for money, a pecuniary legacy for the purposes of s.3(1) of the 1965 Act includes a general and a demonstrative legacy and any other general direction by a testator for the payment of money.[20] As a result, a pecuniary legacy will be paid out of the general estate of a testator unless it is construed as a specific legacy. The beneficiary of personal estate is called a legatee. **5–07**

A specific legacy or bequest is a gift of a particular item of personal property or a certain sum of money: a residuary legacy is a gift of all of a testator's remaining personal property or money not otherwise specifically disposed of in the will. Where the words used in creating a legacy are ambiguous, the court will lean in favour of a general legacy. A general legacy presupposes that the estate of the testator has sufficient assets to pay out the legacy. Where a legacy consists of a money payment, the amount will be payable out of the realised assets of the deceased unless the particular source of payment of the legacy has been indicated by the testator—for instance, where a specific legacy of a specified sum of money is payable out of a repository indicated by the testator in his will and consisting of the precise amount. A general legacy may also consist of a gift of shares in a company where a number of shares are given to a legatee, unless the testator owns a specific number of shares and gives them to the legatee as "my" shares followed by the amount of shares owned by the testator in that particular company, *viz.* "my 1,000 shares in X plc". **5–08**

A demonstrative legacy indicates the actual fund out of which they are to be paid or the particular part of the property of the deceased from which they are to be taken. For instance, a particular bank account may be indicated from which the legacy must be paid or a particular shareholding in a company out of which a number of shares are to be given. Although a particular fund or a particular part of property is indicated for payment or discharge, a demonstrative legacy is also general in effect. In fact, a demonstrative legacy must be general in effect, otherwise it may be deemed a specific **5–09**

17 See Chapter 24 – Wills Precedents; Albert Keating, *Irish Wills Precedents Service* (Dublin: Round Hall, 2009).

18 *ibid.*

19 *ibid.*

20 *ibid.*

legacy which is payable out of a fund indicated by the testator, especially so where that fund contains the exact amount for the payment of the legacy. The essential character of a demonstrative legacy was described by Gibson J. in *Re Connor*[21] as a

> "legacy capable of existence quite independently of the fund, and the direction as to the fund out of which it is payable must be properly be regarded as a subordinate provision of the will. If the source of payment is an integral and inseparable part of the nature of the legacy it cannot be demonstrative, because one of the features of a demonstrative legacy is that it should appear that if the fund prove insufficient the amount of the legacy can be made up out of other assets given by will".

5–10 An annuity is a legacy consisting of a periodic or yearly payment of a sum of money from income arising out of a particular part of the testator's property, usually to be paid out of property in the residuary estate of the testator. An annuity is intended as a source of income for the life of the legatee, although it may be construed as being limited in duration.

Powers of Appointment

5–11 A devise of land may also take the form of a power of appointment. There are three parties involved in the creation and exercise of powers of appointment, *viz.* the donor of the power, i.e. testator, the donee of the power, i.e. the person who is authorised to exercise the power, and the objects of the power, i.e. the beneficiaries of the power. General and special powers are the most common type of testamentary powers. At first glance, powers appear to be similar to trusts, but the main differentiating feature between powers and trusts is that the exercise of a power by the donee is discretionary, whereas a trustee is obliged to carry out the terms of a trust. If this discretionary aspect is absent from a power, it may be construed by the courts as a power in the nature of a trust.

5–12 A general power may be exercised by the donee in favour of any person, including himself. A special power is limited to a specific class of objects and the exercise of the power is confined to that class only. Prior to the 2009 Act, the rule against perpetuities played a prominent role in the creation and exercise of powers of appointment. The operation of the rule depended on whether the power was a general or special power. The rule applied to a general power from the moment of its creation. It applied to a special power from the time of exercising the power. The rule against perpetuities is now abolished by s.16(d) of the 2009 Act. The exercise of a power may also be subject to formal requirements by the donor specifying the instrument that must be used by the donee when exercising the power. If the power is exercised by using another instrument, it may be viewed as a defective exercise of the power. The instrument specified by the donor may itself be

[21] [1969] N.I. 159 at 163–164.

subject to formal requirements for it to take effect, such as where a will is the specified instrument, and if so, it must be executed in compliance with s.78 of the 1965 Act.

Where some doubt exists as to whether the testator intended to create a power of appointment or one in the nature of a trust, the court will construe the language used by him. Where the language suggests that the objects of the power are to receive the property, the power may be construed as creating a power in the nature of a trust.[22] One test employed by the court when determining whether the testator intended to create a power of appointment or a power in the nature of a trust is to ascertain whether there is a gift over in default of appointment by the donee, as this will be an indication that the testator did not intend to create a power in the nature of a trust.[23] The test is not however conclusive.[24] But where the language suggests that the testator intended the objects of the power to benefit by the property, the court may construe the power as one in the nature of a trust and enforce it accordingly.[25] **5–13**

Class Gifts

A devise may take the form of a class gift. A class gift is one where a testator leaves his estate to a designated group of persons, for instance, the children of X. A class gift is also subject to class-closing rules. The basic rule is that the date of distribution of a class gift is the date when the first member of the class becomes entitled to an interest in possession, and it is also at this point that the class closes. The gift will be confined to the children of X born before the death of the testator; any children born after the death of the testator will be excluded unless a contrary intention appears from the will.[26] The class will close at the date of death of the testator. Where however there are no children of the designated class in existence at the date of the testator's death, then all children born after that date will be entitled to a share.[27] A class member may also be a person who becomes a member of a class by statutory definition, for instance, a class gift created for the children of X may include a non-marital child of X by virtue of the Status of Children Act 1987. Prior to the 2009 Act, the rule against perpetuities had also to be observed and, while children of the designated class may be in existence at the date of the testator's death, a gift that infringed the rule against perpetuities was deemed invalid. As already stated, the 2009 Act abolished the rule against perpetuities. **5–14**

---

22 *Re Parker* [1966] I.R. 309.

23 *Re Mills* [1930] 1 Ch. 654; *Re Gestetner Settlement* [1953] Ch. 672.

24 *Re Llewellyn's Settlement* [1921] 2 Ch. 281; *Re Weekes' Settlement* [1897] 1 Ch. 289; *Re Combe* [1925] Ch. 210; *Re Perowne* [1951] Ch. 785.

25 *Re Parker* [1966] I.R. 309.

26 *Re Poe* [1942] I.R. 535 at 537.

27 *Harris v Lloyd* (1823) 1 T. & R. 310; *Weld v Bradbury* (1715) 2 Ver. 705; *Re Chartres* [1927] 1 Ch. 466.

5–15 The creation of a class gift for children may also be made subject to a contingency. For instance, a testator may specify a particular age to be attained before they become entitled under the gift. Where there is a contingency of this nature, the rule is that, once a child of the designated class attains the specified age before the testator's death, the class closes. A child born after the testator's death will be excluded, even though he may attain the specified age. This rule, like the other class-closing rules, is subject to a contrary intention appearing from the will creating the gift. While the class-closing rules may seem unfair to children born subsequent to the testator's death, they at least allow the beneficiaries entitled under the gift to ascertain the minimum value of their shares in the estate. They also facilitate an early administration and distribution of the testator's estate that might otherwise be postponed indefinitely.

5–16 A class gift may also not take immediate effect on the testator's death owing to the existence of a prior or intermediate life estate. Where such is the case, children who are born after the testator's death may become entitled to a share in the estate if they are born during the lifetime of the life tenant. Moreover, the share of a child who predeceases the life tenant will form part of that child's estate. If no children are born into the class at the time of death of the testator or life tenant, the class will remain open to let in children who are born before the death of the person whose children form the objects of the gift.[28] Where there is not only a delayed vesting due to the existence of an intermediate life estate but where the gift is also subject to the contingency of attaining a specified age, the class will remain open to include children who attain that age at the date of death of the life tenant.[29] In the event of no child attaining the specified age at the date of death of the life tenant, the first child who subsequently attains that age will have the effect of closing the class and the gift to which it relates. The share of any child who attains the requisite age and subsequently dies will form part of his estate. Where, however, the vesting of the class gift is accelerated owing to the life tenant predeceasing the testator, the relevant time for ascertaining the members of the class will again be the date of death of the testator. A vesting may also be accelerated by a life tenant's own act, for instance, by disclaimer, and as a result a question may arise in relation to the date of entitlement to a share in a class gift. There are two conflicting English decisions on the matter. In *Re Davies*[30] Vaisey J. was of the opinion that the class closed on the date of the act causing the acceleration and only children born at that time were entitled to a share in the gift. In *Re Harker's Will Trust*[31] Goff J. held that the relevant date for the closing of the class was the death of the erstwhile life tenant, thus allowing children living at that time to share in the gift. It is suggested that the latter view might reflect more the intention

[28] *Re Chartres* [1927] 1 Ch. 466.
[29] See *Re Paul's S.T.* [1920] 1 Ch. 99.
[30] [1957] 1 W.L.R. 922.
[31] [1969] 1 W.L.R. 1124.

of the testator to benefit members of a class following the death of the life tenant, for otherwise he would not have created a life estate.

The class closing rules may not, however, be applicable at all if the objects of the gifts are designated by name, for instance, X, Y and Z being the children of A, rather than generically as the children of A.[32] The rules may also be not applicable where the testator intends to benefit children of a class once born alive, as each child will become entitled to a share in the gift or trust at birth.[33] Where the designated class includes the testator's own children and where one of the children dies before the testator, leaving issue of his own, his share in the gift will not lapse but will go to his surviving issue, unless a contrary intention appears from the will.[34] **5–17**

Joint Tenancies and Tenancies in Common

A devise may also consist of a joint tenancy or a tenancy in common.[35] The words used by the testator when creating the devise will determine the nature of the co-ownership of land by the devisees. Where the word "jointly" is used, a joint tenancy will be created. Where the words "equal shares" or "equally" are used, a tenancy in common will be created. Joint tenants and tenants in common will enjoy co-ownership of the real estate during their lifetimes but, on the death of a joint tenant, his share will pass to the surviving joint tenants by virtue of the right of survivorship. A tenancy in common is not subject to the right of survivorship and, on the death of a tenant in common, his share in the tenancy will become part of his estate. A joint tenancy is characterised by the four unities of possession, interest, title and time, and of course, the right of survivorship. A tenancy in common need only possess the unity of possession, and the equal share of a tenant in common will be determined by the number of tenants entitled to a share in the land. There is no right of survivorship in the case of a tenancy in common. A body corporate may acquire an interest in a joint tenancy in the same way as if it were an individual. A body corporate is also like individuals subject to the right of survivorship and, on dissolution, the property devolves on the surviving joint tenants.[36] Under s.30 of the 2009 Act, there can be no unilateral severance of a joint tenancy without the consent in writing of another joint tenant, but the court may dispense with such consent where it is deemed to be unreasonably withheld.[37] Under s.30(4), the court may **5–18**

---

32 *Re Ramadge* [1969] N.I. 71; *Re Harker's Will Trust* [1969] 1 W.L.R. 1124.

33 *Re Edmondson Will Trust* [1972] 1 W.L.R. 183; *Re Ransome* [1957] Ch. 348; *Re Tom's Settlement* [1987] Ch. 63.

34 See Chapter 9 – The Ademption, Lapse and Modification of Gifts.

35 See Albert Keating, *Keating on Probate* (4th ed) (Dublin: Thomson Round Hall, 2011); Albert Keating, *First Supplement to the Fourth Edition of Keating on Probate* (Dublin: Thomson Round Hall, 2013), Albert Keating, *Irish Wills Precedents Service* (Dublin: Round Hall, 2009), Pt V; s.4(c) of the 1965 Act.

36 s.32(3) of the 2009 Act.

37 s.31(1)(e) of the 2009 Act.

find that all the joint tenants by mutual agreement or by their conduct have severed the joint tenancy in equity.

Trusts

5–19 For a trust to be properly constituted by will, it must, like all trusts, comply with the essential prerequisites for creating trusts, *viz*:

> "the subject-matter must be certain, the objects of the trust must be certain, and the words relied upon as creating the trust must have been used in the imperative mood, so as to show that the testator intended to create an obligation".[38]

5–20 Although there is no set formula of words for creating a trust, the words employed by the testator must be sufficient to manifest an intention to create a trust.[39] The words must also be expressed in the imperative mood so as to make it clear that the person appointed as trustee is holding property in trust for the named beneficiaries.[40] Words that merely request something to be done or words that are "precatory" will not be sufficient to create a trust.[41] Once the testator's intention is made manifest, the next question is whether the property forming the subject matter of the trust and beneficial interest are ascertained or ascertainable. Words describing property as "the bulk of my estate" will not sufficiently identify the subject matter, but words like "a reasonable interest" might be sufficient to ascertain the beneficial interest in the trust estate.[42] The objects or beneficiaries of the trust must also be ascertained or at least ascertainable. This may present very little difficulty if what is called a "fixed" trust is created and all the beneficiaries are named or 'listed' and thus ascertained.[43] Extrinsic evidence may also be admitted to show that the testator intended to include another person as one of the objects of a discretionary trust who would perhaps not normally be a member of that class of objects.[44] Where, however, the definition of beneficiaries for the purposes of the trust is so wide as not to form "anything like a class", it may be deemed "administratively unworkable" and the trust may fail as a result.[45]

5–21 Where a discretionary trust is involved, the trustees will be given a discretion as to how the trust estate is to be distributed among the beneficiaries, and no

---

[38] *Chambers v Fahy* [1931] I.R. 17 at 21 *per* O'Byrne J.; see Albert Keating, *Equitable Succession Rights* (Dublin: Thomson Round Hall, 2005).

[39] *Re Keyford* [1975] 1 All E.R. 604.

[40] *Wright v Atkyns* Turn & R. 143; *Re Humphrey's Estate* [1916] 1 I.R. 21; *Re Sweeney* [1976-77] I.L.R.M. 88)

[41] See *Re Blackwood* [1953] N.I. 23; *Re Coulson* 87 I.L.T.R. 93.

[42] *Re Golay* [1965] 2 All E.R. 660.

[43] *IRC v Broadway Cottages* [1955] Ch. 20.

[44] *Crawford v Lawless*, Unreported, High Court, Smyth J., 6 November 2002.

[45] *McPhail v Doulton* [1970] 2 All E.R. 228; *Morice v Bishop of Durham* 10 Ves.Jun. 522; *Re Baden's Deed Trusts (No.2)* [1972] 2 All E.R. 1304; *Re Manisty's Settlement* [1974] Ch. 17; *Re Hay's Settlement Trust* [1981] 3 All E.R. 786.

member of the class may claim an interest in the trust estate until the trustees exercise their discretion.[46] A testator may wish to create a discretionary trust by empowering his trustees to pay the capital or income of the trust without giving the beneficiary a right to any part of the capital or income of the trust fund or property.[47] A testator may also wish to create a protective trust determinable on the bankruptcy of a beneficiary or in the event of a beneficiary attempting to alienate trust property. Where the event envisaged by the protective trust occurs, it will be transformed into a discretionary trust, though not depriving the beneficiary of the beneficial interest in the trust estate.

TRUSTS OF LAND

Prior to the 2009 Act, the Settled Land Acts 1882-1890 governed all settlements and trusts of land created by testators in their wills. The Settled Land Acts 1882-1890 have now been repealed and replaced by the 2009 Act, and the various kinds of settlements and trusts relating to land will now comprise a "trust of land" for the purposes of s.18 of the 2009 Act. A trust of land covers every kind of settlement (whether or not the instrument creating it creates an express trust), holding trusts and trusts for sale whereby land is to be held for persons in succession to each other, and any other situation where land is subject to a trust, including a constructive or resulting trust declared by a court. The only exception to this rule is in s.18(9), where land is held directly for a charitable purpose. The law relating to charities gives rise to special considerations and they have long been the subject of special legislation such as the Charities Acts 1961, 1973 and 2009. **5–22**

Section 18(1) of the 2009 Act (replacing ss. 2, 59 and 60 of the Settled Land Act 1882) provides that there is trust of land for purposes of Part 4 of the 2009 Act where land is: **5–23**

(a) for the time being limited by an instrument, whenever executed, to persons by way of succession without the interposition of a trust (referred to as a "strict settlement"), and under s.18(2)(a), a strict settlement exists where an estate or interest in reversion or remainder is not disposed of and reverts to the settlor or the testator's successors in title, but does not exist where a person owns a fee simple in possession) or

(b) held, either with or without other property, on a trust whenever it arises and of whatever kind, and under s.18(2)(b), a trust includes an express, implied, resulting, constructive and bare trust and a trust for sale, or

---

46 See *Re Buyley* [1945] I.R. 224; *O'Byrne v Davoren* [1994] 3 I.R. 373; *Re Gulbenkian's Settlement* [1970] A.C. 508; *McPhail v Doulton* [1970] 2 All E.R. 228; *Re Baden's Deed Trusts (No.2)* [1972] 2 All E.R. 1304.

47 See Chapter 24 – Wills Precedents.

(c) vested, whether before or after the commencement of the 2009 Act, in a minor.

5–24 Section 18(3) of the 2009 Act provides that a trust of land is governed by the general law of trusts. The general law comprises the body of law built up by the courts over the centuries relating to, for example, trustees' duties owed to beneficiaries (based on the principle that they must act always in the interests of the beneficiaries, and not seek personal gain) and statute law, such as the provisions of the Trustee Act 1893 dealing with administration of trusts and trustees' powers. Under s.18(4) of the 2009 Act, the conversion of a life estate into an equitable interest under a trust does not affect a life owner's liability for waste. The doctrine of waste was developed by the courts to protect the interests of persons entitled to succeed to land after a prior owner holding a limited interest, like a life estate. It prohibits a prior owner from damaging the property while he or she occupies it. Such an equitable life owner may, under s.20(2) of the 2009 Act, be permitted by the trustees to occupy or use the land. Section 18(5) provides that where, by reason of absence from the State or otherwise, it remains uncertain for a period of at least seven years as to whether a person on whose life an estate or interest depends is alive, it shall continue to be presumed that the person is dead. Section 18(6) goes on to provide that:

> "If such presumption is applied to a person but subsequently rebutted by proof to the contrary, that person may bring an action for damages or another remedy for any loss suffered."

5–25 When hearing such an action under s.18(6), the court may make such order as appears to it to be just and equitable in the circumstances of the case.[48] Section 18(5), (6) and (7) re-enact the substance of the provision in the Life Estates Act 1695 that, after a life owner has been unheard of for at least seven years, there is a presumption that he or she is dead and so it is safe to allow a successor to enjoy the land. Section 18(8) provides that any party to a conveyance is to be presumed to have attained full age.

5–26 Where a strict settlement not involving an express trust exists at the commencement of Part 4, it will become a trust of land under s.18(1)(a). However, in order to preserve some continuity with the previous law governed by the Settled Land Act 1882 (under which the tenant for life had limited powers of dealing with the land, subject to an indirect role of trustees of the settlement), s.19(1)(a) of the 2009 Act provides that the trustees will be the tenant for life, together with the trustees of the settlement. Where a settlement is created after the commencement of Part 4, it will involve a trust, and the instrument creating it should specify the trustees. Section 19(1)(b) lists in order of priority other persons connected with the settlement or trust who may become the trustees if none are specified by the instrument creating the

[48] s.18(7) of the 2009 Act.

trust, such as, in the case of a trust arising under a will, the testator's personal representatives. Section 19(1)(c) applies these provisions to cases where a trust arises under s.18 because the land is vested in a minor. Section 19(d) deals with other trusts of land which do not involve a settlement creating a succession of interests, such as a constructive or resulting trust declared by a court or a bare trust (where land is vested by the owner in a nominee). In all such cases, the person holding the legal title is the trustee. Section 19(3) provides that, as a last resort, an application can be made to court for appointment of a trustee.

Charitable Gifts and Trusts

Where a testator wishes to create a charitable gift or trust, it must be for a charitable purpose recognised by the law of charities.[49] Charitable purposes include the relief of poverty, the advancement of education, the advancement of religion or a purpose beneficial to the community at large. For a charitable trust to be valid and enforceable, it must be created for one or more of these purposes.[50] The Charities Act 2009 introduced significant reforms of the law relating to charities. Since the enactment of the Charities Act 2009, a gift or trust must be for a charitable purpose as defined by s.3 of the Act. The charitable purposes outlined in *Commissioners for Special Purposes of Income Tax v Pemsel*[51] are retained and given statutory recognition by s.3 of the 2009 Act. Once a charitable gift or trust has a charitable purpose, it may be enforced even though the intended charity is no longer in existence, or the testator's intentions are impossible to carry out or are impracticable. In such a case, the court may apply the *cy-près* doctrine to use the trust funds or property for a charitable purpose as near as possible resembling the purpose intended by the testator, and devise a scheme accordingly. The Commissioners of Charitable Donations and Bequests also had a limited jurisdiction under the Charities Act 1961 to frame a scheme for the application *cy-près* of the property comprised in a charitable gift.[52] The Charities Act 2009 provides for the establishment of the Charities Regulatory Authority in place of the Commissioners for Charitable Donations and Bequests, and provides for a system of registration of charitable organisations by the Charities Regulatory Authority. It also contains provisions dealing with the financial regulation and protection of charitable organisations, and the regulation of fund-raising by registered charitable organisations. In relation to charity trustees, s.89(1) of the Charities Act 2009 allows for the remuneration of trustees, s.90 empowers the court to grant relief from liability for breach of trust, and s.91 allows for the provision of indemnity insurance in respect of charity trustees. In practice, however, the majority **5–27**

[49] See Albert Keating, *Equitable Succession Rights* (Dublin: Thomson Round Hall, 2005).

[50] *Commissioners for Special Purposes of Income Tax v Pemsel* [1891] A.C. 531; *Re Worth Library* [1994] 1 I.L.R.M. 161.

[51] [1891] A.C. 531.

[52] See s.29(2) and s.47(1).

of wills contain no charitable provisions at all. Where they do, they usually take the form of gifts to a charity supported by a testator during his lifetime, or for the celebration of Mass for the repose of his soul and for those of his deceased relatives, and do not normally require court intervention.

Secret and Half-Secret Trusts

5–28 A secret trust is one that arises out of a will, although there is no mention of the trust in the will. A half-secret trust in a will is one that discloses the existence of a trust, though not the actual trust itself or the beneficiaries of the trust. The trustee of such trusts is under an equitable obligation to carry out the terms of the trusts.[53] The court will take the view that the testator relied on the express or implied promise of the devisee or legatee to fulfil his wishes after his death and will deal with his property accordingly.[54] Where it is established that, before or at the time of the execution of the will, the testator communicated to the legatee that the legacy is given in trust for another and the legatee consents to this, equity will compel the execution of the trust so communicated.[55]

5–29 In *Re Prendiville*[56] the Court had to determine whether, in the circumstances, there was an enforceable secret trust or a half-secret trust. The facts of the case were as follows. The testator made a will dated 13 October 1961 and died on 21 June 1964. The testator left all his property to his wife "*to be used by her according to my wishes — as she has been advised*". Prior to his death, the testator informed his son, Brendan, that he had written out his wishes regarding the disposal of his estate after his wife's death. He showed Brendan a handwritten document dated 7 May 1961 that contained his wishes. The document included the following provision:

> "Monies to be divided after my wife's death. My wife Mary is to get all my monies, property and debts due, during her lifetime. Billy to get preference of Cluincorrig house — on a reasonable valuation — if he lives or intends to live in Killorglin."

5–30 Billy was also one of the testator's sons. On the reverse side of the document, there was a valuation of the testator's estate and of his wife's. A value of £6,000 was put on the testator's residence. The testator's widow made a statutory declaration on 6 June 1967 acknowledging the acceptance of the terms of the testator's wishes. She made a will on 29 September 1970 leaving her late husband's estate in accordance with his written wishes. She died on 3 January 1986 without having fully administered the testator's estate. In proceedings instituted by Brendan, he claimed that there was an enforceable

[53] *Blackwell v Blackwell* [1929] A.C. 318 at 334; see Albert Keating, *Equitable Succession Rights* (Dublin: Thomson Round Hall, 2005).

[54] *French v French* [1902] 1 I.R. 172 at 230.

[55] *Ward v Lawler* [1944] I.R. 90; *In Re King's Estate* (1888) 21 L.R.Ir.273 at 277; *Blackwell v Blackwell* [1929] A.C. 318.

[56] [1995] 2 I.L.R.M. 578.

fully secret or alternatively a half secret trust under which he had an option to purchase at a reasonable valuation the residence and lands of Cluincorrig House. Barron J. found that the principles of law applicable to secret trusts and half-secret trusts were essentially the same:

> "The only difference between a half-secret trust and a secret trust was that the person named in the will is an express trustee in the first case and a beneficiary in the latter. A person who had on his own behalf agreed to hold an apparently beneficial gift on trust could not in conscience refuse to carry out such trust. That is the position in the case of a secret trust. Should it be the same in the case of a half-secret trust where the beneficiary has not made any such promise to the testator? The answers is, yes and for the reasons set out in the passages from the judgment of *Blackwell v Blackwell* to which I have referred."[57]

Applying the principles to the circumstances of the case before him, Barron **5–31** J. concluded that there was a trust on the face of the will; the terms of it were communicated to the testator's wife and accepted by her during his lifetime; the assent by her was sufficient to validate the half-secret trust. The expression "Cluincorrig House" was a term by which the testator would have referred to both house and land and it was so understood by his wife.

Resulting Trusts

Where an express trust fails, the property comprised in it will revert to the **5–32** estate by way of resulting trust. A resulting trust arises "automatically" by operation of law.[58] In cases of voluntary conveyances of land or transfers of personal property, a resulting trust will be presumed to exist unless the transferor intended to benefit the transferee. Where it is established in evidence that the transferor intended to benefit the transferee, this will be sufficient to rebut the presumption. The presumption of a resulting trust may also be rebutted by reliance on the equitable doctrine of advancement. Where a testator during his lifetime transfers property to his wife or child, the property so transferred may be viewed as an equitable advancement and, as such, the property forming part of the advancement will not form part of a testator's estate.[59]

---

[57] *Re Prendiville* [1995] 2 I.L.R.M. 578 at 585.

[58] *Re Vandervell's Trusts (No.2)* [1974] Ch. 269 at 294; see Albert Keating, *Equitable Succession Rights* (Dublin: Thomson Round Hall, 2005).

[59] See Chapter 11 – *Donationes Mortis Causa*, Joint Bank Accounts and Advancements.

CHAPTER 6

THE ADEMPTION, LAPSE AND MODIFICATION OF GIFTS

INTRODUCTION

Where a testator disposes of the property comprised in a gift during his lifetime, the gift will be adeemed or fail to take effect under the probate doctrine of ademption. A gift may also be adeemed owing to the extent of an alteration to the property comprised in the gift, for instance, where shares in a particular company form the subject matter of the gift, any acquisition or takeover by another company may alter the subject matter of the gift to such an extent that it may be adeemed as a result. A provision in the gift foreseeing the likelihood of such an occurrence may, however, save it from ademption and allow the beneficiary to receive the new investments representing the original shares.[1] Where the subject matter of the gift remains substantially the same, it may not be adeemed, even though the value of shares has been transformed into smaller denominations or the company has undergone a name change.[2] Also, reconstruction of a company after voluntary liquidation may not be substantial enough to alter the subject matter of a gift for the purposes of ademption.[3] Where, however, there is an acquisition of a company resulting in the issue of new shares, this may be viewed as a substantial alteration to the subject matter of a gift and may result in ademption.[4] **6–01**

The equitable doctrine of ademption also becomes applicable when what is called a portion is given to a child of a testator during his or her lifetime and a legacy is also given to the same child, and as a result the legacy will be adeemed by the portion as "equity leans against double portions".[5] Where, **6–02**

1 *Re Lewis's W.T.* [1937] Ch. 118.
2 *Re Clifford* [1912] 1 Ch. 29; *Re O'Brien* (1946) 115 L.J. Ch. 340.
3 *Re Lemming* [1912] 1 Ch. 828.
4 *Re Slater* [1907] 1 Ch. 665.
5 See Albert Keating, "The Effect of Portions and Advancements on Testamentary Gifts to Children: Part One" (2008) 13(2) C.P.L.J.; Albert Keating, "The Effect of

for instance, a portion is given to a child of a testator or a person to whom the testator is *in loco parentis* after the making of the will containing the legacy, the legacy may be adeemed by the portion unless a contrary intention appears in the will. This is because it will be presumed that the portion was given in satisfaction of the legacy.[6] It was stated by Sullivan M.R. in *Curtin v Evans*[7] that

> "when a parent, or one standing *in loco parentis*, gives by will a sum of money to a child, and afterwards a like or greater sum is secured by settlement in the marriage of that child, the law presumes the legacy to be adeemed".

6–03 Advancements under s.63(3) of the Succession Act 1965 (the "1965 Act") may also be said to adeem testamentary gifts which are equal to or greater than the gift which a child of the testator is entitled to receive as, in such circumstances, the child will be precluded from taking the gift, which is more or less the same as ademption of the gift, unless a contrary intention appears in the will.[8]

6–04 Under the doctrine of lapse, where a beneficiary predeceases the testator, the gift to that beneficiary will lapse or fail to take effect, and, as a result, the subject matter of the gift will form part of the testator's residuary estate.[9] The doctrine of lapse may be said to derive from, or is a consequence of, the ambulatory nature of a will, i.e. a will has no effect until the death of the testator and, where a beneficiary predeceases the testator, the gift left to him or her will lapse at the date of the testator's death. The nature of the gift may, however, save it from lapse. Where a gift comprises a joint tenancy and where one of the joint tenants predeceases the testator, the gift will not lapse but will pass by right of survivorship to the joint tenants who survive the testator. Where the gift creates a tenancy in common by which beneficiaries are given equal shares and where one of the beneficiaries predeceases the testator, the equal share of that beneficiary will lapse and, unlike a joint tenancy, the share of the beneficiary will not pass to the surviving tenants in common. The nature of the relationship between testator and beneficiary may also determine whether or not the doctrine of lapse is to apply to a gift. Section 98 provides that, where the predeceased beneficiary is a child or other issue of the testator who leaves issue of his own surviving at the date of death of the testator, the doctrine of lapse will not apply, and the gift will take effect as if the death of that child or other issue had happened immediately after the death of the testator, unless a contrary intention appears from the will.

Portions and Advancements on Testamentary Gifts to Children: Part Two" (2008) 13(3) C.P.L.J. 57.

6 *Weall v Rice* (1831) 2 Russ. & M. 251; *Blundell v Blundell* [1906] 2 Ch. 222.

7 (1872) I.R. 9 Eq. 553, 557; *Re Vaux* [1939] Ch. 465 at 481 *per* Lord Greene M.R.

8 See Chapter 11 – *Donationes Mortis Causa*, Joint Bank Accounts and Advancements.

9 s.91 of the 1965 Act.

Equity may also modify the effect of a testamentary gift by applying one of its doctrines in an appropriate case. The doctrine of satisfaction may be applied where legacies are left in satisfaction of debts, or legacies in satisfaction of other legacies, or portions by legacies.[10] The doctrine of conversion may be applied when a testator directs his personal representatives or trustees to sell his real estate, and this direction to sell will have the effect of converting the real estate into personal estate from the date of the testator's death. **6–05**

The Ademption of Devises and Legacies

Where a testator disposes of the property forming the subject matter of a specific devise or legacy during his lifetime and after the making of his will, the devise or legacy will be adeemed. A specific devise or bequest will also be adeemed where the testator enters into a contract to sell the subject matter of the devise or bequest during his lifetime and after the making of his will, and the purchase money of the sale will form part of the residuary estate.[11] In *Re Sweeting*[12] the testator devised two separate plots of land. Before his death, he entered into two contracts for the sale of the plots but he died before either contract was completed. After his death, the executors completed the sales. The question arose whether the specific devises were adeemed by the contracts of sale. It was held that the devises of the plots of land were converted into personalty and adeemed by the completion of the contracts, and the proceeds of sale fell into the residue. A devisee may, however, be entitled to rents or profits owing and due on the land sold prior to the completion of the contract of sale.[13] Where, however, the contract of sale was entered into prior to the making of the will, the devisee may become entitled to the converted value of the devise in the form of the purchase money.[14] In *Re Calow*[15] the proceeds of sale passed to the specific devisees since the will, having been made after the date of the contract of sale, showed an intention by the testator to pass his interest in the property to the specific devisees. A new will may also save the devise from ademption where the contract for the sale of the land forming the subject matter of the devise was entered into after the making of an earlier will but prior to the making of the new will and especially so where the new will confirms the devise of the land in the earlier will.[16] Furthermore, where a testator makes **6–06**

---

10 See Albert Keating, "The Effect of Portions and Advancements on Testamentary Gifts to Children: Part One" (2008) 13(2) C.P.L.J.; Albert Keating, "The Effect of Portions and Advancements on Testamentary Gifts to Children: Part Two" (2008) 13(3) C.P.L.J. 57.

11 See *Watts v Watts* (1873) L.R. 7 Eq. 217; *Re Galway's W.T.* [1949] 2 All E.R. 419; *Re Sweeting* [1988] 1 All E.R. 1016.

12 [1988] 1 All E.R. 1016.

13 See *Watts v Watts* (1873) L.R. 7 Eq. 217.

14 *Re Calow* [1928] All E.R. 518.

15 [1928] All E.R. 518.

16 *Re Pyle* [1895] 1 Ch. 724; *Sidney v Sidney* L.R. 17 Eq. 65; *MacDonald v Irvine* (1878) 8 Ch.D. 101.

a codicil in the interval between making the will and his death, showing that he intended his interest in lands to pass to the devisee, the proceeds of any sale of such lands by the testator in his lifetime will pass to the devisee.[17]

6–07 A more difficult problem arises where an option to purchase the land forming the subject matter of a devise or to buy shares forming the subject matter of a legacy becomes exercisable after the death of the testator.[18] In *Miley v Carty*[19] Johnston J. stated that:

> "The general rule applicable to the case of a testator who has entered into a conditional contract to sell land which he has dealt with specifically in his will was settled as long ago as 1785 by Kenyon M.R. in *Lawes v Bennett*, and that case has been uniformly followed since that time in a long series of decisions. In such a case the proceeds of the sale of the land devolve as personalty as from the fulfilment of the condition – such as, say, the exercise of an option to purchase."

In *Mooney v M'Mahon*[20] Cherry J. stated that:

> "when, after making a will devising a specific estate, and bequeathing the personal residue to other persons, a testator entered into a contract giving an option of purchase over part of the estate, which option was exercised after the death, the property was converted from the date of the exercise of the option, and went to the residuary legatees".

6–08 In *Re Carrington*[21] the testator bequeathed specific legacies of shares in a company. He also however gave an option to another party to purchase those shares, the option to be exercised within a month of his death. The option was exercised within that time. It was held by the Court of Appeal that, when the option was exercised, there was a conversion of the shares into money and the shares no longer formed part of the testator's estate once this was done, with the result that the specific legacies of the shares were adeemed. A devisee or legatee may however be entitled to the rents or profits or dividends accruing on the property or shares prior to the exercise of the option. A gift of property on condition of paying a price for it is different from a mere option to purchase it. The condition of payment will be viewed as a condition subsequent, i.e. subsequent to the vesting of the property; in other words, the property will already have vested subject to satisfying the condition of payment.[22]

6–09 The sale of shares comprised in a specific legacy during the lifetime of the testator will also result in ademption of the legacy. Where, however, shares undergo a transformation owing to the dealings of the company in which they

---

17 See *Steele v Steele* [1913] 1 I.R. 292.

18 See *Lawes v Bennett* (1785) 1 Cox Eq. 167; *Re Carrington* [1931] All E.R. 658; *Belshaw v Rollins* [1904] 1 I.R. 284; *Re Rose* [1948] 2 All E.R. 971.

19 [1927] I.R. 541 at 543.

20 [1911] 1 I.R. 125 at 134.

21 [1931] All E.R. 658.

22 See *Belshaw v Rollins* [1904] 1 I.R. 284.

are held, the seriousness of the transformation or alteration may determine the ademption or not of the legacy in which they are comprised. It appears that, where shares are merely transformed into smaller denominations, this will not adeem the legacy.[23] It appears also that a specific legacy of shares in a company undergoing reconstruction may not result in ademption of the legacy.[24] But an acquisition or takeover of a company resulting in the issuing of new shares may be a substantial enough event to adeem a legacy, unless there is provision in the legacy anticipating such an event.[25] Where this is the case, no ademption will result, no matter what new investments represent the original shares constituting the subject matter of the legacy.[26] In *Re Lewis*[27] it was held, on a construction of a bequest of shares that underwent alteration, that the words in parenthesis with regard "to investments representing the same at the date of my death if they have been converted into other holdings" were inserted with the intention of preventing ademption. Where a specific legacy comprised of shares is adeemed, it will fall into the residuary estate.

Therefore, where the testator disposes of the subject matter of a specific devise or legacy during his lifetime and after making his will, the devise or legacy will be adeemed. It is a different matter, however, where the testator sells the subject matter of a specific legacy or devise prior to making his will. Where a testator agrees to sell the land forming the subject matter of a specific devise, the purchase money will not replace the devise as the contract of sale will have converted the realty into personalty and will be adeemed accordingly. The purchase money will then form part of the residuary estate. The same occurs in the case of an option to purchase land forming the subject matter of a specific devise that is exercised within a prescribed time period and here also the purchase money will fall into the residue. The same may be said where the option is to purchase shares forming the subject matter of a specific legacy. Where a specific legacy consists of shares in a company, the legacy will not be adeemed by their re-composition or otherwise by the activities or dealings by the company in which they are held, unless the legacy has been substantially altered by such activities or dealings. A provision in the legacy governing such occurrences will, however, save it from ademption. **6–10**

Ademption by Satisfaction

A testamentary gift in the form of a legacy may also be adeemed by virtue of a portion or advancement given to a child during the lifetime of the testator, unless a contrary intention appears in the will. This is one of the consequences of the application of the equitable doctrine of satisfaction to **6–11**

---

23 *Re Clifford* [1912] 1 Ch. 29; *Re O'Brien* (1946) 115 L.J. Ch. 340.
24 *Re Leeming*[1912] 1 Ch. 828.
25 *Re Slater* [1907] 1 Ch. 665.
26 *Re Lewis's W.T.* [1937] 1 All E.R. 227.
27 [1937] 1 All E.R. 227.

portions and legacies.[28] For the doctrine to apply, however, the relationship of father (not mother) and child or a child to whom the testator stands *in loco parentis* must first of all exist.[29] In such circumstances where a portion and legacy are given to a child, the legacy will be adeemed by the portion given in the lifetime of the testator by the equitable doctrine of ademption.[30]

It will be presumed

> "that both gifts were made to fulfil the same natural or moral obligation of providing for the legatee and consequently that the gift *inter vivos* is either wholly or in part a substitution for or an ademption of the legacy".[31]

6–12 But to sustain the presumption, the legacy and the portion must be *ejusdem generis* or of substantially the same nature.[32] It appears, however, there can be no ademption of a legacy where the portion consists of land: "it is elementary that money is not adeemed unless indeed a money value is put upon the gift".[33] The beneficiary is also allowed to choose between the portion and the legacy, but where he or she chooses the portion, the legacy will be adeemed.[34] The presumption of ademption may, however, be rebutted by a testator declaring in his will that the legacy is given in addition to the agreed portion, thus entitling the legatee to receive both portion and legacy. Extrinsic evidence may be adduced to show that the testator intended his child or person to whom he stands *in loco parentis* to receive both legacy and portion.[35]

6–13 While the description of advancements for the purposes of s.63 of the 1965 Act is similar to that of portions, the satisfaction of portions by legacies is expressly excluded from the provisions of the section, and therefore remains an equitable matter.[36] However, the application of the section is not excluded where portions are made in satisfaction of legacies and therefore will be governed by the provisions of the section. Section 63(3) of the 1965 Act provides that:

> "If the advancement is equal or greater than the share which the child is entitled to receive under the will or intestacy, the child or the issue of the child shall be excluded from any such share in the estate."

---

[28] See *Curtin v Evans* (1872) I.R. 9 Eq. 553 at 557.

[29] *Curtin v Evans* (1872) I.R. 9 Eq. 553 at 557; *Re Bannon, Callanan v Ryan (No.2)* [1934] I.R. 701.

[30] *Re Pollock* (1885) 28 Ch.D. 552.

[31] *ibid.* at 555.

[32] *Re Jacques* [1903] 1 Ch. 267; *Hickey v O'Dwyer* [2006] 2 I.L.R.M. 81;*Edgeworth v Johnston* (1877)I.R. 11 Eq. 326; *Pym v Lockyer* (1841) 5 My. & Cr. 29.

[33] *Re Wall's Estate* [1922] 1 I.R. 59 at 61 *per* O'Connor M.R.

[34] See *Hickey v O'Dwyer* [2006] 2 I.L.R.M. 81(where the portion took the form of a life assurance policy).

[35] *Weall v Rice* (1831) 2 Russ. & M. 251.

[36] s.63(9).

Advancements to children under s.63 may lead to the ademption of testamentary gifts whether those gifts comprise vreal or personal estate where they are equal or greater than the value of the gifts, and the gifts will be adeemed accordingly.[37] The application of the provisions of s.63 to testamentary gifts is, however, subject to a contrary intention appearing in the will.[38] **6–14**

The Doctrine of Lapse

Where a beneficiary predeceases the testator, the gift to him or her will lapse and form part of the testator's residuary estate, unless a contrary intention appears from the will. **6–15**

Section 91 of the 1965 Act provides that:

> "Unless a contrary intention appears from the will, any estate comprised or intended to be comprised in any devise or bequest contained in the will which fails or is void by reason of the fact that the devisee or legatee did not survive the testator, or by reason of the devise or bequest being contrary to law or otherwise incapable of taking effect, shall be included in any residuary devise or bequest, as the case may be, contained in the will."

The nature of a gift may also save it from lapse. Where the gift consists of a joint tenancy and one joint tenant predeceases the testator, the gift will not lapse, and the surviving joint tenant will become entitled to the gift by virtue of the right of survivorship. But where the gift creates a tenancy in common, and one of the beneficiaries predeceases the testator, the surviving beneficiary will not become entitled to the share of the predeceased beneficiary, as his or her share in the gift will have lapsed at the date of death of the testator. A later codicil to a will may save a gift from lapse where it confirms a gift to a person identified by description, rather than by name, in the will. Where, for instance, a testator gives a gift to the "husband" of his daughter who predeceases the testator, and the daughter marries again, and a later codicil by the testator confirms the gift to the daughter's "husband", the daughter's current husband will be entitled to the gift as the testator will be taken to have known at the date of the codicil of his daughter's current marital status.[39] A gift may also be saved from lapse where a gift contains substitutive provisions in the event of a beneficiary predeceasing the testator. **6–16**

The nature of the relationship between testator and beneficiary may also determine whether or not the doctrine of lapse is to apply to a gift. Where a child of the testator predeceases him or her, any gift to that child may be **6–17**

[37] See Chapter 10 – *Donationes Mortis Causa*, Joint Bank Accounts and Advancements; Albert Keating, "The Effect of Portions and Advancements on Testamentary Gifts to Children: Part Two" (2008) 13(3) C.P.L.J. 57.

[38] s.63(1).

[39] *Re Hardyman* [1925] Ch. 287.

saved from lapse provided that he or she leaves issue living at the date of death of the testator.[40] Under s.33 of the former 1837 Act, in the absence of a contrary intention appearing from the will, a devise or bequest to a predeceased child of the testator not determinable at or before the death did not lapse if the predeceased child had issue of his or her own living at the date of death of the testator, and the devise or bequest took effect as if the predeceased child or other issue had died immediately after the testator, and the devise or bequest became disposable under the will of the predeceased child. Once the provisions of s.33 were satisfied, the devise or bequest was saved from lapse, and it passed to those beneficially entitled under the predeceased child's will. A contrary intention may appear from the will by the testator providing that, in the event of his child predeceasing him, the gift should then go to the issue of that child. But where no such provision was made by the testator, the predeceased child's issue living at the testator's death had no right to share in the gift, though their existence was vital for saving the gift from lapse, and for the purpose of rendering a will of the predeceased child effective.

6–18 It is interesting to note that, in the U.K. s.33 of the 1837 Act was amended by s.19 of the U.K. Administration of Justice Act 1982. The amended s.33 now provides that:

> "where –
> (a) a will contains a devise or bequest to a child or remoter descendent of the testator; and
> (b) the intended beneficiary dies before the testator, leaving issue; and
> (c) issue of the intended beneficiary are living at the testator's death,
> then, unless a contrary intention appears by the will, the devise or bequest shall take effect as a devise or bequest to the issue living at the testator's death."

6–19 In Northern Ireland, s.33 was amended by Article 22 of the Wills and Administration Proceedings (NI) Order 1994, and Article 22 makes it clear that, subject to a contrary intention appearing from the will, the gift "takes effect as a gift to issue living at the testator's death". The net effect of the amended s.33 by s.19 of the UK Administration of Justice Act 1982 and Article 22 of the Northern Ireland Wills and Administration Proceedings (NI) Order 1994, is that the gift to the predeceased child will take effect as a gift to his or her issue living at the date of death of the testator, unless a contrary intention appears from the will.

6–20 The whole of the 1837 Act, including s.33, was repealed by the 1965 Act. Section 98 of the 1965 Act now provides that:

> "Where a person, being a child or other issue of the testator to whom any property is given (whether by devise or bequest or by the exercise by will of any power of appointment, and whether as a gift to that person as an individual or as a member

[40] See Albert Keating, "The Doctrine of Lapse and Section 98 of the Succession Act" (2013) 31 I.L.T. 181.

> of a class) for any estate not determinable at or before the death of that person, dies in the lifetime of the testator leaving issue, and any such issue of that person is living at the time of the death of the testator, the gift shall not lapse, but shall take effect as if the death of that person had happened immediately after the death of the testator, unless a contrary intention appears from the will."

Under s.98, where property is "given" to a child or other issue of the testator, if:

(a) a will gives property to a child or other issue of the testator, and
(b) the child or other issue predeceases the testator,
(c) issue of the child or other issue are living at the date of death of the testator.

Then, unless a contrary intention appears from the will, the gift will not lapse, but will take effect as if the death of the testator's child or other issue had occurred immediately after the death of the testator. Since the Status of Children Act 1987, the definition of "child or other issue", also includes non-marital children. Under s.3(2) of the 1965 Act, a child *en ventre sa mère* is also included in the definition. It provides that: **6–21**

> "Descendants and relatives of a deceased person begotten before his death but born alive thereafter shall, for the purpose of this Act, be regarded as having been born in the lifetime of the deceased and as having survived him."

Section 98 of the 1965 Act deals with matters formerly governed by s.33 of the 1837 Act, but s.98, besides replacing s.33, also contains marginal notes which state that it deals with "gifts to children or other issue who leave issue living at the testator's death". This helpful pointer appears to suggest that s.98 is capable of a new interpretation, and one that may differ from the interpretation given to the former s.33 of the 1837 Act. The statement in the margin of s.98, i.e. "gifts to children or other issue who leave issue living at the testator's death" can only be taken to mean that the provisions of s.98 relate to such gifts only. If the intent of s.98 were to save a gift from lapse for the purpose of benefiting a predeceased child's estate, why was it necessary to make it conditional on the existence of living issue of the predeceased at the date of the testator's death? The only logical conclusion is that s.98 saves a gift to a predeceased child from lapse, not for the purpose of benefiting all those in his will, but for the benefit of his issue living at the testator's death, unless a contrary intention appears from the will. Section 98 also saves from lapse any property given through the exercise by will of any power of appointment, whether as a gift to that person as an individual or as a member of a class, and will pass to the issue. Section 98 may then be interpreted to allow a gift by the testator to a predeceased child to take effect as a gift to his or her issue living at the date of death of the testator, unless a contrary intention appears from the will. The marginal notes which state that s.98 deals with "gifts to children or other issue who leave issue living at the testator's death" point to such a conclusion, thereby obviating the need for amending legislation similar to s.19 of the U.K. Administration of Justice **6–22**

Act 1982 and Article 22 of the Northern Ireland Wills and Administration Proceedings (NI) Order 1994.

The Modification of Gifts by Equitable Doctrines

6–23 Equity may modify the effect of a testamentary gift by applying one of its doctrines in an appropriate case. The doctrine of satisfaction may be applied where legacies are left in satisfaction of debts, or legacies in satisfaction of other legacies, or portions by legacies.[41] In *Hickey v O'Dwyer*[42] Laffoy J. considered the application of the doctrine of satisfaction *vis-à-vis* the satisfaction of a portion by a legacy. In that case, the testator was the husband of the plaintiff and father of the fourth defendant, who was born on 5 December 1990. The third defendant was the mother of the fourth defendant. The testator and the third defendant were not married. In 1993, the testator took out a life assurance policy and executed a document (the "1993 trust") consisting of a declaration of trust in a standard form produced by the insurer. It was a special condition of the policy that it was issued pursuant to the 1993 trust. In the 1993 trust, the testator declared that the trustees for the time being should hold the policy and the full benefit thereof and all monies which might become payable thereunder on trust, if the benefit under the policy should become payable in consequence of the death of the testator (which happened) for the benefit of all or more of the class of persons named by relationship to the testator (which included the spouse and children of the testator) as the testator in his absolute discretion should by deed or deeds, revocable or irrevocable, appoint. It was expressly provided that no appointment should be made nor any power of revocation exercised after the death of the testator. It was also provided that, in default of and subject to any such appointment, 100% of the trust fund should be held for the absolute benefit of the fourth defendant. The testator did not exercise the power of appointment over the trust fund conferred on him in the 1993 trust during his lifetime. Following his death, the proceeds of the policy, IR£223,350, were paid out by the insurers to two trustees of the trust fund on behalf of the fourth defendant.

6–24 The testator made his will on 26 May 1998. He appointed the plaintiff to be his sole executrix and residuary legatee and devisee. There were two dispositive provisions in the will. The provision which gave rise to the issue in the proceedings was clause 4 wherein the testator devised and bequeathed the sum of IR£100,000 to the first, second and third defendants to be held by them in trust as thereinafter set out for his daughter, the fourth defendant, until she should attain the age of 25 years and then to her absolutely. The first,

[41] See Albert Keating, "The Effect of Portions and Advancements on Testamentary Gifts to Children: Part One" (2008) 13(2) C.P.L.J.; Albert Keating, "The Effect of Portions and Advancements on Testamentary Gifts to Children: Part Two" (2008) 13(3) C.P.L.J. 57.

[42] [2006] 2 I.L.R.M. 81.

second and third defendants were appointed as trustees of that bequest and the trusts on which they were to hold the sum of IR£100,000 were set out. The other dispositive provision was the devise and bequest of the residue to the plaintiff for her own use and benefit absolutely. The executrix, having renounced her right to probate, letters of administration with the testator's will annexed were granted to the first and second defendants on 15 July 2003. The first and second defendants were party to the proceedings in their capacity as personal representatives of the testator. One of the main issues raised in the special summons concerned the entitlement of the fourth defendant to the proceeds of the policy of life assurance and under the will. The court was asked to determine whether the bequest in the testator's will to set up a trust in favour of the fourth defendant in the amount of IR£100,000 was intended to be in whole or in part satisfaction of the monies held on trust for her pursuant to the terms of the 1993 trust funds.

Laffoy J. found that: **6–25**

> "the presumption of satisfaction of a portion by a legacy has traditionally been applied in this jurisdiction where the settlor or testator is the father of, or *in loco parentis*, to the donee, the first gift is a portion and both gifts are substantially of the same nature and in favour of the same person".

She was satisfied that the provision made in 1993 was a portion, in the sense of being a gift of a substantial nature relative to the means of the testator and intended to set up the fourth defendant for life. Moreover, she was satisfied that the provision made in the 1993 trust and the provision made by the testator in his will for the fourth defendant were substantially of the same nature. They were both, essentially, dispositions of money to which the fourth defendant was to be absolutely entitled, albeit in the case of the bequest in the will, the trustees would have control until she attained 25 years of age. Although the provision in the will was substantially smaller than what the policy yielded, the doctrine of satisfaction admits of a lesser provision in a will being satisfaction *pro tanto* of an earlier portion. Laffoy J. thought that the totality of the relevant evidence in relation to the testator's age, marital status and personal circumstances and the state of his assets when he made his will, supported the presumption that the testator did not intend that the fourth defendant should receive both the entirety of the proceeds of the policy and the bequest contained in his will. "In other words, the presumption stands". The consequence of the conclusion that the doctrine of satisfaction applied was that an election had to be made on behalf of the fourth defendant, who was still a minor, between the provision contained in the 1993 trust and the provision under the will. **6–26**

The doctrine of conversion may be applied when a testator directs his personal representatives or trustees to sell his real estate, and this direction to sell will have the effect of converting the real estate into personal estate from the date of the testator's death. The maxim here is that "equity looks **6–27** on that as done which ought to have been done". Where such a direction is given, the real estate will be notionally converted from the date of death of the testator. A power to postpone sale given by a testator to his personal representatives or trustees will have the same effect. A power of sale given to the trustees will notionally convert the property on the date of the testator's death, and the beneficiaries will thereafter become entitled to the proceeds of the sale. The notional conversion of property by equity may, however, be precluded by the beneficiaries relying on another equitable doctrine, namely reconversion. Beneficiaries who prefer to receive the property in its unconverted state may rely on this doctrine and, where such is the case, there will be no notional conversion of the property "as equity, like nature, does nothing in vain". Where, however, an actual conversion takes place by the sale of the property by personal representatives or trustees, the doctrine of reconversion ceases to become operative.

Chapter 7

INTESTATE SUCCESSION

Introduction

Intestacy occurs where a deceased person dies without leaving a will or where a will made by him or her is invalid. Section 3(1) of the Succession Act 1965 (the "1965 Act") provides that an intestate is a person **7–01**

> "who leaves no will or leaves a will but leaves undisposed of some beneficial interest in his estate, and 'intestate' shall be construed accordingly".

Section 3(2) of the 1965 Act provides that:

> "Descendants and relatives of a deceased person begotten before his death but born alive thereafter shall, for the purposes of this Act, be regarded as having been born in the lifetime of the deceased and as having survived him."

While the concept of intestacy existed before and after the 1965 Act, the intestate rules regarding the devolution and distribution of a deceased intestate's property that existed before the 1965 Act were substantially different from those found in that Act, and also issues of devolution and distribution were determined by the nature of property which under the old rules was categorised as realty or personalty.[1] **7–02**

Personalty or a deceased intestate's personal property devolved on his administrator and, after discharging all just debts and funeral expenses, the remainder was distributed in accordance with the provisions of the Statute of Distributions (Ireland) 1695. Realty or a deceased intestate's real property, on the other hand, vested at the date of the deceased's death in his heir-at- **7–03**

---

1 s.2 of the Inheritance Act 1833.

law. The heir-at-law was a blood relative of the deceased intestate traceable from the "last purchaser", i.e. a person who last acquired the realty otherwise than by succession.[2] As a result of s.10(1) of the 1965 Act, a deceased intestate's real and personal estate devolved on and vested in his personal representatives. Part VI of the 1965 Act sets out the rules which govern the distribution of an intestate's estate as amended by the Civil Partnership and Certain Rights and Obligations of Cohabitants Act 2010 (the "2010 Act").

7–04 Under s.15 of the Court of Probate (Ireland) Act 1859, before a grant of letters of administration intestate issued, the deceased intestate's "personal estate and effects" vested in the judge of the Court of Probate for the time being. Section 13 of the Administration of Estates Act 1959 (the "1959 Act") provided that, before a grant issued, the deceased intestate's estate vested in the President of the High Court "in the same manner and to the same extent as formerly in the case of personal estate it vested in the Ordinary". Under s.13 of the 1965 Act, before a grant of letters of administration intestate issues, the deceased's estate vested in the President of the High Court, "who, for this purpose, shall be a corporation sole".[3]

7–05 The distinction between realty and personalty continued to determine the issue of devolution of a deceased intestate's estate until Part IV of the Local Registration of Title (Ireland) Act 1891 assimilated the functions of personal representatives, which were extended to include a deceased's realty. This policy of assimilation was continued by the Administration of Estates Act 1959. Section 12 of the 1965 Act, when dealing with the assimilation of real and personal estate, provides that all enactments—including the 1965 Act and rules of law relating to personal estate—apply equally to real estate "as if it were personal estate". The assimilation of real and personal estate was completed by the 1965 Act.

7–06 It may also be mentioned that the old ecclesiastical jurisdiction governing probate matters ceased to exist by the Probate and Letters of Administration Act (Ireland) Act 1857 and by the transfer of jurisdiction over such matters to the Probate Court under the Court of Probate Act (Ireland) 1859. The jurisdiction of the Probate Court was transferred to the High Court by the Judicature (Ireland) Act 1877, and the current High Court has original jurisdiction to hear such matters. The Circuit Court has a limited jurisdiction in probate matters by virtue of s.6 of the 1965 Act.

---

[2] *ibid.*

[3] s.13 of the Administration of Estates Act 1959 provided for a similar vesting of the deceased's real and personal estate in the President before a grant issued. It was repealed by s.13 of the 1965 Act.

Pre-Succession Act Rules of Intestate Devolution and Distribution

Prior to the 1965 Act, a deceased intestate's property was categorised as realty or personalty. On the death of an intestate, his realty vested immediately in the heir-at-law. The heir-at-law was a blood relative traceable from the "last purchaser", i.e. a person who last acquired the realty otherwise than by succession.[4] Section 19 of the Law of Property Amendment Act 1859 (also known as "Lord St. Leonard's Act") provided that, where there were no remaining heirs of the last purchaser, descent may then be traced from the last person entitled as though he had been a purchaser. The heir-at-law was a lineal successor, such as a child or grandchild of the deceased intestate. Where there were male and female children or grandchildren, sons or grandsons were preferred to daughters or granddaughters. Where there were two or more sons or grandsons, or two or more males, of equal degree of relationship to the deceased, the eldest was the heir-at-law by the feudal rule of primogeniture. Where there were no male heirs, daughters or granddaughters inherited realty as coparceners. A lineal successor who would have succeeded to the intestate's realty had he not predeceased him or inherited the realty was represented by his son by virtue of the doctrine of representation and was entitled as heir-at-law to the realty before, say, a younger son of the deceased intestate. Where no issue survived the deceased intestate, the realty then went to the nearest lineal ancestor and his issue and, for this purpose, the paternal line was preferred to that of the maternal line.[5] Collateral relatives of the half-blood succeeded after relatives of the whole-blood or issue who were in the same degree of relationship to the deceased intestate.[6] As whole-blood relatives were preferred to half-blood, the preference of male over female was no longer applicable and a sister of the deceased intestate was preferred to a brother of the half-blood. All of the foregoing inheritance rules were also subject to the deceased widow's right to dower or, if a widower, his right to curtesy. Realty related to a deceased intestate's fee simple interests in land; though fee tail interests in land were also types of realty, they were governed by different rules of inheritance.[7] **7–07**

As regards personalty, it devolved on the deceased's administrator and, after discharging all just debts and funeral expenses, the deceased's personalty was distributed in accordance with the distributive provisions of the Statute of Distributions (Ireland) 1695.[8] A husband was entitled to receive the whole of his deceased wife's personalty. A widow with children was entitled to one-third of the personalty, with the remainder going to the children, and **7–08**

4 s.2 of the Inheritance Act 1833; see Wylie, J.C.W., *Irish Land Law*, (3rd ed) (London: Butterworths, 1997), p. 853, para. 15.11.

5 ss. 6 and 7 of the Inheritance Act 1833.

6 s.9 of the Inheritance Act 1833.

7 s.11(1) of the Succession Act 1965.

8 See Wylie, J.C.W., *Irish Land Law*, (2nd ed) (London: Butterworths, 1997), p. 852, para. 15.08.

grandchildren were capable of representing their predeceased parent under the doctrine of representation. Where no widow survived, the children of the deceased intestate were entitled to all of the personalty. If no issue survived the deceased intestate, a surviving widow became entitled to one-half of the personalty, and the remainder went to those most related to the deceased intestate by blood. The widow's distributive share of the personalty was increased by the Intestates' Estates Act 1954. Under that Act, a widow was entitled to £4,000 or the whole estate if worth less than £4,000, which was payable rateably out of the real and personal estate of the deceased intestate. If a widow was the sole survivor of the intestate, she became entitled to the whole estate which would otherwise have gone to the State.[9]

7–09 Under s.15 of the Court of Probate (Ireland) Act 1859 it was provided that:

> "From and after the decease of any person dying intestate, and until letters of administration shall be granted in respect of his estate and effects, the personal estate and effects of such deceased person shall vest in the judge of the Court of Probate for the time being, in the same manner and to the same extent as heretofore they vested in the Ordinary."[10]

7–10 It can be seen that the provisions of s.15 of the Court of Probate (Ireland) Act 1859 referred to the personal estate of a deceased person only, and did not cover his real estate. Section 15 of the Court of Probate (Ireland) Act 1859 was repealed and replaced by s.13 of the 1959 Act which covered both the real and personal estate of a deceased person. Section 13 of the 1959 Act provided that:

> "Where a person dies intestate, his real and personal estate, until the administration is granted in respect thereof shall vest in the President of the High Court in the same manner and to the same extent as formerly in the case of personal estate it vested in the Ordinary."

7–11 The first step towards the assimilation of realty and personalty was introduced by Part IV of the Local Registration of Title (Ireland) Act 1891 and, as a result of this assimilation, the functions of personal representatives were extended to include a deceased's realty. This policy of assimilation was continued by s.15 of the 1959 Act by providing that a deceased's personal representatives were entitled to apply for a grant of letters of administration intestate in respect of his real and personal estate.

---

[9] s.6 of the Intestates' Estate Act 1954.

[10] The Probate Act (Ireland) 1857 abolished the jurisdiction and office of the "Ordinary" (i.e. a Church of Ireland bishop) in testamentary and intestate matters of the diocesan courts in Ireland and established a new Court of Probate.

Post Succession Act Rules of Intestate Devolution and Distribution

The old rules of devolution and distribution regarding realty and personalty were abolished by s.11 of the 1965 Act. Section 11 provides that "all existing rules, modes and canons of descent and the devolution of special occupancy are hereby abolished except in so far as they apply to the descent of an estate tail" including "dower and tenancy by the curtesy".[11] Section 10(1) of the 1965 Act now provides that: **7–12**

> "The real and personal estate of a deceased person shall on his death, notwithstanding any testamentary disposition, devolve on and become vested in his personal representatives."[12]

Section 10(3) of the 1965 Act goes on to provide that:

> "The personal representatives shall be the personal representatives of the deceased in regard to his real and personal estate and shall hold as trustees for the persons by law entitled thereto."

In *O'Hagan v Grogan*[13] Macken J., when referring to s.10(1) and s.10(3), stated that: **7–13**

> "Under the provisions of s.10(1) of the Act of 1965 the whole of the intestate estate vests in the personal representative, who nevertheless does not hold the estate on his own behalf, but (under s.10(3)) as a trustee for the persons in law who are entitled to it, and he must act accordingly. Those persons have an immediate beneficial equitable interest in the estate by way of trust, which is nevertheless, subject to rights of the administrator, who has certain powers, including, for example, those for the purposes of disposition. The power to deal with the property of an intestate dates only from the date of grant, however, (as opposed to the position of an executor of a person who dies testate where the property vests on death)."

It appears that, as a result of the decision of the Supreme Court in *O'Hagan v Grogan*, persons entitled to intestate shares in an estate of a deceased person have an immediate beneficial equitable interest in the estate by way of trust, though subject to the rights of the administrator whose powers to deal with the property of an intestate commence from the date of a grant of letters of administration intestate. **7–14**

Part VI of the 1965 Act sets out the rules which govern the distribution of an intestate's estate where the intestate dies after 1 January 1967. Section 66 provides that: **7–15**

---

[11] See Lyall, Andrew, *Land Law in Ireland* (2nd ed) (Dublin: Round Hall, 2000), pp. 1002-1003.

[12] See *O'Hagan v Grogan* [2012] I.E.S.C. 8; Albert Keating, *Keating on Probate* (4th ed) (Dublin: Thomson Round Hall, 2011); Albert Keating, *First Supplement to the Fourth Edition of Keating on Probate* (Dublin: Thomson Round Hall, 2013).

[13] [2012] I.E.S.C. 8.

> "All estate to which a deceased person was beneficially entitled for an estate or interest not ceasing on his death and as to which he dies intestate after the commencement of this Act shall, after payment of all expenses, debts and liabilities and any legal right properly payable thereout, be distributed in accordance with this Part."

7–16 Once the personal representatives have discharged the debts, expenses, liabilities and any legal right share out of the intestate's estate, they may then proceed to distribute the remainder among the beneficiaries in accordance with the rules of intestacy in the 1965 Act. Section 80 of the 2010 Act amended s.109(1) of the 1965 Act by inserting "or civil partner" after "spouse" wherever it appears.[14] Section 72 of the 2010 Act amended s.67 of the 1965 Act by inserting "or civil partner" after "spouse" wherever it appears. Section 73 of the 2010 Act inserts s.67A after s.67 of the 1965 Act. Section 67A(1) provides that, if an intestate dies leaving a civil partner and no issue, the civil partner shall take the whole estate, and (2) goes on to provide that, if an intestate dies leaving a civil partner and issue, subject to subsections (3) to (7), the civil partner shall take two-thirds of the estate, and the remainder shall be distributed among the issue in accordance with s.67B(2). However, s.67A(3) provides that the court may, on the application by or on behalf of a child of an intestate who dies leaving a civil partner and one or more children, order that provision be made for that child out of the intestate's estate only if the court is of the opinion that it would be unjust not to make the order. The court, when making such an order, must ensure that: (a) the amount to which any issue of the intestate is entitled will not be less than that to which he or she would have been entitled had no such order been made; and (b) the amount provided will not be greater than the amount to which the applicant would have been entitled had the intestate died leaving neither spouse nor civil partner. Section 67B(1) and (2) provides that, if an intestate dies leaving issue and no spouse or civil partner, the estate shall be distributed among the issue, and if all the issue are in equal degree of relationship to the deceased, the distribution shall be in equal shares among them; if they are not, it shall be *per stirpes*.[15] Since the enactment of the Status of Children Act 1987, non-marital and adopted children come within the definition of issue and children for the purposes of the *per stirpe* srule.

7–17 Section 13 of the 1959 Act was repealed and replaced by s.13 of the 1965 Act which provides that:

> "Where a person dies intestate, or dies testate but leaving no executor surviving him, his real and personal estate, until administration is granted in respect thereof,

[14] See Albert Keating, *Keating on Probate* (4th ed) (Dublin: Thomson Round Hall, 2011); Albert Keating, *First Supplement to the Fourth Edition of Keating on Probate* (Dublin: Thomson Round Hall, 2013).

[15] See Albert Keating, *Keating on Probate* (4th ed) (Dublin: Round Hall, 2011), Chapter 13 - The Succession Rights of Civil Partners.

> shall vest in the President of the High Court who, for this purpose, shall be a corporation sole."

In *Gleeson v Feehan*[16] Keane J. stated that, in cases of intestacy, the President of the High Court became the "true owner" of the estate of a deceased person until the issuing of a grant of letters of administration. In *O'Hagan v Grogan*[17] Macken J. stated that, in cases of intestacy, the estate vested in the President automatically on the death of the deceased and remained so until a grant of letters of administration was issued "on which event he is divested of the estate, also automatically". The Supreme Court in *Gleeson v Feehan* and *O'Hagan v Grogan* considered the role of the President in circumstances where persons were in adverse possession of the estate of a deceased person. In *Gleeson v Feehan* Keane J. found that, in circumstances where strangers entered on an intestate's lands on the death of the deceased person, their possession was **7–18**

> "at all times adverse to the title of the true owner, the President of the High Court, in whom the entire estate vested pending the raising of representation".

What was extinguished at the end of the limitation period was "the title of the President of the High Court to the land and his right to bring an action to recover the land". However, in *O'Hagan v Grogan* Macken J. found that no beneficial or other estate vested in the President against which a claim to adverse possession can be made. She went on to state that:

> "The President of the High Court does not hold any interest in the property which vests in him temporarily, sufficient to permit a third party to secure rights by means of adverse possession."

At most he has, "on a temporary basis, a bare estate in the property in question". Section 13 neither confers powers, duties nor obligations on him. In *Flack v The President of the High Court*[18] which was decided prior to *Gleeson v Feehan*, Costello J. found that, as the President had no duty or obligation to perform in respect of the estate, the estate vested in him as "a mere matter of necessary convenience and protection". *O'Hagan v Grogan* referred with apparent approval to the judgment of Costello J. in *Flack v The President of the High Court* and, like Costello J., concluded that s.13 was a mere "mechanism of convenience" to ensure that an estate had a "temporary home" pending the grant of administration and that "there is no beneficial or other estate vested in the President, against which a claim to adverse possession can be made".[19] **7–19**

The assimilation of real estate and personal estate of a deceased intestate was **7–20**

---

16 [1997] 1 I.L.R.M. 522.
17 [2012] I.E.S.C. 8.
18 Unreported, High Court, Costello J., 29 November 1983.
19 See Albert Keating, "The Troublesome Section 13" (2012) 17(4) C.P.L.J. 70.

also completed by s.12 of the 1965 Act which provides that all enactments — including the 1965 Act and rules of law relating to personal estate — apply equally to real estate "as if it were personal estate".

7–21 As shown above, prior to the 1965 Act the devolution of property depended on whether it was realty or personalty. Realty vested in the heir-at-law at the date of death of the deceased intestate: personalty devolved on his personal representative. The early rules of inheritance and later the Inheritance Act 1833 identified the heir-at-law as a blood relative of a deceased intestate traceable from the "last purchaser". The rules of distribution and the Statute of Distributions (Ireland) 1695 ascertained those entitled to the personalty of the deceased. The old rules relating to intestate succession to realty and personalty were finally abolished by the 1965 Act. After the enactment of the 1965 Act, a deceased intestate's real and personal estate devolved on and vested in his personal representatives who held the whole estate as trustees for those who were entitled to a share in the intestate estate in accordance with the rules of intestacy in that Act. The 1965 Act was amended by the 2010 Act to include civil partners and the children of civil partners.

7–22 Before a grant of letters of administration intestate issued to the person entitled under the Rules of the Superior Courts 1962, the real and personal estate of the deceased vested in the President of the High Court under s.13 of the 1959 Act. By virtue of s.13 of the 1965 Act, the real and personal estate of the deceased vested in the President of the High Court until a grant issued to the person entitled under Order 79 of the Rules of the Superior Courts 1962, and also by the Rules of the Superior Courts 1986 until a grant issued to the person entitled under Order 79 of those Rules. As a result of *O'Hagan v Grogan,* it now appears that, under s.13 of the 1965 Act, the President of the High Court can no longer be viewed as the true owner of a deceased person's estate for the intervening period between the death of the deceased and the issuing of a grant of administration. As was said by Macken J. in *O'Hagan v Grogan* the section "hovers" over the person of the President for the time being, "by means of a legal fiction, until something else happens". He has no role as a litigant in actions involving the estate as the section provides a mere "mechanism of convenience" before a grant issues, and nothing more.

7–23 The assimilation of the real and personal estate of a deceased intestate, commenced in Part IV of the Local Registration of Title (Ireland) Act 1891 and continued by the 1959 Act, was finally completed by s.12 of the 1965 Act.

7–24 While the 1965 Act abolished the old rules of devolution and distribution of realty and personalty, introduced new rules of intestacy and assimilated the real and personal estates of deceased intestates, the old rules may still have to be considered when resolving questions of title to land where the intestate died before the enactment of the 1965 Act on 1 January 1967.

Surviving Spouses, Civil Partners and Issue

Part VI of the 1965 Act sets down the rules that govern the distribution of an intestate's estate where the intestate dies after 1 January 1967. Section 66 commences Part VI of the 1965 Act by specifying the intestate's estate that is to be made available for distribution among the beneficiaries. It provides that: **7–25**

> "All estate to which a deceased person was beneficially entitled for an estate or interest not ceasing on his death and as to which he dies intestate after the commencement of this Act shall, after payment of all expenses, debts and liabilities and any legal right properly payable thereout, be distributed in accordance with this Part."

Thus after the payment of such expenses as funeral, testamentary and other lawful debts owing and due by the intestate's estate, and any legal right payable out of the estate, the administrator may proceed to distribute the estate among those entitled in accordance with the rules of intestacy in the 1965 Act. **7–26**

Section 67(1) of the 1965 Act provides that: **7–27**

> (1) If an intestate dies leaving a spouse and no issue, the spouse shall take the whole estate.
> (2) If an intestate dies leaving a spouse and issue—
> (a) the spouse shall take two-thirds of the estate, and
> (b) the remainder shall be distributed among the issue in accordance with subsection (4).
> (3) If an intestate dies leaving issue and no spouse, his estate shall be distributed among the issue in accordance with subsection (4).
> (4) If all the issue are in equal degree of relationship to the deceased the distribution shall be in equal shares among them; if they are not, it shall be *per stirpes*.

Section 73 of the 2010 Act amended s.67 of the 1965 Act by inserting a new s.67(A) and s.67(B). Section 67A(1) of the 1965 Act now provides that:

> (1) If an intestate dies leaving a civil partner and no issue, the civil partner shall take the whole estate.
> (2) If an intestate dies leaving a civil partner and issue—
> (a) subject to subsections (3) to (7), the civil partner shall take two-thirds of the estate; and
> (b) the remainder shall be distributed among the issue in accordance with section 67B(2).
> (3) The court may, on the application by or on behalf of a child of an intestate who dies leaving a civil partner and one or more children, order that provision be made for that child out of the intestate's estate only if the court is of the opinion that it would be unjust not to make the order, after considering all the circumstances, including—
> (a) the extent to which the intestate has made provision for that child during the intestate's lifetime,
> (b) the age and reasonable financial requirements of that child,
> (c) the intestate's financial situation, and

(d) the intestate's obligations to the civil partner.

(4) The court, in ordering provision of an amount under subsection (3) shall ensure that—

(a) the amount to which any issue of the intestate is entitled shall not be less than that to which he or she would have been entitled had no such order been made, and

(b) the amount provided shall not be greater than the amount to which the applicant would have been entitled had the intestate died leaving neither spouse nor civil partner.

(5) Rules of court shall provide for the conduct of proceedings under this section in a summary manner.

(6) The costs in the proceedings shall be at the discretion of the court.

(7) An order under this section shall not be made except on an application made within 6 months from the first taking out of representation of the deceased's estate.

A new s.67B of the Succession Act now provides that:

> (1) If an intestate dies leaving issue and no spouse or civil partner, the estate shall be distributed among the issue in accordance with subsection (2).
> (2) If all the issue are in equal degree of relationship to the deceased the distribution shall be in equal shares among them; if they are not, it shall be *per stirpes*.

The *per stirpes* rule may become applicable where issue are not in equal degree of relationship to the deceased. The *per stirpes* rule prescribes that:

> "Where a deceased person's estate or any share therein is to be distributed *per stirpes* among his issue, any issue more remote than a child of the deceased shall take through all degrees, according to their stocks, in equal shares if more than one, the share which the parent of such issue would have taken if living at the death of the deceased, and no issue of the deceased shall take if the parent of such issue is living at the death of the deceased and so capable of taking."[20]

7–28 Applying the rule to s.67(4), the intestate share of a child of the intestate who has predeceased the intestate will be distributed among the issue of his/her child or children where another child survives the intestate. The issue of an intestate will be entitled to shares in the estate *per capita*, i.e. equal shares. Issue of a predeceased intestate's child will be entitled to the share of the predeceased child *per stirpes* where another child of the intestate survives. Since the enactment of the Status of Children Act 1987, non-marital and adopted children come within the definition of issue and children for the purposes of the *per stirpes* rule. Section 67(4) of the 1965 Act provides that:

> "If all the issue are in equal degree of relationship to the deceased the distribution shall be in equal shares among them; if they are not, it shall be *per stirpes*".

Section 67B(2) now provides that, in the case of issue of civil partners:

> "If all the issue are in equal degree of relationship to the deceased the distribution shall be in equal shares among them; if they are not, it shall be *per stirpes*."

[20] See s.3(3) of the 1965 Act.

Sections 64(4) and 67B(2) therefore provide for the distribution of the deceased intestate's estate *per stirpes* among his/her issue if they are not in equal degree of relationship to the deceased. Thus, if a widow, widower or civil partner dies intestate leaving him/her surviving two children and two grandchildren, by applying the *per stirpes* rule, the two surviving children will each be entitled to one-third of the estate, and the two grandchildren will be entitled to the one-third share of their deceased parent and will each receive one-sixth of the estate. However, for the *per stirpes* rule to apply, one of the deceased intestate's children must survive him/her, and one child must predecease the intestate leaving issue him or her surviving.

Surviving Parents

Section 68 of the 1965 Act provides that: **7–29**

> "If an intestate dies leaving neither spouse nor issue, his estate shall be distributed between his parents in equal shares if both survive the intestate, but, if only one parent survives, that parent shall take the whole estate."

Section 74 of the 2010 Act amended s.68 of the 1965 Act by inserting the words "nor civil partner" after "spouse". Thus, the amended s.68 of the 1965 Act now provides that: **7–30**

> "If an intestate dies leaving neither spouse nor civil partner nor issue, his estate shall be distributed between his parents in equal shares if both survive the intestate, but, if only one parent survives, that parent shall take the whole estate."

Surviving Brothers and Sisters

Section 69(1) of the 1965 Act provides that: **7–31**

> "If an intestate dies leaving neither spouse nor issue nor parent, his estate shall be distributed between his brothers and sisters in equal shares, and, if any brother or sister does not survive the intestate, the surviving children of the deceased brother or sister shall, where any other brother or sister of the deceased survives him, take in equal shares the share that their parent would have taken if he or she had survived the intestate."

Section 69(2) goes on to provide that, if an intestate dies leaving neither spouse nor issue, parent, brother nor sister, his estate shall be distributed in equal shares among the children of his brothers and sisters. Section 69 of the Act of 1965 was amended by s.75 of the 2010 Act by inserting "nor civil partner" after "spouse" wherever it appears. Thus, the amended s.69(1) and (2) now provides that: (1) If an intestate dies leaving neither spouse nor civil partner nor issue nor parent, his estate shall be distributed between his brothers and sisters in equal shares, and, if any brother or sister does not survive the intestate, the surviving children of the deceased brother or sister **7–32** shall, where any other brother or sister of the deceased survives him, take in equal shares the share that their parent would have taken if he or she had survived the intestate; and (2) If an intestate dies leaving neither spouse nor civil partner or issue nor parent nor brother nor sister, his estate shall be distributed in equal shares among the children of his brothers and sisters. Brothers and sisters are therefore entitled to their shares in the intestate's estate *per capita*. Brothers and sisters include half-brother and half-sisters, legitimated and adopted brothers and sisters and, since the commencement of the Status of Children Act 1987, non-marital brothers and sisters also.[21]

Surviving Nephews and Nieces

7–33 Section 69(1) of the 1965 Act, having provided that, where brothers and sisters survive the intestate only, his estate will be divided equally among them, goes on to provide that, if any brother or sister does not survive the intestate, the surviving children of the deceased brother or sister will take in equal shares the share that their parent would have taken if he or she had survived the intestate, where any other brother or sister survives the intestate. Thus surviving brothers and sisters will continue to take their shares *per capita*, while surviving children of deceased brothers and sisters will take *per stirpes* the representative share of their parents. If no brother or sister survives, nephews and nieces will become entitled to equal shares *per capita*, and not *per stirpes*.[22] Where no brother or sister survives, there may be a consequent diminution of the share of certain nephews and nieces by the application again of the *per capita* rule, and the larger families of deceased brothers or sisters will benefit more than they would have done had the *per stirpes* rule been applied. Nephews and nieces of half-blood, and adopted and legitimated nephews and nieces are all equally entitled to a share in the intestate's estate.

Surviving Next-of-Kin

7–34 Section 70(1) of the 1965 Act provides that:

> "If an intestate dies leaving neither spouse nor issue nor parent nor brother nor sister nor children of any deceased brother or sister, his estate shall, subject to the succeeding provisions of this Part, be distributed in equal shares among his next-of-kin."

Section 70(2) goes on to provide that:

> "Representation of next-of-kin shall not be admitted amongst collaterals except in the case of children of brothers and sisters of the intestate where any other brother or sister of the intestate survives him."

[21] s.29.

[22] s.69(2) of the 1965 Act.

Section 70(1) of the 1965 Act is now amended by s.76 of the 2010 Act and provides that:

> "If an intestate dies leaving neither spouse nor civil partner nor issue nor parent nor brother nor sister nor children of any deceased brother or sister, his estate shall, subject to the succeeding provisions of this Part, be distributed in equal shares among his next-of-kin."

Section 70(1) of the 1965 Act, as amended by s.76 of the 2010 Act, provides that, where no spouse, civil partner, issue, parents, brother, sister, or children of a brother or sister survive the intestate, his estate will be distributed among his next-of-kin. In ascertaining next-of-kin, lineal descent is preferred to collateral succession, although s.70(2) of the 1965 Act provides for an exception in the case of children of brothers and sisters of the intestate where any other brother or sister survives him. However, this entitlement is further dependent on the continued survival of a brother or sister of the intestate but, where no brother or sister survives, this collateral right to share in the intestate's estate will cease at a point similar to where the relationship of uncle or aunt and nephew or niece ceases. Where the intestate is not survived by any of the above relatives, his estate will be distributed in equal shares among his next-of-kin. **7–35**

The ascertainment of next-of-kin is based on blood relationship to the intestate. Section 71(1) provides that persons who are nearest in blood relationship to the deceased will take as next-of-kin. The degrees of blood relationship from an intestate are parents, brothers and sister, grandparent, great grandparents, uncle and aunt, nephew and niece. The search for a blood relative will commence with a direct lineal ancestor computed by counting upwards from the intestate. If he is the only survivor, he takes the whole estate.[23] Thus, if a grandfather of the intestate is the sole survivor, he will take the whole of the intestate's estate. However, s.71(2) provides that degrees of blood relationship to a direct lineal ancestor are computed by counting upwards from the intestate to that ancestor, and the degrees of blood relationship of any other relative are ascertained by counting upwards to the nearest common ancestor to the intestate, and then downward from that ancestor to the relative. If a direct lineal ancestor and any other relative are found to be within the same degree of blood relationship to the intestate, the other relative will be preferred to the exclusion of the lineal ancestor. If, for argument's sake, the intestate is survived by a great-grandfather and two aunts, the search for the next-of-kin will commence by counting upwards from the intestate to the nearest common ancestor, *viz.* the great-grandfather; the degrees of relationship to the intestate of the great-grandfather and the two aunts are three degrees, and thus equal, but by applying s.71(2), the aunts would be preferred to the great-grandfather. **7–36**

The three steps towards ascertaining next-of-kin as set out in s.70 require: **7–37**

[23] s.71(2) of the 1965 Act.

(a) That a next-of-kin is the nearest blood relative to the deceased;
(b) That the degree of relationship between the intestate and direct lineal ancestor be calculated by counting upwards from the intestate to the direct lineal ancestor, the first degree being a parent, the second degree a grandparent, and the third degree a great-grandparent;
(c) The relationship between other or collateral relatives is determined by counting the degrees up to their common ancestor and down to the other or collateral relative, the first degree being a parent, the second degree a grandparent, and the third degree down to a relative, for instance, an uncle or aunt. The degree of uncle or aunt is the same as that of a great-grandparent, i.e. the third degree.

Partial Intestacy

7–38 Section 74 of the 1965 Act provides that:

> "Where the will of a testator effectively disposes of part only of his estate, the remainder shall be distributed as if he had died intestate and left no other estate."

Section 3 of the 1965 Act defines an intestate as a person who leaves no will or leaves a will but leaves undisposed of some beneficial interest in the estate, and "intestate" should be construed accordingly. Thus, instances of partial intestacy may arise where a testator acquires additional property after making his will and, because of the absence of a residuary clause, it remains undisposed of, or where a gift in a will lapses because a beneficiary predeceases the testator, also in the absence of a residuary clause, or where a beneficiary after the death of the testator disclaims a gift in the will which again contains no residuary clause. The undisposed of share must be distributed in accordance with the rules of intestacy, and the same degrees of relationship to the deceased in a total intestacy are similarly applicable in the case of a partial intestacy. Section 74 makes it clear that the undisposed of estate must be distributed as if the testator died intestate and left no other estate, thus rendering a partial intestacy independent of the provisions of any will of the deceased. Section 63 of the 1965 Act provides that advancements to children of the deceased made during his lifetime are to be taken into account when calculating their entitlements on intestacy or under a will. Thus, in the case of partial intestacies under s.74, any lifetime advancements made to children must be taken into account in calculating their shares under the will and the shares to which they become entitled on a partial intestacy.

7–39 A partial intestacy is also of relevance to the legal right of a surviving spouse or civil partner as s.115(2) provides that, where one spouse or civil partner dies partly testate and partly intestate, the surviving spouse or civil partner may elect to take a share on intestacy, together with any gift under the will.[24] It is of similar relevance to the children of a deceased where the court is asked to reconstruct a will to make proper provision for them and would include the taking into account of undisposed of estate as well.[25]

The State as Ultimate Intestate Successor

In the absence of next-of-kin, the estate of the intestate will pass to the State as "ultimate intestate successor".[26] Section 73 of the 1965 Act replaces the old rules that dealt with the State's right of escheat and *bona vacantia* where an intestate left no surviving next-of-kin. The Minister for Finance, who exercises the right to succeed on behalf of the State, is given a wide discretion by s.73 to waive the right in whole or in part and he may do this in favour of any person, and on such terms and for such money payments as he thinks proper. Unlike the English statutory requirements which give the Crown a limited discretion to provide for dependants of the intestate whether they are related to the intestate or not, and for persons for whom the intestate might reasonably have been expected to make provision,[27] the Minister for Finance has an unfettered discretion and is not obliged to take into account any particular category of persons when exercising a waiver of the State's rights. When administration of an estate is granted for the use and benefit of the State, any legal proceedings by or against the personal representatives for the recovery of the estate, or any share in the estate, must be conducted in the same way and subject to the same rules of law and equity as if the grant had been made to the personal representatives of the person beneficially entitled to the estate. **7–40**

In proceedings involving questions of private international law and the State's entitlement to foreign movables belonging to the intestate who died domiciled in Ireland, the State's right to succeed will be based on succession, and not on any form of escheat or *bona vacantia* which would not entitle the State to succeed to the intestate's foreign movables on jurisdictional grounds. In *Re Maldonado*[28] the English courts considered the question of a foreign State's succession to the movables of an intestate who died domiciled in Spain. The Spanish authorities applied for a grant of administration to the intestate's movable property located in England on the grounds that Spanish law treated the State as an intestate successor. Barnard J. held that, as Spanish law provided for the intestate succession of the State, it was entitled to succeed to the movable property belonging to the estate of the deceased intestate in England. It was suggested by the Court that the decision would have been different if the Spanish authorities had based their claim on a **7–41**

24 See Chapter 8 – The Legal Right of Spouses and Civil Partners and Applications by Qualified Cohabitants.
25 See Chapter 9 – The Moral Duty of Testators.
26 s.73(1) of the 1965 Act.
27 U.K. Administration of Estates Act 1925, s.46(1)(vi).
28 [1953] 2 All E.R. 579.

bona vacantia or escheat. Irish law, by virtue of s.73 of the Succession Act, gives the State similar rights of succession to moveable property abroad of a deceased intestate who died domiciled in Ireland.

7–42 Section 73(1) of the 1965 Act provides that, in the absence of next-of-kin, the estate of a deceased person who dies intestate will pass to the State as ultimate intestate successor. Under Ord.79, r.5(1)(m) of the Rules of the Superior Court 1986 a nominee of the State (the Chief State Solicitor or Solicitor for the Attorney General) may apply for a grant of letters of administration intestate by lodging the usual proofs for such grants, with the exception of an administration bond. Section 34(5) of the 1965 Act provides that the Chief State Solicitor or Solicitor for the Attorney General is not required to give an administration bond when applying for or obtaining administration for the use or benefit of the State.

7–43 Section 65(1) of the 1965 Act provides that:

> "Where administration of an estate is granted for the use and benefit of the State (whether to the Chief State Solicitor, the Solicitor for the Attorney General or any other person), any legal proceedings by or against the administrator for the recovery of the estate or any share thereof shall be of the same character and be instituted and carried on in the same manner, and be subject to the same rules of law and equity in all respects, as if the grant had been made to the administrator as a person beneficially entitled to a share of the estate."[29]

[29] See *O'Hagan v Grogan* [2012] I.E.S.C. 8; Chapter 23 – The Limitation of Actions and Striking Out of Proceedings.

CHAPTER 8

THE LEGAL RIGHT OF SPOUSES AND CIVIL PARTNERS AND APPLICATIONS BY QUALIFIED COHABITANTS

INTRODUCTION

Since the enactment of the Succession Act 1965 (the "1965 Act"), a surviving spouse has a legal right to a share in his or her deceased spouse's estate.[1] The estate of a deceased spouse means all of his or her estate to which he or she was beneficially entitled "for an estate or interest not ceasing on his death remaining after payment of all expenses, debts, and liabilities, (other than estate duty), properly paid out".[2] Since the Civil Partnership and Certain Rights and Obligations of Cohabitants Act 2010 (the 2010 Act), a surviving civil partner also has a legal right to a share in his or her deceased partner's estate. Section 80 of the 2010 Act amended s.109(1) of the 1965 Act by inserting "or civil partner" after "spouse" wherever it appears. Section 69 of the 2010 Act amends s.3(1) of the 1965 Act by providing that a civil partner has the meaning assigned to it by the 2010 Act, and that legal right means the right of a spouse under s.111 to a share in the estate of a deceased person, and the right of a civil partner under s.111A to a share in the estate of a deceased person. Section 80 of the 2010 Act amends the 1965 Act by inserting s.111A after s.111 of the 1965 Act. Section 112 of the 1965 Act provides that the legal right of a spouse or civil partner will have priority over devises, bequests and shares on intestacy. Section 82 of the 2010 Act amended s.112 of the 1965 Act by inserting "or the right of a civil partner". **8–01**

[1] Enacted on 1 January 1967.
[2] See s.109(2) of the 1965 Act.

In *H v O*[3] Henchy J., when referring to the priority of the legal right of one-half or one-third share in the estate of the testator, stated that:

> "In the general context of the Act of 1965, it must be assumed that the legislative intention was that the legal right (where elected for) is to be discharged in the same manner as if the one-half or one-third of the estate had been expressly given in the will in priority over all devises and bequests."

8–02 Under s.114 (1) of the 1965 Act, where a gift left by one spouse to another is expressed in the will to be made in addition to the share representing the legal right, the surviving spouse will become entitled on the death of the testator to a sum equal to the value of the legal right, and also the gift left to him or her in the will. Section 84 of the 2010 Act amends s.114 of the 1965 Act by the insertion of "or civil partner" after "spouse" wherever it appears. Section 115(1)(a) of the 1965 Act provides that:

> "Where, under the will of a deceased person who dies wholly testate, there is a devise or bequest to a spouse, the spouse may elect to take either that devise or bequest or the share to which he is entitled as a legal right."

8–03 Section 85 of the 2010 Act amended s.115 of the 1965 Act (a) by inserting "or civil partner" after "spouse" wherever it appears, and (b) in subsection (5), by inserting "or civil partner's" after "spouse's".

8–04 A surviving spouse or civil partner is also the only person who may exercise the legal right. In *Reilly v McEntee*[4] Murphy J. stated that:

> "But it is not the value of this right which is in issue. It is the identity of the person by whom it is exercisable. The statute confers it on the surviving spouse and no reference has been made to any provision in the Act or any other authority which would justify the proposition that the right so conferred may be extended or transmitted to any other person."

8–05 In *O'Dwyer v Keegan*[5] Barron J. stated that the legal right has the same quality as an interest arising under a will or a share arising on intestacy. Barron J., when deciding whether the right given by s.111 of the 1965 Act created an interest in the property of a deceased testator or merely a right personal to the surviving spouse who may elect to take such interest, stated that:

> "First, the surviving spouse has a right to a share in the estate, and secondly, this right has the same quality as an interest arising under a will or a share arising on intestacy. The two latter interests vest on death. In my view, the former does so also."

8–06 The legal right may be extinguished by renunciation by a spouse or civil

[3] [1978] I.R. 194 at 203-204.
[4] [1984] I.L.R.M. 572 at 575-576.
[5] [1997] 2 I.L.R.M. 401.

partner, by divorce or dissolution of a civil partnership, by decree of the court in judicial separation proceedings, or where the limitation period of six years has expired.[6] The legal right may be renounced under s.113 of the 1965 Act by a spouse or civil partner by

> "an ante-nuptial contract made in writing between the parties to an intended marriage or may be renounced in writing by the spouse after marriage and during the lifetime of the testator".[7]

Section 83 of the 2010 Act amended s.113 of the 1965 Act by inserting the following section after s.113: **8–07**

> "113A The legal right of a civil partner may be renounced in an ante-civil-partnership registration contract made in writing between the parties to an intended civil partnership or may be renounced in writing by the civil partner after registration and during the lifetime of the testator."

The new status of qualified cohabitant introduced by the 2010 Act does not give rise to legal rights similar to spouses and civil partners. However, by s.194 of the 2010 Act, surviving qualified cohabitants may apply to the court for provision to be made for them out of the net estate of a deceased cohabitant.[8] Under s.194(11), the net estate of a deceased cohabitant means the estate that remains after the payment of debts, funeral and testamentary expenses, and the discharge of the legal rights and intestate succession rights of spouses or civil partners. The court, when considering an application by a surviving cohabitant under s.194 of the 2010 Act, may also take into account other court orders made during the lifetime of cohabitants under ss.174, 175, 187 of the 2010 Act, and the provisions of any cohabitants' agreement.[9] **8–08**

The Legal Right Share of Spouses and Civil Partners

For the legal right of a surviving spouse or civil partner to take effect, two conditions must be satisfied: first, the surviving spouse or civil partner is the lawful spouse or civil partner of the deceased, and secondly, the deceased spouse or civil partner must have died "wholly or partly testate".[10] The legal right is also an absolute statutory right and takes effect on the death of the testator. The amount of the legal right share will depend on whether or not there are also surviving children. Sections 111 and s.111A of the 1965 **8–09**

---

6 s.126(10) of the 1965 Act.

7 s.113 of the 1965 Act; see Chapter 26 – Succession Act Precedents; Albert Keating, *Keating on Probate* (4th ed) (Dublin: Thomson Round Hall, 2011); Albert Keating, *First Supplement to the Fourth Edition of Keating on Probate* (Dublin: Thomson Round Hall, 2013).

8 See s.173(1) of the 2010 Act; Albert Keating, *Keating on Probate* (4th ed) (Dublin: Thomson Round Hall, 2011); Albert Keating, *First Supplement to the Fourth Edition of Keating on Probate* (Dublin: Thomson Round Hall, 2013).

9 See s.202 of the 2010 Act.

10 See s.109(1) of the 1965 Act.

Act provide that, where the testator leaves a spouse or civil partner and no children, the spouse or civil partner will have a right to one-half of the estate, but where the testator leaves a spouse or civil partner and children, the spouse or civil partner will have a right to one-third of the estate. Section 111 of the 1965 Act provides that:

> "(1) If the testator leaves a spouse and no children, the spouse shall have a right to one-half of the estate.
>
> (2) If the testator leaves a spouse and children, the spouse shall have a right to one-third of the estate."

8–10 Section 80 of the 2010 Act amends the 1965 Act by inserting the following section after s.111of the 1965 Act:

> "111A (1) If the testator leaves a civil partner and no children, the civil partner shall have a right to one-half of the estate. (2) Subject to section 117(3A), if the testator leaves a civil partner and children, the civil partner shall have a right to one-third of the estate."

Section 112 of the 1965 Act adds:

> "The right of a spouse under section 111 (which shall be known as a legal right) shall have priority over devises, bequests and shares on intestacy."

8–11 Section 82 of the 2010 Act is amended by s.112 of the 1965 Act by the insertion of the words "or the right of a civil partner under section 111A" after "section 111".

The legal right may be renounced by:

> "an ante-nuptial contract made in writing between the parties to an intended marriage or may be renounced in writing by the spouse after marriage and during the lifetime of the testator".[11]

8–12 Since the enactment of the 2010 Act, the legal right may be renounced by an ante-civil partnership contract made in writing between the parties to an intended civil partnership or may be renounced in writing by the civil partner after the civil partnership was entered into and during the lifetime of the testator.[12]

8–13 Where a testamentary gift left by one spouse to another is expressed to be made in addition to the share representing the legal right that spouse will become entitled on the death of the testator to a sum equal to the value of the legal right, and also the gift left to that spouse in the will. But in all other cases a gift by will to a spouse "shall be deemed to have been intended by

---

[11] s.113 of the 1965 Act; see Chapter 26 – Succession Act Precedents.

[12] *ibid.*

the testator to be in satisfaction of the share as a legal right of the spouse". Section 114(1) of the 1965 Act provides that:

> "Where property is devised or bequeathed in a will to a spouse and the devise or bequest is expressed in the will to be in addition to the share as a legal right of the spouse, the testator shall be deemed to have made by the will a gift to the spouse consisting of (a) a sum equal to the value of the share as a legal right of the spouse, and (b) the property so devised or bequeathed."

Section 114(2) goes on to provide that:

> "In any other case, a devise or bequest in a will to a spouse shall be deemed to have been intended by the testator to be in satisfaction of the share as a legal right of the spouse."

Section 84 of the 2010 Act amended s.114 of the 1965 Act by inserting "or civil partner" after "spouse" wherever it appears in s.114.

The date for valuation of the legal right share of a surviving spouse or civil partner is the date of distribution, since it is the only date on which the true nature and extent of one-half or one-third of the net estate of the deceased can be determined.[13] **8–14**

The Right of Election by Spouses and Civil Partners

A surviving spouse is also given the concomitant right of election under s.115 of the 1965 Act, and he or she may elect to take the gift left by will or the value of the legal right share.[14] Section 115(1)(a) provides that: **8–15**

> "Where, under the will of a deceased person who dies wholly testate, there is a devise or bequest to a spouse, the spouse may elect to take either that devise or bequest or the share to which he is entitled as a legal right."

It was said in one case that the condition precedent for the acquisition of the legal right under s.115 is the exercise of the right of election by the surviving spouse.[15] Also, the right of election is a personal right and can only be exercised by the surviving spouse. Nobody else may exercise it on his or her behalf, and this includes a surviving spouse's personal representatives.[16] In the event of the death of the surviving spouse after exercising the right of election, the property representing the value of the legal right will form part of the spouse's estate.[17] The personal representatives of the deceased spouse have a duty to notify the surviving spouse in writing of the right of election and the right must be exercised within six months from the date of **8–16**

---

13 *Strong v Holmes* [2010] I.E.H.C. 70.
14 See Chapter 26 – Succession Act Precedents.
15 *Re Urquhart* [1974] I.R. 197.
16 *Reilly v McEntee* [1984] I.L.R.M. 572.
17 *Re Cummins* [1997] 2 I.L.R.M. 401.

notification of the right, or one year from the first taking out of a grant of probate or letters of administration with the will annexed.[18] Section 115(4) provides that:

> "It shall be the duty of the personal representatives to notify the spouse in writing of the right of election conferred by this section. The right shall not be exercisable after the expiration of six months from the receipt by the spouse of such notification or one year from the first taking out of representation of the deceased's estate, whichever is the later."[19]

8–17 When exercising the right of election, the spouse may take a gift left to him or her in the deceased spouse's will in partial satisfaction of the legal right, with the balance payable out of the deceased spouse's estate.

8–18 Section 85 of the 2010 Act amended s.115 of the Act of 1965: (a) by inserting "or civil partner" after "spouse" wherever it appears; and (b) in subsection (5), by inserting "or civil partner's" after "spouse's". Section 115(1)(a) of the 1965 Act as amended by s.85 of the 2010 Act, provides that where, under the will of a deceased person who dies wholly testate, there is a devise or bequest to a civil partner, the civil partner may elect to take either that devise or bequest or the share to which he is entitled as a legal right. The right of election of a civil partner, like that of a surviving spouse, is a personal right, and it may not be exercised by another person on behalf of a surviving civil partner, or by a personal representative on behalf of a surviving civil partner's estate.[20] Section 115(2)(a) provides that, where a person dies partly testate and partly intestate, a civil partner may elect to take either: (i) his or her share as a legal right; or (ii) his or her share under the intestacy, together with any devise or bequest to him or her under the will of the deceased. In default of election, the civil partner will be entitled to take his or her share under the intestacy, together with any devise or bequest to him or her under the will, and he or she will not be entitled to take any share as a legal right.[21] Section 115(2)(a)(ii) is applicable to a partial intestacy under s.74 of the 1965 Act which provides that, where the will of a testator disposes of part only of his estate, the remainder will be distributed as if he had died intestate and left no other estate. Section 3 of the 1965 Act defines an intestate as a person who leaves no will or leaves a will but leaves undisposed of some beneficial interest in the estate, and "intestate" should be construed accordingly.[22] Thus, instances of partial intestacy may arise where a testator acquires additional property after making his will and, because of the absence of a residuary clause, it remains undisposed of, or where a gift in a will lapses because a beneficiary predeceases the testator. A partial intestacy may also arise in the absence of a residuary clause, or

---

18 s.115(4) of the 1965 Act.

19 See Chapter 26 – Succession Act Precedents.

20 *Reilly v McEntee* [1984] I.L.R.M. 572.

21 s.115(2)(b) of the 1965 Act.

22 See Chapter 7 – Intestate Succession.

where a beneficiary after the death of the testator disclaims a gift in the will which contains no residuary clause. The undisposed of share must be distributed in accordance with the rules of intestacy, and the same degrees of relationship to the deceased in a total intestacy are applicable in the case of a partial intestacy. Section 74 makes it clear that the undisposed of estate must be distributed as if the testator died intestate and left no other estate, thus rendering a partial intestacy independent of the provisions of any will of the deceased. Thus, by virtue of s.115(2)(a)(ii), where there is a partial intestacy, a surviving civil partner may elect to take his or her share under the intestacy, together with any devise or bequest to him or her under the will of the deceased. Section 115(3) provides that a civil partner, in electing to take his share as a legal right, may further elect to take any devise or bequest to him or her less in value than the share in partial satisfaction thereof. The surviving civil partner under s.115(3) also has the right to elect to take any devise or bequest to him or her less in value than the share in partial satisfaction. Where he or she does so, the legal right will be comprised of the testamentary gift in partial satisfaction of the right, with the balance payable out of the estate. The personal representatives of the deceased civil partner have a duty to notify the surviving civil partner in writing of this right of election, and the right must be exercised within six months from the date of notification or one year from the first taking out of a grant of probate or letters of administration with the will annexed.[23]

The Right of Appropriation by a Spouse and Civil Partner

Section 56 (1) of the 1965 Act provides that: **8–19**

> "Where the estate of a deceased person includes a dwelling in which, at the time of the deceased's death, the surviving spouse was ordinarily resident, the surviving spouse may, subject to subsection (5), require the personal representatives in writing to appropriate the dwelling under section 55 in or towards satisfaction of any share of the surviving spouse."

By s.56(2), the surviving spouse may also require the personal representatives in writing to appropriate any household chattels in or towards the satisfaction of the share of the surviving spouse, and by s.56(3), if the share of a surviving spouse is insufficient to enable an appropriation to be made, the right may also be exercised in relation to the share of any minor for whom the surviving spouse is trustee under s.57 of the 1965 Act or otherwise.[24] Under s.56(4), the personal representatives have a duty to notify the surviving spouse in writing of the rights conferred by s.56. **8–20**

Section 56 (5) provides that: **8–21**

[23] s.115(4) of the 1965 Act; see Chapter 26 – Succession Act Precedents.

[24] See Chapter 26 – Succession Act Precedents.

"A right conferred by this section shall not be exercisable –

(a) after the expiration of six months from the receipt by the surviving spouse of such notification or one one year from the first taking out of representation of the deceased's estate, whichever is the later, or

(b) in relation to a dwelling, in any of the cases mentioned in subsection (6), unless the court, on application made by the personal representatives or the surviving spouse, is satisfied that the exercise of that right is unlikely to diminish the value of the assets of the deceased, other than the dwelling, or to make it more difficult to dispose of them in due course of administration and authorises its exercise."

8–22 In *H v H*[25] Parke J., when construing the provisions of s.56(5)(b), stated that:

"the onus of proof rests on the applicant to satisfy the court that the exercise of the right of appropriation is unlikely to diminish the value of the assets of the deceased, other than the dwelling, or to make it more difficult to dispose of them in due course of administration".

8–23 When construing the meaning of the words "the value of the assets of the deceased, other than the dwelling," he found that the words of s.56(5)(b) "are clear and intelligible as they stand" and that they refer "plainly" to all the assets of the deceased, other than the dwelling, and the fact that "the dwelling is the only exclusion seems to me to remove any doubt which might exist as to the comprehensiveness of the word 'all'". The next step is to determine the meaning and effect of the word "or" which separates the expressions "to diminish the value of the assets of the deceased, other than the dwelling," and "to make it more difficult to dispose of them in due course of administration". He stated that the Court must be satisfied "that *neither* of the specified eventualities is likely to happen". In *H v H,* the testator left all of his property to the second defendant, subject to the right of his widow to reside in part of the dwelling which was situated on the devised property for her life. The property consisted of agricultural land. There were no children of the marriage. The widow, who was the plaintiff, elected to take her legal right share pursuant to s.115 of the 1965 Act, instead of the life interest given to her in the will. She then applied to the High Court under s.56 of the 1965 Act for an order directing the personal representative to appropriate the dwelling to her in satisfaction of her legal right share in the estate. The second defendant in the case objected to this appropriation on the grounds that it would diminish the value of the agricultural land which was left to him. Parke J. for the Supreme Court held that the widow had failed to establish her right to appropriate under s.56 of the 1965 Act.[26] Where a surviving spouse exercises the right of appropriation under s.56 of the 1965 Act, the relevant date for evaluating the assets of the estate is the date of the appropriation, and not the date of death of the deceased.[27]

---

[25] [1978] I.R. 138 at 147-148.

[26] See *H v O* [1978] I.R. 194.

[27] See also *Re Charteris* [1917] 2 Ch. 379; *Robinson v Collins* [1975] 1 W.L.R. 309; *Re Gollin's Declaration of Trust* [1969] 1 W.L.R. 1858.

The relevant date for evaluating the assets of the estate for the purposes of appropriation under s.56(5)(b) of the 1965 Act and s.71 of the 2010 Act is the date of the appropriation, and not the date of death of the deceased. Murphy J. said in *Strong v Holmes*[28] that the relevant date for evaluating the assets of the estate for the purposes of appropriation is the date of the appropriation, and not the date of death of the deceased. In *Robinson v Collins*[29] Pennycuick V.C. stated, in relation to the power of appropriation and the valuation date in relation to the U.K. Administration of Estates Act 1925, that: **8–24**

> "There can be no doubt that where a personal representative exercises the statutory power of appropriation under s.41 of the Act of 1925 he must do so at the value of the property appropriated as at the date of appropriation."

As was said by Murphy J. in *Strong v Holmes*:

> "While there are differences in the statutory provisions in *Robinson* and under the provisions of the Succession Act, it seems clear, that in the absence of any statutory provision, that the valuation date is the actual date of appropriation."

THE EXTINGUISHMENT OF THE LEGAL RIGHT

The legal right may be extinguished by renunciation by a spouse or civil partner, by divorce or dissolution of a civil partnership, by decree of the court in judicial separation proceedings, or where the limitation period of six years has expired.[30] The legal right may be renounced under s.113 of the 1965 Act by a spouse or civil partner by **8–25**

> "an ante-nuptial contract made in writing between the parties to an intended marriage or may be renounced in writing by the spouse after marriage and during the lifetime of the testator".[31]

Section 83 of the 2010 Act amended s.113 of the 1965 Act by inserting the following section after s.113: **8–26**

> "113A The legal right of a civil partner may be renounced in an ante-civil-partnership registration contract made in writing between the parties to an intended civil partnership or may be renounced in writing by the civil partner after registration and during the lifetime of the testator."

When a decree of divorce is granted, the legal right share of a spouse or **8–27**

---

[28] [2010] I.E.H.C. 70.

[29] [1975] 1 W.L.R. 309 at 313 and cited with approval by Murphy J. in *Strong v Holmes*.

[30] s.126(1) of the 1965 Act; see Chapter 10 – The Cessation of Succession and Legal Rights; Chapter 23 – The Limitation of Actions and Striking Out Proceedings.

[31] s.113 of the 1965 Act; see Albert Keating, *Keating on Probate* (4th ed) (Dublin: Thomson Round Hall, 2011); Albert Keating, *First Supplement to the Fourth Edition of Keating on Probate* (Dublin: Thomson Round Hall, 2013).

a share on intestacy ceases contemporaneously with the dissolution of the marriage, but the court, when making such a decree, will take such inheritance matters into account.[32] However, under s.18 of the Family Law (Divorce) 1996 Act, a divorced spouse may apply to the court for provision to be made for him or her out of the other divorced spouse's estate. When considering such applications by divorced spouses, the court will have regard to the rights of all persons who have an interest in the estate of the deceased. It must be satisfied that it was not possible for proper provision to be made for the applicant during the lifetime of the deceased when the court was making ancillary orders under Part III of the 1996 Act, and that this was not because of the misconduct of the applicant.[33] The time limit for making such applications is six months from the first taking out of representation to the deceased's estate. Section 18 of the Family Law (Divorce) Act 1996 is amended by s.155 of the 2010 Act to include civil partners.

8–28 The court at the time of granting a decree of judicial separation, or at any time thereafter, may make an order extinguishing the legal right share of a spouse or the share to which that spouse is entitled to on an intestacy.[34] There is no need for the court to make any such order in the case of a decree of divorce being granted as a spouse ceases to be a spouse from the date of the decree.[35] However, the court on granting a decree of judicial separation and when deciding whether or not to extinguish a spouse's legal right share or share on intestacy must be satisfied that:

1. Adequate and reasonable financial provision exists or can be made under sections 8, 9, 10(1)(a), 11, 12, or 13 of the Family Law Act 1995 for the spouse whose succession rights are in question; or
2. The spouse concerned is a spouse for the support of whom the court refused to make an order under sections 8, 9, 10(1)(a), 11, 12, or 13 of the 1995 Act; or
3. The spouse concerned is not a spouse for whose benefit the court would, if an application were made to it in that behalf, make an order under sections 8, 9, 10(1)(a), 11, 12, or 13 of the 1995 Act.[36]

8–29 The court will have regard to all the circumstances of the case when deciding whether to make an extinguishment order and will endeavour to ensure if making such an order that it is made in the interests of justice.[37] The Family Law Act 1995 is amended by Part 14 of the 2010 Act to include civil partners.

8–30 The legal right of a surviving spouse or civil partner may also be extinguished by the expiration of the limitation period of six years, which is the period

---

[32] s.18(3) of the Family Law (Divorce) Act 1996.
[33] *ibid.*
[34] s.14 of the Family Law Act 1995.
[35] See s.18 of the Family Law (Divorce) Act 1996.
[36] s.14 of the Family Law Act 1995.
[37] ss.16(1) and 5 of the Family Law Act 1995,

prescribed by s.126 of the 1965 Act for bringing an action against the estate of a deceased spouse or civil partner claiming the legal right. Section 126(1) of the 1965 Act provides that no action in respect of any claim to the estate of a deceased person or to any share or interest in such estate, whether under a will, on intestacy or under s.111 of the of the 1965 Act, may be brought after the expiration of six years from the date when the right to receive the share or interest accrued. Section 126(1) of the 1965 Act was amended by s.89 of the Civil Partnership and Certain Rights and Obligations of Cohabitants Act 2010 (the "2010 Act") by inserting "or section 111A" after "section 111".

Qualified Cohabitants

Section 171 of the 2010 Act provides that "cohabitant" has the meaning assigned to it in s.172 of the 2010 Act. A cohabitant is defined as: **8–31**

> "one of two adults (whether of the same or the opposite sex) who live together as a couple in an intimate and committed relationship and who are not related to each other within the prohibited degrees of relationship or married to each other or civil partners of each other."[38]

For the purposes of s.172, two adults are within a prohibited degree of relationship if they would be prohibited from marrying each other in the State, or are in a relationship referred to in the Third Schedule to the Civil Registration Act 2004 inserted by s.26 of the 2010 Act.[39] Section 172(5) provides that: **8–32**

> "a qualified cohabitant means an adult who was in a relationship of cohabitation with another adult and who, immediately before the time that that relationship ended, whether through death or otherwise, was living with the other adult as a couple for a period: (a) of 2 years or more, in the case where they are the parents of one or more dependent children, and (b) of 5 years or more, in any other case".

Section 171 also provides that a "dependent child", in relation to a cohabitant or a couple of cohabitants, means any child of whom both the cohabitants are the parents and who is: (a) under the age of 18 years; or (b) 18 years of age or over and is (i) receiving full-time education or instruction at any university, college, school or other educational establishment and is under the age of 23 years or (ii) incapable of taking care of his or her own needs because of a mental or physical disability. **8–33**

When determining whether or not two adults are cohabitants, the court may take into account all the circumstances of the relationship and in particular will have regard to the following: **8–34**

> "(a) the duration of the relationship;

[38] s.172(1) of the 2010 Act.
[39] s.172(4) of the 2010 Act.

(b) the basis on which the couple live together;
(c) the degree of financial dependence of either adult on the other and any agreements in respect of their finances;
(d) the degree and nature of any financial arrangements between the adults including any joint purchase of an estate or interest in land or joint acquisition of personal property;
(e) whether there are one or more dependent children;
(f) whether one of the adults cares for and supports the children of the other; and
(g) the degree to which the adults present themselves to others as a couple."[40]

8–35 Section 172(3) also provides that a relationship does not cease to be an intimate relationship for the purpose of s.172 merely because it is no longer sexual in nature.

8–36 Qualified cohabitants who are financially dependent may apply to the court for a property adjustment order under s.174 of the 2010 Act, a compensatory maintenance order under s.175 of the 2010 Act and a pension adjustment order under s.187 of the 2010 Act. Section 173(1) of the 2010 Act provides that a qualified cohabitant may, subject to any cohabitants' agreement under s.202, apply to the court, on notice to the other cohabitant, for a property adjustment order under s.174, for a compensatory maintenance order under s.175 or for a pension adjustment order under s.187 or any of them, but only if the qualified cohabitant first satisfies the court that he or she is financially dependent on the other cohabitant and that the financial dependence arises from the relationship or the ending of the relationship. The court may, if satisfied that it is just and equitable to do so in all the circumstances, make the order concerned.[41] Such orders once made may, however, be taken into account when the court is making provision for a surviving cohabitant out of a deceased cohabitant's estate under s.194. Section 173(7) goes on to provide that:

> "Where the court makes an order under s.174, 175(1)(c) or 187 in favour of a qualified cohabitant, the court may, in the same proceedings or at any later date, on the application of either of the qualified cohabitants concerned, order that either or both of them will not, on the death of the other, be entitled to apply for an order under section 194."

Section 194 Applications by Surviving Qualified Cohabitants

8–37 Under s.194 of the 2010 Act, surviving qualified cohabitants may apply to the court for provision to be made for them out of the "net estate" of a deceased cohabitant. The court, when considering an application by a surviving cohabitant under s.194 of the 2010 Act, may also take into account other court orders made during the lifetime of cohabitants under ss. 174, 175, 187

[40] s.172(2) of the 2010 Act.
[41] s.173(2) of the 2010 Act.

of the 2010 Act, and the provisions of any cohabitants' agreement.[42] Under s.174(1), the court may order, *inter alia*,

> "the transfer by either of the cohabitants to or for the benefit of the other, of specified property in which the cohabitant has an interest either in possession or reversion".

Under s.175(1), the court may order one cohabitant to make periodical payments to the other. Section 187 deals with issues relating to pensions and applications for pension adjustment orders, and any order made by the court in relation to such matters may also be taken into account by the court when deciding the question of provision for a surviving cohabitant under s.194. Under s.202(1) of the 2010 Act, cohabitants may enter into a cohabitants' agreement "to provide for financial matters during the relationship or when the relationship ends, whether through death or otherwise". Where such an agreement exists, it may be taken into account by the court when making an order under s.194. An application by a surviving qualified cohabitant under s.194 must be made within six months from the first taking out of a grant of representation to the estate. **8–38**

Qualified cohabitants do not have a legal right to a share in any part of a deceased cohabitant's estate or intestate rights of succession to the estate of deceased cohabitants similar to spouses or civil partners. In fact, s.194(11) of the 2010 Act provides that the "net estate" of a deceased cohabitant means the estate that remains after discharging: **8–39**

(a) Other liabilities of the estate having priority over the rights referred to in paragraphs (b) and (c);
(b) Any rights, under the 1965 Act, of any surviving spouse of the person; and
(c) Any rights, under the 1965 Act, of any surviving civil partner of the person.

Under s.194(11), the net estate of a deceased cohabitant means the estate that remains after the payment of debts, funeral and testamentary expenses, and the discharge of the legal rights and intestate succession rights of spouses or civil partners. The amount of the legal right of a surviving spouse or civil partner depends on whether or not there are surviving children also, as s.111 of the 1965 Act provides that, if the testator leaves a spouse or civil partner and no children, the spouse or civil partner will have a right to one-half of the estate, and if the testator leaves a spouse or civil partner and children, the spouse or civil partner will have a right to one-third of the estate. Section 67 of the 1965 Act provides that, where an intestate dies leaving a spouse or civil partner and no issue, the spouse or civil partner will take the whole estate, but if an intestate leaves a spouse or civil partner **8–40**

---

[42] See s.202 of the 2010 Act.

and issue, the spouse or civil partner shall take two-thirds of the estate, and the remainder will be distributed among the issue. A surviving spouse or civil partner may also exercise a right of election under s.115 of the 1965 Act. Section 115(1)(a) of the 1965 Act provides that:

> "Where, under the will of a deceased person who dies wholly testate, there is a devise or bequest to a spouse, the spouse may elect to take either that devise or bequest or the share to which he is entitled as a legal right."

8–41 Thus, where there is a surviving spouse or civil partner, the succession rights which he or she enjoys under the 1965 Act must first be deducted from the estate of a deceased cohabitant and whatever estate remains is the net estate out of which provision may be made for a surviving cohabitant under s.194 of the 2010 Act. But where there is no spouse or civil partner, the court may make provision out of the net estate that remains after the payment of debts, funeral and testamentary expenses. Where such is the case, the maximum provision that can be made by the court for a surviving cohabitant is equivalent to the value of a legal right share or share on intestacy of a surviving spouse or civil partner under the 1965 Act.[43] Therefore, it can be seen that the amount of the net estate out of which provision can be made for a surviving cohabitant by the court under s.194 may be considerably reduced by the existence of a surviving spouse or civil partner, whether or not a deceased cohabitant leaves a will and, of course, the existence of children of a deceased cohabitant, who also have succession rights to the estate.

8–42 The children may also under s.117 of the 1965 Act apply to the court for proper provision to be made for them out of the net estate of a deceased cohabitant. They must first establish that the moral duty has not been fulfilled before the court can make provision for them. Section 194 of the 2010 Act does not provide for a moral duty and an application under that section is simply for provision to be made out of the net estate of a deceased cohabitant for the surviving cohabitant, subject to the various factors that must be taken into account by the court under the 2010 Act and the 1965 Act when making an order under s.194. But the court, when making proper provision for children under s.117 of the 1965 Act, cannot affect the legal right of a spouse and, to a more limited extent, the legal right of a civil partner. Provision for them can only be made out of the remaining net estate. Where a surviving spouse or civil partner exists, that also is the estate out of which provision may be made for a surviving cohabitant. Where the court makes provision for children under s.117 out of that estate, the provision may be further reduced insofar as a surviving cohabitant is concerned. It is suggested that, in the event of applications by a surviving cohabitant under s.194 and children under s.117, both applications might be joined to ensure a more equitable distribution of the net estate. But where there is no surviving spouse or civil partner or children, the net estate is the estate that remains

---

[43] See s.194(7) of the 2010 Act.

after the payment of debts, funeral and testamentary expenses. Where such is the case, the maximum amount of provision that can be made by the court for a surviving cohabitant is equivalent to the value of a legal right share or share on intestacy of a surviving spouse or civil partner under the 1965 Act.[44] Therefore, it can be seen that the amount of the net estate out of which provision can be made for a surviving cohabitant by the court under s.194 may be considerably reduced by the existence of a surviving spouse or civil partner and whether or not a deceased cohabitant leaves a will. It may even be further reduced where the court decides to make provision for the children of the deceased cohabitant under s.117. On the other hand, where there is no surviving spouse or civil partner or children, the amount of the estate available for making provision for a surviving cohabitant will be significantly increased, but the maximum amount of provision that can be made by the court for a surviving cohabitant in such circumstances is equivalent to the value of a legal right share or share on intestacy of a surviving spouse or civil partner under the 1965 Act.[45] It is also important to bear in mind that the court, when considering an application under s.194, may take into account other court orders made during the lifetime of cohabitants under ss. 174, 175, 187 of the 2010 Act, and the provisions of any cohabitants' agreement.[46]

By s.194(3) of the 2010 Act, the court may make "appropriate" provision **8–43**
for a qualified cohabitant if it is satisfied

> "that proper provision in the circumstances was not made for the applicant during the lifetime of the deceased for any reason other than conduct by the applicant that, in the opinion of the court, it would in all the circumstances be unjust to disregard".

It appears from s.194(3) that the court may take into account the conduct **8–44**
of an applicant cohabitant when making an order under s.194. Where it appears that the misconduct by the applicant cohabitant was the reason for the deceased cohabitant not making proper provision for him or her during his or her lifetime, such misconduct may be considered by the court when considering an application under s.194. For instance, the desertion by the applicant cohabitant during the lifetime of the deceased cohabitant may be "conduct" which may be taken into account by the court under s.193(3).

Under s.202(1) of the 2010 Act, cohabitants may enter into a cohabitants' **8–45**
agreement "to provide for financial matters during the relationship or when the relationship ends, whether through death or otherwise". Where such an agreement exists, it may be taken into account by the court when making an order under s.194. Section 202(1) of the 2010 Act provides that:

> "Notwithstanding any enactment or rule of law, cohabitants may enter into a

44 *ibid.*
45 s.194(7) of the 2010 Act.
46 See s.202 of the 2010 Act.

cohabitants' agreement to provide for financial matters during the relationship or when the relationship ends, whether through death or otherwise."

8–46 A cohabitants' agreement will not be valid unless:

"(a) the cohabitants—
  (i) have each received independent legal advice before entering into it, or
  (ii) have received legal advice together and have waived in writing the right to independent legal advice,
(b) the agreement is in writing and signed by both cohabitants, and
(c) the general law of contract is complied with."[47]

8–47 Subject to s.202(4), a cohabitants' agreement may provide that neither cohabitant may apply for an order for redress referred to in s.173 of the 2010 Act, or an order for provision from the estate of his or her cohabitant under s.194 of the 2010 Act.[48] Under s.202(4), the court is empowered to vary or set aside a cohabitants' agreement in exceptional circumstances, where its enforceability would cause serious injustice. By s.202(5), a cohabitants' agreement that meets the other criteria of s.202 may be deemed to be a cohabitants' agreement under s.202, even if entered into before the cohabitation has commenced.

[47] See s.202(2) of the 2010 Act.
[48] See s.202(3) of the 2010 Act.

Chapter 9

THE MORAL DUTY OF TESTATORS

Introduction

Section 117(1) of the Succession Act 1965 (the "1965 Act") provides that: **9–01**

> "Where, on application by or on behalf of a child of a testator, the court is of opinion that the testator has failed in his moral duty to make proper provision for the child in accordance with his means, whether by his will or otherwise, the court may order that such provision shall be made for the child out of the estate as the court thinks just."

Prior to 1987, such applications could only be made by children coming within the definition of children in the 1965 Act.[1] Since the enactment of the Status of Children Act 1987, a non-marital child of a testator may also apply to the court under s.117. In the context of s.117(2), the expression "other children" has been held to mean any other child other than the applicant who is a beneficiary in the will and whose testamentary benefit may be affected by a court order.[2] Section 117(1A)(a) of the 1965 Act provides that: **9–02**

> "An application made under this section by virtue of Part V of the Status of Children Act, 1987, shall be considered in accordance with subsection (2) irrespective of whether the testator executed his will before or after the commencement of the said Part V."

Section 117(1A)(b) provides that:

---

1 See *O'B v S* [1984] I.R. 316.

2 *MFH v WBH* [1984] I.R. 599 at 606; See Albert Keating, *Keating on Probate* (4th ed) (Dublin: Thomson Round Hall, 2011); Albert Keating, *First Supplement to the Fourth Edition of Keating on Probate* (Dublin: Thomson Round Hall, 2013).

> "Nothing in paragraph (a) shall be construed as referring to a right to apply under this section in respect of a testator who dies before the commencement of the said Part V."

9–03 The moral duty of testators in s.117 arises out of the relationship of testator and child and, even though it is "transposed" into "a legal duty enforceable in the terms laid down in section 117", it does not bestow any legal right to a share in a deceased testator's estate, similar to the legal rights of spouses and civil partners.[3] The moral description of the duty may suggest that parents ought to make provision for their children in their wills, and accordingly, s.117(1) of the 1965 Act gives children a form of natural right to a share in the estate. While this may be a correct description from a natural law point of view, it is a view not shared by the courts which described the moral duty as a positivist and legal duty enforceable in the terms laid down in s.117.[4]

9–04 In *A v C & Anor*[5] Laffoy J. stated that "the court's function in adjudicating on an application under s.117 of the 1965 Act is a two-stage process". The first stage is that the court must decide whether the testator has failed in his moral duty to make proper provision for the applicant child. That decision is made by reference to the circumstances which prevailed at the date of death of the testator. It is only when the applicant child overcomes the "relatively high onus" of proof that there has been a positive failure in the moral duty that the court proceeds to the second stage, which is to decide what provision is to be ordered for the applicant child.[6] Laffoy J. also referred to the judgment of Carroll J. in *MPD v MD*[7] for the statement that:

> "when the court moves to the second stage, the provision must be just at the time the court makes its order, so that the court must have regard to the value of the entire estate at the date of the hearing".

9–05 While a court order under s.117 of the 1965 Act will not affect any benefit or gift given to children during the lifetime of the testator, it may be a factor taken into account by the court when determining whether a testator was in breach of his moral duty, especially, when considering the question of proper provision for the applicant child. Section 117 provides that proper provision for a child may also be made for a child "otherwise" than by way of a will. Section 117(3) provides that an order made under s.117 shall not affect the legal right of a surviving spouse or, if the surviving spouse is the mother or father of the applicant child, any devise or bequest to the spouse or any share to which the spouse is entitled on intestacy. Section 117(3) was amended by s.86 of the Civil Partnership and Certain Rights and Obligations of Cohabitants Act 2010 (the "2010 Act") by inserting a new s.117(3)(A)

---

3 See *EB v SS* [1998] 2 I.L.R.M. 141.
4 *ibid.*
5 [2007] I.E.H.C. 120.
6 *Re IAC* [1990] 2 I.R. 143.
7 [1981] I.L.R.M. 179 at 188.

which provides that an order under s.117 shall not affect the legal right of a surviving civil partner:

> "unless the court, after consideration of all the circumstances, including the testator's financial circumstances and his or her obligations to the surviving civil partner, is of the opinion that it would be unjust not to make the order".

The time prescribed for instituting proceedings under s.117(6), as amended by s.46 of the Family Law (Divorce) Act 1996, is six months from the first taking out of a grant of representation.[8] The provisions of s.117 apply only to cases where a parent dies testate or partly testate, but not where he or she dies wholly intestate.[9] **9–06**

The Moral Duty of Testators

Under s.117 of the 1965 Act, the court must first be satisfied that the testator has failed in his moral duty to make proper provision for the child in accordance with his means.[10] When considering the nature of the moral duty in s.117 in *In the Goods of GM: FM v TAM*[11] Kenny J. stated that, because a testator may leave the whole of his estate to his spouse (or civil partner), the moral duty created by s.117 is not an absolute one, "nor is it an obligation to each child to leave him something". *In the Goods of GM: FM v TAM* is the first case that considered in depth the factors that may be taken into account by the court when considering an application under s.117, and is usually the starting point for any discussion of the provisions of s.117. In that case Kenny J. thought that the moral duty of a testator was one based on the relationship between testator and child and arises out of such a relationship though "does not of itself and without regard to other circumstances create a moral duty to leave anything to a child". He went on to state that the existence of the testator's moral duty to make proper provision for his children will be determined by the facts existing at the date of death of the testator. It **9–07**

> "must depend upon:- (a) the amount left to the surviving spouse or the value of the legal right if the survivor elects to take this, (b) the number of the testator's children, their ages and their positions in life at the date of the testator's death, (c) the means of the testator, (d) the age of the child whose case is being considered and his or her financial position and prospects in life, (e) whether the testator has already in his lifetime made proper provision for the child. The court must decide whether the duty exists and the view of the testator that he did not owe any is not decisive."

---

8 See *S1 and S2 v PR1 and PR2* [2013] I.E.H.C. 407; Albert Keating, "A Constructive Interpretation of Section 117(6) of the Succession Act 1965 (2014) 19(2) C.P.L.J. 33.

9 *MPD v MD* [1981] I.L.R.M. 179.

10 See Albert Keating, "The Moral Duty and "New Model" Constructive Trusts" (2007) 12(3) C.P.L.J. 79.

11 (1970) 106 I.L.T.R. 82 at 87.

9–08 In *In the Goods of GM: FM v TAM,* the testator left all his property in Ireland on trust for his wife for life and after her death for two nephews. Although there were no children of the marriage, the testator's wife decided to adopt a boy without informing the testator until the boy, who was English, came to live with the testator and his wife in Ireland. There was no formal system of adoption in Ireland at the time. However, with the enactment of the Adoption Act 1952, a formal system of adoption was introduced into Ireland. Two years after the 1952 Act, the plaintiff was legally adopted by the testator and his wife. At the time when the plaintiff applied to the court under s.117, he was 32 years, married and had two children of his own. In holding that the testator had failed in his moral duty to make proper provision for his adopted son, Kenny J. ordered that proper provision be made out of the estate and that the question must be decided from the point of view of a prudent and just parent. On this basis, he ordered that the plaintiff be given one-half of the estate, excluding any immoveable property owned by the testator in England.

9–09 In *EB v SS*[12] Keane J. (as he then was) stated that the Oireachtas had transposed the moral duty into a legal duty owing by parents to their children and enforceable in the terms laid down in s.117, thereby suggesting that the relationship of parent and child creates the legal duty, and that that relationship activates the provisions of s.117 for the purposes of deciding whether a testator had failed to fulfil this duty by will or otherwise to make proper provision for his children in accordance with his means. In the course of his judgment, he stated that the Oireachtas

> "has transposed the moral obligation which she, in common with all parents, owed to their children into a legal duty enforceable in the terms laid down in section 117".

He also remarked, however, that the "extremely ample provisions" afforded to the children of a testator under s.117 were not to be extended to grandchildren and that therefore the needs of the plaintiff's children were not a factor to be taken into consideration by the Court. In *EB v SS,* the testatrix, before her death, divided the shares she held in a company among her children. The plaintiff sold his shares which realised £275,000. In a subsequent will, the testatrix left the bulk of her estate to charity. Before she made the subsequent will, the testatrix was aware that the plaintiff had dissipated all of his money and that he was experiencing financial and marital problems, but he was nevertheless excluded from her will. Keane J. was of the view that, although the Court "cannot disregard the fact that parents must be presumed to know their children better than anyone else" and in many cases that obvious fact "would be of little weight where it is established that a child had been treated in a manner which points clearly to a failure of the moral duty," in the present case knowledge of the plaintiff's

[12] [1998] 2 I.L.R.M. 141.

circumstances was of "considerable significance" where, even the most favourable view of the plaintiff's case, it cannot be suggested that he was treated with anything other than generosity and support by both his parents up to the time the shares were transferred to him. Against the plaintiff's background the testatrix's decision

> "not to make further provision for him may well have been prompted, not merely by the concern that her money should go where she could be sure it could do most good, but also by the belief that, since the provision of significant financial assistance had not in the past produced the best results, it might not have been in his own interest to provide him with further funds, even through the mechanism of a trust".

In the circumstances, Keane J. concluded that the plaintiff had failed to establish that the testatrix had not fulfilled her moral duty to him.

In *McDonald v Norris*[13] McCracken J., following the reasoning of Keane J., said that there is an assumption in the 1965 Act that a moral duty exists in general for a testator to make provision for his children, and that the provisions of s.117 (2) must also be considered when deciding whether there has been a failure of such duty. Section 117 (2) provides that: **9–10**

> "The court shall consider the application from the point of view of a prudent and just parent, taking into account the position of each of the children of the testator and any other circumstances which the court may consider of assistance in arriving at a decision that will be as fair as possible to the child to whom the application relates and to the other children."

When assessing whether a testator has failed in his moral duty, the court may also take into consideration the behaviour, or rather misbehaviour, of the child towards him during his lifetime. The kind of misbehaviour envisaged here is not of the criminal variety which is governed by s.120 of the 1965 Act and which precludes the making of an application under s.117.[14] It is a kind of behaviour engendered by "bad feeling" between testator and child, and may be taken into account by the court when deciding whether a testator has failed to fulfil his moral duty in regard to a particular child. Although a testator is not obliged to treat all his children on an equal basis, the reason for his not doing so may be of importance when deciding whether he has failed to fulfil his moral duty relation to a particular child. **9–11**

In *CF v WC*[15] Finlay C.J., when considering the onus of proof in s.117 applications, thought that the phrase "failed in his moral duty to make proper provision for the child in accordance with his means" placed a relatively high onus of proof on an applicant seeking relief under s.117. He also approved of the general guidelines adumbrated by Kenny J. in *In the Goods of GM:* **9–12**

---

13 [1999] 1 I.L.R.M. 270.

14 See Chapter 10 – The Cessation of Succession and Legal Rights.

15 [1989] I.L.R.M. 815 at 819.

FM v TAM "as being a correct statement of the law". He went on to add that it was not sufficient:

> "to establish that the provision made for a child was not as great as it might have been, or that compared with generous bequests to other children or beneficiaries in the will, it appears ungenerous. The court should not, I consider, make an order under the section merely because it would on the facts proved have formed different testamentary dispositions".

He emphasised that a "positive failure in moral duty must be established".[16]

The Estate of a Deceased Testator

9–13 Once a grant of probate or letters of administration with the will annexed issues, then the court will be in a position to identify the estate of the deceased testator for the purposes of determining whether or not to make an order under s.117(1). In *S. 1 and S. 2 v P.R. 1 and P.R. 2*[17] Laffoy J. stated that:

> "(a) the terms of the last will, including any codicils, of the testator must have been proved either by a grant of probate or a grant of letters of administration with the will annexed, and
> (b) the estate of the testator must be identifiable.
>
> Otherwise, the court could not form a view as to
> (i) what provision had been made by the testator either by his will or otherwise, his will meaning his last will validly executed in accordance with law, hence the necessity for requirement (a), or
> (ii) whether the testator had made proper provision for the child applicant in accordance with his means, hence the necessity for requirement (b)."

Proper Provision

9–14 Once the court has determined that a testator has failed to fulfil the moral duty towards his children, it must then decide what provision should be made for them out of the estate.[18] The question of proper provision for children will be considered from the point of view of a prudent and just parent:

> "taking into account the position of each of the children of the testator and any other circumstances which the court may consider of assistance in arriving at a decision that will be as fair as possible to the child to whom the application relates and to the other children".[19]

9–15 A parent must weigh up carefully all his or her moral obligations and these obligations are not necessarily confined to the children of a testator. They

---

16 See also *A v C & Anor* [2007] I.E.H.C. 120.
17 [2013] I.E.H.C. 407.
18 See *L v L* [1978] I.R. 288.
19 s.117(2) of the 1965 Act.

may involve the moral obligations that a testator may have towards aged and infirm parents who are dependent on him and to whom he owes a moral duty of support. It was held by Costello J. in *L v L*[20] that a testator, when acting as a prudent and just parent towards his children,

> "would have to bear in mind his obligations to his own parents who are dependent on him and that the provision he makes for his children may have to be reduced because of these other obligations."

However, the moral duty which a testator may owe to parents who are dependent on him is a circumstance only which the court may take into consideration in assessing the quantum of what is proper provision for the children of a testator under s.117(2), and it is not a legal duty similar to that which a testator owes to his children under s.117(1).

Among the children themselves, the moral duty owing to each of them may **9–16**
also vary with their circumstances in life. For instance, an exceptionally bright child may make it morally wrong not to foster his intellectual talents, or a child who is mentally retarded may require greater provision to be made for him to ensure that he enjoys a reasonable quality of life. The view of Costello J., that all moral obligations and all claims on his resources thereby arising must be taken into account, was approved of by McWilliam J. in *JH v Allied Irish Banks*,[21] and was also referred to by Barron J. in *MFH v WBH*[22] as demonstrating the approach which the Court adopts "in the exercise of its jurisdiction under the section". In exercising its jurisdiction the court is required by s.117(2) to look at matters from the point of view of a prudent and just parent, and to take into account the position of each of the children and any other circumstances which it may consider of assistance. Once this is done, the court must then reach a decision that is as fair as possible to the applicant child and, where there are other children, to those other children also. The expression "other children" used in s.117(2) was held by Barron J. in *MFH v WBH* to mean

> "any other child who is also an applicant or who is a beneficiary under the will and whose benefit thereunder may be affected by the exercise of the court's powers".

It must be emphasised, however, that the duty under s.117 is not to make **9–17**
adequate provision, but rather to provide proper provision in accordance with the testator's means. This matter was considered in *XC v RT*.[23] In that case, the plaintiffs made an application under s.117 for an order that proper provision be made for them out of their father's estate. The testator set up a discretionary trust in which all of the plaintiffs and the first two defendants were named as beneficiaries. The trustees of the trust were also the executors

---

20 [1978] I.R. 288.
21 Unreported, High Court, McWilliam J., 17 November 1978.
22 [1984] I.R. 599 at 606.
23 [2003] 2 I.R. 250.

and beneficiaries under the will and, because of this, the plaintiffs claimed that a clear conflict of interests arose in the circumstances. Kearns J. held that the only question which the Court had to resolve was whether, in the circumstances, the testator when making his will, and having regard to the requirement that the moral duty be assessed at the date of death, by setting up a discretionary trust in which all the plaintiffs and the first two defendants were named as beneficiaries, discharged his moral duty under s.117 to his children. The question of conflict of interests by executors in the administration of estates and trustees discharging their duties to beneficiaries of a trust required separate causes of action in cases where failures are established, and did not form the subject matter of an application under s.117. The setting up of the discretionary trust in this instance completed the discharge of the testator's moral duty to his children and making proper provision for them in accordance with his means.[24] The court, when considering whether a testator has made proper provision, may also engage in balancing circumstances against the needs of children. In *DS v KM and D,*[25] the testator devised and bequeathed to his son, a farm, house, plot of land and a sum of money. He provided a site for his daughter, the plaintiff, out of the plot of land left to his son for the purposes of building a house, and she was also left a sum of money. Carroll J., having taken account of the position of the son who undoubtedly had the greater need, held that the failure of the testator could be remedied by leaving the entire building site comprising approximately one acre to the daughter. The son's ability to continue with his farming would not be affected by this provision.

Summary of Section 117 Principles

9–18 In *XC v RT*[26] Kearns J. (as he then was) provided a useful summary of the principles applied by the courts in former decisions when deciding whether or not a testator has discharged his moral duty towards his children by making proper provision for them in accordance with his means. Kearns J. stated that the following legal principles derive from former decisions of the courts involving s.117 applications:

> "(a) The social policy underlying s.117 is primarily directed to protecting those children who are still of an age and situation in life where they might reasonably expect support from their parents, against the failure of parents who are unmindful of their duties in that area.
>
> (b) What has to be determined is whether the testator, at the time of his death, owes any moral obligation to the applicants and, if so, whether he has failed in that obligation.

[24] See *CK and FC v FC*, Unreported, High Court, Carroll J., 16 December 2003, where the testatrix had failed in her moral duty towards the plaintiffs to make proper provision for them under the terms of a secret trust.

[25] Unreported, High Court, Carroll J., 19 December 2003.

[26] [2003] 2 I.R. 250.

(c) There is a high onus of proof placed on an applicant for relief under s.117 that requires the establishment of a positive failure in moral duty.
(d) Before a court can interfere, there must be clear circumstances and a positive failure in moral duty must be established.
(e) The duty created by s.117 is not absolute.
(f) The relationship of parent and child does not itself and without regard to other circumstances creates a moral duty to leave anything by will to the child.
(g) Section 117 does not create an obligation to leave something to each child.
(h) The provision of an expensive education for a child may discharge the moral duty, as may other gifts or settlements during the lifetime of the testator.
(i) Financing a good education so as to give a child the best start in life possible, and providing money, which if properly managed, should afford a degree of financial security for the rest of one's life, does amount to making proper provision.
(j) The duty under s.117 is not to make adequate provision but to provide proper provision in accordance with the testator's means.
(k) A just parent must take into account, not just his moral obligations to his children and to his wife, but all his moral obligations, for instance, to aged and infirm parents.
(l) In dealing with a s.117 application, the position of an applicant child is not to be taken in isolation. The court's duty is to consider the entirety of the testator's affairs and to decide on the application in the overall context. In other words, while the moral claim of a child may require a testator to make a particular provision for him, the moral claims of others may require such provision to be reduced or omitted altogether.
(m) Special circumstances giving rise to a moral duty arise if a child is induced to believe that by, for example, working a farm he will ultimately become the owner of it, thereby causing him to shape his upbringing, training and life accordingly.
(n) Another example of special circumstances might be a child who had a long illness or an exceptional talent that it would be morally wrong not to foster.
(o) Special needs would also include physical or mental disability.
(p) Although the court has very wide powers both as to when to make provisions for an applicant child and as to the nature of such provision, such powers must not be construed as giving the court a power to make a new will for the testator.
(q) The test to be applied is not which of the alternative courses open to the testator the court itself would have adopted if confronted with the same situation, but rather whether the decision of the testator to opt for the course he did, of itself and without more, constituted a breach of moral duty to the plaintiff.
(r) The court must not disregard the fact that parents must be presumed to know their children better than anyone else."

The application of these principles may also involve the courts in balancing the circumstances and needs of a testator's children.[27] In *CW v LW*[28] O'Sullivan J. asked, when deciding whether the testator discharged his moral obligation to the applicant, "do I credit him with the prescient foreknowledge that the applicant will in due course inherit a large sum from her mother?" When answering, he took the testator as having been **9–19**

[27] *DS v KM and D*, Unreported, High Court, Carroll J., 19 December 2003.
[28] Unreported, High Court, O'Sullivan J., 23 February 2005.

aware that the applicant would inherit, not only the bequest to her under his own will, but also a substantial sum from her mother. It was on this basis that he went on to consider whether the testator had discharged his moral duty to the applicant. He would, however, be guided by the jurisprudence which has been extensively opened during the hearing and not least by the comprehensive list of principles set out by Kearns J. in *XC v RT*. In *A v C & Anor*[29] Laffoy J. when reviewing the law in an application under s.117 referred to the judgment of Kenny J. in *In the Goods of G M: FM v TAM*[30] and the guidelines laid down by him in relation to an application under s.117, and the judgment of Kearns J. in *XC v RT* who set down 18 relevant legal principles derived from the authorities in former cases involving s.117, bearing in mind that the moral duty is to make "proper provision" for the applicant in accordance with the testator's means, not to make adequate provision.

9–20 In *H (A Minor) v H*[31] an application was made to the court pursuant to s.117 of the 1965 Act by the plaintiff (H), a minor who sued in the name of her mother and next friend to make just provision for her out of her deceased father's estate. The defendant was the widow and executrix of the deceased's estate and was also his sole beneficiary. A grant of probate was issued to the defendant as sole executrix. The defendant, who had been making payments for the education and maintenance of the plaintiff since the death of the deceased, simplified the task of the Court by conceding that the court should make an order making proper provision for the plaintiff. Accordingly, the parties agreed that this was the only matter to be decided by the Court.

9–21 The background to the case was that the plaintiff's mother was in a long-term relationship with the deceased when the plaintiff was born. The deceased then went to work in the United States where he met the defendant and subsequently married her. The relationship between the deceased and the plaintiff's mother ended. The plaintiff and her mother, who had been living on a farm that the deceased subsequently inherited, had to vacate the farm and went to live in rented corporation property. The defendant and the deceased remained in the United States and they had two children. The plaintiff's mother had no assets of her own, save a weekly income. The plaintiff's mother was her sole carer and provided for all her needs out of her own resources, other than sporadic maintenance payments made by the deceased during his lifetime. Payments had been made out of the deceased's estate for the plaintiff's education since the deceased's death. At the time of the deceased's tragic early death, he had returned to Ireland to make proper provision for the plaintiff. The deceased had assets in Ireland and the United States. The assets in Ireland consisted of a farm valued at €1.7 to €2 million. The defendant since inheriting the farm had been receiving a net income

---

[29] [2007] I.E.H.C. 120.

[30] (1970) 106 I.L.T.R. 82.

[31] [2008] I.E.H.C. 163.

from it of €18,548 per annum. The assets in the United States consisted of partnership assets valued at $75,000 and a vehicle valued at $8,000. There were also two insurance policies for the benefit of the defendant with a total value of $250,000, one of which was used by the defendant to clear the mortgage on the family home in the United States which was valued at $175,000 at the time of the deceased's death. The defendant was a schoolteacher by profession and mother of the deceased's other two children. One of the children was diagnosed with a lifelong medical condition that required full-time assistance for all of her daily activities and rendered her financially dependent for her lifetime. The defendant's annual teacher's salary was $38,347, out of which she also had to pay a neighbour $125 a week for assisting her with her daughter.

Sheehan J. referred to the decision of Kearns J. in *XC v RT* in which Kearns **9–22**
J. set out a number of general principles which the Court should follow when considering what amounts to proper provision. He considered that the principles set out at (g), (i), (l), (n) and (o) in *XC v RT* to be particularly relevant to the case before him and set them out as follows:

> "(g) Section 117 does not create an obligation to leave something to each child.
> (i) Financing a good education so as to give a child the best start in life possible, and providing money, which if properly managed, should afford a degree of financial security for the rest of one's life does amount to making 'proper provision'.
> (l) In dealing with an s.117 application, the position of an applicant child is not to be taken in isolation. The court's duty is to consider the entirety of the testator's affairs and to decide upon the application in the overall context. In other words, while the moral claim of a child may require a testator to make a particular provision for him, the moral claims of others may require such provision to be reduced or omitted altogether.
> (n) Another example of special circumstances might be a child who had a long illness or an exceptional talent that it would be morally wrong not to foster.
> (o) Special needs would also include physical or mental disability."

In *K & Ors v D & Anor*[32] the testator was survived by two sons MK and **9–23**
PK, and by his daughter PA, the plaintiffs in these proceedings. All of the plaintiffs were of full age at the date of the testator's death. PA had severe epilepsy since infancy. She lived with her mother AK. Judicial separation proceedings involving the deceased and his wife AK were settled, as a result of which AK's entitlement to any interest in the estate of the testator was extinguished. AK made no claim against the estate of the testator. The defendant was the partner of the deceased at the time of his death and had been in a relationship with him since 1983. She lived with the testator during the last three years of his life. The testator suffered two strokes in 1997 and the evidence of the defendant was that she took time off work to look after him and eventually left work to take care of him on a full-time basis. Under the terms of the will, the testator devised a house site on lands

[32] [2011] I.E.H.C. 22.

owned by him to the defendant for her absolute use and benefit. Subsequent to the making of his will, the testator transferred the house site to himself and the defendant as joint tenants, and subsequently a bungalow was built on that site in which the testator and the defendant resided. On the death of the testator, the defendant became solely entitled to the bungalow by right of survivorship. The bungalow was a substantial one having five bedrooms and it came with a garden of approximately one acre. At the date of death it was valued at €378,000 with bank loans amounting to €26,000 leaving a net value at the time of €352,330. The premises were at the date of the proceedings valued at €400,000.

9–24 The testator was also the owner of a number of acres of agricultural land. At various stages, the acreage involved had been estimated at eight or ten acres. Prior to his death, he had entered into a contract to sell a site comprising approximately half an acre to a third party. This transaction gave rise to litigation and the sale was completed after his death. By his will, the testator devised a house site of half an acre out of the agricultural land to each of his sons, MK and PK. The testator expressly provided that the devise was to be subject to his sons obtaining planning permission within two years of the date of his death. The planning permission was not obtained by either son within the time prescribed. The application for planning permission by both sons failed following an objection which had been lodged by the defendant. Subsequently, her solicitors confirmed that she was not consenting to the extension of the time set out in the will for procuring planning permission. The testator also owned a yard comprising three commercial units which at the time of his death were producing a rental income, though in the case of one unit, the rent was significantly in arrears. By his will, he devised this property, which he described as his "commercial yard", to his sons MK and PK, his daughter PA and the defendant in equal shares absolutely. The testator's residuary estate consisted of household contents and machinery and tools and money, including the proceeds of the sale of the site. He devised the residue of his estate to the defendant.

9–25 When arriving at his decision, Birmingham J. referred to the legal principles involved in s.117 cases derived by Kearns J. in the case of *XC v RT*[33] from former decisions on the matter. In seeking to apply these principles, it was necessary in the first instance to identify the value of the estate both at the time of death and at the present time. Birmingham J stated that:

> "It has consistently been stated in the case law that the relevant date for ascertaining whether there has been a failure to make proper provision is the date of the testator's death."

9–26 In *In the Goods of G M: FM v TAM*[34] Kenny J. stated that "the existence of a moral duty to make proper provision by will for a child must be judged

[33] [2003] 2 I.R. 250 at 262.
[34] [1970] 106 I.L.T.R. 82 at 87.

by the facts existing at the date of death". As of the date of death, the net value of the estate was approximately €815,800. Of this, the sum of approximately €417,000 was attributable to the commercial premises and €330,031 to the agricultural land. The personal representatives averred that each of the sites devised to the sons of the testator had a value at the time of death of approximately €88,881 with the benefit of planning permission. Birmingham J. went on to state that:

> "the decided cases indicate that if the stage is reached where a court has to decide what provision should be made for children regard has to be had to the value of the entire estate not only at the date of death but also at the date of the hearing".

In *MPD v MD*[35] Carroll J. held:

> "in deciding what provision the court should make for the children regard must be had to the value of the entire estate, not only at the date of death but also at the date of hearing."

It was estimated that the assets at the time of the hearing had a value of €543,450, made up as to €310,000 for the industrial units (€250,000 with vacant possession) €165,000 in respect of the agricultural land, €63,450 cash and €5,000 contents/farm machinery. It was also necessary to consider the circumstances of relevant parties as of the date of death and as of the date of hearing. **9–27**

Birmingham J. was firmly of the view that there was a clear failure on the part of the testator to make proper provision for his daughter. Given his daughter's medical situation and her inability to care and provide for herself, there was a moral imperative for the testator to address his daughter's needs and make proper provision for her. The quarter share in the commercial yard along with a valuable residential site, which was what the testator sought to achieve in his will, amounted to proper provision for his two sons. Although the testator had no statutory obligations towards the defendant, in a situation where they were partners and where she had re-arranged her working and domestic life to support him after he became ill, Birmingham J. believed that there was a moral obligation to make provision for her. He also said that he did not believe that the testator was acting immorally or wrongly or capriciously in seeking to make provision for the defendant. As Clarke J. stated in *AC (A Minor) v JF, FG & P McE*[36]: **9–28**

> "it is clear from a number of the authorities that the persons in respect of whom a deceased may owe a moral duty are not confined to those persons in respect of whom a legal obligation arises".

In considering what was required if proper provision was to be made for his children, the testator erred in failing to have regard to the fact that, **9–29**

---

35 [1981] I.L.R.M. 179 at 188.

36 [2007] I.E.H.C 399.

in providing that the defendant would acquire the bungalow by right of survivorship, he was conferring a significant benefit on the defendant. Birmingham J. ordered that all of the assets in the estate should be converted into cash, and directed that the net assets should then be distributed on the basis of 50% for PA and 16.66% each for MK, PK and the defendant.

Advancements Fulfilling the Moral Duty

9–30 It will be remembered that s.117(1) of the 1965 Act provides that where, on application by or on behalf of a child of a testator, the court is of opinion that the testator has failed in his moral duty to make proper provision for the child in accordance with his means, whether by his will *or otherwise*, the court may order just provision. It would seem, therefore, that, where a testator makes advancements within the meaning of s.63 of the 1965 Act to his children during his lifetime, such advancements might be viewed by the courts as the fulfilment of the moral duty towards his children by making proper provision for them otherwise than by will.[37]

The Effect of an Order of Court on the Legal Right of Surviving Spouse or Civil Partner

9–31 Section 117(3) of the 1965 Act provides that an order made under s.117 shall not affect the legal right of a surviving spouse or, if the surviving spouse is the mother or father of the applicant child, any devise or bequest to the spouse or any share to which the spouse is entitled on intestacy. As a result of s.117(3), the following comments may be made:

(i) An order under s.117 shall not affect the legal right of a surviving spouse, whether or not the surviving spouse is the father or mother of the applicant child;
(ii) An order under s.117 shall not affect a devise or bequest to a surviving spouse who is the father or mother of the applicant child;
(iii) An order under s.117 may affect a devise or bequest to a surviving spouse who is not the father or mother of the applicant child, viz. a step-parent;
(iv) An order under s.117 shall not affect any share to which the surviving spouse is entitled on intestacy where the surviving spouse is the father or mother of the applicant child. In the context of s.117, this means a share on partial intestacy as there must be a will for a child to make an application under s.117;
(v) An order under s.117 may affect any share to which a surviving

[37] See Chapter 11 – *Donationes Mortis Causa*, Joint Bank Accounts and Advancements.

spouse is entitled on partial intestacy where the surviving spouse is not the father or mother of the applicant child, viz. a step-parent;

(vi) An applicant child under s.117 may be the legitimate, adopted or non-marital child of the testator;

(vii) Section 117(3) was amended by s.86 of the 2010 Act by inserting a new s.117(3)(A) which provides that an order under s.117 shall not affect the legal right of a surviving civil partner "unless the court, after consideration of all the circumstances, including the testator's financial circumstances and his or her obligations to the surviving civil partner, is of the opinion that it would be unjust not to make the order";

(viii) By s.117(3)(A), an order under s.117 may affect the legal right of a surviving civil partner if just in the circumstances;

(ix) By s.117(3)(A), an order under s.117 may affect any devise or bequest to a surviving civil partner or any share to which the surviving civil partner is entitled on partial intestacy having regard to the provisions of s.117(1) and s.117(2) only;

(x) Section 117(3)(A) does not make a distinction between parents and step-parents in the case of civil partners;

(xi) There is no authoritative decision by the courts interpreting the provisions of s.117(3) or s.117(3)(A);

(xii) The Oireachtas had the opportunity to amend the provisions of s.117(3) of the 1965 Act by the 2010 Act, but inserted a new s.117(3)(A) dealing with civil partners only.

Time Limits

The limitation period for bringing applications under s.117(6), as amended **9–32**
by s.46 of the Family Law (Divorce) Act 1996, is six months from the first taking out of representation.[38] It is clear that, where a grant of probate or a grant of letters of administration with will annexed has issued from the Probate Office or a District Probate Registry, it will be viewed as the first taking out of representation for the purpose of s.117(6) and also that the limitation period of six months will commence to run from the date of issue. The same may be said in the case of a grant of letters of administration with the will annexed that issued from the Probate Office or a District Probate Registry in pursuance of a court order under s.27(4) of the 1965 Act. Section 3 of the 1965 Act provides that "representation" means probate or administration. Therefore the context of Part IX of the 1965 Act requires that "the first taking out of representation of the deceased's estate" for the purposes of s.117(6) must be taken to mean that the limitation period will commence to run from the time a grant of probate or a grant of letters of

[38] See Albert Keating, "A Constructive Interpretation of Section 117(6) of the Succession Act 1965 (2014) 19(2) C.P.L.J. 33; Chapter 10 – The Cessation of Succession and Legal Rights where the interaction between s.117 and s.121 of the 1965 Act is discussed; Chapter 23 – The Limitation of Actions and Striking Out Proceedings.

administration with the will annexed has issued. This includes a grant of letters of administration with the annexed that issued pursuant to an order of the court under s.27(4) of the 1965 Act. But where the type of grant of administration ordered to be made by the court under s.27(4) of the 1965 Act is for limited purposes only, for instance, a grant *ad litem* for defending proceedings brought against the estate of the deceased testator, such a grant may not be viewed as the first taking out of representation to the estate of a deceased testator for the purposes of the running of the limitation period in s.117(6).[39] A person to whom a grant of administration *ad litem* has issued by order of the court may not administer or distribute the estate of the deceased testator, as his or her role is limited to instituting or defending specified proceedings only. The grant *ad litem*:

> "will state on its face that it is limited for the purposes of defending named proceedings, and may also further recite further limitations depending on what is contained in the court order".[40]

Section 27(4) of the 1965 Act provides that:

> "Where by reason of any special circumstances it appears to the High Court (or, in a case within the jurisdiction of the Circuit Court, that Court) to be necessary or expedient to do so, the Court may order that administration be granted to such person as it thinks fit."[41]

9–33 Section 27(5) of the 1965 Act provides that:

> "On administration being granted, no person shall be or become entitled without a grant to administer any estate to which that administration relates."

The administrator appointed by the court pursuant to s.27(4) must apply for a grant and

> "the fact that an order under the section has been made shall be stated in the oath of the administrator, in the grant of administration and in the administration bond".[42]

Thus, it appears, that, while a person may be appointed administrator by the court under s.27(4),in order for him or her to have representative capacity to act for and on behalf of the estate, he or she must by virtue of s.27(5) first obtain a grant to entitle him or her to do so, or at least have submitted the proofs for obtaining a grant at the time when he or she acts in a representative capacity.[43] The same may be said in a case where a plaintiff applies to the

---

39 See *S1 and S2 v PR1 and PR2* [2013] I.E.H.C. 407.

40 See Probate Update issued by the Probate Office on 6 July 2012.

41 See Chapter 20 – Probate Motions and Section 27(4) Applications.

42 See s.27(5) of the Succession Act 1965; Rules of the Superior Courts 1986, Ord. 79 r.22 (Probate Office); Ord. 80 r.26 (District Probate Registry).

43 *Bank of Scotland v Gray and Doyle* [2012] I.E.H.C. 545; see Albert Keating, "The Representative Capacity of Administrators and Section 9(2) of the Civil Liability Act 1961" (2013) 2(1) I.P.L.J. 2.

court for the appointment of an administrator *ad litem* for the purposes of defending proceedings against the estate of a deceased person. The estate of the deceased will not vest in him until he applies for and obtains a grant in accordance with the Rules of the Superior Courts, although when doing he is not required to include an inland revenue affidavit among the proofs.[44] In *S. 1 and S. 2 v P.R. 1 and P.R. 2*[45] the grant of letters of administration *ad litem* pursuant to a court order under s.27(4) was made to a creditor bank for the purposes of instituting proceedings against the estate. The *ad litem* grant that issued was limited in effect to actions by the creditor bank against the estate only, and did not extend to other types of actions or claims, including claims by children of the deceased testator under s.117. Laffoy J. stated that:

> "Further and significantly, under the limited grant of 15th October, 2010, the authority of A.A.L. was limited for the purpose of defending the proceedings which the creditor bank intended to bring against the estate of the testator. If an application under s. 117 was initiated against A.A.L., as defendant as representing the estate of the testator, it could not be prosecuted because A.A.L. had no authority from the court or otherwise to defend such an application."

Accordingly, it seemed to her that:

> "when one considers subs. (6) of s. 117 in the context of the Act of 1965 as a whole, the intention of the Oireachtas cannot have been that a grant of administration *ad litem* would trigger the commencement of the limitation period provided for in s. 117(6)".

Therefore, taking out a grant of administration *ad litem* could not be viewed as the first taking out of representation for the purposes of the limitation period in s.117(6). Laffoy J., when construing the provisions of s.117(6), stated that: **9–34**

> "When one looks at s.117(6) on its own but incorporating the definitions contained in s. 3 of the Act of 1965, 'first taking out of representation'" reads as follows: first taking out probate of a will or letters of administration, whether with or without a will annexed, and whether granted for special or limited purposes. Such a reading would mean that, once a grant for a limited purpose, such as a grant to substantiate proceedings of the type granted to A.A.L. was extracted, time would start to run for the purposes of s.117(6). However, when one looks at the Act of 1965 as a whole, as one is required to do at common law and under s.5 of the Interpretation Act 2005, to ascertain the intention of the Oireachtas, it becomes obvious that the Oireachtas could not have intended that a grant limited for a purpose, such as a grant of administration *ad litem*, would start time running against a prospective applicant under s.117."

In *S. 1 and S. 2 v P.R. 1 and P.R. 2* the Court had to consider as a preliminary issue whether it had jurisdiction to grant the relief sought by the plaintiffs pursuant to s.117 of the 1965 Act, the proceedings having issued more than six months after the first taking out of representation to the estate of the **9–35**

[44] See Probate Office Update, 6 July 2012.

[45] [2013] I.E.H.C. 407.

testator, and also whether the grant of representation was a valid one for the purposes of the limitation period set out in s.117(6) of the 1965 Act. S.1 was the plaintiff in the plenary proceedings, and the plaintiff in the related special summons proceedings was S.2; S.1 and S.2 were brothers and the adult sons of the deceased testator.

9–36 Laffoy J., having identified the principles of construction that were applicable to cases involving s.117(6),and having applied them to the foregoing time line of events, found that:

> "(a) S. 1, by having made the application for relief under s. 117 of the Act of 1965 by plenary summons which issued within six months of the issue of the grant of probate of the will of the Testator on 28th March, 2011, made that application within the time limited in s. 117(6) of the Act of 1965 and the court does have jurisdiction to hear it;
> (b) S. 2 by having made the application for relief under s. 117 of the Act of 1965 by special summons which issued within six months of the issue of the grant of probate of the will of the Testator on 28th March, 2011, made that application within the time limited in s. 117(6) of the Act of 1965 and the court does have jurisdiction to hear it."

Section 117 and Partial Intestacy

9–37 Section 117 of the 1965 Act applies only to cases where a parent dies testate or partly testate. Even where a deceased parent's will is wholly ineffective due to the predecease of beneficiaries and his or her entire estate devolves as on intestacy, the deceased parent will still be deemed a testator for the purposes of s.117 by virtue of the provisions of s.109 of the 1965 Act. Section 109(1) provides that:

> "Where, after the commencement of this Act, a person dies wholly or partly testate leaving a spouse or children or both spouse and children, the provisions of this Part shall have effect."

In *MPD v MD*[46] Carroll J. stated that:

> "The state of testacy does not depend on the effectiveness of the will. It depends on the effectiveness of the execution of the will. If testacy is established, then in my opinion it follows that the person must die wholly or partly testate. There is no third state of testacy – that is, a state of testacy which is neither total nor partial."

Section 117 does not apply in the case of "a pure intestacy".[47]

---

46 [1981] I.L.R.M. 179.
47 See *RG v PSG and JRG* [1980] I.L.R.M. 225.

THE DISCOVERY OF DOCUMENTS

In *G.P. v G.R. and P.M.*[48] the plaintiff's solicitors made a request for voluntary discovery of certain documents by letter to the defendants' solicitors in order to assess the plaintiff's entitlement to any provision from the estate of the testator under s.117(1) of the 1965 Act. The response of the testator's solicitors was that the categories of documents sought were neither relevant nor necessary. The plaintiff applied to the court requiring the defendants to make discovery of the document sought. **9–38**

The defendants relied on the judgment of Barron J. in *In the Goods of J.H.*[49] when he stated at p. 606 that: **9–39**

> "In the exercise of its jurisdiction, the section requires the court to approach its decision from the point of view of a prudent and just parent, and to take into account the position of each of the children and any other circumstances which it may consider to be of assistance. Having taken these matters into account, it must reach a decision which is as fair as possible to the applicant child, and, where there are other children, to those other children also. In this context, the expression 'other children' means any other child who is also an applicant or who is a beneficiary under the will and whose benefit thereunder may be affected by the exercise of the court's powers. The court should not be required to take into account provision or lack of provision made for children not in either of these categories. The provision made for such children cannot be affected by its order. It must strike a balance, where necessary, between the children before the court on the basis of what is just having regard, as well as to the other matters it has to take into account, to the means of the testator passing by his will."

The plaintiff relied on the decision of Kearns J. (as he then was) in *X.C. v R.T.*[50] In that case Kearns J. at p. 262 set out the legal principles to be derived from previous authorities on the application of s.117. However, Laffoy J., having considered those principles, stated that: "I am not satisfied that any of them displaces what was stated by Barron J. in the *J.H.* case". She said that it was important to emphasise that all the court was concerned with at this stage was to determine whether the documentation sought by the plaintiff met the "relevant" and "necessary" criteria which must be established before an order for discovery is made. **9–40**

Further that:

> "what the court has to decide is whether the documents sought are relevant to any matter in question in the proceedings and whether they are necessary for disposing fairly of the cause or matter or for saving costs".

She went on to find that:

> "As regards the 'relevant' criterion, it is difficult to see how the means or assets

48 [2013] I.E.H.C. 333.
49 [1984] I.R. 599.
50 [2003] 2 I.R. 250.

of B.P. or A.P. during the lifetime of the testator or at or since his death are of any relevance to the issues raised on the s. 117 application, given that neither is an applicant under s. 117 nor benefits under the Will of the testator, and both were independent adults at the date of the testator's death. Aside from that, most, if not all, of the documentation sought is not, as a matter of probability, in the possession or procurement of the defendants, who are sued in their capacity as personal representatives of the testator. Were the defendants to ask B.P. and A.P., for example, for their tax returns for the past ten years, B.P. and A.P. would be fully justified in telling the defendants to 'mind their own business'. As regards the 'necessary' criterion, the burden, scale and cost of making discovery of the documentation sought in relation to B.P. and A.P., even if it was relevant, which it is not, would be likely to be disproportionate in the context of the disposing of the proceedings in a fair and just manner."

She concluded by stating that:

> "it must be understood that the focus of s. 117 is on the position as at the death of the testator and each and every category of the thirteen categories sought, even in relation to the widow, is far too wide".

Accordingly, she dismissed the application for discovery of documents.

The Duty of Solicitors

9–41 Solicitors owe a duty:

> "to advise and assist the personal representative in the due and proper administration of the estate in accordance with the directions contained within the testator's will".[51]

The duty does not however extend to informing the children of a testator of their right to make an application under s.117 of the 1965 Act, or indeed, a personal representative who is also a child of the testator. There is further no duty imposed on a solicitor to assess the personal circumstances of beneficiaries for the purposes of establishing if they have a potential claim under s.117, or to advise them that they may have such a claim and ought to seek separate and independent legal advice. Where, however, a personal representative receives an enquiry from a child of the testator regarding a potential claim by that child against the estate under s.117, the personal representative may owe a duty to the estate and "possibly" to the child to inform him or her to seek separate and independent legal advice on the matter.[52]

[51] See *Rojack v Taylor and Buchalter*, Unreported, High Court, Quirke J., 10 February 2005.

[52] *ibid.*

Chapter 10

THE CESSATION OF SUCCESSION AND LEGAL RIGHTS

Introduction

A beneficiary may be excluded from succession to property by virtue of the provisions of s.120 of the Succession Act 1965 (the "1965 Act"). Section 120(1) of the 1965 Act provides that: **10–01**

> "A sane person who has been guilty of the murder, attempted murder or manslaughter of another shall be precluded from taking any share in the estate of that other, except a share arising under a will made after the act constituting the offence, and shall not be entitled to make an application under section 117."

In *In the Estate of Glynn*[1] McCarthy J, when commenting on the provisions of s.120(1), stated that, on grounds of public policy, a person who is proved to be guilty of murder or manslaughter of the testator cannot claim to take under the testator's will, and that this was given statutory force by s.120 of the 1965 Act. In *Nevin v Nevin*[2] Kearns P. when referring to s.120(1) stated that it is declaratory of a public policy that the perpetrator of the crime of murder should not be its beneficiary. While both McCarthy J. and Kearns P. acknowledge that s.120(1) is declaratory of a public policy, Kearns P. found that the wording of s.120(1) was so uncertain and indeterminate that it could not be interpreted to preclude a person from taking a share in the estate of a deceased for the offences specified in its present form because of the omission of words requiring that a person be found guilty of an offence by a court of competent jurisdiction. Furthermore, he found that s.120(1) was inconsistent with the provisions of s.120(4) which required a finding of guilt in the case of lesser offences. Under s.120(2) of the 1965 Act, a spouse **10–02**

---

1 [1992] 1 I.R. 361 at 364.
2 [2013] I.E.H.C. 80.

guilty of desertion which has continued up to the death for two years or more shall be precluded from taking any share in the estate of the deceased as a legal right or on intestacy. Section 120(4) provides that a person "who has been found guilty" of an offence against the deceased, or against the spouse or civil partner or any child of the deceased, including an adopted child or a person to whom the deceased was *in loco parentis* at the time of the offence, punishable by imprisonment for a maximum period of at least two years or by a more severe penalty, will be precluded from taking any share in the estate as a legal right or from making an application under s.117 of the 1965 Act. Section 120(5) of the 1965 Act provides that any share which a person is precluded from taking under s.120 will be distributed as if that person had died before the deceased. Section 120 of the 1965 Act was amended by s.87 of the Civil Partnership and Certain Rights and Obligations of Cohabitants Act 2010 (the "2010 Act") to include civil partners.

10–03 It is worth noting that 120(5) may not be used by analogy to joint tenancies in circumstances where one joint tenant causes the death of another joint tenant. In *Cawley v Lillis*[3] Laffoy J. stated that:

> "In particular, I do not consider that it would be proper to determine, by analogy to s.120(5), that the ownership of the joint assets following the death of the deceased should be determined on the basis that the defendant should be deemed to have pre-deceased the deceased. Section 120 deals with the distribution of property owned by the deceased person, not with the distribution of property in which an unworthy potential successor has rights."

10–04 Section 121 of the 1965 Act provides that, where a person disposes of his property three years before his death for the purpose of defeating or substantially diminishing the share of his spouse or children, such disposition is deemed "to be a devise or bequest made by him by will and to form part of his estate, and to have had no other effect". The section applies to:

> "a disposition of property (other than a testamentary disposition, or a disposition to a purchaser) under which the beneficial ownership of the property vests in possession in the donee within three years before the death of the person who made it or on his death or later".

A disposition for the purposes of s.121 also expressly includes a *donatio mortis causa*.[4] Section 121 of the 1965 Act was amended by s.88 of the 2010 Act by the insertion of "or civil partner" after "spouse" wherever it appears.

10–05 Section 82(1) of the 1965 Act as amended by s.77 of the 2010 Act provides that, where a beneficiary or his or her spouse or civil partner witnesses a

---

[3] [2011] I.E.H.C. 515.

[4] s.121(10) of the 1965 Act; see Chapter 11 – *Donationes Mortis Causa*, Joint Bank Accounts and Advancements.

will, the gift to him or her will be nullified.[5] A will may be invalidated and all succession rights created by it will cease to exist where it fails to comply with the rules for the execution of wills in s.78 of the 1965 Act,[6] or where the testator lacks testamentary capacity,[7] or where it is shown that the will was made as a result of undue influence being exerted on the testator by another person,[8] or where it is shown that a will was procured and prepared by a person who is also a beneficiary, or where it is shown that it was made as a result of fraud.[9] The legal right of a spouse or civil partner may be voluntarily renounced under s.113 of the 1965 as amended by the 2010 Act or it may be extinguished by the courts.[10] A beneficiary may voluntarily disclaim a gift in a will or share on intestacy and, on doing so, his or her succession rights will cease from the date of disclaimer.

Section 120(1)

In *Nevin v Nevin*[11] Kearns P., commenting on the text of s.120(1) of the 1965 Act, stated that it was deficient because of the omission of a finding of guilt as a prerequisite for precluding a person from taking a share in a deceased's estate. He stated that: **10–06**

> "it was an extraordinary omission for which it is difficult to find any rational explanation, given that a 'finding of guilt' is required under s.120 (4) for lesser offences and having regard further to the fact that 'guilt' is a finding appropriate to the criminal rather than the civil process. One is left not knowing what the section is to mean, unless one supplies the word 'found' to subsection (1) where in the text it does not appear."

As a result of this uncertainty, Kearns P. went on to state that:

> "given that the section is undoubtedly punitive and conclusive in both nature and effect, its terms must clearly be subject to rules of strict construction in favour of the person against whom it is sought to enforce it".

The defendant therefore:

> "must be the beneficiary of this ambiguity so I am satisfied that the issue before the court cannot be resolved by reference to the specific provisions of section 120 (1)".

---

5 s.82 of the 1965 Act as amended by s.77 of the Civil Partnership and Certain Rights and Obligations of Cohabitants Act 2010.

6 See Chapter 2 – The Execution of Wills.

7 See Chapter 3 – Testamentary Capacity.

8 See Chapter 21–Probate and Administration Actions and Costs.

9 *ibid.*

10 See Chapter 8 – The Legal Right of Spouses and Civil Partners and Applications by Qualified Cohabitants.

11 [2013] I.E.H.C. 80.

10–07 Having decided that the issue cannot be resolved by reference to s.120(1), Kearns P. posed the questions:

> "Is a criminal conviction for murder admissible in a later civil proceeding brought against a person convicted of that murder? If not admissible, then it would follow that a defendant in a civil case would be in precisely the same position as a person who was acquitted or never charged with the offence in question. The conviction could not be used in any way whatsoever in the civil case. If on the other hand the conviction is admissible, is it conclusive of the fact that the defendant murdered her husband or is it simply *prima facie* evidence of that fact, leaving to the defendant the right to argue that she should not have been convicted?"

10–08 When answering the question Kearns P. first referred to *Re Crippin*,[12] and in particular the statement of Sir Samuel Evans who, when addressing the question of the admissibility of a conviction for murder in later civil proceedings, stated that:

> "In my opinion, where a convicted felon, or the personal representative of a convicted murderer who has been executed, brings any civil proceeding to establish claims, or to enforce rights, which result to the felon, or to the convicted testator from his own crime, the conviction is admissible in evidence, not merely as proof of the conviction, but also as presumptive proof of the commission of the crime."

10–09 However, the Court of Appeal in *Hollington v Hewthorn*[13] overruled *Crippin* on this point, and held that, on principle and authority, evidence of a conviction was inadmissible in subsequent civil proceedings. In that case Goddard L.J. stated:

> "In truth, the conviction is only proof that another court considered that the defendant was guilty of careless driving. Even were it proved that it was the accident that led to the prosecution, the conviction proves no more than what has just been stated. The court which has to try the claim for damages knows nothing of the evidence that was before the criminal court. It cannot know what arguments were addressed to it, or what influenced the court in arriving at its decision."[14]

He went on to state that the issue in criminal proceedings is not identical with that raised in a claim for damages, and

> "it is obvious that once the defendant challenges the propriety of the conviction the court, on the subsequent trial, would have to retry the criminal case to find out what weight ought to be attached to the result".[15]

10–10 The decision in *Hollington v Hewthorn* was later criticised by Lord Denning

[12] [1911] P. 108 at 115.
[13] [1943] 1 K.B. 587.
[14] *ibid* at 594.
[15] *ibid.*

M.R. in *McIlkenny v Chief Constable of West Midlands Police Force*[16] where he stated that:

> "Beyond doubt, *Hollington v Hewthorn* was wrongly decided. It was done in ignorance of previous authorities. It was done *per incuriam*. If it were necessary to depart from it today, I would do so without hesitation. But it is unnecessary. It has been replaced by s.11 of the Civil Evidence Act 1968."

Section 11(2) of the UK Civil Evidence Act 1968 now provides that:

> "In any civil proceedings in which by virtue of this section a person is proved to have been convicted of an offence by or before any court in the United Kingdom or by a court-martial there or elsewhere-
>
> (a) he shall be taken to have committed that offence unless the contrary is proved."

In *Nevin v Nevin* Kearns P. was also critical of the rule in *Hollington v Hewthorn*, stating that it "was contrary to logic and common sense and offended any reasonable person's sense of justice and fairness". He added that: **10–11**

> "There is the clearest public policy consideration for so holding and it is set out starkly and unambiguously in s.120 of the Succession Act 1965. That policy consideration may be characterised as being no more and no less than that the perpetrator of the crime of murder should not be the beneficiary of it."

He also said that the Irish courts in this jurisdiction were spared the consequences and confusion created by the decision in *Hollington v Hewthorn* which gave rise to the passing of the UK Civil Evidence Act 1968. **10–12**

He went on to refer to *Re Crippin*[17] and the New Zealand Court of Appeal decision in *Jorgensen v News Media (Auckland) Ltd.*[18] He preferred to base his view **10–13**

> "on the proposition that the admissibility of the murder conviction is either authorised on foot of the decision in *Crippen's* case or comes within an exception to the hearsay rule as suggested and found by the Court of Appeal in New Zealand in *Jorgensen's* case".

His reasons for doing so were:

> "(a) that there can be no real doubt that a certificate of conviction constitutes unimpeachable evidence not only of the fact that a person was convicted, but also that the court did in fact consider the person guilty of the crime (in other words any of the usual objections to hearsay — that the version given in court

---

16 [1980] 2 All E.R. 227 at 237; see also *Hunter v Chief Constable of the West Midlands Police & Ors.* [1982] A.C. 529 at 543.

17 [1911] P. 108 at 115.

18 [1969] N.Z.L.R. 961.

> may be unsatisfactory as false, unreliable, biased, untested by cross-examination etc — simply do not arise) and (b) any objection that the court may have been wrong is more than addressed by the requirement that the court before convicting must be satisfied beyond all reasonable doubt that the person was guilty of the crime charged."

10–14 He concluded that this legal principle rested "most comfortably" with the view that the conviction should be seen as *prima facie* evidence only of guilt. Evidence of the conviction of the defendant for murder was admissible in the plaintiff's civil claim against the defendant but he

> "would go no further than did the Court of Appeal in New Zealand to say that the conviction is *prima facie* evidence only that the defendant murdered her husband".

There is no doubt a clear need for amending legislation to rid s.120(1) of the 1965 Act of the ambiguity identified by Kearns P. to render it certain, determinate and consistent with the other provisions of s.120. Alternatively, new legislation may be introduced, akin to the UK Civil Evidence Act 1968, allowing for the admission of evidence of a conviction in *all* subsequent civil proceedings, where the person convicted of the offence "shall be taken to have committed that offence unless the contrary is proved".

10–15 It may be noted however that as, s.120(1) does not contain provisions precluding persons who have been guilty of the specified offences from applying for grants of probate or letters of administration with the will annexed or intestate, the subsection appears to have no relevance to an application to the court under s.27(4) of the 1965 Act by a person seeking a grant of administration to a deceased person's estate in place of an executor or person entitled to apply for a grant under the Rules of the Superior Courts who has been convicted of, say, the murder of the deceased or a fellow beneficiary. In *In the Estate of Glynn*[19] McCarthy J. when granting administration of the deceased's estate to the Chief State Solicitor under s.27(4) of the 1965 Act, stated that it would be "utterly wrong" for a beneficiary in a will who was also the executor and who had been convicted of the murder of the testator's sister in order to accelerate his succession in remainder "should be permitted, even in the most formal manner, to administer the estate". In the course of his judgment McCarthy J. referred to *Re Crippin*[20] and the decision of Sir Samuel Evans where he stated that:

> "In the present case a man who has been convicted of the wilful murder of his wife has, after his conviction, made a will appointing a person his executrix, to administer the murdered wife's estate, and as legatee to be entitled to the murdered wife's property. These are, surely, 'special circumstances'. I therefore pass over and decline to appoint the executrix; and I appoint the applicant as attorney of the deceased woman's sister to be administrator of the deceased's woman's estate

[19] [1992] 1 I.R. 361at 364.
[20] [1911] P. 108 at 111-112.

on the sister's behalf. If I am right in this exercise of the discretion of the court, there remains nothing which is necessary for me to decide upon this motion."

Desertion by Spouse or Civil Partner

Under s.120(2) of the 1965 Act, **10–16**

> "a spouse against whom the deceased obtained a decree of divorce *a mensa et thoro*, a spouse who failed to comply with a decree of restitution of conjugal rights obtained by the deceased and a spouse guilty of desertion which has continued up to the death for two years or more shall be precluded from taking any share in the estate of the deceased as a legal right or on intestacy".

Section 120(2) of the 1965 Act was amended by s.42(1) of the Judicial Separation and Family Law Reform Act 1989 to exclude a decree of divorce *a mensa et thoro* and a decree of restitution of conjugal rights from the provisions of s.120(2), thus leaving desertion as the only non-criminal ground for precluding a spouse from taking a share in the estate of the deceased as a legal right or on intestacy.[21] Section 120(3) provides that a spouse who was guilty of conduct which justified the deceased in separating and living apart from that spouse will be deemed to be guilty of desertion within the meaning of s.120(2). It appears that s.120(3) extends the meaning of desertion to include constructive desertion. Section 120(2) therefore precludes a spouse from taking a legal right share or a share on intestacy on the grounds of desertion, though it does not preclude the deserting spouse from taking a gift left to him or her by the deceased spouse in his or her will. Section 120 of the 1965 Act was amended by s.87 of the 2010 Act to include civil partners by inserting the following subsection after subsection (2):

> "(2A) A deceased's civil partner who has deserted the deceased is precluded from taking any share in the deceased's estate as a legal right or on intestacy if the desertion continued up to the death for two years or more."

And by inserting the following subsection after subsection (3):

> "(3A) A civil partner who was guilty of conduct which justified the deceased in separating and living apart from him or her is deemed to be guilty of desertion within the meaning of subsection (2A)."

Desertion must be shown for the purposes of s.120(1) to have existed for **10–17** a period of two years or more before the death of the deceased spouse. This time period may commence at any time after the marriage.[22] Proof of desertion may be an easy matter if it is based simply on the physical separation of the spouses for a period of two years or more, but where the deserting spouse alleges that he was justified in leaving, the onus of proof

---

[21] See also s.42(2) of the Judicial Separation and Family Law Reform Act 1989.

[22] See *Wells v Wells* [1940] N.I. 880.

is on him to show that the misconduct of the deceased spouse caused him to leave.[23] There must be some form of serious misconduct to cause a spouse to leave the other spouse, and eccentricities or character traits no matter how "vexatious and trying" may not be a sufficient reason for leaving.[24]

10–18 The desertion provisions in s.120(2) of the 1965 Act are applicable only to spouses and civil partners. Section 120 does not include cohabitants. However, where qualified cohabitants are concerned, s.194(3) of the 2010 Act provides that the court may make provision for a qualified cohabitant if it is satisfied

> "that proper provision in the circumstances was not made for the applicant during the lifetime of the deceased for any reason other than conduct by the applicant that, in the opinion of the court, it would in all the circumstances be unjust to disregard".[25]

10–19 When entertaining an application by a qualified cohabitant under s.194(3), the court may take into account the conduct by an applicant cohabitant towards the deceased cohabitant during his or her lifetime, and such conduct may be interpreted to include desertion.

Section 120(4)

10–20 Under s.120(4) of the 1965 Act, a person who has been found guilty of an offence against the deceased, or against the spouse or any child of the deceased, including an adopted child or a person to whom the deceased was *in loco parentis* at the time of the offence, punishable by imprisonment for a maximum period of at least two years or by a more severe penalty, will be precluded from taking any share in the estate as a legal right or from making an application under s.117 of the 1965 Act. Section 120(4) was amended by the 2010 Act by the insertion of "or civil partner" after "spouse". Since the enactment of the Status of Children Act 1987, a non-marital child would also be deemed a child for the purposes of s.120 of the 1965 Act. Thus, where a spouse or civil partner has been found guilty of an offence against the deceased, or any child of the deceased, including an adopted child or a person to whom the deceased was *in loco parentis* at the time of the offence, punishable by imprisonment for a maximum period of at least two years or by a more severe penalty, he or she will be precluded from taking any share in the estate as a legal right. Any child of the deceased found guilty of the same offence will be precluded from making an application under s.117 of the 1965 Act. While s.194(3) of the 2010 Act does not preclude a qualified

---

[23] See *P v P*, Unreported, High Court, Barrington J., 12 March 1980; *Buchler v Buchler* [1947] 1 All E.R. 319.

[24] *P v P*, Unreported, High Court, Barrington J., 12 March 1980; *AB v JB and MB* [1991] 2 I.R. 501.

[25] See Chapter 8 – The Legal Right of Spouses and Civil Partners and Applications by Qualified Cohabitants.

cohabitant from making an application under s.194 for offences similar to those found in s.120 of the 1965 Act, the courts may take such similar type offences into account when deciding whether or not to make adequate provision for him or her out of the estate of the deceased cohabitant.[26]

The Effect of Section 120(5)

Section 120 (5) of the 1965 Act provides that: **10–21**

> "Any share which a person is precluded from taking under this section shall be distributed as if that person had died before the deceased."

As a consequence of the impugned s.120(1) by Kearns P. in *Nevin v Nevin*[27] **10–22** it appears that the effect of "a person precluded from taking under this section" under s.120(5) ceases to have any relevance to s.120(1). Under s.120(2) and (3), a spouse or civil partner will be precluded from taking any share in the deceased's estate as a legal right or on intestacy, and under the predecease rule in s.120(5), his or her share in the deceased's estate will be distributed as if that spouse or civil partner had died before the deceased. It appears, however, that a spouse or civil partner found guilty of an offence under s.120(4), though expressly precluded from taking any share in the estate as a legal right, is not precluded from taking a share in the deceased's estate in the event of intestacy. Any child of the deceased found guilty of an offence under s.120(4) will be precluded from making an application under s.117 of the 1965 Act, but not precluded from taking a share on intestacy. Thus, where the deceased for the purposes of s.120(4) dies leaving a will, a surviving spouse or civil partner will be precluded from taking a legal right share, and a child will be precluded from making a s.117 application, and the predecease rule in s.120(5) will become applicable, but where the deceased dies intestate the predecease rule in s.120(5) is not applicable, and a surviving spouse or civil partner or child will be entitled to a share on intestacy in the deceased's estate.

Section 121 Dispositions

Section 121(1) of the 1965 Act applies to: **10–23**

> "a disposition of property (other than a testamentary disposition or a disposition to a purchaser) under which the beneficial ownership of the property vests in possession in the donee within three years before the death of the person who made it or on his death or later".

The definition of "disposition" for the purposes of s.121 expressly includes a *donatio mortis causa* which is an *inter vivos* gift effective on the death

---

[26] *ibid.*

[27] [2013] I.E.H.C. 80.

of the donor.[28] Under s.121(2) of the 1965 Act, where the court is satisfied that a disposition within the definition of s.121(1) was made for the purpose of defeating or substantially diminishing the share of his spouse, whether as a legal right or on intestacy, or the intestate share of any of his or her children, or of leaving any of his or her children insufficiently provided for, the disposition may be deemed in whole or in part "to be a devise or bequest made by him by will and to form part of his estate, and to have had no other effect".[29] Section 121 of the Act of 1965 was amended by s.88 of the 2010 Act by inserting "or civil partner" after "spouse" wherever it appears. It follows then that any disposition of property other than by way of a gift by will or a disposition to a purchaser that is made by a person three years before his death for the purpose of defeating or substantially diminishing the share of his spouse or civil partner, whether as a legal right or on intestacy, or the intestate share of any of his or her children, or of leaving any of his or her children insufficiently provided for, may be deemed in whole or in part to be a devise or bequest made by him by will and to form part of his estate, and to have had no other effect. Therefore, the type of disposition envisaged by s.121(1) is a voluntary gift of property that vests in possession in the donee, made within a period of three years before the donor's death or on his death, for instance, a *donatio mortis causa*, or later. In *LC (a minor) v HS*[30] Clarke J., when considering what constituted a disposition for the purposes of s.121(1), stated that "the person who engaged in the disposition was the owner of the land being disposed of", that the disposition was not a mortgage of the property, and that it was not "an acquisition of property by purchase or otherwise".

10–24 It must be shown that the disposition was made by the deceased for the purpose of defeating or substantially diminishing the share of the disponer's spouse or civil partner, whether as a legal right or on intestacy, or the intestate share of the deceased's children, or for the purpose of leaving any of his children insufficiently provided for. If the court is satisfied that this was the purpose for making the disposition, it may order that the disposition in whole or in part be deemed to be a devise or bequest made by the deceased by will and to form part of his estate. Once an order is made by the court, the donee of the property, or any person deriving title under him, will be deemed to be a debtor of the estate for such amount as the court orders.[31] The court is also empowered to make such further orders as may appear to be just and equitable having regard to the circumstances of the case.[32] An order may be made in the interest of the spouse or civil partner on the application of the spouse or civil partner or personal representative of the deceased within one year from the first taking out of a grant of representation to the estate and in the interest of a child of the deceased on an application

---

[28] See Chapter 11 – *Donationes Mortis Causa*, Joint Bank Accounts and Advancements.

[29] s.121(2).

[30] [2014] I.E.H.C. 32.

[31] s.121(3).

[32] s.121(4)

under s.117.[33] Dispositions made by the deceased in favour of a spouse or civil partner or child within three years of his death cannot form the subject matter of an application under s.121, except in the case of a child who is a child of the disponer, but not the child of the spouse or civil partner.[34] Ever since the passing of the Status of Children Act 1987, this apparently includes a non-marital child of the disponer. Where a disposition is made in favour of a spouse or civil partner only, the court will not make an order under s.121 on an application by a child of the disponer who is also a child of the spouse or civil partner, and this includes adopted and legitimated children.

By virtue of s.121(7) the court will not make an order where it would affect a disposition made in favour of a child and in circumstances where: **10–25**

(a) the spouse or civil partner of the disponer was dead when the disposition was made;
(b) the spouse or civil partner was alive when the disposition was made but was a person who, if the disponer had then died, would have been precluded under s.120 from taking a share in his estate; or
(c) the spouse or civil partner was alive when the disposition was made and consented in writing to it.

The interaction between s.117 and s.121 of the 1965 Act was discussed by Carroll J. in *MPD v MD*.[35] Section 121(5) of the 1965 Act, as amended, provides that an order may be made under s.121 either (a) in the interests of the spouse or civil partner, on the application of the spouse or civil partner or the personal representative, made within one year of the first taking out of representation, or (b) in the interest of a child, on an application made under s.117. No time limit is expressly imposed in the case of an application made by a child, but Carroll J. held that only one set of proceedings is necessary to bring an application under ss.117 and 121, and that the time limit of six months from the taking out of representation imposed by s.117(6) applies equally to an application under s.121.[36] In *LC (a Minor) v HS*[37] Clark J. stated that: **10–26**

> "It is clear from *MPD v MD* that the six month time limit applicable to s.117 applications applies equally to s.121 applications, which can only be sought as a relief in s.117 proceedings in cases where the order is sought in the interest of a child of the deceased."

In *LC (a Minor) v HS*, Clark J. referred to the finding by Carroll J. in *MPD* **10–27**

---

[33] s.121(5); see Chapter 9 – The Moral Duty of Testators.
[34] s.121(6).
[35] [1981] I.L.R.M. 179.
[36] See Chapter 9 – The Moral Duty of Testators.
[37] [1981] I.L.R.M. 179.

v MD that one set of proceedings is sufficient to mount a claim under s.117 and 121:

> "is a recognition of their connection under the 1965 Act but is not a licence to use one set of proceedings to stay any statutory time limitations for the other."

But she continued:

> "That is *not* to say that in an appropriate case, in order to ensure that proper provision has been made for the child of a testator in accordance with Section 117, the Court could not grant an order under Section 121, as part of its inherent jurisdiction to provide just relief, even if no such claim was made. The Court's discretion would clearly depend on a number of pre-conditions being met; i.e. that (1) the Section 117 proceedings were commenced within the statutory time; (2) it would be unjust to ignore the disinheriting disposition; (3) there would otherwise be little or no estate available to provide just provision for the child; and (4) as soon as reasonably possible after becoming aware of the disputed disposition, the Plaintiff put the Defendant on notice that he / she would be seeking to have the disposition treated as a bequest or devise made by will and treated as part of the estate, in the context of the Section 117 proceedings. An order may only be made under Section 117 '*on application by or on behalf of the child of a testator*' and cannot generally be made if the deceased died intestate. However, as previously mentioned, Section 121 is not subject to that limitation and where an order is made under Section 121, the deceased is treated as though he made a bequest or devise by will, which potentially brings Section 117 into play even if the deceased otherwise died intestate (see the judgment of Carroll J. in *MPD v MD*)."

Clark J. concluded that:

> "Although the Section 117 proceedings were brought within time they were not appropriate to an intestacy and they did not include a claim under Section 121 nor was any claim brought to amend the pleadings within a reasonable time after the Plaintiff was aware that W.S. had died intestate and that it had been asserted by the Defendant that his estate did not comprise any real property. In those circumstances it is clear that her claim falls to be dealt with under the intestacy rules under Section 67, and it would be unconscionable for the Court to exercise its inherent jurisdiction to make an order under Section 121. The Court is satisfied that the action is statute barred."

10–28 Section 127 of the 1965 Act which extends the disability provisions of the Statute of Limitations 1957 relating to minority and unsound mind to actions in respect of a claim to the estate of the deceased person or a share in the estate does not apply to applications by children under s.117 or s.121.[38] This reflects the principle, identified by the Supreme Court in *Moynihan v Greensmyth*,[39] that there is a public interest in the speedy administration of estates.[40]

---

[38] *M.P.D. v M.D.* [1981] I.L.R.M. 179.

[39] [1977] 1 I.R. 55.

[40] See *LC (a Minor) v HS* [2014] I.E.H.C. 32.

THE ANNULMENT OF GIFTS

Where a beneficiary or his or her spouse or civil partner witnesses a will, the gift to him or her will be nullified.[41] Section 82(1) of the 1965 Act as amended by s.77 of the 2010 Act provides that: **10–29**

> "If a person attests the execution of a will, and any devise, bequest, estate, interest, gift, or appointment, of or affecting any property (other than charges and directions for the payment of any debt or debts) is given or made by the will to that person or his spouse or civil partner, that devise, bequest, estate, interest, gift, or appointment shall, so far only as concerns the person attesting the execution of the will, or the spouse or the civil partner of that person, or any person claiming under that person or spouse or civil partner, be utterly null and void."

Where there are three witnesses and one of them is also a beneficiary, it will be presumed that the beneficiary signed with the intention of attesting the will.[42] The presumption may be rebutted where it is shown that the third witness did not sign with the intention of attesting the will, and as a result his or her signature may be omitted from probate.[43] A later codicil may save a gift given to a beneficiary who has signed an earlier will as witness, as long as the later codicil containing the same gift is not attested by either the beneficiary or his spouse or civil partner. The same applies to a later codicil which simply confirms a gift given in any earlier will which was witnessed by the beneficiary or his spouse or civil partner.[44] However, a later codicil witnessed by him which merely increases the value of a gift made to him in an earlier will which was not witnessed by him may not prevent him from taking the increased value of the gift in the later instrument, although it appears that any direct gift to him will again fall foul of the rule in s.82 of the 1965 Act.[45] Where a trustee signs a will as a witness, although the trust will remain unaffected, the personal gift made to him or her may be nullified under s.82 of the 1965 Act.[46] Where a witness later discovers that he or she is a beneficiary by virtue of a secret trust arising out of the will, the fact that he or she was a witness to the will may not prevent him or her from benefiting under the provisions of the secret trust.[47] In English law, where three witnesses sign a will and one is a beneficiary or the spouse of a beneficiary, the signature of the beneficiary or his spouse may be omitted from the probate of the will if the execution of the will remains unaffected by the omission. But where two of three witnesses receive a gift, the **10–30**

---

41 s.82 of the 1965 Act as amended by s.77 of the Civil Partnership and Certain Rights and Obligations of Cohabitants Act 2010.

42 See *Re Parker* (1905) 39 I.L.T.R. 6; *In the Goods of Willis* (1927) 61 I.L.T.R. 48; *In the Goods of Shaw* [1944] Ir. Jur. Rep. 77.

43 *In the Goods of Shaw* [1944] Ir. Jur. Rep. 77; *In the Goods of Willis* (1927) 61 I.L.T.R. 48.

44 See *Re Trotter* [1899] 1 Ch. 764.

45 See *Guerney v Guerney* (1855) 3 Drew. 208.

46 See *Re Ray's W.T.* [1936] Ch. 520.

47 *O'Brien v Condon* [1905] 1 I.R. 51; *Re Young* [1951] Ch. 344.

presumption of signing with the intention of attesting will be applied.[48] A nullified gift under s.82 of the 1965 Act will form part of the residuary estate or, in the absence of a clause disposing of the residuary estate, will be distributed on intestacy.

The Invalidation of Wills

10–31 A will may be invalidated on the grounds of undue influence, or that it was unlawfully procured or made as a result of fraud.

Undue Influence

10–32 Where undue influence is alleged, there must be positive proof that the testator was coerced by another party into making a will.[49] In *Wingrove v Wingrove*[50] Sir James Hannen stated that, for undue influence in the eyes of the law, there must be — to sum it up in a word — coercion: "It is only when the will of the person who becomes a testator is coerced into doing that which he or she does not desire to do that it is undue influence". However, persuasion does not amount to coercion where limited to that which

> "appeals to the affection or ties of kindred, to sentiment of gratitude for past service, or pity for future destitution, or the like — these are all legitimate, and may fairly be pressed on a testator".[51]

10–33 But pressure of whatever character, "whether acting on the fears or the hopes, if so exerted as to overpower the volition without convincing the judgement, is a species of restraining under which no valid will can be made".[52] Where it is shown that coercion was limited to part only of the will, the impugned part may be excluded from probate.[53] There was also a time when particulars of undue influence in probate were not obligatory[54] but such particulars must now be furnished in the same way as in all other cases where undue influence is alleged.[55]

10–34 The basis of an allegation of undue influence in probate law is that the testator was coerced into making a will which was not "the offspring of his own volition". For a will to be impugned on the grounds of undue influence,

48 See UK Wills Act 1968, s.1.
49 Chapter 21 – Probate and Administration Actions and Costs.
50 (1885) 11 P.D. 81 at 82 *per* Sir. J. Hannen.
51 *Hall v Hall* (1868) L.R. 1 P. & D. 481 at 482 *per* Sir J.P. Wilde; see also *Wingrove v Wingrove* (1885) 11 P.D. 81 at 82 *per* Sir J. Hannen.
52 *Hall v Hall* (1868) L.R. 1 P. & D. 481 at 482.
53 *Allen v M'Pherson* (1847) 1 H.L.C. 191 at 209; *Farrelly v Corrigan* [1899] A.C. 563.
54 See *Wallace v McDowell* [1920] 2 I.R. 194.
55 *In the Goods of Rutledge* [1981] I.L.R.M. 198.

there must be positive proof of coercion overpowering the volition of the testator.[56] While a testator may be persuaded to make a will

> "which you may condemn, really and truly to intend to give his property to another, though you may disapprove of the act, yet it is legitimate in the sense of its being legal,"

coercion of whatever character,

> "whether acting on the fears or the hopes, if so exerted as to overpower the volition without convincing the judgement, is a species of restraining under which no valid will can be made".[57]

An exception may be made in the case of a will made as a result of "natural influence" by a parent, child or guardian, and the existence of such influence may not impugn a will so long as the testator thoroughly understands what he is doing and is a free agent.[58] The character of the testator may also be taken into account and, where threats are made which the testator has not had the moral courage to resist, or which the testator complies with for the sake of peace and quiet, or if the pressure used **10–35**

> "is carried to a degree in which the free play of the testator's judgement, discretion or wishes is overborne, it will constitute undue influence, though no force is either used or threatened".[59]

Where, however, there is a suspicion only of undue influence without positive proof of coercion, it is "inadvisable" to pursue a claim based on undue influence. **10–36**

The onus of proof at all times rests on the party alleging the undue influence. There is no presumption of undue influence in probate law based on the nature of the relationship between the testator and the party allegedly exerting the coercion. This is different from the law relating to *inter vivos* transactions, for instance in the case of contracts, where a presumption of undue influence will arise out of the existence of a fiduciary or similar type of relationship between contracting parties.[60] As was stated by Murphy J. in *Lambert v Lyons*[61] Irish law **10–37**

> "recognises a distinction between the proof of undue influence in the context of

---

[56] See Albert Keating, "Undue Influence in Probate Law" (2011) 29 I.L.T. 61; Albert Keating, "A Plea of Want of Knowledge and Approval as an Alternative to Undue Influence" (2008) 13(1) C.P.L.J. 10.

[57] *Hall v Hall* (1868) L.R. 1 P. & D. 481at 482 *per* Sir J.P. Wilde; see also *Wingrove v Wingrove* (1885) 11 P.D. 81 at 82.

[58] *Boyse v Rossborough* (1857) 6 H.L.C. 2.

[59] See *Elliot v Stamp*, Unreported, High Court, Murphy J., 7 November 2006.

[60] *Carroll v Carroll* [1999] 4 I.R. 241; *Prendergast v Joyce* [2009] I.E.H.C. 199; *Bourke v O'Donnell & Ors* [2010] I.E.H.C. 348.

[61] [2010] I.E.H.C. 29.

> wills and in the context of transactions *inter vivos*, the burden of proof is on the plaintiffs and there is no presumption of undue influence arising from special relationships".

10–38 But in both cases, for undue influence to exist there must be positive proof of coercion, and, as was said by Murphy J. in *Elliot v Stamp*[62] in relation to wills, a mere suspicion of undue influence without positive proof of coercion would render it "inadvisable" to pursue an action in undue influence.

The Procurement of Wills

10–39 A matter related to undue influence, and one that may be pleaded as an alternative to it, is the requirement of a beneficiary who has prepared and procured the execution of a will in circumstances that arouse the vigilance of the court to show the "righteousness of the transaction" to the satisfaction of the court.[63] In such a case, the propounding party must adduce evidence, not only to remove the suspicion, but also to satisfy the court that the testator knew and approved of the contents of the will.[64] The onus of proof in such circumstances will be the same for all beneficiaries, and no distinction will be made between strangers and near relatives of the testator.[65]

10–40 When the principle of knowledge and approval becomes an issue, it must be shown that the testator knew and approved of the contents of his will either at the time of giving instructions or at the time of executing it.[66] Where, however, the principle is raised as an issue, the circumstances surrounding a case will determine the approach to be adopted by the courts. Where it is shown that a will was procured and prepared by a person who was also a beneficiary, or who had a benefit increased by a subsequent codicil, the vigilance of the court will be aroused. It will view such circumstances as suspicious and the onus of proof will rest on such person to satisfy the court of the righteousness of the transaction. This onus may be discharged by evidence establishing that the testator knew and approved of the contents of the will at the time of execution. Where no such circumstances exist yet there is some doubt as to whether a testator knew and approved of the contents owing to his state of health or age, the issue of whether he knew and approved may involve an evaluation of his intellectual capacity by the court. The evidence adduced will determine whether he had sufficient intellectual

[62] Unreported, High Court, Murphy J., 7 November 2006.

[63] See Albert Keating, "A Plea of Want of Knowledge and Approval as an Alternative to Undue Influence" (2008) 13(1) C.P.L.J.10.

[64] *In the Goods of Corboy* [1969] I.R. 148; *Tyrrell v Painton* [1894] P. 151; *Barry v Butlin* (1838) 2 Moo. P.C. 480; *Fulton v Andrew* (1875) L.R. 7 H.L. 448; *Brown v Fisher* (1890) 63 L.T. 465; *Re Begley* [1939] I.R. 479.

[65] *Hegarty v King* (1880) 7 L.R. Ir. 18 at 22; see also *Donnelly v Broughton* [1891] A.C. 435.

[66] See Chapter 2 – The Execution of Wills; Albert Keating, "The Principle of Knowledge and Approval: A Judicial Term of Art" (2005) 10(2) C.P.L.J. 30; Chapter 21 – Probate and Administration Actions and Costs.

capacity to know and approve of the contents of his will. Evidence showing that a testator knew and approved of the instructions given for his will may be sufficient to satisfy the court that he knew and approved of the contents of his will "provided that the circumstances were such as would enable the court to say that he knew the will had been drawn according to his instructions".[67] Where a testator is merely confirming instructions already given, it may not be necessary to show that he knew and approved of contents at the time of execution, provided that he understood that he was executing a will.[68]

Fraud

Fraud will always render a testamentary gift, or indeed the whole will, invalid. Fraud, however, eludes definition. Indeed, so varied are the acts that may constitute fraud that any attempt to define it would bind the hands of the courts in their effort to counter newly-devised fraudulent schemes if the courts were confined to the terms of a definition. There are no rules specifying what acts constitute fraud for the purposes of rendering a will invalid, although the relevant time for ascertaining the presence of an act which is alleged to be fraudulent is the time when the testator executes his will. While there is no presumption of fraud, the probability of its presence in the circumstances may be so strong that the court may infer it and thereby place the onus of proof on the propounding party to dispel it. The difference between undue influence and fraud is that, in the case of undue influence, a testator is coerced into making a will, while, in the case of fraud, he is deceived into doing so. Where fraud is established, it will, like undue influence, invalidate the gift or will. A gift will be void for fraud where, for instance, the testator was deceived by a fraudulent assumption by a beneficiary in the will. Where a person fraudulently assumes a character and is left a gift in a will on the basis of the character assumed, the gift may be invalidated if the testator had been deceived by the fraudulent assumption.[69] Fraud must be established on the balance of probabilities by the party alleging its existence. Fraud is a separate plea to undue influence and cannot be raised directly under a plea of undue influence. The onus of proof rests on the person who alleges the fraud.[70] **10–41**

Renunciation or Extinguishment of the Legal Right

The legal right will cease to exist where it is renounced or extinguished. A legal right may be renounced by **10–42**

[67] See *Glynn v Glynn* [1990] 2 I.R. 326; *In the Estate of Blackall*, Unreported, Supreme Court, 1 April 1998.

[68] *Ibid.*

[69] *Re Posner* [1953] 1 All E.R. 1123.

[70] See *Banco Ambrosiano SpA v Ansbacher and Co. Ltd.* [1987] I.L.R.M. 669; Chapter 21 – Probate and Administration Actions and Costs.

> "an ante-nuptial contract made in writing between the parties to an intended marriage or may be renounced in writing by the spouse after marriage and during the lifetime of the testator."[71]

10–43 Since the enactment of the 2010 Act, the legal right may be renounced by an ante-civil partnership contract made in writing between the parties to an intended civil partnership or may be renounced in writing by the civil partner after the civil partnership was entered into and during the lifetime of the testator.[72] The legal right may be extinguished by a decree of judicial separation[73] or a decree of divorce, and the legal right of a spouse or civil partner will cease contemporaneously with the dissolution of the marriage or civil partnership.[74] The legal right of a surviving spouse or civil partner may also become statute-barred under s.126 of the 1965 Act.[75]

Disclaimer of Gifts and Intestate Shares

10–44 A beneficiary cannot be forced to take a gift in a will and it is for him to accept or disclaim it. Where a beneficiary wishes to disclaim a gift, he may do so by deed of disclaimer or by some other form of writing, or he may be held to have disclaimed by conduct. Once a beneficiary disclaims a gift, it falls into the residue, provided that there is a residuary clause in the will. In the absence of such a clause, the disclaimed gift will be distributed on intestacy. It may also have the effect of accelerating future interests if, say, a life interest is disclaimed. Although the beneficiary is not obliged to give a motive for disclaiming a gift, a disclaimer is usually made out of self-interest, especially where the gift carries with it certain responsibilities that a beneficiary is unwilling to accept, although a beneficiary may have a genuine altruistic motive for disclaiming a valuable gift where, for instance, it would benefit a more needy relative.[76] A beneficiary will not, however, be allowed to disclaim once he has commenced to receive some benefit from the gift and he will not be allowed to withdraw his disclaimer once another person commences to receive some advantage from the gift.[77] It may happen that a beneficiary who is left two gifts in the same will may wish to disclaim one and take the other. He may do this as long as the two gifts are separate and distinct but he will not be allowed to pick and choose among the assets contained in a single gift.[78]

[71] s.113 of the 1965 Act; see Chapter 8 – The Legal Right of Spouses and Civil Partners and Applications by Qualified Cohabitants; Chapter 26 – Succession Act Precedents.

[72] s.113 of the 1965 Act.

[73] See Chapter 8–The Legal Right of Spouses and Civil Partners and Applications by Qualified Cohabitants; Family Law Act 1995, s.14.

[74] See Family Law (Divorce) Act 1996: The Legal Right of Spouses and Civil Partners and Applications by Qualified Cohabitants.

[75] See Chapter 23 – The Limitation of Actions and Striking Out Proceedings.

[76] See *Re Hodge* [1940] Ch. 260.

[77] See *Re Cranstoun* [1949] Ch. 523.

[78] *Re Joel* [1943] Ch. 311.

Prior to the enactment of s.72A of the 1965 Act as inserted by s.6 of the Family Law (Miscellaneous Provisions) Act 1997 (the 1997 Act), some doubt existed over the entitlement to a disclaimed intestate share.[79] The question was whether the share reverted to the estate of the deceased intestate for further distribution among the other beneficiaries, or whether the State was entitled to the share as ultimate intestate successor under s.73 of the 1965 Act. S.72A of the 1965 Act as inserted by s.6 of the 1997 Act removed all such doubt. It provides that: **10–45**

> "Where the estate, or part of the estate, as to which a person dies intestate is disclaimed after the passing of the 1997 Act (otherwise than by s.73 of this Act), the estate or part, as the case may be, shall be distributed in accordance with this Part–(a) as if the person disclaiming had died immediately before the death of the intestate; and (b) if that person is not the spouse or a direct lineal ancestor of the intestate, as if that person had died without leaving issue."

It may be noted however that the section is applicable only to disclaimers made after the passing of the 1997 Act.

After the passing of the 1997 Act, the Conveyancing Committee of the Law Society of Ireland issued a Practice Note together with a precedent disclaimer on intestacy. The Practice Note stated that, not only does the person who disclaims lose all entitlement to a share in the intestate's estate, but also he loses his entitlement in the order of priority to apply for a grant of letters of administration under Ord 79, r.5 of the Rules of the Superior Courts 1986. Where the entitled person applies for a grant and then disclaims his interest, the application for the grant must be discontinued as he no longer has the necessary beneficial interest in the estate entitling him to apply for the grant in the first place. The next person entitled to apply for a grant must, however, exhibit the disclaimer in the administrator's oath when applying for a grant. Where there are two or more persons equally entitled to apply for a grant and one of those persons disclaims, it is not necessary for the applicant to exhibit the disclaimer. It seems that, in the case of separated spouses with no children, a disclaimer made by a surviving spouse will take effect as though the surviving spouse had predeceased the spouse who had died intestate. The Note, however, cautions that it would be a mistake for a relative, like a brother of the deceased, to think that a disclaimer made by him would pass his share in the deceased's estate to his children; once a share is disclaimed it reverts to the estate and is then distributed among those who are already entitled to a share. **10–46**

---

[79] See *Re Scott* [1975] 2 All E.R. 1033.

CHAPTER 11

DONATIONES MORTIS CAUSA, JOINT BANK ACCOUNTS AND ADVANCEMENTS

INTRODUCTION

A *donatio mortis causa* is an *inter vivos* gift of property effective on death. For a valid *donatio mortis causa* to come into existence and receive the recognition of the courts, it must be made in contemplation of the death of the donor. The property forming the subject matter of the *donatio* must be delivered to the donee at the time of its creation. The delivery of the property may be performed by the donor handing it over to the donee. Once these requirements are satisfied, the property forming the subject matter of the *donatio* will become the property of the donee on the death of the donor.[1] But where the existence of a *donatio mortis causa* is challenged, the onus of proof rests on the donee to show that the conditions for its creation existed at the time the *donatio* was made.[2] **11–01**

The opening of a joint bank account is a form of contract between the joint holders that gives a surviving account holder a legal interest in the monies on deposit. Formerly, as a result of the Supreme Court decision in *Owens v Greene*[3] joint bank accounts gave rise to a presumption of a resulting trust for the benefit of the deceased depositor's estate and, unless the presumption was rebutted, a surviving joint account holder was not entitled to claim the monies in the account and the monies on account reverted to the deceased depositor's estate.[4] Since the decision of the Supreme Court in **11–02**

---

1 See Albert Keating, "*Donationes Mortis Causa* in Irish Law" (2005) 10 (3) C.P.L.J. 62; Albert Keating, *Keating on Probate* (4th ed) (Dublin: Thomson Round Hall, 2011); Albert Keating, *First Supplement to the Fourth Edition of Keating on Probate* (Dublin: Thomson Round Hall, 2013).

2 *Bentham v Potterton*, Unreported, High Court, Barr J., 28 May 1998.

3 [1932] I.R. 225.

4 See *Owens v Greene* [1932] I.R. 225; *McCabe v Ulster Bank Ltd* [1939] I.R. 1; *Re Walsh* [1942] I.R. 403; *McDonnell v McNeilly* [1917] 1 I.R. 117; *Doyle v Byrne* (1922) 56 I.L.T.R. 125.

Lynch v Burke[5] the opening of a joint bank account no longer gives rise to a presumption of a resulting trust but instead is viewed as a contract between the joint account holders and the bank, giving a surviving account holder a legal interest in the monies on deposit based on the contract.

11–03 Where a husband voluntarily transfers property to his wife, the presumption of advancement will become applicable and will override any presumption of a resulting trust. As a result, the property will become the property of the wife. It is basically the relationship of husband and wife that gives rise to the presumption of advancement in circumstances where a husband transfers property to his wife: no such presumption will arise where a wife transfers property to her husband. It was stated by Keane J. (as he then was) in *JC v JHC*[6] that the presumption of a resulting trust

> "may however be rebutted; and in particular the circumstances in whose name the property is conveyed being the wife of the person advancing the money may be sufficient to rebut the presumption under the doctrine of advancement".

Equity will also presume that an absolute gift was intended in circumstances where the transferor is the father of the transferee, or when the transferor is a person who is *in loco parentis* to a child.[7] For the equitable doctrine of advancement to apply in such circumstances, the relationship of father and child, or person *in loco parentis* to a child, must exist. A voluntary *inter vivos* transfer of property by a father to a child or a person who stands *in loco parentis* to a child will be sufficient to invoke the doctrine. An advancement made by a mother to her child will not be an advancement under the equitable doctrine of advancement. An advancement under the equitable doctrine will not be governed by s.63 of the Succession Act 1965 (the "1965 Act"), unless it was made for one of the purposes for making advancements under s.63. Where it was, it may then be taken into account when computing the value of the child's testate or intestate share in the estate.

11–04 An advancement coming within the meaning of s.63 of the 1965 Act may be taken into account when computing the value of a child's testate or intestate share in the estate of a deceased person. Section 63(1) of the 1965 Act provides that any advancement made to the child of a deceased person during his lifetime, the issue of the child or a person to whom the deceased was *in loco parentis* will

> "be taken as being made in or towards satisfaction of the share of such child in the estate of the deceased or share which such child would have taken if living at the death of the deceased, and as between the children shall be brought into account in distributing the estate".[8]

---

5 [1996] I.L.R.M. 114.

6 Unreported, High Court, Keane J., 4 August 1982.

7 *Bennet v Bennet* (1879) 10 Ch.D. 474; *O'Brien v Sheil* (1873) I.R. 7 Eq. 255.

8 s.63(1) of the 1965 Act.

But for such advancement to be taken into account, it must be for one of the purposes set out in s.63 of the 1965 Act.

Donationes Mortis Causa

For a *donatio mortis causa* to be effective on death, it must satisfy two primary requirements or conditions: first, it must be made in contemplation of death, and secondly there must be a delivery of the property forming the subject matter of the *donatio mortis causa* to the donee during the lifetime of the donor. Where the validity of a *donatio mortis causa* is challenged, the onus of proof rests on the donee to show that the conditions for the creation of a *donatio mortis causa* have been satisfied. The *donatio* must be made in contemplation of death. An instance of the latter would be where a person is diagnosed as suffering from a terminal illness and makes a gift in contemplation of death from the illness. Once a donor is diagnosed as suffering from a particular kind of terminal illness, and he or she makes a gift in contemplation of death from that illness, that will be sufficient to create a valid *donatio*, and the *donatio* will not be defeated where his or her death is caused by some other illness, as he or she possessed the necessary state of mind to make a valid *donatio mortis causa*. Furthermore, once a gift is made in contemplation of death from a terminal illness, the gift will take effect as a *donatio mortis causa* even if the donor later commits suicide.[9] **11–05**

The *donatio* must also be delivered by the donor with the intention of transferring dominion over the property. This may be carried out by the donor himself or he or she may appoint an agent to act on his or her behalf. The donee may also appoint an agent to accept delivery on his or her behalf. The mode of delivery may also depend on the nature of the property to be transferred, for instance, goods may be delivered by simply them handing over to the donee. They must, however, be handed over with the intention of transferring dominion over the goods, and not just for safekeeping. The subject matter of the *donatio* must also be capable of delivery and, in the case of items of personal property, they may be delivered by handing them over to the donee at the time of making the *donatio*, for instance, jewellery or a painting. But choses in action consisting of a post office savings book, a deposit receipt or third party cheques are all capable of delivery in their original state, though not cheques drawn on the donor's account or an insurance policy. There are other forms of chose in action which are not capable of delivery by merely handing them over to the donee, for instance, an IOU, a certificate of building society shares, a contract note for the purchase of stocks and shares or post office saving certificates, as distinct from a savings book. Where shares in a company form the subject matter of a *donatio*, the relevant transfer documentation must first be prepared and **11–06**

[9] *Mills v Shields and Kelly* [1948] I.R. 367at 370; *Agnew v Belfast Banking Company* [1896] 2 I.R. 204; *Wilkes v Allington* [1931] 2 Ch. 104; *Re Craven's Estate* (No.1) [1937] Ch. 423.

executed to pass good title to the donee. The onus of proof rests on the party claiming the *donatio* to satisfy the Court on the balance of probabilities that all the requisite conditions for the creation of a valid *donatio mortis causa* have been met.[10]

JOINT BANK ACCOUNTS

11–07 The opening of a joint bank account gives rise to a contract between the joint account holders and the bank, no matter what the relationship between the joint holders themselves. In *Lynch v Burke*[11] O'Flaherty J. considered the legal effect of opening a joint bank account. He was of the view that opening such an account gave rise to a contract between the joint account holders and the bank. He referred to *Russell v Scott*,[12] a decision of the High Court of Australia concerning the devolution of a joint bank account on death, for the statement that:

> "The contract between the bank and the customers constituted them joint creditors. They had, of course, no rights of property in any of the moneys deposited with the bank. The relation between the bank and its customers is that of debtor and creditor. The aunt and the nephew upon opening the joint bank account became jointly entitled at common law to a chose in action. The chose in action consisted in the contractual right against the bank, i.e. in a debt, but a debt fluctuating in amount as moneys might be deposited and withdrawn. At common law this chose in action passed or accrued to the survivor."

It was held in that case that the balance standing to the credit of the account on the death of the aunt devolved and vested in the nephew. In relation to the case before him, O'Flaherty J. stated:

> "I believe that at law the niece had a legal interest in the monies on deposit either by reason of the contractual relationship of the parties or, in the alternative, as a gift which admittedly was not a completed gift in the conventional sense but is nonetheless one that should be upheld as being a gift subject to a contingency *viz.* that of the death of the donor which contingency does not disqualify it as being a proper gift."[13]

11–08 He went on to overrule *Owens v Greene*,[14] and found that the concept of the resulting trust was devised primarily to defeat the misappropriation of property as a consequence of potentially fraudulent or improvident transactions, and was not to be used to defeat the clear intention of the depositor to benefit the surviving account holder on death. The overruling of *Owens v Greene* after so long a period of time

---

10 *Bentham v Potterton*, Unreported, High Court, Barr J., 28 May 1998.
11 [1996] I.L.R.M. 114.
12 (1936) 55 C.L.R. 440.
13 *Lynch v Burke* [1996] I.L.R.M. 114 at 121.
14 [1932] I.R. 225.

> "restores equity to the high ground which it should properly occupy to ameliorate the harshness of common law rules on occasion rather than itself be an instrument of injustice".

In *O'Meara v Bank of Scotland PLC*[15] Laffoy J. stated that, as a result of *Lynch v Burke*, the legal effect of opening a joint bank account was that the bank became contractually bound to both account holders and, as a matter of contract, between the surviving account holder and the bank, the surviving account holder became entitled to the balance in the account on the death of the deceased account holder. The balance in the account accrued to the surviving account holder by the right of survivorship. A surviving account holder was entitled to withdraw the balance in the account on demand. Furthermore, any claims to set-offs by a bank against the joint account in relation to loans of a deceased joint holder must be mutually agreed between the account holders and the bank during the negotiations for the setting up of such an account before the courts will entertain such claims. In the absence of such agreement regarding set-offs, the surviving account holder will become entitled to the balance in the account free of set-off. In *O'Meara v Bank of Scotland PLC* the proceedings related to the ownership of monies in two deposit accounts in the joint names of the plaintiff's deceased husband and herself. The primary relief sought by the plaintiff was a declaration that all monies standing in both accounts on the date of death of her husband belonged to her by way of survivorship. The defendant denied such ownership, and further claimed a right of set-off on foot of a loan account in her deceased husband's sole name against the monies standing to the credit of the joint accounts. Laffoy J. stated that if, the defendant had a valid right of set-off against the joint accounts, that right was exercisable notwithstanding the death of the plaintiff's husband, and the plaintiff's entitlement by way of survivorship would have been subject to it. But as the date of the set-off post-dated the negotiations and agreement for the opening of the joint account between the defendant and the plaintiff's deceased husband and herself, the claim by the defendant to a set-off was invalid. When considering the validity of the defendant's claim to a set-off against the joint account, it was held by Laffoy J. that the defendant was not be entitled to a set-off claimed after the negotiations and agreement for the opening of a joint bank account between it and the plaintiff's deceased husband and plaintiff had taken place. In relation to the ownership of the joint bank account and the bank's right of set-off Laffoy J. stated that: **11–09**

> "As regards joint deposit account No. 101, I have come to the conclusion that the monies in that account were jointly beneficially owned by Mr. O'Meara and the plaintiff and that they passed to the plaintiff by right of survivorship on the death of Mr. O'Meara. I have further concluded that the defendant was not entitled to set-off the monies due on loan account No. 128 against those monies, as it purported to do in January 2010. Accordingly, the plaintiff is entitled to a declaration that all the monies which were standing to the credit of that account on 28th November, 2009 are the property of the plaintiff."

---

[15] [2011] I.E.H.C. 402.

11–10 Laffoy J., affirming *Lynch v Burke,* stated that the legal effect of opening a joint bank account was that the bank became contractually bound to both account holders and, as a matter of contract between the surviving account holder and the bank, the surviving account holder became entitled to the balance in the account on the death of the deceased account holder.[16]

11–11 A right of set-off may be exercised by a bank against a joint account on the death of an account holder who has a loan account with the bank and, where the right is exercised, a surviving joint holder's entitlement to the monies in the joint account may become subject to the right of set-off. But where a right of set-off is claimed after the negotiations and agreement for the opening of a joint account have been concluded, it will not be enforced by the courts. Laffoy J. stated that, as the date of the set-off claimed by the defendant bank post-dated the negotiations and agreement for the opening of the joint account between the defendant bank and the plaintiff's deceased husband and herself, the claim by the defendant to a set-off was invalid, and the plaintiff became entitled to the monies in the joint account on the date of death of her husband by way of survivorship.

Equitable Advancements

11–12 The presumption of advancement is also applicable to all forms of property, including joint bank accounts.[17] Professor Delany in *Equity and the Law of Trusts in Ireland*[18] states that:

> "where money is deposited by a husband in an account in their joint names the presumption of a resulting trust in these circumstances may be rebutted by the presumption of advancement and *prima facie* the relationship between the parties will usually result in the wife taking the balance remaining in the account beneficially".

11–13 In *O'Meara v Bank of Scotland PLC*[19] Laffoy J. commented that it was reasonable to infer that, by opening the joint account, the plaintiff's deceased husband intended to make provision for her should he predecease her. The doctrine of advancement may also be relied on by a child where there is a voluntary transfer of property that would normally give rise to a presumption of a resulting trust but for the fact that the transferor is the father (not the mother) of the child. It was stated by O'Sullivan M.R. in *O'Brien v Sheil*[20] that

> "a lodgment by a father in the joint names of himself and his child is as powerful

[16] See Albert Keating "The Devolution of Joint Bank Accounts" (2012) 17(2) C.P.L.J. 29.

[17] See *O'Meara v Bank of Scotland PLC* [2011] I.E.H.C. 402.

[18] (5th ed) (Dublin: Round Hall, 2011), p 162.

[19] [2011] I.E.H.C. 402.

[20] (1873) I.R. 7 Eq. 255.

> and strong an indication of advancement as a lodgment in the name of the child alone. Now, what is the effect of that doctrine of advancement attaching on a sum lodged in the joint names of father and child (the latter surviving), or in the name of the child alone, unexplained by any evidence? It is a gift of the property to the child in the one case immediately, and in the other if the child survives".

The presumption of advancement may be rebutted by showing a contrary intention. The doctrine of advancement raises a presumption only and it is one that may be rebutted by acts or statements made before or at the time of making the advancement showing that no advancement was intended.[21] In such cases, the onus is on the husband or father to show **11–14**

> "by reference to acts or statements before or around the transaction, that a beneficial interest was not intended to be conveyed in the circumstances relied on".[22]

Acts done or statements made after the making of the advancement will not, however, be admitted in evidence to support a rebuttal of the presumption.[23] In *RF v MF*[24] Henchy J. treated a wife's subsequent refusal to live with her husband as sufficient grounds for rebutting the presumption of advancement. He stated:

> "If the relevant circumstances show that the paper result achieved by the conveyance conceals the real intention of the husband in entering the transaction, so that the benefit contended for by the wife was not intended, the court will hold that the presumption of advancement is rebutted."[25]

The courts, however, will be slow to rebut the presumption, and will only do so where there is evidence of acts or statements that go towards showing that no advancement was intended, or that the circumstances of the case show, as in *RF v MF*, the existence of an arrangement between husband and wife and of her subsequent breach of the arrangement. Where it is discovered, however, that the husband made the advancement for an illegal purpose, evidence of the illegal purpose cannot be adduced for the purposes of rebutting the presumption.[26] **11–15**

As regards the relationship of father and child and the presumption of advancement, Jessel M.R. said in *Bennet v Bennet*[27] that a father **11–16**

> "is under that obligation from the mere fact of his being the father, and therefore no evidence is necessary to show the obligation to provide for his child".

---

[21] *Shepherd v Cartwright* [1955] A.C. 431.
[22] *RF v MF* [1995] 2 I.L.R.M. 572 at 576-577.
[23] *RF v MF* [1995] 2 I.L.R.M. 572.
[24] *ibid.*
[25] *ibid* at 577.
[26] *Parker v Parker* [1980] I.L.R.M. 137.
[27] (1879) 10 Ch.D. 474 at 476.

He went on to say that, in the case of a father, "you have only to prove that he is the father" and, once that is done, the obligation at once arises. It is the nature of the relationship that gives rise to the presumption of advancement and rebuts the presumption of a resulting trust. The intention of a father or person *in loco parentis* to make an advancement may be gathered from

> "contemporaneous acts, and even contemporaneous declarations of the parent, may amount to such evidence, has often been decided. Subsequent acts and declarations of the parent are not evidence to support the trust, although subsequent acts and declarations of the child may be so; but generally speaking we are to look to what was said and done at the time".[28]

11–17 A gift made by a mother to her child will not be an advancement for the purposes of the equitable doctrine,[29] nor apparently a gift made by a father to his illegitimate child, although it may be a valid one if it can be shown that the father was also *in loco parentis* to such a child. The presumption of advancement may, however, be rebutted where a contrary intention is evident.[30] For the equitable doctrine to apply, there must be a voluntary *inter vivos* transfer of property, and the transferor must be a father, or a person who is *in loco parentis* to a child.

Statutory Advancements

11–18 An advancement for the purposes of s.63 of the 1965 Act means a gift intended for establishing a child in a profession, vocation, trade or business, or for the education of a child to a standard higher than that provided by the transferor for any other of his or her children, or intended to make permanent provision for a child and this includes an advancement by way of portion or settlement, including any life or lesser interest and including property covenanted to be paid or settled, and will not be taken into account where the child is left a gift in the father's or mother's will or his or her share on intestacy. Where an advancement of real or personal property is made for any of the purposes in s.63, it will be taken as being made in satisfaction of a gift in a will, or share on intestacy, and will be brought into account in distributing the estate.[31] Advancements will be "reckoned" as part of the estate and their value will be "reckoned" at the date of the advancement.[32] If the advancement coming within the provisions of s.63 is equal to or greater than the share which a child is entitled to receive under the will or intestacy, the child, or indeed issue of the child, will be excluded from

---

[28] *Sidmouth v Sidmouth* (1840) 2 Beav. 447 at 455; see *O'Brien v Sheil* (1873) I.R. 7 Eq. 255.

[29] *Bennet v Bennet* (1873) I.R. 7 Eq. 255.

[30] See *O'Brien v Sheil* (1873) I.R. 7 Eq. 255; *Shephard v Cartwright* [1955] A.C. 431; *Marshall v Crutwell* (1875) L.R. 20 Eq. 328; *RF v MF* [1995] 2 I.L.R.M. 572.

[31] s.63(1).

[32] s.63(2).

taking his or her testate or intestate share in the estate.[33] Where, however, the advancement is less than the legacy or share on intestacy, the child will be entitled to receive in satisfaction of the legacy or share so much only of the estate as, when added to the advancement, is sufficient, as nearly as can be estimated, to make up the full amount of the share.[34] For the provisions of s.63 of the 1965 Act to come into play, the relationship of father or mother and child or issue of a child or a person to whom the testator or intestate stands *in loco parentis* must exist. It appears that the definition of child for advancement purposes under s.63 also includes non-marital, or non-civil partnership children by virtue of the Status of Children Act 1987. The onus of proving that an advancement was made to a child rests on the person so asserting unless the advancement has been expressed in writing by the deceased.[35] However, the provisions under s.63 will not become applicable where a contrary intention is expressed or appears from the circumstances of the case.[36]

Section 63(9) of the 1965 Act provides that nothing in the section shall affect any rule of law as to the satisfaction of portion debts by legacies.[37] While the purposes for giving an advancement under s.63 and that of a portion are similar, the prerequisites regarding relationships are different. For a portion, the relationship must be between father and child, including a person to whom the deceased was *in loco parentis* only: for the purposes of an advancement under s.63, the relationships may be father or mother of a child or issue of a child, or a person to whom the deceased was *in loco parentis*, including non-marital, or non-civil partnership children since the status of Children Act 1987. Similar to advancements, the value of the portion will must be shown to be substantial enough to carry out the intended purpose, i.e. to make permanent provision for a child. It is also expressly provided in s.63(8) that nothing in the section shall prevent a child retaining the advancement and abandoning his or her right to a share under the will or on intestacy. So, like satisfaction of a legacy by a portion, a child under s.63(8) may elect between the advancement and gift in the will or a share on intestacy.[38] **11–19**

Advancements to children of a testator may also be taken into account by the Court under s.117(1) of the 1965 Act when determining whether the testator **11–20**

[33] s.63(3).

[34] s.63(4).

[35] s.63(5).

[36] s.63(1).

[37] See Chapter 6 – The Ademption, Lapse and Modification of Gifts; Albert Keating, "The Effect of Portions and Advancements on Testamentary Gifts to Children, Part One" (2008) 13(2) C.P.L.J. 40; Albert Keating, "The Effect of Portions and Advancements on Testamentary Gifts to Children, Part Two" (2008) 13(3) C.P.L.J. 57.

[38] See Chapter 6 – The Ademption, Lapse and Modification of Gifts.

has fulfilled his or her moral duty to make proper provision for the applicant child by his or her will "or otherwise".[39] Section 117(1) provides that:

> "Where, on application by or on behalf of a child of a testator, the court is of opinion that the testator has failed in his moral duty to make proper provision for the child in accordance with his means, whether by his will or otherwise, the court may order that such provision shall be made for the child out of the estate as the court thinks just."

11–21 Even where an advancement within the meaning of s.63 of the 1965 Act is expressly excluded by a clause in a will, the value of it may yet be taken into account by the Court when determining whether a testator has fulfilled his or her moral duty to make proper provision for his or her children by will or otherwise under s.117(1). Although an advancement may be taken into account by the Court under s.117(1), a child of the testator may still succeed in having his or her share in the estate re-computed to his or her advantage, especially where the other beneficiaries are not children of the testator. It may also be mentioned here that advancements made by a father to his child under the equitable doctrine of advancement may be taken into account in an application under s.117(1) in the same way as portions, legacies and advancements covered by s.63.

[39] See Chapter 9 – The Moral Duty of Testators.

CHAPTER 12

EQUITABLE PROPERTY RIGHTS

INTRODUCTION

Equitable property rights may be acquired by a person who satisfies the prerequisites of the equitable doctrine of proprietary estoppel and, when established, may impinge on the succession rights of beneficiaries in a will or arising out of intestacies. The doctrine of proprietary estoppel was developed by equity to furnish a remedy to a person who acts on foot of assurances or representations made to him or her by an owner of land in relation to future property rights to that land, and the person to whom the assurances or representations were made suffers some form of detriment by relying on them.[1] While the element of detriment is an essential ingredient of proprietary estoppel, the fundamental principle that equity will prevent unconscionable conduct permeates all the elements of the concept.[2] In *Thorner v Major*[3] Lord Walker stated that the concept of proprietary estoppel is based on three fundamental elements: **12–01**

> "a representation or assurance made to the claimant; reliance on it by the claimant; and detriment to the claimant in consequence of his (reasonable) reliance".[4]

Lord Walker also stated that a claim based on the existence of a proprietary estoppel requires the claimant to prove a promise or assurance that he will acquire a proprietary interest in specified property. In *Naylor v Maher*[5] O'Keeffe J. referred with approval to the decision in *Thorner v Major* and the three fundamental elements for establishing a proprietary estoppel,

---

1 See *Greasley v Cooke* [1980] 1 W.L.R. 1306; *McDonagh v Denton*, Unreported, High Court, 15 April 2005; *Smyth v Halpin* [1997] 2 I.L.R.M. 38.

2 *Gillett v Holt* [2001] Ch. 210; see also *Greasley v Cooke* [1980] 1 W.L.R. 1306.

3 [2009] U.K.H.L. 18.

4 See also *Snell's Principles of Equity* 28th edn, (London: Sweet & Maxwell, 1982) referred to by Blayney J. in *Haughan v Rutledge* [1988] I.R. 295 at 300 and O'Sullivan J. in *McDonagh v Denton*, Unreported, High Court, 15 April 2005.

5 [2012] I.E.H.C. 408.

and also the judgment of Murphy J. in *McCarron v McCarron*[6] who, when commenting on the nature of detriment, stated that in

> "a suitable case it may well be argued that a plaintiff suffers as severe a loss or detriment by providing his own labours or services in relation to the lands of another and accordingly should equally qualify for recognition in equity".

The onus of proof rests on the claimant to show that all of the elements necessary for establishing a proprietary estoppel have been satisfied.

12–02 Equitable property rights may also be acquired by a new model constructive trust.[7] The courts may impose such a trust to prevent a person from acting in breach of good faith,[8] and may be compelled to hold property in trust for another where equity and good conscience demands it[9] and, in the case of unjust enrichment, where the restoration of a benefit can only be achieved by giving the plaintiff an interest in property, a new model constructive trust may be imposed as an equitable remedy "to restore to the plaintiff the benefit of which he has been deprived".[10]

12–03 In *Thorner v Major*[11] Lord Scott stated that he

> "would prefer to keep proprietary estoppel and constructive trust as distinct and separate remedies, to confine proprietary estoppel to cases where the representation, whether express or implied, on which the claimant has acted is unconditional and to address the cases where the representations are of future benefits, and subject to qualification on account of unforeseen future events, via the principles of remedial constructive trusts".[12]

He further stated that:

> "The possibility of a remedial constructive trust over property, created by the common intention or understanding of the parties regarding the property on the basis of which the claimant has acted to his detriment, has been recognised at least since *Gissing v Gissing* [1971] AC 886 (see particularly Lord Diplock, at p 905). The 'inheritance' cases, of which *Gillett v Holt* [2001] Ch. 210, *In re Basham* [1986] 1 W.L.R. 1498 and *Walton v Walton* (1994 C.A. unreported) and, of course, the present case are good examples, are, to my mind, more comfortably viewed as constructive trust cases."

---

6 Unreported, Supreme Court, 13 February 1997.

7 *Hussey v Palmer* [1972] 3 All E.R. 744; Judge Ronan Keane, *Equity and the Law of Trusts in the Republic of Ireland* (London: Butterworths, 1988); *Kelly v Cahill* [2001] 2 I.L.R.M. 205.

8 *N.A.D. v T.D.* [1985] I.L.R.M. 153.

9 *H.K.N. Invest OY v Incotrade PVT Ltd.* [1993] 3 I.R. 152.

10 Judge Ronan Keane, *Equity and the Law of Trusts in the Republic of Ireland* (London: Butterworths, 1988); *Kelly v Cahill* [2001] 2 I.L.R.M. 205; see See Albert Keating, "The Moral Duty and New Model Constructive Trusts" (2007) 12(3) C.P.L.J. 79.

11 [2009] U.K.H.L. 18.

12 See Albert Keating, "The Primacy of a Proprietary Estoppel or Remedial Constructive Trusts in Inheritance Cases" (2013) 18(1) C.P.L.J. 9.

Proprietary Estoppel

The effect of a proprietary estoppel may be immediate once the conditions for creating it have been established to the satisfaction of the Court. The conditions set out in *Snell's Principles of Equity*[13] for establishing a proprietary estoppel were adopted by Blayney J. in *Haughan v Rutledge*[14] and by O'Sullivan J. in *McDonagh v Denton*.[15] In *Snell,* four conditions must be satisfied for a proprietary estoppel to arise: **12–04**

(i) The person claiming must have incurred expenditure or otherwise have prejudiced himself or acted to his detriment;
(ii) The person relying on the concept must have acted as though he already owned a sufficient interest in the property to justify the expenditure or that he would obtain such an interest;
(iii) The person relying on the concept must have been encouraged by the other person's agent or predecessor in title;
(iv) No equity will arise if to enforce the right the claim would contravene some statute, or prevent the exercise of a statutory discretion or prevent or excuse the performance of a statutory duty.

In *Haughan v Rutledge*, Blayney J. thought that *Snell* provided: **12–05**

> "a correct statement of the law and that if these four conditions are satisfied then an equity will arise which can be enforced against the owner of the land."

Applying the *Snell* conditions to the facts in *Haughan v Rutledge,* Blayney J. found that the second and third conditions (expectation and encouragement) had not been satisfied because the plaintiffs spent money on the construction of a racetrack **12–06**

> "in the hope and expectation that the defendant would continue to make lettings of the track to them, but as that hope and expectation was not created or encouraged by the defendant, the plaintiffs have no claim which can be enforced by law or equity".[16]

In *McDonagh v Denton,* O'Sullivan J. found that all four of the *Snell* conditions were satisfied because: **12–07**

(1) the plaintiff had prejudiced himself or acted to his detriment in the sense indicated in contracting to sell the disputed plot of ground and thereby exposing himself to specific performance proceedings;
(2) he acted in the belief that he already owned a clear and transferable title in the property conveyed to him;

---

[13] (28th ed) (London: Sweet & Maxwell, 1982).
[14] [1988] I.R. 295 at 300.
[15] Unreported, High Court, O'Sullivan J., 15 April 2005.
[16] [1988] I.R. 295 at 300 at 303; see also *Ramsden v Dyson* (1866) L.R. 1 H.L. 129.

(3) he was encouraged in this belief by the silence of the defendants' solicitor when confronted with an assertion of the plaintiff's title; and (4) there was no bar to the equity.

12–08 As it would be unjust and inequitable if the defendants were able to assert their prior registered title to the disputed plot of ground as against the plaintiff, O'Sullivan J. restrained the defendants from interfering with the plaintiff's beneficial ownership. In *McDonagh v Denton,* O'Sullivan J. also referred to *Greasley v Cooke*[17] where Lord Denning M.R., when dealing with the question of detriment, said that "in many cases of proprietary estoppel there has been a money expenditure. But that is not a necessary element". It will be

> "sufficient if the party, to whom the assurance is given, acts on the faith of it, in such circumstances that it would be unjust and inequitable for the party making the assurance to go back on it: see *Moorgate Mercantile Company Limited v Twitchings* [1976] 1 Q.B. 225 and *Crabb v Arun District Council* [1976 1 Ch. 179, 188".

12–09 In *Smyth v Halpin,*[18] a claim was made against the deceased's estate by way of proprietary estoppel. The plaintiff built an extension to the deceased's cottage at his own expense following statements made by the deceased who was his father and owner of the cottage to the effect that he would be left the entire cottage after the death of his mother. The question for the Court to decide was

> "whether in the light of the authorities on proprietary estoppel the facts of this case give rise to a proper recourse to that principle and if so, whether the application of the principle of proprietary estoppel in this case actually requires that this court make an order directing a transfer of the reversionary interest. The granting of the latter remedy would effectively involve permitting the estoppel to be used as a sword and not merely a shield and would also be an exceptional inroad into the well established principle that equity will not complete an uncompleted gift".[19]

The plaintiff having successfully established all of the essential criteria necessary for a proprietary estoppel, Geoghegan J. ordered the transfer of the reversionary interest in the cottage to him.

12–10 In *Thorner v Major,*[20] Lord Walker, when considering whether the appellant acquired a proprietary estoppel in the deceased's estate, stated that the doctrine was based on three main elements:

(i) a representation or assurance made to the claimant;
(ii) a reliance on it by the claimant;

---

17 [1980] 1 W.L.R. 1306.
18 [1997] 2 I.L.R.M. 38.
19 *ibid* at 42-43.
20 [2009] U.K.H.L. 18.

(iii) a detriment to the claimant in consequence of his reasonable reliance on the representation or assurance.

In that case, the appellant David Thorner did substantial work without pay on the farm of his father's cousin Peter Thorner for nearly thirty years. The evidence showed that, from 1990 until his death in 2005, Peter encouraged David to believe that he would inherit the farm and that David acted in reliance on this assurance. Peter died without making a will. David claimed that, by reason of the assurances made by Peter and his reliance on them, Peter's estate was estopped from denying that he had acquired the beneficial interest in the farm. Lord Hoffmann, when dealing with the date when an assurance became unequivocal, said: **12–11**

> "I do not think that the judge was trying to pin point the date at which the assurance became unequivocal and I think it would be unrealistic in a case like this to try to do so. There was a close and ongoing daily relationship between the parties. Past events provide context and background for the interpretation of subsequent events and subsequent events throw retrospective light upon the meaning of past events. The owl of Minerva spreads its wings only with the falling of the dusk. The finding was that David reasonably relied upon the assurance from 1990, even if it required later events to confirm that it was reasonable for him to have done so."

While changes in the character or extent of the property in question are relevant to the relief which equity will provide, such changes will not exclude a remedy in proprietary estoppel once the property forming the subject matter of the proprietary estoppel can be identified. In relation to this matter, Lord Walker stated that: **12–12**

> "changes in the character or extent of the property in question are relevant to the relief which equity will provide but do not exclude such a remedy where there is still an identifiable property. In the present case, I see no reason to question the judge's decision that David was entitled to the beneficial interest in the farm and the farming business as they were at Peter's death."

Lord Neuberger thought that:

> "It would represent a regrettable and substantial emasculation of the beneficial principle of proprietary estoppel if it were artificially fettered so as to require the precise extent of the property the subject of the alleged estoppel to be strictly defined in every case."

The detriment occasioned by the claimant need not take the form of a money expenditure on the land as it "is not a necessary element". It will be

> "sufficient if the party, to whom the assurance is given, acts on the faith of it, in such circumstances that it would be unjust and inequitable for the party making the assurance to go back on it".

A plaintiff

> "suffers as severe a loss or detriment by providing his own labours or services in relation to the lands of another and accordingly should equally qualify for recognition in equity".

12–13 In *Naylor v Maher*[21] the plaintiff worked on the deceased's lands for minimal remuneration over a period of thirty years. The deceased during his lifetime gave assurances to the plaintiff that he would devise the lands to him. In fact the deceased made a will in 2005 under which he devised the lands to the plaintiff. He however made another will in 2006 by which he devised the lands to the defendant. The plaintiff submitted that the defendant was estopped from denying that the plaintiff had an interest in the lands. He also challenged the validity of the 2006 will leaving the lands to the defendant, but failed in his attempt to do so.

12–14 During the course of his judgment, O'Keeffe J. referred with approval to the House of Lords decision in *Thorner v Major*, especially the speeches of Lord Walker, Lord Hoffman and Lord Neuberger. When dealing with the issue of detriment, he accepted the *dicta* of Murphy J. in *McCarron v McCarron*[22] who stated that, in

> "a suitable case it may well be argued that a plaintiff suffers as severe a loss or detriment by providing his own labours or services in relation to the lands of another and accordingly should equally qualify for recognition in equity".

He found that the plaintiff's claim to the lands by way of proprietary estoppel was established.

12–15 In *Coyle v Finnegan and Finnegan*[23] Laffoy J. when referring to the three main elements which form the basis of the doctrine of proprietary estoppel in the context of the facts of the case, stated:

> "(a) In this case, unlike many cases, there was an express representation or assurance by the deceased to the plaintiff that, if the plaintiff assisted the deceased in running the farm, the deceased would leave the farm to the plaintiff in his will. Not only that, but, in accordance with that representation, the deceased made the August 1991 will to fulfil that assurance and he told the plaintiff that he had made it. Further, he told the plaintiff that, if he were to change his mind, he would tell the plaintiff. It was reasonable for the plaintiff to assume that, if the deceased did change his mind, he would recognise that the plaintiff should be rewarded for the assistance given by him to the deceased up to that time. Indeed, in view of the provision in the amount of €5,000 made by the deceased for the plaintiff in the August 2003 will, it is reasonable to assume that the deceased considered that it was fair and just that the plaintiff should be rewarded for the services he had rendered post-1991.
>
> (b) Between 1991 and 2000 the plaintiff acted in reliance on the assurances given

---

[21] [2012] I.E.H.C. 408.

[22] Unreported, Supreme Court, 13 February 1997.

[23] [2013] I.E.H.C. 463.

to him by the deceased both before and after August 1991, in particular, the assurance he gave him on the day following the making of the August 1991 will and the confirmation on the way home from the seminar on early retirement schemes.

(c) The plaintiff did suffer a detriment in consequence of his reasonable reliance on the deceased's assurances and such detriment was of the type envisaged by Murphy J. in *McCarron v McCarron*, in that the plaintiff suffered a loss or detriment by providing his own labours and services to assist the deceased in running the farm without any remuneration for his endeavours. As Murphy J. pointed out, that type of detriment should qualify for recognition in equity and, in my view, in this case it does."

She went on to state that "it would be unconscionable if the plaintiff was not recompensed for the labours and services he provided to the deceased over the period from 1991 to 2000" and that equity required that "the plaintiff be reasonably remunerated for the labours and services which he gave the deceased". She agreed with the suggestion in the judgment of Murphy J. in *McCarron v McCarron*: **12–16**

> "that a charge or lien on the lands for a sum equivalent to reasonable remuneration for services rendered might constitute adequate compensation, in my view, is particularly suitable to the situation here and meets the equity of this case. I propose adopting that course here. It remains to determine the measure of reasonable remuneration".

In *Coyle v Finnegan and Finnegan* Laffoy J. not only accepted the re-formulated elements for establishing the estoppel in *Thorner v Major*, but she also adopted the extended meaning given to the element of detriment by Murphy J. in his *obiter* statement in *McCarron v McCarron*.[24] **12–17**

A New Model Constructive Trust

A constructive trust has been described as a trust imposed by equity in order to satisfy the demands of justice and good conscience, without reference to any express or presumed intentions of the parties, and "in its traditional form, arises because of equity's refusal to countenance any form of fraud".[25] Such a trust was described by Lord Denning M.R. in *Hussey v Palmer*[26] as "a trust imposed by law whenever justice and good conscience require it" and as: **12–18**

> "a liberal process, founded on large principles of equity, to be applied in cases where the defendant cannot conscientiously keep the property for himself alone, but ought to allow another to have the property or a share in it".

---

24 See Albert Keating, "The Recognition of Services as a Detriment for Proprietary Estoppel" (2014) 19(1) C.P.L.J. 2.

25 Judge Ronan Keane, *Equity and the Law of Trusts in the Republic of Ireland* (London: Butterworths, 1988) p. 186, para.13.10.

26 [1972] 3 All E.R. 744 at 747; see also *Binions v Evans* [1972] 2 All E.R. 70; *Eves v Eves* [1975] 3 All E.R. 768.

12–19 He also described it as "an equitable remedy by which the court can enable an aggrieved party to obtain restitution".[27] This description of a "new model" constructive trust was later approved in a number of Irish decisions. In *N.A.D. v T.D.*[28] Barron J. thought that: "Its imposition is dependent upon the conduct of the person upon whom the trust is imposed and prevents him from acting in breach of good faith." In *H.K.N. Invest OY v Incotrade PVT Ltd.*[29] Costello J., referring to *Hussey v Palmer,* stated that the principle was that:

> "where a person who holds property in circumstances which in equity and good conscience should be held and enjoyed by another he will be compelled to hold the property in trust for another".

12–20 Judge Ronan Keane in his book *Equity and the Law of Trusts in the Republic of Ireland*[30] states that the constructive trust:

> "in its traditional form, arises because of equity's refusal to countenance any form of fraud: in this wider modern guise it is imposed by law whenever justice and good conscience require it".

12–21 He went on to say that it "is imposed by the court as an equitable remedy intended to restore the plaintiff the benefit of which he has been deprived".[31] In *Kelly v Cahill*[32] Barr J. referred with apparent approval to the judgments of Lord Denning M.R. in *Hussey v Palmer* and Costello J. in *H.K.N. Invest OY v Incotrade PVT Ltd* although he preferred the explanation of this type of trust by Judge Ronan Keane in *Equity and the Law of Trusts in the Republic of Ireland.* He was of the view that:

> "a 'new model' constructive trust of that nature the purpose of which is to prevent unjust enrichment is an equitable concept which deserves recognition in Irish law".

12–22 In *Hussey v Palmer*[33] the plaintiff sold her house and was invited to live with her daughter and son-in-law, the defendant in the case. As the defendant's house was too small for all three of them, he arranged for the building of an extension to the house to be used as a bedroom by the plaintiff. The plaintiff paid the costs of the extension to the builder. There was no arrangement between the plaintiff and the defendant for the repayment of the costs of the extension. Owing to differences later arising between the plaintiff and her daughter and the defendant, she went to live elsewhere. She needed money and asked the defendant for financial assistance but he refused. She then asked for the repayment of the money spent by her on the extension, but

27 See also Judge Ronan Keane, *Equity and the Law of Trusts in the Republic of Ireland* (London: Butterworths, 1988) p 186, para.13.10.

28 [1985] I.L.R.M. 153 at 160; see *Murray v Murray* [1996] 3 I.R. 25.

29 [1993] 3 I.R. 152 at 162.

30 Judge Ronan Keane, *Equity and the Law of Trusts in the Republic of Ireland* (London: Butterworths, 1988) p. 186, para.13.10.

31 *ibid* at p.187, para. 13.12.

32 [2001] 2 I.L.R.M. 205.

33 [1972] 3 All E.R. 744.

this request was refused also. She sued the defendant for the repayment of her money, alleging that there was a resulting trust. The case finally came before the Court of Appeal.

Lord Denning M.R., allowing the appeal, held that the trust in the case was more in the nature of a constructive trust and one that "is imposed by law whenever justice and good conscience require it". He described it as a liberal process: **12–23**

> "founded on large principles of equity, to be applied in cases where the defendant cannot conscientiously keep the property for himself alone, but ought to allow another to have the property or a share in it. The trust may arise at the outset when the property is acquired, or later on, as the circumstances may require".

In *Murray v Murray*[34] the plaintiff was the defendant's nephew, who had lived in a property belonging to the defendant. The plaintiff's mother, who had also lived in the property, had paid the mortgage instalments and most of the outgoings on the house. After the death of the plaintiff's mother, the plaintiff claimed that, as her nearest kin, he was entitled to the beneficial interest in the property and argued that, in the circumstances, it would be unconscionable for the defendant to rely on his legal title. Barron J. held: **12–24**

> "It is I think quite clear that the law will impose a constructive trust in all circumstances where it would be unjust and unconscionable not to do so."

Barron J. referred to *Hussey v Palmer* as an authority for the proposition that, where equity required it, "a debt could be secured by the device of a constructive trust on the property created by the money involved". The absence of any evidence that the plaintiff's mother intended to create a beneficial interest as a result of her actions precluded Barron J from holding that a resulting trust arose, so he therefore made use of the more flexible constructive trust to provide a remedy. **12–25**

In *Kelly v Cahill*[35] the testator devised all of his property to his wife and brother as joint tenants for life, with remainder to trustees in trust for his nephew. He died without revoking his will. His brother died two years later. Two years before his death, he attended his solicitor and informed him that he no longer wished to benefit his nephew and wished instead to leave all of his property to his wife absolutely without any remainder provision. However, instead of altering his will, a deed of transfer was prepared which transferred the testator's registered lands from his sole ownership to that of himself and his wife. By inadvertence, certain of the registered lands were not included in the transfer deed. As the testator had not revoked his will, a question arose as to whether the registered lands excluded through inadvertence from the deed of transfer passed under the terms of the will or whether, in the light **12–26**

[34] [1996] 3 I.R. 25.
[35] [2001] 2 I.L.R.M. 205.

of the circumstances, the nephew named as remainderman in the will held the lands as a constructive trustee for the testator's widow. Barr J. found that the net issue to be addressed was whether a constructive trust arose in relation to and comprising the lands that were not transferred in the way intended by the testator.

12–27 In his judgment, Barr J. referred to the concept of the new model constructive trust as explained by Judge Ronan Keane in his book *Equity and the Law of Trusts in the Republic of Ireland*,[36] and as described by Lord Denning M.R. in *Hussey v Palmer*,[37] but he adopted the assessment of the new model constructive trust by Judge Keane. In relation to such trusts, Keane thought:

> "the principle of unjust enrichment requires the restoration by the defendant to the plaintiff of a benefit which it would be unjust for him to retain. Sometimes this can be done by a simple award of money, e.g., the refund of money paid under a mistake of fact. But sometimes the restoration of the benefit can only be achieved by giving the plaintiff an interest in property. Thus, the constructive trust is imposed by the court as an equitable remedy intended to restore to the plaintiff the benefit of which he has been deprived."

12–28 The "kernel of the question" was whether the evidence established "a clear, positive intention on the part of the testator that his wife should inherit all of his property on his death." The "essential element" was that the testator had changed his mind regarding the disposition of his estate after his death and he took appropriate steps to give effect to that intention. That having been established to the satisfaction of the Court, it followed that "justice and good conscience" required that the nephew should not be allowed to inherit any part of the testator's property and that his interest in remainder under the will should be deemed a constructive trust in favour of the testator's widow. Barr J. concluded by saying that:

> "a new model constructive trust of that nature the purpose of which is to prevent unjust enrichment is an equitable concept which deserves recognition in Irish law".

12–29 In *In the Matter of Varko Limited and In the Matter of an Application by the Executors of Charlotte McCoy Deceased Pursuant to Section 21(10) of the Companies Act 1963*,[38] Gilligan J., having referred to the foregoing Irish and English authorities, applied the doctrine of a new model constructive trust to the facts of the case before him as follows:

> "It is the case at the point in time when the loan was drawn down from First Active and Mrs. McCoy's home was mortgaged that her son, James McCoy was a joint tenant by the consent of the late Charlotte McCoy but all the surrounding circumstances including the ongoing behaviour of James McCoy, assist in demonstrating the type of person that he is and in the absence of any denial

---

[36] Judge Ronan Keane, *Equity and the Law of Trusts in the Republic of Ireland* (London: Butterworths, 1988) pp. 186-187.

[37] [1972] 3 All E.R. 744.

[38] [2012] I.E.H.C. 278.

> as regards the facts contended for in the affidavit of Charlotte McCoy in the proceedings bearing Record No. 2010 8282P that led to judgment being obtained against James McCoy and the company and the various other affidavits as referred to herein, the applicants discharge the onus of satisfying this Court that on the balance of probabilities the manner in which the mortgage of Mrs. McCoy's home in Kinsale was obtained from First Active Building Society was unconscionable and that unfair advantage was taken of the late Mrs. McCoy and that the demands of justice and good conscience dictate that as regards the sum of €200,000.00 being part of the aforesaid mortgage, such said sum was at all material times in the circumstances as herein as outlined held by the company Varko Limited in trust for the late Charlotte McCoy and on her death forms part of her estate and is not available for distribution in the voluntary winding up of the company."

The Relationship between Proprietary Estoppel and Remedial Constructive Trusts

In *Thorner v Major*[39] Lord Scott considered the relationship between a proprietary estoppel and constructive trust and their respective roles in providing remedies where representations about future property interests had been made and relied on. He stated that: **12–30**

> "There are many cases in which the representations relied on relate to the acquisition by the representee of an immediate, or more or less immediate, interest in the property in question. In these cases a proprietary estoppel is the obvious remedy. The representor is estopped from denying that the representee has the proprietary interest that was promised by the representation in question."

He then went on to illustrate this by reference to past decisions of the courts where proprietary estoppel was shown to be the more appropriate remedy. The decision in *Crabb v Arun District Council*[40] seemed to him a clear example of such a case. In that case, the council had represented that Crabb would be entitled to have access to the private road at gateway B and had confirmed that representation by erecting gateposts and a gate across the gateway. Once Crabb, in reliance on that representation, had acted to his detriment in selling off a portion of his land so that his only means of access to and egress from his retained land was via gateway B, it was too late for the council to change its mind. The council was estopped from denying that Crabb had the necessary access rights. Lord Scott also cited *Ramsden v Dyson*[41] and stated that: **12–31**

> "In cases where the owner of land stands by and allows a neighbour to build over the mutual boundary, representing either expressly or impliedly that the building owner is entitled to do so, the owner may be estopped from subsequently asserting his title to the encroached upon land. This, too, seems to me straightforward proprietary estoppel. There are many other examples of decided cases where representations acted on by the representee have led to the representor being

---

[39] [2009] U.K.H.L. 18.

[40] [1976] 1 Ch. 179, 188; [1975] 3 All E.R. 865.

[41] (1866) L.R. 1 H.L. 129.

estopped from denying that the representee had the proprietary interest in the representor's land that the representation had suggested. Constructive trust, in my opinion, has nothing to offer to cases of this sort."

But in cases where the relevant representation has related to inheritance prospects, Lord Scott found it difficult

"to square with the principles of proprietary estoppel established by the *Ramsden v Dyson* and *Crabb v Arun District Council* line of cases and, for my part, I find them made easier to understand as constructive trust cases".

He preferred

"to keep proprietary estoppel and constructive trust as distinct and separate remedies, to confine proprietary estoppel to cases where the representation, whether express or implied, on which the claimant has acted is unconditional and to address the cases where the representations are of future benefits, and subject to qualification on account of unforeseen future events, via the principles of remedial constructive trusts".

12–32 *Thorner v Major* was, according to Lord Scott, also a good example of this, and may be "more comfortably" viewed as a constructive trust case. He thought that the facts in *Thorner v Major* would have justified relief by remedial constructive trust. He then went on to identify former decisions of the courts where the remedial constructive trust was held to be the more appropriate remedy. He said:

"The possibility of a remedial constructive trust over property, created by the common intention or understanding of the parties regarding the property on the basis of which the claimant has acted to his detriment, has been recognised at least since *Gissing v Gissing* [1971] AC 886 (see particularly Lord Diplock, at p 905)."[42]

He concluded:

"But in my judgment, at all events where the belief is that A is going to be given a right in the future, it is properly to be regarded as giving rise to a species of constructive trust, which is the concept employed by a court of equity to prevent a person from relying on his legal rights where it would be unconscionable for him to do so."

12–33 According to Lord Scott, the imposition of a remedial constructive trust is more appropriate in inheritance cases involving unconscionable behaviour regarding assurances which have future effect than a proprietary estoppel, which is more suitable for dealing with immediate circumstances. In *Naylor v Maher,* O'Keeffe J. made no such distinction between proprietary estoppel and remedial constructive trusts as he was satisfied that a proprietary estoppel, though it may be said of the inheritable variety, existed following the persuasive authority of *Thorner v Major*, and regarding detriment, also

[42] See also *Gillett v Holt* [2001] Ch. 210, *In Re Basham* [1986] 1 W.L.R. 1498.

the *dicta* of Murphy J. in *McCarron v McCarron*. It is interesting to note that, in *Naylor v Maher,* the plaintiff further submitted if the Court found that the plaintiff had not established a claim in proprietary estoppel that the defendant held the lands on a constructive trust for the plaintiff, and he based this submission for the existence of a remedial constructive trust on the conclusions of Lord Scott in *Thorner v Major*. However, no such distinction is made between inheritance cases and those with "immediate circumstances" by the Irish courts when determining the existence of a proprietary estoppel or, indeed, when imposing a new model constructive trust "in all circumstances where it would be unjust and unconscionable not to do so".

CHAPTER 13

APPLICATIONS FOR GRANTS OF PROBATE

INTRODUCTION

Executors are the only persons entitled to apply for a grant of probate. An executor's entitlement to apply for a grant of probate derives from the will. In the case of all other grants, the applicant's entitlement to apply for a grant of representation will be determined by Ord.79 of the Rules of the Superior Courts 1986 (the "1986 Rules"). Where the executors decide to apply for a grant of probate, the necessary proofs must be prepared and lodged in the Probate Office or a District Probate Registry.[1] The following are the essential proofs that must be submitted by the executors when applying for a grant of probate: **13–01**

1. Form S1 (postal application form);
2. The will (and codicils, if any);
3. A certified copy of the will;
4. Oath of executor;
5. A copy oath of executor;
6. The Inland Revenue Affidavit (Form CA 24 (2010 edition) where the deceased died after 5 December 2001 or Form CA24 (2000 edition) where the deceased died before 5 December 2001); and
7. Death certificate of the testator.

Additional proofs may consist of an affidavit of an attesting witness, affidavit of plight and condition, affidavit of mental capacity of a testator by his **13–02**

[1] See Chapter 25 – Probate Precedents; Albert Keating, *Irish Probate Precedents Service* (Dublin: Round Hall, 2009); Albert Keating, *Keating on Probate* (4th ed) (Dublin: Round Hall, 2011); Albert Keating, *First Supplement to the Fourth Edition of Keating on Probate* (Dublin: Thomson Round Hall, 2013).

medical practitioner or an affidavit of mental capacity of a testator by his solicitor.[2] Applications for grants may be made to the Seat Office division of the Probate Office either personally or through town agents, pursuant to Ord.79 r.3 of the 1986 Rules, or a District Probate Registry within whose area the deceased testator had a fixed place of abode at the time of his death.[3]

13–03 The Seat Office will now accept a photocopy of the original oath of executor or administrator which replaces the need for a formal notice of application for a grant. Photostat copies of wills will also be acceptable for grants of probate or letters of administration with the will annexed but, where the original will is not totally legible, a typewritten version of the original must be made, and all copy wills must be certified by the solicitors for the applicant as being a true copy of the original will.

13–04 Where a will contains charitable bequests a charitable bequest form setting out the details of the bequest should be lodged with the papers when applying for a grant. These forms are available in the Seat Office of the Probate Office. Copies of vouching documents like bank statements and the like are not required to be lodged with the copy Schedule of Assets. Where, however, a question on the Inland Revenue Affidavit CA24 is answered by stating "see attached", a copy of the attached document should be lodged with the other proofs. The copy Schedule of Assets should be certified by the solicitor for the applicant to be a true copy of the original. Corrective affidavits should also not be lodged with the application for a grant as they only become relevant after a grant has issued. The grant of probate made by the Probate Office or a District Probate Registry is known as a grant in common form. An official copy of a grant of probate or letters of administration will be sufficient evidence of such grant.

Executors

13–05 A person may be appointed an executor by simply naming him or her in the will as executor. There must, however, be no ambiguity surrounding the appointment of an executor, and where there is some doubt surrounding his or her identity, sufficient evidence may have to be adduced establishing his or her true identity to the satisfaction of the court. Where, for instance, a surname is omitted through inadvertence, evidence of identity has to be adduced.[4]

13–06 The Succession Act 1965 (the "1965 Act") also allows for the appointment of

[2] See Albert Keating, *Irish Probate Precedents Service* (Dublin: Round Hall, 2009); Albert Keating, *Keating on Probate* (4th ed) (Dublin: Round Hall, 2011); Albert Keating, *First Supplement to the Fourth Edition of Keating on Probate* (Dublin: Thomson Round Hall, 2013).

[3] See Ord. 80 of the Rules of the Superior Courts 1986.

[4] See *Re Kehoe* [1940] Ir. Jur. Rep. 35.

a trust corporation as sole executor or jointly with others. Where a will and codicil appoint two different executors and the executor appointed by the will refuses or fails to act, the executor appointed by the codicil may apply for probate of the will and codicil. The appointment of executors by a subsequent codicil does not necessarily revoke the appointment of executors by the will: executors appointed by subsequent codicil are treated as additional to those named in the will, and not substitutive. A presumption of substitution may arise where the executor appointed in the subsequent codicil is described as sole executor.[5] A testator may provide for the substitution of an executor on a specified event occurring, for instance, in the event of an executor predeceasing him or renouncing. Where no executor is appointed but a beneficiary in the will is given functions that would normally be carried out by an executor, he or she may be viewed as an executor *according to the tenor*, and may apply for a grant of probate.

Applicants for Grants of Probate

The applicant for a grant of probate may be a sole executor, or may be one of two executors or a trust corporation. Where a trust corporation is the applicant for a grant, the person nominated by the trust corporation to apply for a grant must swear an affidavit exhibiting the resolution of the trust corporation appointing him or her to apply for the grant, and that affidavit must be included in the proofs when applying for the grant.[6] Where a sole or surviving executor renounces his entitlement to apply for a grant of probate, that will be the end of the line of applicants for a grant of probate, and the next person entitled to apply for a grant will be determined by the 1986 Rules and may apply for a grant of letters of administration with the will annexed, and not a grant of probate.[7] **13–07**

Essential Proofs

Form S1 (postal application form) must be lodged with all applications submitted by post: **13–08**

1. The original will (and codicils, if any);
2. Certified copy of will (and codicils, if any);
3. Oath of the executor;
4. Copy oath of executor;
5. Inland Revenue Affidavit (CA 24 (2010 edition) for deaths after 5 December 2001 and CA24 (2000 edition) where the deceased died before 5 December 2001);

[5] See *Re McCarthy* [1941] Ir. Jur. Rep. 31.

[6] Ord.79, rr.17, 18 and 19 of the Rules of the Superior Courts 1986.

[7] See Chapter 14 – Applications for Grants of Letters of Administration with Will Annexed.

6. Death certificate of the testator;
7. Charitable bequest form (A form PAS3 is required where there are charitable bequests in the will relating to Irish charities. Money bequeathed for Masses should be inserted. Exact wording as per will must be inserted).

Original Will (and Codicils, if any) and Certified Copies

13–09 A photocopy of a will or codicil or typed engrossment must be certified by a solicitor to be a true copy. Every will, or copy of a will, exhibited in the oath of the executor, must be marked by the executor and by the person before whom it is sworn. Any such marking is usually made on the back of the will so as not to interfere with the will or the attestation of it. Copies of wills must be written in a legible hand, or printed, typewritten or photocopied, subject to the directions of the probate officer. If there is no attestation clause in a will submitted for probate or letters of administration with the will annexed, or if the attestation clause is insufficient, an affidavit from at least one of the attesting witnesses will be required confirming that the provisions of the 1965 Act regarding the execution of wills have been complied with, and a note signed by the probate officer will be made on the copy of the will to the effect that such an affidavit has been filed. The rules laid down by Ord. 40 of the 1986 Rules for the preparation of affidavits generally will also apply to affidavits required filing or using in the Probate Office. In every case where an affidavit is made by an attesting witness to a will for the purpose of proving due execution, that witness must depose as to the mode in which the will of the testator was executed and attested. Where the affidavit evidence of an attesting witness discloses that the provisions of the 1965 Act dealing with due execution have not been satisfied, the probate officer may refuse to issue a grant of probate of the will. If it transpires that both attesting witnesses are dead or, for some other reason, no affidavit can be obtained from either of them, other persons who were present at the execution of the will may instead swear an affidavit deposing to the facts surrounding the execution of the will. As a last resort, evidence on affidavit may be procured of the handwriting of the deceased testator and of the attesting witnesses which may be sufficient as a substitute to raise the presumption of due execution. Where, however, the probate officer is not satisfied with the affidavit evidence of the circumstances surrounding the execution of the will, he or she may require that an order of the Court be sought to determine the formal validity of the will. The probate officer will not allow probate of the will or letters of administration with the will annexed of any blind or illiterate person to issue unless he or she is satisfied, by evidence on affidavit, that the will was read over to the testator before its execution or that the testator had at the time knowledge of its contents. Where a will is written in a language other than Irish or English, a translation must be provided and the probate officer may make a grant of probate of the will "in terms of a translation" in either the Irish or English language.

Where interlineations or other alterations appear on the face of the will, affidavit evidence may be required to show that they appeared on the will before its execution, unless such interlineations or alterations were themselves duly executed by the testator and attesting witnesses or were recited in or identified by the attestation clause. Alterations that are deemed to be of "small importance" will be acceptable once verified by the initials of the attesting witnesses. An interlineation or other alteration made after the execution of a will may be invalid unless it is duly executed in the manner required by the 1965 Act, or by re-execution of the will, or by a subsequent codicil referring to it. Alterations in the form of erasures or obliterations are also invalid unless they were made prior to the execution of the will; or were duly executed by the testator and witnesses after its execution; or were rendered valid by re-execution of the will by the testator or by a subsequent codicil referring to them. However, if no satisfactory evidence is forthcoming as to the time when such erasures were made and the words appear not to be totally erased or obliterated, and can be ascertained, they must form part of probate. Any significant erasure or obliteration of words must be verified by affidavit evidence. **13–10**

Where documents are incorporated by reference to them in the will, for instance, where a reference is made to a deed, memorandum, inventory or other instrument, and a question arises as to whether they are to form part of the probate of the will, such documents must be produced, and if they are not produced, their absence must be accounted for. If it transpires that the document referred to in the will was not in existence at the time the will was executed, it will not be admitted to probate with the will. Where it appears that the will itself or some document referred to by the will is totally or partially written in pencil, it must be copied and the original pages or sheets containing the pencil writing must be written in red ink and filed in the Probate Office. Where it appears from marks or otherwise made on the face of the will that a paper or document was attached to it, such paper or document must be produced and, if not produced, its absence must be accounted for. **13–11**

Oath of Executor

The oath of the executor must be subscribed and sworn as an affidavit and filed in the Probate Office. Where a trust corporation is one of the executors, the official appointed by the trust corporation to act on its behalf may swear an affidavit exhibiting the resolution of the trust corporation appointing him to act on its behalf and it must be included in the application for the grant. Every will or copy of a will exhibited in the oath of executor must be marked by the executor and by the person before whom the oath is sworn, and any **13–12** such marking must be made on the back of the will so as to distinguish it from the will itself and the attestation clause. The probate officer may, where he or she deems it necessary, require further proof of the identity of the deceased or of the party applying for the grant, in addition to the information contained in the oath. The correct name and address of the executor must appear in the oath and, where a misspelled version appears in the will, this must be corrected by the oath–for instance, if the executor's name is John Browne and he is named "John Brown" in the will. It may also be required to elaborate on a description given in the will, for instance, the testator may appoint "my wife" as executrix and, if that is the case, the oath should state that the executrix is the lawful wife of the deceased testator. If the executor has changed his name by deed poll since the time of his appointment by the will, the deed poll should be referred to and produced. It may happen that an executrix appointed by the will may have married since the death of the testator and, if that is the case, the executrix may have to depose as to her former and present name and description. If a person is appointed executor of the will by a subsequent codicil, both the will and codicil have to be referred to when ascertaining his appointment, name and address. The name, address and description of the deceased testator must also appear in the oath and, where the deceased used an alias when making his will, his correct name and alias must be stated in the oath. Where an alias was used for a particular reason, for instance, for the purposes of acquiring property that is now part of his estate, the alias should be added to his correct name. The address and description of the deceased must appear also, and if the deceased lived at a different address from that mentioned in the will, the oath should show that he or she formerly lived at the address stated in the will. Where a foreign address of the testator appears in the will, a statement should be included in the oath to the effect that the deceased died domiciled in Ireland. The description of the deceased testator must be included and, strictly speaking, if he or she changed his or her occupation since the date of the will, this must be referred to in the oath of the executor.

13–13 The relationship between the executor and the deceased testator, if one exists, must appear in the oath. If the relationship is inconsistent with that stated in the will, the correct relationship should appear in the oath. In the case of children, where the relationship is other than legitimate, the nature of the relationship should be stated: legitimated and adopted children should be stated as such, and in the case of non-marital children, they may be described as the natural son or daughter of the testator. Where the testator describes the executor as "my son" in his will and if the executor is the non-marital, or non-civil partnership son of the testator, he may be described as the natural son of the testator in the oath.

13–14 The oath must also confirm that the testator did not "intermarry" (or enter a civil partnership) after the making of his will. The main reason for including this statement in the oath is that, if the testator had married (or entered into a civil partnership) after the making of his will, the subsequent marriage (or civil partnership) would have revoked his will, unless it was established that his will was made in contemplation of that marriage (or civil partnership). Any doubt on the matter may have to be resolved by an application to the court.

For instance, in *In the Estate of Baker*[8] the testator made a will in 1951 in which he devised and bequeathed all his real and personal estate to Margaret Gaffrey. In 1954, the testator married Margaret Gaffrey. He died in 1983 and was survived by his wife, Margaret Gaffrey. The executor appointed by the 1951 will applied to the court claiming that the deceased's will was not revoked by his marriage to Margaret Gaffrey as it was made in contemplation of his marriage to her. Gannon J., in the course of his judgment, said: **13–15**

> "There is nothing in the evidence on this application which would enable a court to draw an inference of probability that the will was made in contemplation of any particular marriage. Had the will been made in contemplation of some marriage, it is probable that the person taking the instructions for the making of the will would have received some intimation of that nature and could give evidence to that effect."

Where the testator did "intermarry" (or enter a civil partnership) after making a will, the subsequent marriage (or civil partnership) will revoke the will unless it is established that it was made in contemplation of that marriage (or civil partnership) but where there is some doubt in relation to this, the executor may have to seek an order of the court to ascertain the true position, and provide sufficient evidence that the will was in fact made in contemplation of that marriage (or civil partnership).[9] **13–16**

The precise date of death of the testator must be stated in the oath. A duly authenticated death certificate must be produced to provide evidence of death. The place of death should also be included in the oath. Where leave of the court has been obtained to swear death, the oath should state that the deceased died on or since the date he or she was last known to be alive, and the particulars of the court order must also be given. Where there is no death certificate or sufficient alternative evidence of death, an order may have to be sought from the court presuming the death of the testator. For the court to presume the death of a testator, it must first be established that seven years have elapsed since the testator was last heard of. It must further be established that persons who would normally have heard of him have not heard of him over the period of seven years. Proper inquiries and investigations must also be carried out in the place where the testator's residence was located, and if inquiries there show that he or she disappeared without any trace, death may be presumed by the court.[10] Inquiries may **13–17**

8 [1985] I.R. 101.

9 See *In the Estate of Fleming* [1987] I.L.R.M. 638; Chapter 4 – The Revocation and Revival of Wills.

10 See *In the Goods of Freytag* (1909) 43 I.L.T.R. 116; *In the Goods of Inkerman Brown* (1932) 36 I.L.T.R. 173; *In the Goods of Doherty* [1961] I.R. 219.

include the placing of advertisements in newspapers circulating at or near the place where the testator was last known to reside, or at the place he or she was last heard of or might be found. However, in certain cases, for instance, "disappearance" cases, leave may be sought to presume death even though less than seven years have elapsed. In *In the Goods of Matthews*[11] the Court gave leave to presume death after three years had elapsed from the disappearance of the testator. The presiding judge held that "very ample" inquiries had been carried out. Thus the thoroughness of inquiries and the circumstances surrounding the disappearance may allow the court to give leave to presume death within a shorter period of time. In *In the Goods of Griffin*[12] even judicial knowledge of the circumstances giving rise to the presumption was taken into account in presuming the death of the deceased: the trial judge had knowledge of the facts surrounding the case from a case that he himself had heard prior to the application to presume death by the widow of the deceased. A coroner's interim death certificate will be accepted where the final death certificate is not yet issued.

13–18 The oath must contain a statement of gross value of the estate of the testator without any deductions for debts. This gross value appearing in the oath should be that of current value and not necessarily that appearing in the Inland Revenue Affidavit.

13–19 Where there are two executors appointed by the will and one of them wishes to renounce his office, he or she must sign a renunciation form and this must be referred to and exhibited in the oath by the remaining executor who is applying for the grant of probate. An executor who renounces his right to probate will cease to be an executor and his right of representation will devolve as if that person had not been appointed executor by the testator. An executor who renounces his office will not be allowed to obtain representation to the same deceased in another character; for instance, he or she will also lose his entitlement to apply for a grant of letters of administration with the will annexed, unless the court orders otherwise. Where probate is granted to one or two executors, all powers conferred on executors by the 1965 Act or otherwise by law may be exercised by the executors who were granted probate or by the survivor of them. An executor who has renounced may be permitted to withdraw his renunciation to apply for a grant, and the grant will take effect without prejudice to any dealings by prior personal representatives who had previously taken out representation, and a memorandum of the subsequent probate will be endorsed on the original grant. Otherwise a renunciation is final after the date of filing.

[11] [1898] P. 143.

[12] (1931) 65 I.L.T.R. 108.

OATH OF EXECUTOR

THE HIGH COURT
PROBATE

The Probate Office/The District Probate Registry at

In the estate of (name of testator) late of (address) deceased.

I, (name of executor) of (address) aged eighteen years and upwards, make oath and say that I believe the paper writing hereto annexed, and marked by me, to contain the true and original last will [*or* last will with codicils] of (name of testator) late of [address and description] deceased; that same was made by the said after attaining the age of eighteen years, and that he or she did not intermarry with any person after the making of same; that I am the [state relationship; if not a blood relation, insert *stranger in blood*] of the said (name of testator) and the sole executor named in the said will; that I will faithfully administer the estate of the said testator, by paying his just debts and the legacies bequeathed by his said will [*or* will and codicils], so far as the same shall thereto extend and the law bind me; that I will exhibit a true inventory of the said estate, and render a true account thereof, whenever required by law so to do; that the testator died at on the day of [*where application is made in District Probate Registry add*] and that the testator has at the time of his death a fixed place of abode at within the district of and that the whole of the estate which devolves on and vests in his legal personal representative amounts in value to [*the gross assets, without any deductions for debts*] and no more, to the best of my knowledge, information and belief.

Sworn, &c.

INLAND REVENUE AFFIDAVIT

Before an application for a grant of probate can be made, an Inland Revenue Affidavit must be prepared by the executor setting out the particulars and assets of the estate of the deceased testator. The Inland Revenue Affidavit must be sent directly to the Probate Office (or a District Probate Registry) with the other proofs. The Affidavit must be submitted in duplicate and, once the grant has issued, one of the duplicates must be forwarded to the Revenue Commissioners with a copy of the will.[13] The Finance Act 2010 introduced significant changes to the Capital Acquisitions Tax Consolidated Act 2003. The Act removes the requirement for certification of the Inland Revenue Affidavit CA24 (2010 edition) by the Revenue Commissioners before the issue of a grant of probate or letters of administration with will annexed or intestate. It introduces a 'pay and file' regime for gift and inheritance tax. It abolishes secondary accountability for personal representatives of a deceased person,thereby ending the process and compliance costs of issuing personal clearance certificates. Forms CA11, CA44, and IT10 will no longer be issued **13–20**

[13] s.147 of the Finance Act 2010.

by the Revenue Commissioners. From 14 June 2010, it is no longer required to present an Inland Revenue Affidavit to the Revenue Commissioners for certification prior to an application for a grant to the Probate Office or a District Probate Registry. The Inland Revenue Affidavit may be submitted in duplicate directly to the Probate Office or a District Probate Registry, together with all of the other necessary proofs required for a grant.

13–21 Form CA24 (2010 edition) is the appropriate form of the Inland Revenue Affidavit to use where the deceased died on or after 5 December 2001. The form must be completed by computer and two copies must be printed for swearing prior to an application for a grant to the Probate Office or a District Probate Registry. The printed copies of Form CA24 must be legible otherwise they will not be accepted. Printed copies that are completed manually will also not be accepted. Photocopies will not be sufficient substitutes for the printed version. The font used to complete Form CA24 must not be altered. Both affidavits must be submitted to the Probate Office or the appropriate District Probate Registry. The Revenue Commissioners will receive all of the relevant data from either the Probate Office or district Probate Registry. Form CA24 (2000 edition) may also be downloaded and completed on screen and should be used only for applications for grants where the deceased died before 5 December 2001. There are no changes to the form and procedures in respect of applications for grants prior to 5 December 2001. The values of the estate existing at death must be entered in the Inland Revenue Affidavit.

13–22 Any copies of vouching documents should not be included, except where any question is answered by stating "see attached". A copy of "attached" document should be lodged. The downloaded version of CA24 must be completed on computer. The hard copy version must be completed in blue pen. Both copies must be identical. A schedule of lands (CA6 or Part 6 of CA24, depending on version) is required for deaths before 5 December 2001 if there is property in the estate. Date of death value and tenure must be inserted.

Corrective Inland Revenue Affidavits

13–23 Where any material error or omission was made in the Inland Revenue Affidavit, the executor may be required to swear a further affidavit correcting the error or omission. Where additional assets of the deceased are discovered after the grant has issued, a corrective affidavit must be prepared taking account of those assets. The corrective affidavit must be prepared in duplicate and sent to the Probate Office or District Probate Registry, and from there a copy will be sent to the Revenue Commissioners. Form CA26 (2010 edition) may be downloaded and completed on screen, and may be used only where the deceased died on or after 5 December 2001. Form CA26 may also be downloaded and completed on screen where the deceased died before 5 December 2001.

The same type of affidavit may become necessary on a re-evaluation of assets already taken into account. An original and copy of the affidavit must be prepared and approved by the Revenue Commissioners. The original and copy affidavit must then be produced in the Probate Office or the District Probate Registry from which the grant issued. Additional probate fees may become payable as a result of a reassessment and either the Probate Officer or District Probate Registrar will sign the certificate on the original affidavit and retain the copy. The original affidavit must be returned to the Revenue Commissioners together with payment of any additional tax. **13–24**

If the deceased died on or after 5 December 2001, the following items should be lodged in the Probate Office: **13–25**

1. Corrective affidavit (two originals and one copy);
2. Original grant of representation;
3. Additional fees (if relevant). This will apply if the net value of the estate has increased to such an extent that additional fees would be payable;
4. Bond (if relevant). This will apply in administration cases where the value of the estate has increased. The penal sum in the new bond must be for double the gross additional assets;
5. A letter confirming the grantee(s) is/are still alive is required only if more than six months have elapsed since the grantee(s) signed the corrective affidavit.

When the Probate Office has assessed the above papers (and assuming no queries arise), the probate officer will sign the certificate at the foot of the corrective affidavit and will forward same to the Revenue Commissioners. A copy will be returned to the solicitors. **13–26**

If the deceased died before 5 December 2001, the following proofs must be lodged in the Probate Office: **13–27**

1. Corrective affidavit together with a copy (check www.revenue.ie for the appropriate form); and
2. Proofs referred to at 2, 3, 4, and 5 above.

The Probate Office will confirm the amount of additional fees payable, and the certificate on the original corrective affidavit will be signed by the probate officer (or district probate registrar). The copy affidavit will be retained by the Probate Office and the original affidavit will be returned to solicitors for onward transmission to the Revenue Commissioners.[14] **13–28**

---

[14] Probate Office Update: 6 July 2012.

Death Certificate

13–29 Every application for a grant of probate must include the death certificate of the deceased testator among the documents required for obtaining a grant of probate. However, a coroner's interim death certificate will be accepted where the final death certificate is not yet issued. In the absence of a death certificate, other evidence which tends towards proving that the testator was buried may be acceptable in place of a death certificate, for instance, a photograph of a headstone or tombstone or the production of mortuary cards.

Unadministered and Double Probate

13–30 Where a grant of probate has been made to one of two executors with a power reserved to the other executor to apply for a grant, a grant of unadministered probate may be made on the death of the proving executor to the surviving executor. When a grant of probate is made to one of two executors and a right is reserved to the other executor also to apply for a grant, where that other executor applies for a grant during the lifetime of the executor to whom probate was first granted, he or she will be issued with a grant known as a double probate. Until a grant of double probate is made, the executor to whom the original probate was granted may exercise all the powers of a personal representative. An instance of a double probate may arise where one of two executors applies for and obtains a grant of probate but the other does not wish to renounce nor is cited to apply or renounce. A power will be reserved to him later to apply for a grant of double probate.

CHAPTER 14

APPLICATIONS FOR GRANTS OF LETTERS OF ADMINISTRATION WITH WILL ANNEXED

INTRODUCTION

Where a testator fails to appoint an executor, or the appointment of an executor fails by his or her predecease or renunciation, or he or she is cleared off as a result of a citation or has been otherwise removed, the person entitled under Ord.79, r.5(6) of the Rules of the Superior Court 1986 (the "1986 Rules") may apply for a grant of letters of administration with the will annexed. Order 79, r.5(6) of the 1986 Rules sets out the order of priority of persons who are entitled to apply for a grant of letters of administration with the will annexed.[1] Order 79, r.5(6) is read in conjunction with the will, and the beneficiary in the will who is first entitled under Ord.79, r.5(6) may apply for a grant — for instance, the residuary legatee and devisee. There are apparently four species of residuary legatee and devisee who may apply for a grant in Ord.79, r.5(6). Where no residuary legatee and devisee is named in the will, the person next entitled may apply for a grant. A person with prior entitlement to a grant cannot be compelled to apply for one, even where it is shown that he or she has intermeddled in the estate of the deceased. Where a person renounces his or her entitlement to a grant, the person next in order of priority will be entitled to apply for a grant. A person may also be deemed to have renounced his or her entitlement to apply for a grant if he or she fails to enter an appearance to a citation to accept or **14–01**

1 See Chapter 25 – Probate Precedents; Albert Keating, *Irish Probate Precedents Service* (Dublin: Round Hall, 2009); Albert Keating, *Keating on Probate* (4th ed) (Dublin: Round Hall, 2011); Albert Keating, *First Supplement to the Fourth Edition of Keating on Probate* (Dublin: Thomson Round Hall, 2013).

refuse administration.[2] The current order of priority of persons entitled to apply for a grant of letters of administration with the will annexed is set out in Ord.79, r.5(6) of the 1986 Rules. Before the introduction of the 1986 Rules, the Rules of the Superior Courts 1962 (the "1962 Rules") governed the order of priority of persons entitled to apply for a grant. The 1962 Rules are applicable to deaths occurring prior to 1 January 1967; the 1986 Rules are applicable to deaths occurring after that date. An application for a grant of letters of administration with the will annexed may be made to the Probate Office or a District Probate Registry within whose area the deceased testator had a place of residence at the time of his death.

14–02 The following are the essential proofs that must be submitted by the person entitled under Ord.79, r.5(6) when applying for a grant of letters of administration with the will annexed:

1. Form S1 (postal application form);
2. The will (and codicils, if any);
3. A certified copy of the will;
4. The oath of administrator with the will annexed;
5. A copy of the oath of administrator with the will annexed;
6. The Inland Revenue Affidavit (Forms CA 24 (2010 edition) where the deceased died after 5 December 2001 or Form CA24 (2000 edition)where the deceased died before 5 December 2001); and
7. Death certificate of the testator.

14–03 Additional proofs may consist of an affidavit of an attesting witness, affidavit of plight and condition, affidavit of mental capacity of a testator by his medical practitioner, or an affidavit of mental capacity of a testator by his solicitor.[3] As in the case of applications for grants of probate, the Seat Office will accept a photocopy of the original oath of executor or administrator which replaces the need for a formal notice of application for a grant. Photostat copies of wills will also be acceptable for grants of probate or letters of administration with the will annexed, but where the original will is not totally legible, a typewritten version of the original must be made, and all copy wills must be certified by the solicitors for the applicant as being a true copy of the original will.

Applicants for Grants under the 1962 Rules

14–04 Under Ord.79, r.5(1) of the 1962 Rules the following persons are entitled to apply for a grant of letters of administration with the will annexed:

---

2 Ord.79, r.57 of the 1986 Rules.

3 See Albert Keating, *Keating on Probate* (4th ed) (Dublin: Round Hall, 2011); Albert Keating, *First Supplement to the Fourth Edition of Keating on Probate* (Dublin: Thomson Round Hall, 2013).

(i) A residuary legatee and a residuary devisee are equally entitled to a grant;
(ii) A residuary devisee in trust is entitled in priority to a residuary legatee and a residuary legatee in trust is entitled in priority to a residuary devisee;
(iii) A residuary legatee or devisee is entitled in priority to the next-of-kin and heir-at-law;
(iv) A residuary devisee is entitled in priority to the representative of a deceased residuary legatee and a residuary legatee is entitled in priority to the representative of a deceased residuary devisee;
(v) A residuary legatee or devisee for life is entitled in priority to a remainderman and
(vi) The next-of-kin and heir-at-law are equally entitled.

Applicants for Grants under the 1986 Rules

Under Ord.79, r.5(6) of the 1986 Rules, the following persons are entitled to apply for a grant of letters of administration with the will annexed: **14–05**

(i) The residuary legatee or devisee holding in trust for other persons;
(ii) The residuary legatee or devisee with a life interest;
(iii) Any other residuary legatee or devisee or the personal representative of any residuary legatee or devisee;
(iv) Any residuary legatee or devisee for life jointly with any ultimate residuary legatee or devisee on the renunciation or consent of the remaining residuary legatees or devisees for life;
(v) Where the residue is not in terms wholly disposed of, the probate officer may, if he or she is of opinion that the testator has nevertheless disposed of the whole or substantially the whole of the estate as ascertained at the time of the application for a grant, allow a grant to be made to any legatee or devisee entitled to, or to share in, the estate so disposed of, without regard to the person entitled to share in any residue not disposed of by the will;
(vi) Where the residue is not wholly disposed of by the will, any person (other than a creditor) entitled to a grant in the event of a total intestacy, according to the order of priority set out in sub-rules (1) to (5) of Ord. 79 of the 1986 Rules; and
(vii) Any legatee or devisee or any creditor or the personal representative of any such person.

Essential Proofs

1. Form S1 (postal application form) must be lodged with all applications submitted by post; **14–06**
2. The original will (and codicils, if any);

3. Certified copy of will (and codicils, if any);
4. Oath of administrator will annexed;
5. Copy oath of administrator will annexed;
6. Administration bond;
7. Inland Revenue Affidavit (CA 24 (2010 edition) for deaths after 5 December 2001 and CA24 (2000 edition) where the deceased died before 5 December 2001);
8. Affidavit of market value or certificate of market value;
9. Death certificate of testator.

Original Will (and Codicils, if any) and Certified Copies

14–07 Every will, or copy of a will, exhibited in the oath of administrator will annexed, must be marked by him or her and by the person before whom it is sworn.[4]

Oath of Administrator with Will Annexed

14–08 The entitlement or capacity of the applicant to apply for a grant must be clearly stated in the oath of administrator, and any person with prior entitlement to the applicant must first be cleared off. The will exhibited in the oath of administrator must be marked on the back by the person applying for the grant and by the person before whom it is sworn. Any such marking is usually made on the back of the will so as not to interfere with the will or the attestation of it. Copies of wills must be written in a legible hand, or printed, typewritten or photocopied, subject to the directions of the probate officer.

14–09 The probate officer, where he or she deems it necessary, may require further proof of the identity of the deceased or of the party applying for the grant, in addition to the information contained in the oath. The correct name and address of the administrator must appear in the oath. The name, address and description of the deceased testator must also appear in the oath and, where the deceased used an alias when making his will, his correct name and alias must be stated in the oath. Where an alias was used for a particular reason, for instance, for the purposes of acquiring property that is now part of his estate, the alias should be added to his correct name. The address and description of the deceased must appear also and, if the deceased lived at a different address from that mentioned in the will, the oath should show that he formerly lived at the address stated in the will. The relationship between the administrator and the deceased testator, if one exists, must appear in the oath.

[4] See Chapter 13 – Applications for Grants of Probate.

The oath must also confirm that the testator did not "intermarry" or civil partnership after the making of his or her will. The main reason for including this statement in the oath is that a subsequent marriage or civil partnership revokes a will, unless it was established that the will was made in contemplation of that marriage or civil partnership. Any doubt on the matter may have to be resolved by an application to the court. **14–10**

The precise date of death must be stated in the oath. However, the date of death appearing in the oath is not conclusive evidence of the death of the deceased. A duly authenticated death certificate must be produced to provide evidence of death. The place of residence of the testator should also be included in the oath where an application for a grant is made at a District Probate Registry. Where the deceased died on board a ship on the high seas, the name of the ship should be stated, together with the fact that he died and was buried at sea, and the same must be duly authenticated by the ship's records. Where the testator is known to have died but the precise date of his death is unascertainable, the oath should state when the deceased was last seen alive and when and where his body was discovered. Where leave of the court has been obtained to swear death, the oath should state that the deceased died on or since the date he was last known to be alive, and the particulars of the court order must also be given. Where there is no death certificate or sufficient alternative evidence of death, an order may have to be sought from the court presuming the death of the testator. For the court to presume the death of a testator, it must first be established that seven years have elapsed since the testator was last heard of or seen alive. It must further be established that persons who would normally have heard of him have not heard of him over the period of seven years. Proper inquiries and investigations must also be carried out in the place where the testator's residence was located, and if inquiries there show that he disappeared without any trace, death may be presumed by the court. Inquiries may include the placing of advertisements in newspapers circulating at or near the place where the testator was last known to reside, or at the place he was last seen alive. **14–11**

The oath must also contain a statement of gross value of the estate of the testator without any deductions for debts. This gross value appearing in the oath should be current value and not necessarily the gross value appearing in the Inland Revenue Affidavit. **14–12**

The oath must also refer to any court order where the leave of the court was sought and obtained to apply for a grant of letters of administration with the will annexed. Where an executor named in the will renounces his office, or the person next entitled to apply for a grant of letters of administration with the will annexed renounces his right to apply for a grant, he must sign a renunciation form and this must be referred to and exhibited in the oath of administrator with the will annexed. **14–13**

OATH OF ADMINISTRATOR WITH THE WILL

THE HIGH COURT
PROBATE

In the estate of (name of deceased testator) late of (address) deceased.

> I, [name of applicant] of [address] aged eighteen years and upwards, make oath and say, that I believe the paper writing hereunto annexed, and marked by me, to contain the true and original last will [*or* last will with codicils] of late of [address and description], deceased, and that same was made by the said after attaining the age of eighteen years and upwards, and that he did not intermarry with any person after the making of same, and that [title of the applicant] and that I will well and faithfully administer the estate of the said testator, by paying his just debts and the legacies bequeathed by his said will [*or* will and codicils] and distributing the residue of his estate according to law; and that I will exhibit a true and perfect inventory of the said estate, and render a true account thereof whenever required by law so to do; and that the testator died at on the day of [where application is made in a District Probate Registry, add: and had at the time of his death a fixed place of abode at within the district of] and that the whole of the personal estate of the said testator amounts in value to the sum of [the gross personal estate, without any deductions for debts] and that the whole of the real estate of the said testator which devolves on and vests in his legal personal representative is of the market value of [the amount shown in the affidavit of market value] and no more to the best of my knowledge, information and belief.
>
> Sworn, &c.

Administration Bond

14–14 The entitlement or capacity of the person applying for a grant stated in the bond must reflect that as stated in the oath of administrator. The person who applies for a grant of administration must enter into a bond for the benefit of the President of the High Court, and if the High Court, the probate officer or a District Probate Registrar so requires, with one or more sureties conditioned for collecting, getting in and administering the estate of the deceased. The administration bond must be in a penalty of double the amount at which the estate of the deceased is sworn unless the court, probate officer or District Probate Registrar directs it to be reduced. While the necessity for an administration bond when applying for grants of letters of administration with the will annexed remains a statutory requirement, the practice regarding the discretionary requirement for one or more sureties under s.34(1) of the 1965 Act has been altered as a result of a Practice Directive. The Practice Directive provides that:

> "it shall not be required of a person applying for administration to furnish a surety or sureties in addition to an administration bond unless required to do so by the High Court, the Probate Officer, or in the case of a grant from a District Probate Registry, the District Probate Registrar," (effective from 1 September 2004).

The State as applicant for a grant is not required to give an administration bond. An administration bond issued by a guarantee society or insurance company approved by the President of the High Court will be acceptable for the purposes of s.34. The probate officer must ensure that the sureties to a bond where they are required are responsible persons, and must then justify in the gross amount at which the estate of the deceased testator is valued. **14–15**

Administration bonds may be attested by the probate officer, the assistant probate officer or by a District Probate Registrar, or by a Commissioner for Oaths or such other person authorised to take affidavits. The same person who attested the oath of administrator must also attest the signature of the administrator to the bond. **14–16**

The form of administration bond prescribed by the President of the High Court is the document that must be used in the case of the testator dying on or after 1 January 1967. The current form is set out in Appendix Q, Part II of the Rules of the Superior Courts 1986. In the case of testators dying before 1 January 1967, the forms prescribed by the Rules of the Superior Courts 1962 must be used. **14–17**

ADMINISTRATION BOND **14–18**

THE HIGH COURT

The Probate Office/The District Probate Registry at [place]

I/We [insert name address and description of applicant and surety/ies if applicable] am/are each liable in full to pay to the President of the High Court the sum of [insert penal sum twice gross assets of estate reflecting current market value of immovable property] for which payment we bind ourselves and each of us and our executors, administrators and successors and sealed with our seal(s) and dated the [insert day of signing bond] day of [insert month and year of signing bond]. The condition of this obligation is that if the above-named [insert name of applicant] of [insert name, address and description of deceased] deceased, and the intended administrator/administratix of the estate of the said deceased, do, when lawfully called on in that behalf, make or cause to be made a true inventory of the said estate which has or shall come into his/her hands, possession or knowledge, or into the hands, possession or control of any other person for him/her;

do exhibit the said inventory or cause it to be exhibited in the Probate Office [or in the district probate registry at] whenever required by law to do so; do well and truly administer the said estate according to law, paying all the debts owed by the deceased at the time of his death, all death duties payable in respect of the estate of the deceased for which the personal representative is accountable and all income tax and surtax payable out of the estate,

distributing all shares in the estate to those entitled by law thereto and as the law requires him/her; and further, do make or cause to be made a true account of the said administration whenever required by law to do so;

then this obligation shall be void and no effect, but shall otherwise remain in full force and effect.

Signed, Sealed and Delivered by the within-named	Applicant(s) signature and seal
Name of applicant and surety/ies if applicable	Surety's/sureties' signature and seal (if applicable)

In the presence of
(Insert Commissioner's/Solicitor's name)

Commissioner/Solicitor to sign here

Commissioner/Solicitor

Applicant(s) should execute bond before Commissioner/Solicitor on Oath.[5]

Inland Revenue Affidavit

14–19 Form CA24 (2010 edition) is the appropriate form of the Inland Revenue Affidavit to use where the deceased died on or after 5 December 2001. The form must be completed by computer and two copies must be printed for swearing prior to an application for a grant to the Probate Office or a District Probate Registry. The printed copies of Form CA24 must be legible otherwise they will not be accepted. Printed copies that are completed manually will also not be accepted. Photocopies will not be sufficient substitutes for the printed version. The font used to complete Form CA24 must not be altered. Both affidavits must be submitted to the Probate Office or the appropriate District Probate Registry. The Revenue Commissioners will receive all of the relevant data from either the Probate Office or district Probate Registry. Form CA24 (2000 edition) may also be downloaded and completed on screen and should be used only for applications for grants where the deceased died before 5 December 2001. There are no changes to the form and procedures in respect of applications for grants prior to 5 December 2001. The values of the estate existing at death must be entered in the Inland Revenue Affidavit; current values must be entered in the oath of administrator and, in the case of real estate, the values as stated in the affidavit of market value or certificate of market value.[6]

Affidavit or Certificate of Market Value

14–20 An affidavit of market value must also be sworn in the case of an application

[5] See Ord.79, r.29, Rules of the Superior Courts.

[6] See Chapter 13 – Applications for Grants of Probate–Corrective Inland Revenue Affidavits.

for letters of administration with the will annexed where the real estate of the deceased includes agricultural land, and a valuation of such land must include any milk quota attached to it. The affidavit must state the current value of the land and will be valid for six months only. Where, however, the real estate is non-agricultural and consists of a dwelling on less than half an acre of land, a certificate of market value in the form of a letter by the applicant's solicitors will be a sufficient substitute for the affidavit of market value.

Death Certificate

Every application for a grant of letters of administration with the will annexed must include the death certificate of the deceased testator among the proofs required for obtaining such a grant. **14–21**

CHAPTER 15

APPLICATIONS FOR GRANTS OF LETTERS OF ADMINISTRATION INTESTATE

INTRODUCTION

Where a deceased dies intestate, the type of grant that must be sought to administer his or her estate is a grant of letters of administration intestate. The order of priority of applicants entitled to a grant of letters of administration intestate is set out in Ord. 79, r.5(1) of the Rules of the Superior Courts 1962 (the "1962 Rules") for deaths occurring on or after 1 June 1959.[1] The order of priority of persons entitled to a grant in the 1962 Rules more or less reflects the old devolution and distributive rules relating to succession to realty and personalty, and the provisions of the Intestates' Estates Act 1954, and also those of the Administration of Estates Act 1959 (the "1959 Act"). The 1962 Rules continued to determine the order of priority of applicants for grants for deaths occurring on or after 1 January 1967[2] until finally replaced by the Rules of the Superior Courts (the "1986 Rules"). Order 79, r.5(1) of the 1986 Rules replaced Ord. 79, r.5(1) of the 1962 Rules and now determines the order of priority of persons entitled to apply for letters of administration intestate to estates of persons who died on or after 1 January 1967. The 1986 Rules apply to deaths occurring on or after 1 January 1967. The priority of applicants entitled to a grant of letters of administration intestate is that as set out in Ord. 79, r.5(1) of the 1986 Rules for deaths occurring on or after the 1 January 1967. The order of priority of persons entitled to a grant in the 1986 Rules is more or less the same as that of persons entitled to receive a distributive share in the intestate's **15–01**

[1] Date of enactment of the Administration of Estates Act 1959.
[2] Date of enactment of the Succession Act 1965.

estate in accordance with the intestate rules of succession and distribution in the 1965 Act.[3] Since the Status of Children Act 1987, non-marital or non civil partnership children have equal entitlement to apply for a grant with other children of the deceased intestate. Since the Civil Partnership Act and Certain Rights and Obligations of Cohabitants Act 2010 (the "2010 Act"), a civil partner, like a spouse, is the first in the order of priority to apply for a grant. Applications for grants may be made to the Seat Office division of the Probate Office either personally or through town agents pursuant to Ord.79, r.3 of the 1986 Rules, or a District Probate Registry within whose area the deceased testator had a fixed place of abode at the time of his death.[4]

15–02 The following are the essential proofs that must be submitted by the person entitled under Ord.79, r.5(1) of the 1986 Rules when applying for a grant of letters of administration intestate:

1. Form S1 (postal application form);
2. Oath of administrator intestate;
3. Copy oath of administrator intestate;
4. Administration bond;
5. Inland Revenue Affidavit (CA 24 (2010 edition) for deaths after 5 December 2001 and CA24 (2000 edition) where the deceased died before 5 December 2001);
6. Affidavit of market value or certificate of market value;
7. Death certificate.

Applicants for Grants under the 1962 Rules

15–03 Since the enactment of the 1959 Act, a widow of a deceased intestate became entitled to apply for a grant of letters of administration intestate by virtue of Ord. 79, r.5(1) of the 1962 Rules which relates to deaths occurring on or after 1 June 1959. Ordrt 79, r.5(1)(f) provides that the next-of-kin of the deceased and heir-at-law are equally entitled to a grant of letters of administration intestate. This reflects s.7(4) of the 1959 Act which provides that, where an intestate dies possessed of real estate, his heir-at-law, if not one of the next-of-kin, will be equally entitled to the grant with the next-of-kin. While the deceased's heir-at-law and his next-of-kin are equally entitled to apply for a grant of letters of administration intestate, it appears that a surviving widower or widow has the "first right" to apply for a grant, as Ord. 79, r.5(1)(g) provides that the widower or widow of an intestate had the first right to a grant. Since the 1959 Act, a widower and widow became equally entitled to apply to a grant. Order 79, r.5(1)(h) provides that, notwithstanding paragraph (f) of r.5(1) which provides

---

[3] See Chapter 25 – Probate Precedents; Albert Keating, *Irish Probate Precedents Service* (Dublin: Round Hall, 2009); Albert Keating, *Keating on Probate* (4th ed) (Dublin: Round Hall, 2011); Albert Keating, *First Supplement to the Fourth Edition of Keating on Probate* (Dublin: Thomson Round Hall, 2013).

[4] See Ord.80 of the Rules of the Superior Courts 1986.

that the next-of-kin and heir-at-law are equally entitled to a grant, where the widower of an intestate renounces his title to a grant, the heir-at-law will be entitled in priority to next-of-kin. But when the widow of an intestate renounces, the next-of-kin are entitled equally with the heir-at-law to apply for a grant. Under r.5(1)(j), the heir-at-law and next-of-kin are entitled to apply for a grant in priority to a person who (though not one of the next-of-kin) is entitled in distribution to a share of the personal estate. By r.5(1)(k) the heir-at-law of an intestate is entitled to apply for a grant in priority to the representative of a deceased next-of-kin.

The heir-at-law was a blood relative traceable from the "last purchaser", i.e. a person who last acquired the realty otherwise than by succession.[5] He was a lineal successor as child or grandchild of the deceased intestate. Where there were two or more sons or grandsons or of equal degree of relationship to the deceased, the eldest was the heir-at-law by the feudal rule of primogeniture. Where there were no male heirs, daughters or granddaughters inherited realty as coparceners. A lineal successor who would have succeeded to the intestate's realty had he not predeceased him or inherited the realty was represented by his son by virtue of the doctrine of representation and was entitled as heir-at-law to the realty before, say, a younger son of the deceased intestate. Where no issue survived the deceased intestate, the realty then went to the nearest lineal ancestor and his issue, and for this purpose, the paternal line was preferred to that of the maternal line.[6] **15–04**

Under the old rules, a widower became entitled to the whole of his deceased wife personalty. A widow, on the other hand, received one-third or one-half of her deceased husband's personalty, depending on whether or not there were surviving next-of-kin. The next-of-kin were blood relatives traceable from the deceased intestate. They were his children and grandchildren and, if there were no children or grandchildren, the next-of-kin most related to him by blood. Under the Statute of Distributions (Ireland) 1695, a widow with children was entitled to one-third of the personalty, with the remainder going to the children, and grandchildren were capable of representing their predeceased parent under the doctrine of representation. Where no widow survived, the children of the deceased intestate were entitled to all of the personalty. If no issue survived the deceased intestate, a surviving widow became entitled to one-half of the personalty, with the remainder going to those most related to the deceased intestate by blood. The widow's distributive share of the personalty was increased by the Intestates' Estates Act 1954. Under that Act, a widow was entitled to £4,000 or the whole estate if worth less than £4,000, and the £4,000 was payable rateably out of the real and personal estate of the deceased intestate: if a widow was the sole survivor of the intestate, she became entitled to the whole estate which would **15–05**

---

5 s.2 of the Inheritance Act 1833; see Wylie, J.C.W., *Irish Land Law* (3rd ed) (London: Butterworths 1997), p. 853, para. 15.11.

6 s. 6 and s.7 of the Inheritance Act 1833.

otherwise have gone to the State.[7] Since the Act of 1959, notwithstanding the old rules relating to the distribution of personalty, a widower and widow became equally entitled to apply for a grant.

15–06 Order 79, r.28(1) of the 1962 Rules provides that, in the case of estates of persons dying on or before 31 May 1959, the oath of administrator shall be so worded as to clear off all persons having a prior right to the grant. The grant shall show on its face how the prior interests have been cleared off, and the oath shall set forth, when the fact is so, that the party applying is the only next-of-kin or one of the next-of-kin of the deceased. Order 79, r.28(2) provides that, in the case of estates of persons dying on or after 1 June 1959 (i.e. the date of enactment of the 1959 Act), the oath of administrator intestate should be so worded as to clear off all persons having a prior right to the grant. But where it is sworn that the deceased died without being possessed of any real estate (other than freehold land registered under Part IV of the Registration of Title Act 1891), the grant may be made without clearing off the heir-at-law. The oath must state that the party applying is only next-of-kin or one of the next-of-kin or the heir-at-law of the deceased. Where there are prior interests, the grant will show on its face how they have been cleared off. Where the grant is made to the heir-at-law, the relationship to the deceased need not be stated in the grant. Under r.28(4) of the same Order, the value of the property stated in the oath must be verified by other affidavits if required by the probate officer. The 1962 Rules are still applicable to deaths occurring on or before 1 January 1967, and applications for grants before that date must be made in compliance with the 1962 Rules.

15–07 Order 79, r.5(2) of the 1962 Rules provides that nothing in r.5 shall affect the powers of the High Court under the 1959 Act, s.12, to appoint an administrator of the estate of a deceased intestate where, by reason of special circumstances, it appears necessary or expedient to do so.

15–08 The 1962 Rules reflected the statutory order of things before and after the 1959 Act and prescribed the order of applicants for grants of letters of administration intestate. For deaths intestate occurring prior to 1 June 1959, the husband as surviving spouse was the only person entitled to a grant and, on his death, the person next entitled was his personal representative. Where the wife was the surviving spouse, her title to apply for a grant intestate to her deceased's husband's estate lasted only for three months and after that period of time, the next-of-kin became equally entitled to a grant. The next-of-kin were equally entitled to a grant where the wife as surviving spouse died or renounced her title to a grant. By s.7(4) of the 1959 Act, where an intestate dies possessed of real estate, his heir-at-law, if not one of the next-of-kin, will be equally entitled to the grant with the next-of-kin. While the deceased's heir-at-law and his next-of-kin are equally entitled to apply for a grant of letters of administration intestate, it appears that a

[7] s.6 of the Intestates' Estate Act 1954.

surviving widower or widow has the "first right" to apply for a grant. While the Succession Act 1965 (the "1965 Act") abolished the canons of descent and the status of heir-at-law and repealed the 1959 Act, and introduced new rules of devolution and distribution regarding intestate estates, the 1962 Rules continued to be operative as regards the entitlement of applicants for grants, and the oath of administrator prescribed by the 1962 Rules must be used. The 1986 Rules replaced the 1962 Rules, and the 1986 Rules from the date of their introduction are now applicable to deaths occurring on or after 1 January 1967 and the oath of administrator prescribed by the 1986 Rules must be sworn by the applicant entitled to a grant under the 1986 Rules.

Even though the 1965 Act set out the rules which govern the devolution and distribution of an intestate's estate for deaths occurring on or after 1 January 1967 as amended by the 2010 Act,[8] the 1962 Rules continued to govern the order of priority of persons entitled to apply for a grant of letters of administration intestate until the introduction of the 1986 Rules. The 1986 Rules are expressed to apply to deaths occurring on or before 1 January 1967. The 1986 Rules reflect the radical changes introduced by the 1965 Act which abolished the old rules relating to intestate succession to realty and personalty and repealed the 1959 Act. The 1962 Rules reflected the statutory order of things before and after the 1959 Act and prescribed the order for applicants for grants of letters of administration intestate. For deaths intestate occurring prior to 1 June 1959, the husband as surviving spouse was the only person entitled to a grant, and on his death, the person next entitled was his personal representative. **15–09**

Where the wife was the surviving spouse, her title to apply for a grant intestate to her deceased's husband's estate lasted only for three months and, after that period of time the next-of-kin became equally entitled to a grant. The next-of-kin were equally entitled to a grant where the wife as surviving spouse died or renounced her title to a grant. By s.7 (4) of the 1959 Act, where an intestate dies possessed of real estate, his heir-at-law, if not one of the next-of-kin, will be equally entitled to the grant with the next-of-kin. While the deceased's heir-at-law and his next-of-kin are equally entitled to apply for a grant of letters of administration intestate, it appears that a surviving widower or widow has the "first right" to apply for a grant. While the 1965 Act abolished the canons of descent and the status of heir-at-law and repealed the 1959 Act, and introduced new rules of devolution and distribution regarding intestate estates, the 1962 Rules continued to be operative as regards the entitlement of applicants for grants, and the oath of administrator prescribed by the 1962 Rules must be used. The 1986 Rules replaced the 1962 Rules, and the 1986 Rules from the date of their introduction are now applicable to deaths occurring on or after 1 January 1967 and the oath of administrator prescribed by the 1986 Rules must be sworn by the applicant entitled to a grant under the 1986 Rules. **15–10**

---

[8] See Part VI of the Succession Act 1965.

15–11 The order of priority of persons entitled to apply for a grant of letters of administration intestate is that as set out in Ord.79, r.5(1) of the 1986 Rules. The order of priority of such persons is more or less the same as that of persons entitled to receive a distributive share in the intestate's estate in accordance the intestate rules of succession.[9] Since the Status of Children Act 1987, non-marital or non civil partnership children have equal entitlement to apply for a grant with other children of the deceased intestate. Since the 2010 Act, a civil partner, like a spouse, is the first in the order of priority to apply for a grant. Where the person entitled under Ord.79, r.5(1) decides to apply for a grant of letters of administration intestate, the necessary proofs required for such a grant must be prepared. The following are the essential proofs that must be submitted by the person entitled under Ord.79, r.5(1) when applying for a grant of letters of administration intestate:

1. the oath of administrator intestate;
2. a copy of the oath of administrator intestate;
3. the Inland Revenue Affidavit (Forms CA 24 (2010 edition) where the deceased died after 5 December 2001 or Form CA24 (2000 edition) where the deceased died before 5 December 2001; and
4. death certificate of the deceased intestate.

15–12 The application for a grant of letters of administration intestate may be made to the Probate Office or a District Probate Registry within whose area the deceased testator had a fixed place of abode at the time of his death.

Applicants for Grants under the 1986 Rules

15–13 Order 79, r.5(1) of the 1986 Rules provides that, in determining the order of priority of persons entitled to apply for letters of administration to estates of persons who died on or after 1 January 1967 (the enactment date of the 1965 Act) wholly intestate and domiciled in Ireland, the persons having a beneficial interest in the estate will be entitled to apply for a grant in the following order:

(i) The surviving spouse or civil partner;
(ii) The surviving spouse or civil partner jointly with a child of the deceased nominated by the surviving spouse or civil partner. The obvious advantage to be derived here is that, if the surviving spouse or civil partner is elderly, assistance in the administration may be required and a child may be nominated for this purpose. It also dispenses with the need for further grants should the death

---

[9] See Chapter 7 – Intestate Successi..; see Albert Keating, *Irish Probate Precedents Service* (Dublin: Round Hall, 2009); Albert Keating, *Keating on Probate* (4th ed) (Dublin: Round Hall, 2011, Chapter 37); Albert Keating, *First Supplement to the Fourth Edition of Keating on Probate* (Dublin: Thomson Round Hall, 2013).

of the surviving spouse or civil partner occur during the course of the administration;

(iii) The child or children of the deceased. This rule was amended by S.I. No. 2 of 1989: Rules of the Superior Courts (No. 2) 1989 by providing: "The child or children of the deceased (including any person entitled by virtue of the Status of Children Act, 1987, to succeed to the estate of the deceased.)";

(iv) The issue of any child who has died during the lifetime of the deceased;

(v) The father or mother of the deceased intestate. This rule was amended by S.I. No. 2 of 1989: Rules of the Superior Courts (No. 2) 1989 by providing: "The father or mother of the deceased or where the presumption contained in Section 4A(2) of the Succession Act, 1965 (inserted by s.29 of the status of Children Act, 1987) applies, the mother.";

(vi) The brothers and sisters of the deceased, whether of the whole or half-blood;

(vii) Where any brother or sister survived the intestate, the children of a predeceased brother or sister;

(viii) The nephews and nieces of the intestate (whether of the whole or half-blood).

(ix) The grandparents of the intestate;

(x) The uncles or aunts (whether of the whole or half-blood) of the intestate;

(xi) The great-grandparents of the intestate;

(xii) Other next-of-kin of the nearest degree (whether of the whole or half-blood) preferring collaterals to direct lineal ancestors;

(xiii) The nominee of the State.

Rule 5(2) provides that the executor or administrator of any of the above persons, excluding the personal representative of the nominee of the State, will have the same entitlement to a grant as the person whom he represents, save only that a grant will be made to a living member of a class entitled to a grant in preference to the executor or administrator of a member of that class who has died after the intestate, unless the court or probate officer otherwise directs. The reason for this, apparently, is that live interests are preferred to dead interests. **15–14**

Rule 5(3) provides that, where there are conflicting claims for a grant between members of a class with equal entitlement to apply, the grant will be made to such of the claimants as the probate officer may select, having given not less than 21 days' notice to all rival claimants. If any objection is made to the probate officer's selection within that period, the court may make the selection. The suitability of a person for the office of administrator and the one who best serves the interests of the estate are the main criteria used when making a selection among rival claimants. **15–15**

15–16 Rule 5(4) provides that, if all of the persons entitled to apply for a grant have been cleared off, a grant may be made to a creditor of the deceased, or to the executor or administrator of a creditor. A citation to accept or refuse a grant of administration may be used by a creditor to clear off persons with a prior entitlement and, in the event of persons cited failing to apply for a grant, the creditor may himself apply for a grant.

15–17 Rule 5(5) provides that the Adoption Acts 1952-1988 will apply in determining the title to apply for a grant as they apply to the devolution of an estate on intestacy. On production of the necessary affidavit exhibiting the birth certificate and adoption order for the purposes of establishing relationship to the intestate, a grant will issue. This rule was amended by S.I. No. 2 of 1989: Rules of the Superior Courts (No. 2) 1989 by providing:

> "The provisions of the Adoption Acts, 1952-1988, (as construed in accordance with Section 27(3) of the Status of Children Act, 1987) shall apply in determining the title to a grant as they apply to a devolution of property on intestacy."

15–18 Where a father and non-marital (or non-civil partnership) child are involved, s.46(3) of the Status of Children Act 1987 presumes the father registered on the birth certificate to be the father of the child unless the contrary is proved on the balance of probabilities. A declaration of parentage may be sought from the Circuit Court under s.35 of the 1987 Act.

Essential Proofs

15–19

1. Form S1 (postal application form) must be lodged with all applications submitted by post;
2. Oath of administrator intestate;
3. Copy oath of administrator intestate;
4. Administration bond;
5. Inland Revenue Affidavit (CA 24 (2010 edition) for deaths after 5 December 2001 and CA24 (2000 edition) where the deceased died before 5 December 2001);
6. Affidavit of market value or certificate of market value;
7. Death certificate.

The Oath of Administrator Intestate

15–20 The entitlement or capacity of the applicant for the grant must be clearly stated in the administrator's oath and any person with prior title should first be cleared off. The oath of the administrator intestate must be subscribed and sworn as an affidavit and filed in the Probate Office. Where it is deemed necessary, the probate officer may require further proof of the identity of the deceased or of the party applying for the grant, in addition to the information contained in the oath. The correct name and address of the administrator must appear in the oath. The name, address and description of the deceased intestate must also appear in the oath, as well as the relationship between the administrator and the deceased intestate.

The precise date of death must be stated in the oath. A duly authenticated death certificate must be produced to provide evidence of death and the place of death should also be included in the oath. Where the deceased died on board a ship on the high seas, the name of the ship should be stated together with the fact that he died and was buried at sea and, if such should be the case, the same being duly authenticated by the ship's records. Where the intestate is known to have died but the precise date of his death is unascertainable, the oath should state when the deceased was last seen alive and when and where the body was discovered. Where leave of the court has been obtained to swear death, the oath should state that the deceased died on or since the date he was last known to be alive, and the particulars of the court order must also be given. Where there is no death certificate or sufficient alternative evidence of death, an order may have to be sought of the court presuming the death of the testator. **15–21**

The oath must contain a statement of gross value of the estate of the testator without any deductions for debts. This gross value of the estate appearing in the oath should be the current gross value, though not necessarily that provided by the Inland Revenue Affidavit. The oath must also refer to any court order where the leave of the court was sought and obtained to apply for a grant of letters of administration intestate. Where the person entitled to apply for a grant of letters of administration with the will annexed renounces his right, he or she must sign a renunciation form and this must be referred to and exhibited in the oath of administrator intestate. **15–22**

OATH OF ADMINISTRATOR

THE HIGH COURT
PROBATE

In the estate of [name of intestate] late of [address] deceased.

I, [name of applicant] of [address] aged eighteen years and upwards, make oath and say that late of [address and description], deceased, died intestate and that [title of the applicant] and that I will well and faithfully administer the estate of the said deceased by paying his just debts and distributing the residue of said estate according to law, and that I will exhibit a true inventory of the said estate and render a true account thereof, whenever required by law so to do; that the said deceased died at on the day of [month and year] [where application is made in a District Probate Registry, add: and that the said deceased had at the time of his death a fixed place of abode at within the district of] and that the whole of the personal estate of the said deceased amounts in value to the sum of [the gross personal estate without any deductions for debts] and that the whole of the real estate of the said deceased which devolves on and vests in his legal personal representatives is of the market value of [the amount shown in the affidavit of market value] and no more to the best of my knowledge, information and belief.

Sworn, &c.

15–23 Where a divorced person dies intestate, the oath of administrator must state that the deceased died intestate and

> "was divorced by virtue of order of the Court dated day of 20 [and relationship of the applicant to the deceased in accordance with succession rights of the applicant]."

15–24 All of the other proofs for the grant remain the same. A copy of the court order need not be included among the proofs for the grant.

15–25 Where a separated person (whether under a deed or judicial separation) dies intestate and issue of the deceased apply for a grant, the surviving separated spouse must execute a renunciation and it must be exhibited and included among the proofs submitted for the grant. The renunciation of succession rights clause usually inserted in deeds of separation will not be sufficient by itself to allow the next-of-kin of the deceased spouse to extract a grant to that person's estate. Furthermore, where the applicant is other than issue of the deceased, a disclaimer by the surviving spouse must be exhibited in the oath of the administrator and must be included among the proofs for the grant. Where a renunciation or disclaimer is not forthcoming, an application must be made to the court pursuant to s.27(4) of the 1965 Act to allow the applicant to apply for a grant. The procedure is by way of notice of motion grounded on an affidavit and must issue from the Rules Office section of the Probate Office.[10]

15–26 Where a person who has been granted a foreign divorce dies intestate and issue of that person apply for a grant, a renunciation from the divorced surviving spouse must be exhibited in the oath of administrator and included among the proofs for the grant. Where the applicant for the grant is other than issue, a disclaimer from the divorced surviving spouse must be exhibited in the oath of administrator and included among the proofs for the grant. Where no renunciation or disclaimer is forthcoming, an application must be made to the Court pursuant to s.27(4) of the 1965 Act by way of notice of motion grounded on an affidavit.[11]

Administration Bond

15–27 The applicant for the grant must enter into a bond to inure for the benefit of the President of the High Court, and if the High Court, the probate

[10] See Chapter 20 – Probate Motions and Section 27(4) Applications.
[11] *ibid.*

officer or the District Probate Registrar so requires, with one or more sureties conditioned for collecting, getting in and administering the estate of the deceased. The administration bond must be in a penalty of double the amount at which the estate of the deceased is sworn unless the court, probate officer or District Probate Registrar directs it to be reduced. While the necessity for an administration bond when applying for grants of letters of administration intestate remains a statutory requirement, the practice regarding the discretionary requirement for one or more sureties has been altered as a result of a High Court Practice Directive. The Practice Directive provides that

> "it shall not be required of a person applying for administration to furnish a surety or sureties in addition to an administration bond unless required to do so by the High Court, the Probate Officer, or in the case of a grant from a District Probate Registry, the District Probate Registrar".[12]

The probate officer must ensure that the sureties to the bond, where they are required, are responsible persons. The sureties to the bond must then justify in the gross amount at which the estate of the deceased testator is sworn, unless the court or the probate officer otherwise orders. The State as applicant for a grant is not required to give an administration bond. Where the applicant for the grant is a trust corporation, no sureties are required. An administration bond issued by a guarantee society or insurance company approved by the President of the High Court will be acceptable for the purposes of s.34 of the 1965 Act.

All administration bonds may be attested to by the probate officer, the assistant probate officer or by a District Probate Registrar, or by a commissioner for oaths or other person authorised to take affidavits. The person who administers the oath must attest the signature of the administrator to the bond. **15–28**

ADMINISTRATION BOND

THE HIGH COURT

The Probate Office/The District Probate Registry at

I/We [Insert name address and description of applicant and surety/sureties if applicable] am/are each liable in full to pay to the President of the High Court the sum of [insert penal sum twice gross assets of estate, reflecting current market value of immoveable property] for which payment we bind ourselves and each of us and our executors, administrators and successors and our sealed with our seal(s) and dated the [insert day of signing bond] day of [insert month and year of signing bond]. The condition of this obligation is that if the above-named [insert name of applicant] of [insert name address and description of deceased] deceased, and the intended administrator/administratix of the estate of the said

[12] Effective from 1 September 2004.

deceased, do, when lawfully called on in that behalf, make or cause to be made a true inventory of the said estate which has or shall come into his/her hands, possession or knowledge, or into the hands, possession or control of any other person for him/her;do exhibit the said inventory or cause it to be exhibited in the Probate Office [or in the District Probate Registry at] whenever required by law to do so; do well and truly administer the said estate according to law, paying all the debts owed by the deceased at the time of his death, all death duties payable in respect of the estate of the deceased for which the personal representative is accountable and all income tax and surtax payable out of the estate, distributing all shares in the estate to those entitled by law thereto and as the law requires him/her; and further, do make or cause to be made a true account of the said administration whenever required by law to do so;and further do, if so required, render and deliver up the letters of administration in the High Court if it shall hereafter appear that any will was made by the deceased which is exhibited in the said Court, with a request that it be allowed and approved accordingly;

then this obligation shall be void and no effect, but shall otherwise remain in full force and effect.

Signed, sealed and delivered by the within-named	Applicant(s) signature and seal
Name of applicant and surety/sureties if applicable	Surety's/sureties' signature(s) and seal (if applicable)

In the presence of
(Insert Commissioner's/Solicitor's name)

Commissioner/Solicitor to sign here
Commissioner/Solicitor

Applicant(s) should execute the bond before a Commissioner/Solicitor on oath.[13]

Inland Revenue Affidavit

15–29 The Finance Act 2010 removes the requirement for certification of the Inland Revenue Affidavit CA24 (2010 edition) by the Revenue Commissioners before the issue of a grant of letters of administration intestate. It introduces a "pay and file" regime for gift and inheritance tax. It abolishes secondary accountability for personal representatives of a deceased person and thereby ends the process and compliance costs of issuing personal clearance certificates. Forms CA11, CA44, and IT10 will no longer be issued by the Revenue Commissioners. From 14 June 2010, it is no longer required to present an Inland Revenue Affidavit to the Revenue Commissioners for certification prior to an application for a grant to the Probate Office or a District Probate Registry. The Inland Revenue Affidavit may be submitted

[13] See Ord.79, r.29, Rules of the Superior Courts.

in duplicate directly to the Probate Office or a District Probate Registry together with all of the other necessary proofs required for a grant.

Form CA24 (2010 edition) is the appropriate form of the Inland Revenue Affidavit to use where the deceased died on or after 5 December 2001. The form must be completed by computer and two copies must be printed for swearing prior to an application for a grant to the Probate Office or a District Probate Registry. The printed copies of Form CA24 must be legible otherwise they will not be accepted. Printed copies that are completed manually will also not be accepted. Photocopies will not be sufficient substitutes for the printed version. The font used to complete Form CA24 must not be altered. Both affidavits must be submitted to the Probate Office or the appropriate District Probate Registry. The Revenue Commissioners will receive all of the relevant data from either the Probate Office or district Probate Registry. Form CA24 (2000 edition) may also be downloaded and completed on screen and should be used only for applications for grants where the deceased died before 5 December 2001. There are no changes to the form and procedures in respect of applications for grants prior to 5 December 2001. The values of the estate existing at death must be entered in the Inland Revenue Affidavit: current values must be entered in the oath of administrator and, in the case of real estate, the values as stated in the affidavit of market value or certificate of market value.[14] **15–30**

Affidavit of Market Value or Certificate of Market Value

An affidavit of market value must also be sworn in the case of an application for letters of administration intestate where the real estate of the deceased includes agricultural land, and a valuation of the land must include any milk quota attached to it. The affidavit must state the current value of the land and will be valid for six months only. Where, however, the real estate is non-agricultural and consists of a dwelling on less than half an acre of land, a certificate of value in the form of a letter by the applicant's solicitors will be a sufficient substitute for the affidavit of value. **15–31**

Death Certificate

Every application for a grant must include the death certificate of the deceased intestate among the proofs submitted for the grant. **15–32**

[14] See Chapter 13 – Applications for Grants of Probate–Corrective Inland Revenue Affidavits.

Chapter 16

APPLICATIONS FOR GRANTS BY GUARDIANS, COMMITTEES AND ATTORNEYS

Introduction

Although there is no age requirement for a person to be appointed an executor, there is one for applying for a grant of probate. The general rule is that anybody who is capable of making a will is capable of acting as executor, and as a person under the age of eighteen years cannot make a valid will, an executor who is under the age of eighteen years cannot apply for a grant of probate. Though the appointment of a person under the age of eighteen years as executor will be a valid appointment, he or she has not the legal capacity to apply for a grant while still a minor, and a guardian has to be appointed to apply for a grant on his or her behalf. A grant of letters of administration with the will annexed may be made to the guardian of a minor and the guardian will remain the personal representative of the estate **16–01** of the deceased person until the minor attains the age of majority and applies for a grant himself or herself.[1]

16–02 A testator may also appoint his executors and/or trustees to be the guardians of his infant children and, on his death, they may act jointly with a surviving parent as guardians.[2] Where, however, the surviving parent objects to the testamentary guardian appointed by the deceased testator, or where the testamentary guardian alleges that the surviving parent is unfit to act as guardian, the court may decide that the surviving parent should be the sole guardian, or that both surviving parent and testamentary guardian act jointly, or that the testamentary guardian should be the sole guardian. Where the person entitled has no testamentary guardian or a guardian appointed by the court, or by or under the provisions of the Guardianship of Infants Act 1964 (the "1964 Act"), a guardian may be assigned by order of the court or of the probate officer.

16–03 According to a Probate Update issued from the Probate Office in August 2012 concerning applications for grants by guardians:

> "This type of grant will state on its face that it is limited for the use and benefit of the named minor and limited until he reaches the age of 18 years or, having attained that age, until the said minor has applied for a full grant. (Rules of the Superior Courts, Ord.79, rrs.24 and 25) Generally a probate officer's order is required before applying for this type of grant. Where the person entitled to extract a grant is a minor, and where the minor does not have a testamentary guardian, or where a guardian has not been appointed by the court, a probate officer's order may be sought appointing a person as guardian of the minor for the purpose of extracting a grant in the estate. The most commonly appointed guardians would be the natural mother or father of the minor. The grant that issues is limited for the use and benefit of the said minor."

16–04 A person of unsound mind is also incapable of applying for a grant and, in such cases, the committee appointed by the probate officer may apply for a grant on behalf of the person entitled to apply for a grant. Order 79, r.26 of the Rules of the Superior Courts 1986 (the "1986 Rules") provides that a grant of letters of administration with the will annexed or intestate may be made to a committee of a person of unsound mind for such person's use and benefit and during his or her incapacity.

16–05 According to a Probate Office Update in August 2012 dealing with grants to committees:

> "This type of grant will state on its face that it is limited for the use and benefit of the named individual (who is entitled to extract the grant but who is incapacitated) and that it is limited during the incapacity of that individual. Where the incapacitated person is not a ward of court, a probate officer's order may be obtained to appoint a committee. Where a person entitled to extract a grant is

[1] See Albert Keating, "Beneficial Grants of Representation" (2008) 13(4) C.P.L.J. 85.

[2] See Chapter 24 – Wills Precedents.

> already a ward of court, a letter of consent must be obtained from the Registrar of Wards of Court allowing the committee already appointed to proceed with the application for a grant. Where the incapacitated person is a ward of court, the committee in the wardship matters may apply without a probate officer's order. However, the Probate Office will require proof that the Registrar of the Wards of Court is on notice that the committee intends applying for the grant. The Probate Office will accept the following items as proof:
>
> 1. An attested copy wards of court order giving the named committee liberty to extract the grant in a particular estate.
> 2. A letter from the Wards of Court Office consenting to the application for a grant in the particular estate.
>
> A person who is of full capacity and is equally entitled to a grant with a person of unsound mind is entitled to extract the grant in priority to the committee of such person (Order 79, Rule 5(9)(c)). The probate officer does have discretion to set aside this priority if he/she deems it appropriate in the circumstances of the case. The following proofs are required to be lodged in the Probate Office:
>
> 1. Affidavit from the proposed committee setting out the facts i.e. name, address, date of death of deceased, entitlement of person of unsound mind to grant, domicile of person of unsound mind, no other person equally entitled to grant, assets within the jurisdiction and request for order appointing him committee. (If the executor is incapacitated the appropriate committee is the residuary legatee and devisee; If the person entitled to administration is incapacitated, the appropriate committee is his/her next of kin; If the residuary legatee and devisee is incapacitated, the appropriate committee is his/her next of kin.)
> 2. Affidavit from a medical practitioner giving evidence of the person's mental incapacity.
> 3. A letter of consent from the Wards of Court Office.
> 4. Fees (probate officer's orders carry fees, and so do any necessary affidavits. The fees must accompany the application).
>
> Where the application for the grant is made through a District Probate Registry, the probate officer's order application may be lodged in the relevant registry, and the registry will then forward the application to the Dublin Probate Office for consideration by the probate officer."

Where the executor appointed by the will, or the person entitled to apply for a grant under Ord.79 of the 1986 Rules, is residing outside the jurisdiction, a grant may be made to his or her attorney until he or she returns to the jurisdiction. A grant may also be issued to an attorney where it is shown to the satisfaction of the court or the probate officer that the person entitled to the grant is suffering from a severe and continuing physical disability.[3] **16–06**

According to a Probate Office Update in August 2012 dealing with applications for grants by attorneys: **16–07**

---

[3] See Albert Keating, *Irish Probate Precedents Service* (Dublin: Round Hall, 2009); Albert Keating, *Keating on Probate* (4th ed) (Dublin: Round Hall, 2011); Albert Keating, *First Supplement to the Fourth Edition of Keating on Probate* (Dublin: Thomson Round Hall, 2013).

> "The form of power used is specific to the administration of the estate in question. A form of a general nature is not acceptable as all general powers are now governed by the Powers of Attorney Act 1996 which precludes donors of such powers delegating trustee/legal personal representative powers. A donee of an enduring power of attorney is not entitled to extract a grant of representation on behalf of a donor of such power. Section 16 of the Powers of Attorney Act 1996 indicates that the donor of such powers cannot delegate functions which they may have as trustee, or personal representative."

Applications for Grants by Guardians

16–08 Generally a probate officer's order is required before a guardian applies for a grant. However, a probate officer's order will not be required if:

1. A testamentary guardian has been appointed by will;
2. A guardian has been appointed by the President of the High Court;
3. A guardian has been appointed under the 1964 Act.

16–09 Where the person entitled to apply for a grant is a minor, and where the minor does not have a testamentary guardian, or where a guardian has not been appointed by the court, a probate officer's order may be sought appointing a person as guardian of the minor for the purpose of applying a grant in the estate.

16–10 The most commonly appointed guardians would be the natural mother or father of the minor. The grant that issues is limited for the use and benefit of the minor.

16–11 Proofs required (to be lodged in the Probate Office):

1. Petition from proposed guardian;
2. Election may be required (where the child is over 12 years and someone other than the parent is the applicant);
3. Proof of parentage may be required (long form birth certificate is required or a declaration of parentage where the father's name is not on the birth certificate);
4. Fees.[4]

16–12 This type of grant will state on its face that it is limited for the use and benefit of the named minor and limited until he or she reaches eighteen years or, having attained such age, until he or she has applied for a full grant.[5]

16–13 The application to the probate officer (in the form of a petition) for the assignment of a guardian under Ord.79, r.25 of the 1986 Rules must be

---

[4] See Probate Office Update, August 2012.

[5] See Ord. 79, r.24 and r.25 of the 1986 Rules; Appendix Q, Form 17, of the 1986 Rules.

grounded on an affidavit showing the amount of assets, the age of the minor and the name of the person with whom he or she resides, and also showing that the proposed guardian is the nearest relative of the minor, or that the nearest relative has renounced his or her right to the guardianship, or is consenting to the assignment of the proposed guardian, and that such proposed guardian is ready to undertake guardianship. In considering the assignment of the guardian, the probate officer may have regard to the expressed wishes of any minor over the age of twelve years. Generally, the nearest relative of a minor will be the preferred guardian. Minors between the ages of seven and eighteen years may elect a guardian, subject to the approval of the court or the probate officer.

The Guardian of a Minor

Order 79, r.24 of the 1986 Rules provides that a grant of administration may be made to a guardian of a minor for the minor's use. Order 79, r.25 provides that, where any minor has no testamentary guardian or guardian appointed by the court, or by or under the provisions of the 1964 Act, a guardian must be assigned by order of the court or of the probate officer. **16–14**

A guardian may be any one of the following: **16–15**

1. The father and mother jointly, provided they are married;
2. A surviving parent;
3. A surviving parent jointly with a testamentary guardian appointed by the deceased parent, or a guardian appointed by deed during the lifetime of the deceased. Both parents are entitled to appoint a guardian by deed or by will to act jointly with the surviving parent;
4. Where the surviving parent objects to a testamentary guardian appointed by the deceased parent, or where the testamentary guardian alleges that the surviving parent is unfit to act as guardian, an application may be made to the Circuit Court or High Court and the court may decide that the surviving parent be the sole guardian, or that both surviving parent and testamentary guardian act jointly, or that the testamentary guardian or a guardian appointed by deed be the sole guardian;
5. Where there is no surviving parent, the testamentary guardian or a guardian appointed by deed will be the sole guardian;
6. If the guardian appointed by deed or will is dead or refuses to act, the court is empowered to appoint a guardian and the court is also empowered to remove a guardian appointed by the parents;
7. Section 11 of the Status of Children Act 1987 (the "1987 Act") replaced s.6(4) of the 1964 Act with the following:

   > "Where the mother of an infant has not married the infant's father, she, while living, shall alone be the guardian of the infant unless there is in

> force an order under s.6A (inserted by the Act of 1987) of this Act or a guardian has otherwise been appointed in accordance with this Act."

16–16 The term "parent" as used in the 1964 Act excluded the father of an non-marital (or non-civil partnership) child. But s.12 of the 1987 Act inserting s.6A(1) of the 1964 Act now provides that:

> "Where the father and mother of an infant have not married each other, the court may, on the application of the father, by order appoint him to be a guardian of the infant."

16–17 The appointment by the court of the father as guardian will not, however, affect the prior appointment of any person as a guardian under s.8(1) of the 1964 Act, unless the court orders otherwise. The 1987 Act gives the natural father a right only to apply to the court to be appointed guardian, though not a "right to be guardian". The court, when exercising its discretion to make an appointment, will always treat the welfare of the child as the first and paramount consideration. The mother may, however, consent in writing to the appointment of the father as guardian if the father subsequently registers himself as the father of the child under the Births and Deaths Registration Acts 1863-1987, and such consent and registration could be used in support of any application made by him to the court to be appointed guardian. In the case of void marriages, the father may not have to apply to the court to be appointed guardian under the new s.6A of the 1964 Act where it is shown that he reasonably believed at the appropriate time that he was lawfully married to the mother, or in the case of a voidable marriage which is later annulled, that he reasonably held this belief after the child was conceived. In the case of a void marriage, it will be presumed that the father reasonably believed that the marriage was a valid one until the contrary is shown. Since the Children Act 1997, s.4, a court application for guardianship by a natural father may not be necessary where the natural father and mother of the child make a statutory declaration to the effect that they are not married to each other, that both are the parents of the child and it is agreed between them that the natural father be appointed a guardian of the child, and that an arrangement has been made regarding the custody and access to the child.

16–18 Section 30 of the 1987 Act provides for a rebuttable presumption that, where a non-marital relationship affects the title to a grant, all those persons who would be entitled to apply for a grant on the basis of that non-marital relationship have predeceased the deceased. The long form of birth certificate must be exhibited in the oath for administrator intestate. Where a mother and non-marital child are involved, this is accepted as conclusive. Where a father and non-marital or non civil partnership child are involved, s.46(3) of the 1987 Act presumes that the father registered on the birth certificate is the father of the child, unless the contrary is proved on the balance of probabilities. Where the father's name does not appear on the birth certificate, an application may be made *ex parte* to the probate officer in his list. If he is not convinced, an application will have to be made to court. A declaration of parentage may be sought from the Circuit Court under s.35 of the 1987 Act. Minors may elect an uncle/aunt to be their guardian for the purpose of applying for a grant of letters of administration intestate.

Applications for a Grant of Letters of Administration with Will Annexed by a Guardian

The guardian of a minor may apply for a grant for the minor's use and benefit until he or she attains the age of eighteen years, and the grant issued to the guardian will be limited to the minority of the person entitled to the grant. Where there is no guardian appointed, one may be assigned by the court or by the probate officer for the purposes of applying for a grant. **16–19**

Essential Proofs

1. Form S1 (postal application form) must be lodged with all applications submitted by post; **16–20**
2. The original will (and codicils, if any);
3. Order of probate officer appointing the applicant as guardian of the minor;
4. Certified copy of will (and codicils, if any);
5. Oath of administrator with will annexed by guardian;
6. Copy oath of administrator with will annexed by guardian;
7. Administration bond;
8. Inland Revenue Affidavit (Form CA 24 (2010 edition));
9. Death certificate;
10. Affidavit of market value or certificate of market value.

OATH OF ADMINISTRATOR WITH THE WILL

The High Court
Probate

The Probate Office/The District Probate Registry at

In the estate of late of deceased.

I, of aged eighteen years and upwards, make oath and say, that I believe the paper writing hereunto annexed, and marked by me, to contain the true and original last will [*or* last will with codicils] of late of [address and description], deceased, and that same was made by the said after attaining the age of [enter age] years, and that he did not intermarry with any person after the making of same, and that I am the guardian lawfully appointed by order of the probate officer dated the [insert day] day of [insert month and year]. limited to the use and benefit of CD the named sole executor in the said will and during his minority and that I will well and faithfully administer the estate of the said testator, by paying his just debts and the legacies bequeathed by his said will [*or* will and codicils] and distributing the residue of his estate according to law; and that I will exhibit a true and perfect inventory of the said estate, and render a true account thereof whenever required by law so to do; and that the testator died at [insert address] on the day of [where application is made in a District Probate Registry, add: and had at the time of his death a fixed place of abode at within the district of] and that the whole of the personal estate of the said testator amounts in value to the sum of [the gross personal estate, without any deductions for debts] and that the whole of the real estate of the said testator which devolves on and vests in his legal personal representative is of the market value of [the amount shown in the affidavit of market value] and no more to the best of my knowledge, information and belief.

Sworn, &c.

ADMINISTRATION BOND

THE HIGH COURT

The Probate Office/The District Probate Registry at

I [insert name, address and description of applicant and surety/sureties if applicable] am liable in full to pay to the President of the High Court the sum of [insert penal sum twice gross assets of estate reflecting current market value of immovable property] for which payment I bind myself, my executors, administrators and successors and sealed with my seal and dated the [insert day of signing bond] day of [insert month and year of signing bond]. The condition of this obligation is that, if the above-named [insert name of applicant] the guardian of CD [insert name] and the said CD [name] is named sole executor in the will of (I[insert name, address and description of deceased]) deceased, and the intended administrator/ administratix of the estate of the said deceased, do, when lawfully called on in that behalf, make or cause to be made a true inventory of the said estate which has or shall come into his/her hands, possession or knowledge, or into the hands, possession or control of any other person for him/her;

do exhibit the said inventory or cause it to be exhibited in the Probate Office [or in the District Probate Registry at] whenever required by law to do so; do well and truly administer the said estate according to law, paying all the debts owed by the deceased at the time of his death, all death duties payable in respect of the estate of the deceased for which the personal representative is accountable and all income tax and surtax payable out of the estate,

distributing all shares in the estate to those entitled by law thereto and as the law requires him/her; and further, do make or cause to be made a true account of the said administration whenever required by law to do so;

then this obligation shall be void and no effect, but shall otherwise remain in full force and effect.

Signed, sealed and delivered by the within-named	Applicant(s) signature and seal
Name of applicant and surety/ sureties if applicable	Surety's/sureties' signature and seal [if applicable]

In the presence of
[insert Commissioner's/Solicitor's name]

Commissioner/Solicitor to sign here
Commissioner/Solicitor

Applicant(s) should execute bond before Commissioner/Solicitor on oath.[6]

Applications for a Grant of Letters of Administration Intestate by a Guardian

The following are the essential proofs that must be submitted by the guardian of a minor entitled to apply for a grant of letters of administration intestate under Ord.79, r.5(1): **16–21**

1. Form S1 (postal application form);
2. The order of the probate officer assigning a guardian to the minor to apply for a grant;
3. The election by minors;
4. The oath of administrator intestate by guardian;
5. A copy of the oath of administrator intestate by guardian,
6. The Inland Revenue Affidavit (Forms CA 24 (2010 edition) where the deceased died after 5 December 2001 or Form CA24 (2000 edition) where the deceased died before 5 December 2001,
7. Death certificate of the deceased intestate and
8. Affidavit or certificate of market value.

The application by the guardian for a grant of letters of administration intestate may be made to the Probate Office or a District Probate Registry within whose area the deceased testator had a fixed place of abode at the time of his death. **16–22**

6 See Ord.79, r.29 of the Rules of the Superior Courts.

Application for a Grant of Letters of Administration Intestate by a Grandparent as Guardian of a Son/Daughter of the Deceased

16–23 OATH OF ADMINISTRATOR

THE HIGH COURT
PROBATE

The Probate Office/The District Probate Registry at

In the estate of [name of deceased] late of [address] deceased.

I, [name of guardian] of [address] aged eighteen years and upwards, make oath and say that [name of deceased], late of [address and description], deceased, died intestate leaving AB [name of widow] his lawful widow and CD [name of surviving child] his lawful son/daughter him surviving and that the said AB[name of widow] has since died and that I am the guardian of the said CD [name of child] lawfully appointed by order of the probate officer dated the day of 20 limited to the use and benefit of the said CD[name of child] and during his/her minority and that I will well and faithfully administer the estate of the said deceased by paying his just debts and distributing the residue of said estate according to law, and that I will exhibit a true inventory of the said estate and render a true account thereof, whenever required by law so to do; that the said deceased died at on the day of [and that the said deceased had at the time of his death a fixed place of abode at within the district of] and that the whole of the personal estate of the said deceased amounts in value to the sum of [the gross personal estate without any deductions for debts] and that the whole of the real estate of the said deceased which devolves on and vests in his legal personal representatives is of the market value of [the amount shown in the affidavit of market value] and no more to the best of my knowledge, information and belief.

Sworn, &c.

ADMINISTRATION BOND

THE HIGH COURT

The Probate Office/The District Probate Registry at

I [insert name address and description of guardian and surety/sureties if applicable] am liable in full to pay to the President of the High Court the sum of [insert penal sum twice gross assets of estate reflecting current market value of immovable property] for which payment I bind myself and my executors, administrators and successors and sealed with my seal and dated the [insert day of signing bond] day of [insert month and year of signing bond]. The condition of this obligation is that if the above-named [insert name of applicant] the lawful guardian of CD [name,] the lawful son/daughter of [insert name, address and description of deceased]

deceased, and the intended administrator/administratix of the estate of the said deceased, do, when lawfully called on in that behalf, make or cause to be made a true inventory of the said estate which has or shall come into his/her hands, possession or knowledge, or into the hands, possession or control of any other person for him/her;

do exhibit the said inventory or cause it to be exhibited in the Probate Office [or in the District Probate Registry at] whenever required by law to do so; do well and truly administer the said estate according to law, paying all the debts owed by the deceased at the time of his death, all death duties payable in respect of the estate of the deceased for which the personal representative is accountable and all income tax and surtax payable out of the estate,

distributing all shares in the estate to those entitled by law thereto and as the law requires him/her; and further, do make or cause to be made a true account of the said administration whenever required by law to do so;

and further do, if so required, render and deliver up the letters of administration in the High Court if it shall hereafter appear that any will was made by the deceased which is exhibited in the said Court with a request that it be allowed and approved accordingly;

then this obligation shall be void and no effect, but shall otherwise remain in full force and effect.

Signed, sealed and delivered by the within-named	Applicant(s) signature and seal
Name of applicant and surety/ sureties if applicable	Surety's/sureties' signature and seal [if applicable]

In the presence of
[insert Commissioner's/Solicitor's name]

Commissioner/Solicitor to sign here
Commissioner/Solicitor

Applicant(s) should execute bond before Commissioner/Solicitor on oath.

Applications for Grants by Committees

Order 79, r.26 of the 1986 Rules provides that a grant of letters of administration with the will annexed or intestate may be made to a committee of a person of unsound mind for such person's use and benefit and during his incapacity.[7] By Ord.79, s.27 of the 1986 Rules, where a person of unsound mind has no such committee, a grant may issue to such person as the probate **16–24**

[7] See Albert Keating, *Keating on Probate* (4th ed) (Dublin: Round Hall, 2011); Albert Keating, *First Supplement to the Fourth Edition of Keating on Probate* (Dublin: Thomson Round Hall, 2013).

officer may by order assign with the consent of the Registrar of Wards of Court. Where an executor, or the person entitled to apply for a grant, is of unsound mind, a grant may be made to a committee for his use and benefit and limited to his mental incapacity. Where there is no committee, one may be appointed by the court or by order of the probate officer with the consent of the Registrar of the Wards of Court for the purposes of extracting a grant. The person desiring to be appointed the committee of the person of unsound mind must first petition the probate officer showing the amount of the assets, the age and residence of the person of unsound mind and his or her relationship to the applicant, together with an affidavit of a medical practitioner identifying the nature of the mental incapacity of such person. Where, however, two persons are equally entitled to apply for a grant and a committee has been appointed for one of them, the grant will be made to the other person in preference to the committee. All the necessary proofs required when applying for a grant in ordinary circumstances must likewise be prepared and submitted by the committee appointed by the probate officer. The order of the probate officer assigning the committee must be included among the proofs.

Applications for Grants of Letters of Administration with Will Annexed by a Committee

16–25 The following are the essential proofs that must be submitted by the committee assigned by the probate officer when applying for a grant of letters of administration with the will annexed on behalf of the person entitled under Ord.79, r.5(6):

1. The order of the probate officer appointing committee;
2. Affidavit of medical practitioner;
3. Letter of consent of the Registrar of Wards of Court;
4. Form S1 (postal application form);
5. Original will (and codicils, if any);
6. Certified copy of will;
7. Oath of administrator with the will annexed by committee;
8. Copy of oath of administrator with the will annexed by committee;
9. An administration bond;
10. Inland Revenue Affidavit (Form CA 24 (2010 edition));
11. Death certificate;
12. Affidavit of market value or certificate of market value.

16–26 The Inland Revenue Affidavit (Forms CA 24) (2010 edition) will be required where the deceased died after 5 December 2001 or Form CA24 (2000 edition) where the deceased died before 5 December 2001. Additional proofs may consist of an affidavit of an attesting witness, affidavit of plight and condition, affidavit of mental capacity of a testator by his medical practitioner, or an affidavit of mental capacity of a testator by his solicitor.

Where the incapacitated person is a ward of court, the committee in the wardship matter may apply without a probate officer's order. However, the Probate Office will require proof that the Registrar of the Wards of Court is on notice that the committee intends applying for the grant. **16–27**

The Probate Office will accept the following items as proof: **16–28**

- Attested copy wards of court order giving the named committee liberty to extract the grant in a particular estate;
- Letter from the Wards of Court Office consenting to the application for a grant in the particular estate.

OATH OF ADMINISTRATOR WITH THE WILL

THE HIGH COURT
PROBATE

In the estate of late of deceased.

I, of aged eighteen years and upwards, make oath and say, that I believe the paper writing hereunto annexed, and marked by me, to contain the true and original last will [*or* last will with codicils] of late of [address and description], deceased, and that same was made by the said after attaining the age of [age] years, and that he did not intermarry with any person after the making of same, and did therein name as sole executor CD [child's name] and that the said CD [child's name] is incapable in law of taking upon himself probate of the estate of the said deceased and that I am the lawfully appointed committee of the said CD [child's name] by order of the probate officer dated the day of 20 limited to the use and benefit of the said CD [child's name] during his incapacity that I will well and faithfully administer the estate of the said testator, by paying his just debts and the legacies bequeathed by his said will [*or* will and codicils] and distributing the residue of his estate according to law; and that I will exhibit a true and perfect inventory of the said estate, and render a true account thereof whenever required by law so to do; and that the testator died at on the day of [where application is made in a District Probate Registry, add: and had at the time of his death a fixed place of abode at within the district of] and that the whole of the personal estate of the said testator amounts in value to the sum of [the gross personal estate, without any deductions for debts] and that the whole of the real estate of the said testator which devolves on and vests in his legal personal representative is of the market value of [the amount shown in the affidavit of market value] and no more to the best of my knowledge, information and belief.

Sworn, &c.

ADMINISTRATION BOND

THE HIGH COURT

The Probate Office/The District Probate Registry at

I [insert name address and description of applicant and surety/sureties if applicable] am liable in full to pay to the President of the High Court the sum of [insert penal sum twice gross assets of estate reflecting current market value of immovable property] for which payment I bind myself and my executors, administrators and successors and sealed with my seal and dated the [insert day of signing bond] day of [insert month and year of signing bond]. The condition of this obligation is that if the above-named [insert name of applicant] the lawfully appointed committee of CD [child's name] by order of the probate officer dated the day of 20 and that the said CD [child's name] is named sole executor in the will of [insert name, address and description of deceased] deceased, and the intended administrator/ administratix of the estate of the said deceased, do, when lawfully called on in that behalf, make or cause to be made a true inventory of the said estate which has or shall come into his/her hands, possession or knowledge, or into the hands, possession or control of any other person for him/her;

do exhibit the said inventory or cause it to be exhibited in the Probate Office [or in the District Probate Registry at] whenever required by law to do so; do well and truly administer the said estate according to law, paying all the debts owed by the deceased at the time of his death, all death duties payable in respect of the estate of the deceased for which the personal representative is accountable and all income tax and surtax payable out of the estate,

distributing all shares in the estate to those entitled by law thereto and as the law requires him/her; and further, do make or cause to be made a true account of the said administration whenever required by law to do so;

then this obligation shall be void and no effect, but shall otherwise remain in full force and effect.

Signed, sealed and delivered by the within-named	Applicant(s) signature and seal
Name of applicant and surety/ sureties if applicable	Surety's/sureties' signature and seal [if applicable]

In the presence of
[insert Commissioner's/Solicitor's name]

Commissioner/Solicitor to sign here
Commissioner/Solicitor

Applicant(s) should execute bond before Commissioner/Solicitor on oath.[8]

8 See Ord 79, r.29 Rules of the Superior Courts.

Applications for Grants of Letters of Administration Intestate by a Committee

The following are the essential proofs that must be submitted by the committee assigned by the probate officer person when applying for a grant of letters of administration intestate on behalf of the person entitled under Ord.79, r.5(1): the order of the probate officer appointing the committee, affidavit of medical practitioner, letter of consent of the Registrar of Wards of Court, Form S1 (postal application form), oath of administrator intestate by committee, copy of oath of committee administrator intestate by committee, administration bond, Inland Revenue Affidavit (Form CA 24 (2010 edition)), death certificate, affidavit of market value or certificate of market value. The Inland Revenue Affidavit (Forms CA 24) (2010 edition) will be required where the deceased died after 5 December 2001 or Form CA24 (2000 edition) where the deceased died before 5 December 2001, and death certificate of the deceased intestate. The application by the committee for a grant of letters of administration with the will annexed or letters of administration intestate may be made to the Probate Office or a District Probate Registry within whose area the deceased testator had a fixed place of abode at the time of his death.[9] **16–29**

OATH OF ADMINISTRATOR

THE HIGH COURT
PROBATE

In the estate of late of deceased.

I, of aged eighteen years and upwards, make oath and say that late of [address and description], deceased, died intestate a bachelor leaving CD his lawful brother/sister him surviving and that the said CD is incapable in law of taking upon himself/herself letters of administration of the estate of the said deceased and that I am the lawfully appointed Committee of the said CD by order of the probate officer dated the day of 20 limited to the use and benefit of the said CD during his/her incapacity and that I will well and faithfully administer the estate of the said deceased by paying his just debts and distributing the residue of said estate according to law, and that I will exhibit a true inventory of the said estate and render a true account thereof, whenever required by law so to do; that the said deceased died at on the day of [where application is made in a District Probate Registry, add: and that the said deceased had at the time of his death a fixed place of abode at within the district of] and that the whole of the personal estate of the said deceased amounts in value to the sum of [the gross personal estate without any deductions for debts] and that the whole of the real estate of the said deceased which devolves on and vests in his legal personal representatives is of the market value of [the amount shown in the affidavit of market value] and no more to the best of my knowledge, information and belief.

Sworn, &c.

---

[9] See Albert Keating, *Keating on Probate* (4th ed) (Dublin: Round Hall, 2011); Albert Keating, *First Supplement to the Fourth Edition of Keating on Probate* (Dublin: Thomson Round Hall, 2013).

ADMINISTRATION BOND

The High Court

The Probate Office/The District Probate Registry at

I [insert name, address and description of applicant and surety/sureties if applicable] am liable in full to pay to the President of the High Court the sum of [insert penal sum twice gross assets of estate reflecting current market value of immovable property] for which payment I bind myself and my executors, administrators and successors and sealed with my seal and dated the [insert day of signing bond] day of [insert month and year of signing bond]. The condition of this obligation is that if the above-named [insert name of applicant] the lawfully appointed committee of CD by order of the probate officer dated the day of 20 and that the said CD is the lawful nephew/niece of [insert name address and description of deceased] deceased, and the intended administrator/administratix of the estate of the said deceased, do, when lawfully called on in that behalf, make or cause to be made a true inventory of the said estate which has or shall come into his/her hands, possession or knowledge, or into the hands, possession or control of any other person for him/her;

do exhibit the said inventory or cause it to be exhibited in the Probate Office [or in the District Probate Registry at] whenever required by law to do so; do well and truly administer the said estate according to law, paying all the debts owed by the deceased at the time of his death, all death duties payable in respect of the estate of the deceased for which the personal representative is accountable and all income tax and surtax payable out of the estate,

distributing all shares in the estate to those entitled by law thereto and as the law requires him/her; and further, do make or cause to be made a true account of the said administration whenever required by law to do so;

and further do, if so required, render and deliver up the letters of administration in the High Court if it shall hereafter appear that any will was made by the deceased which is exhibited in the said Court with a request that it be allowed and approved accordingly;

then this obligation shall be void and no effect, but shall otherwise remain in full force and effect.

Signed, sealed and delivered by the within-named	Applicant(s) signature and seal
Name of applicant and surety/ sureties if applicable	Surety's/sureties' signature and seal [if applicable]

In the presence of
[insert Commissioner's/Solicitor's name]

Commissioner/Solicitor to sign here
Commissioner/Solicitor

Applicant(s) should execute bond before Commissioner/Solicitor on oath.[10]

Applications for Grants by Attorneys

Where the executor appointed by the will, or the person entitled to apply for a grant under Ord.79 of the 1986 Rules, is residing outside the jurisdiction, a grant may be made to his or her attorney until he or she returns to the jurisdiction.[11] The attorney, once a grant is issued, will have all the powers of a general administrator until the executor or person entitled to apply for a grant of letters of administration has returned to the jurisdiction. The attorney's powers of administration will cease on the return of the executor or person entitled to a grant to the jurisdiction or on his or her death. On the death of the executor or person entitled who is residing out of the jurisdiction, the attorney's powers to administer the estate will cease. The person next entitled may apply for a grant *de bonis non* to continue with the administration of the estate. The grant issued to the attorney is limited to the period of residence abroad by the executor or person entitled to a grant. A grant may also be issued to an attorney where it is shown to the satisfaction of the court or the probate officer that the person entitled to the grant is suffering from a severe and continuing physical disability. The application by the attorney for a grant must be accompanied by an affidavit of the medical practitioner of the executor or the person entitled to a grant of letters of administration with the will annexed or intestate specifying the nature of the physical disability that renders him or her incapable of carrying out the functions of a personal representative. It is important to note that the grant to the attorney in this instance is made because the person entitled is suffering from a physical disability, as opposed to mental incapacity, as the latter will require the appointment of a committee to apply for a grant. **16–30**

The power of attorney is a document which the person giving/delegating the power (known as the donor) executes, in which he names another person (known as the donee of the power) to carry out the necessary functions attaching to the office in question. The form of power used is specific to the administration of the estate in question. A form of a general nature is not acceptable, as all general powers are now governed by the Powers of Attorney Act 1996 which precludes donors of such powers delegating trustee/legal personal representative powers. A donee of an enduring power of attorney is not entitled to extract a grant of representation on behalf of a donor of such power. Section 16 of the Powers of Attorney Act 1996 indicates that the donor of such powers cannot delegate functions which they may have as trustee, or personal representative.[12]

---

10 See Ord.79, r.29, Rules of the Superior Courts.

11 See Albert Keating, *Keating on Probate* (4th ed) (Dublin: Round Hall, 2011); Albert Keating, *First Supplement to the Fourth Edition of Keating on Probate* (Dublin: Thomson Round Hall, 2013).

12 Probate Office Update, August 2012.

Applications for a Grant of Letters of Administration with Will Annexed by an Attorney

Essential Proofs

16–31
1. Form S1 (postal application form) must be lodged with all applications submitted by post;
2. The power of attorney;
3. Original will (and codicils, if any);
4. Certified copy of will;
5. Oath of administrator with will annexed by attorney;
6. Copy oath of administrator with will annexed by attorney;
7. Administration bond by attorney;
8. Inland Revenue Affidavit (Form CA 24 (2010 edition));
9. Affidavit of mvalue or certificate of market value;
10. Death certificate.

OATH OF ADMINISTRATOR WITH THE WILL

THE HIGH COURT
PROBATE

In the estate of [name of deceased] late of [address] deceased.

I, [name of attorney] of [address] aged eighteen years and upwards, make oath and say that I believe the paper writing hereunto annexed, and marked by me, to contain the true and original last will [*or* last will with codicils] of [name of deceased], late of [address and description], deceased, and that same was made by the said [name of deceased] after attaining the age of years, and that he did not intermarry or entering a civil partnership with any person after the making of same, e.g. and that he did therein name CD [executor's name] sole executor who is aged eighteen years and upwards and is now residing at [full foreign address] [description] and that I am the attorney lawfully appointed of the said CD [executor's name] under power of attorney dated upon which I have signed my name and marked the letter 'A' prior to the swearing hereof and that I will well and faithfully administer the estate of the said testator, by paying his just debts and the legacies bequeathed by his said will [*or* will and codicils] and distributing the residue of his estate according to law; and that I will exhibit a true and perfect inventory of the said estate, and render a true account thereof whenever required by law so to do; and that the testator died at on the day of [where application is made in a District Probate Registry, add: and had at the time of his death a fixed place of abode at within the district of] and that the whole of the personal estate of the said testator amounts in value to the sum of [the gross personal estate, without any deductions for debts] and that the whole of the real estate of the said testator which devolves on and vests in his legal personal representative is of the market value of [the amount shown in the affidavit of market value] and no more to the best of my knowledge, information and belief.

Sworn, &c.

ADMINISTRATION BOND

THE HIGH COURT

The Probate Office/The District Probate Registry at

I [insert name address and description of attorney and surety/sureties if applicable] am liable in full to pay to the President of the High Court the sum of [insert penal sum twice gross assets of estate reflecting current market value of immovable property] for which payment I bind myself and my executors, administrators and successors and sealed with my seal and dated the [insert day of signing bond] day of [insert month and year of signing bond]. The condition of this obligation is that if the above-named [insert name of applicant] the attorney lawfully appointed of CD [name of executor] sole executor in the will of [insert name address and description of deceased] deceased, and the intended administrator/administratix of the estate of the said deceased, do, when lawfully called on in that behalf, make or cause to be made a true inventory of the said estate which has or shall come into his/her hands, possession or knowledge, or into the hands, possession or control of any other person for him/her;

do exhibit the said inventory or cause it to be exhibited in the Probate Office [or in the District Probate Registry at] whenever required by law to do so; do well and truly administer the said estate according to law, paying all the debts owed by the deceased at the time of his death, all death duties payable in respect of the estate of the deceased for which the personal representative is accountable and all income tax and surtax payable out of the estate,

distributing all shares in the estate to those entitled by law thereto and as the law requires him/her; and further, do make or cause to be made a true account of the said administration whenever required by law to do so;

then this obligation shall be void and no effect, but shall otherwise remain in full force and effect.

Signed, sealed and delivered by the within-named	Applicant(s) signature and seal
Name of applicant and surety/ sureties if applicable	Surety's/sureties' signature and seal [if applicable]

In the presence of
[insert Commissioner's/Solicitor's name]

Commissioner/Solicitor to sign here
Commissioner/Solicitor

Applicant(s) should execute bond before Commissioner/Solicitor on oath.[13]

[13] See Ord.79, r.29, Rules of the Superior Courts.

Applications for a Grant of Letters of Administration Intestate by an Attorney

16–32 The following are the essential proofs that must be lodged in the Probate Office or a District Probate Registry by the attorney of the person to apply for a grant of letters of administration intestate under Ord.79, r.5(1):

1. Form S1 (postal application form) must be lodged with all applications submitted by post;
2. Power of attorney;
3. Oath of administrator intestate by attorney;
4. Copy oath of administrator intestate by attorney;
5. Administration bond by attorney;
6. Inland Revenue Affidavit (Form CA 24 (2010 edition));
7. Death certificate; and
8. Affidavit of market value or certificate of market value.

16–33 The Inland Revenue Affidavit (Forms CA 24 (2010 edition) will be required where the deceased died after 5 December 2001, or Form CA24 (2000 edition) where the deceased died before 5 December 2001. The application by the attorney for a grant of letters of administration with the will annexed or letters of administration intestate may be made to the Probate Office or a District Probate Registry within whose area the deceased testator had a fixed place of abode at the time of his death.[14]

Application by an Attorney for a Grant of Letters of Administration Intestate for the Use and Benefit of the Person Entitled to a Grant Who is Residing out of Jurisdiction

16–34 OATH OF ADMINISTRATOR

THE HIGH COURT
PROBATE

In the estate of [name of deceased] late of [address] deceased.

I, [name of attorney] of [address] aged eighteen years and upwards, make oath and say that [name of deceased] late of [address and description], deceased, died intestate leaving him surviving his lawful widow CD [widow's name] who is aged eighteen years and upwards and is now residing at [full foreign address] [description] and that I am the attorney lawfully appointed of the said CD [widow's name] under power of attorney dated upon which I have signed my name and marked the letter 'A' prior to the swearing hereof and that I will

[14] See Albert Keating, *Irish Probate Precedents Service* (Dublin: Round Hall, 2009).

well and faithfully administer the estate of the said deceased by paying his just debts and distributing the residue of said estate according to law, and that I will exhibit a true inventory of the said estate and render a true account thereof, whenever required by law so to do; that the said deceased died at on the day of [where application is made in a District Probate Registry, add: and that the said deceased had at the time of his death a fixed place of abode at within the district of] and that the whole of the personal estate of the said deceased amounts in value to the sum of [the gross personal estate without any deductions for debts] and that the whole of the real estate of the said deceased which devolves on and vests in his legal personal representatives is of the market value of [the amount shown in the affidavit or certificate? of market value] and no more to the best of my knowledge, information and belief.

Sworn, &c.

ADMINISTRATION BOND

THE HIGH COURT

The Probate Office/The District Probate Registry at

I [insert name, address and description of attorney and surety/sureties if applicable] am liable in full to pay to the President of the High Court the sum of [insert penal sum twice gross assets of estate reflecting current market value of immovable property] for which payment I bind myself and my executors, administrators and successors and sealed with my seal and dated the [insert day of signing bond] day of [insert month and year of signing bond]. The condition of this obligation is that if the above-named [insert name of applicant] the attorney lawfully appointed of CD [widow's name] the lawful widow of [insert name address and description of deceased] deceased, and the intended administrator/administratix of the estate of the said deceased, do, when lawfully called on in that behalf, make or cause to be made a true inventory of the said estate which has or shall come into his/her hands, possession or knowledge, or into the hands, possession or control of any other person for him/her;

do exhibit the said inventory or cause it to be exhibited in the Probate Office [or in the District Probate Registry at] whenever required by law to do so; do well and truly administer the said estate according to law, paying all the debts owed by the deceased at the time of his death, all death duties payable in respect of the estate of the deceased for which the personal representative is accountable and all income tax and surtax payable out of the estate,

distributing all shares in the estate to those entitled by law thereto and as the law requires him/her; and further, do make or cause to be made a true account of the said administration whenever required by law to do so;

and further do, if so required, render and deliver up the letters of administration in the High Court if it shall hereafter appear that any will was made by the deceased which is exhibited in the said Court with a request that it be allowed and approved accordingly;

then this obligation shall be void and no effect, but shall otherwise remain in full force and effect.

Signed, sealed and delivered by the within-named	Applicant(s) signature and seal
Name of applicant and surety/ sureties if applicable	Surety's/sureties' signature and seal [if applicable]

In the presence of
[insert Commissioner's/Solicitor's name]

Commissioner/Solicitor to sign here
Commissioner/Solicitor

Applicant(s) should execute bond before Commissioner/Solicitor on oath.

CHAPTER 17

APPLICATIONS FOR *DE BONIS NON* GRANTS

INTRODUCTION

Where the person to whom a grant of letters of administration with the will annexed has issued dies during the administration of the estate, a subsequent grant of letters of administration with the will annexed *de bonis non* will become necessary to continue with the administration of the deceased's estate.[1] The applicant for the *de bonis non* grant in this case will be the person next entitled in accordance with the order of priority of persons entitled to apply for a grant of letters of administration with the will annexed in Ord.79, r.5(6) of the Rules of the Superior Courts (the "1986 Rules"). It may be noted that, where a *de bonis non* grant is sought in the case of the death of a sole or surviving executor, the applicant for the grant will be the *first* person entitled to apply under Ord.79, r.5(6) but, in the case of the death of the person to whom a grant of letters of administration with the will annexed has issued, the person *next* entitled under Ord.79, r.5(6) may apply for a *de bonis non* grant.[2] Where, for instance, the initial grant is made to the residuary legatee and devisee but that person dies during the course of administering the estate, the person next entitled under Ord.79, r.5(6) may apply for a *de bonis non*.[3] **17–01**

---

1 See Albert Keating, *Irish Probate Precedents Service* (Dublin: Round Hall, 2009); Albert Keating, *Keating on Probate* (4th ed) (Dublin: Round Hall, 2011); Albert Keating, *First Supplement to the Fourth Edition of Keating on Probate* (Dublin: Thomson Round Hall, 2013).

2 See Chapter 13 – Applications for Grants of Probate; Chapter 14 – Applications for Grants of Letters of Administration with Will Annexed; Chapter 15 – Applications for Grants of Letters of Administration Intestate.

3 See Albert Keating "Subsequent Grants of Administration" (2009) 14(2) C.P.L.J. 46.

17–02 Applications for *de bonis non* grants must be made to the Probate Office or District Probate Registry, as the case may be, out of which the original grant of letters of administration with the will annexed first issued. The original will, death certificate and any affidavits that accompanied the application for the initial grant of letters of administration with the will annexed will already have been lodged in the Probate Office or District Probate Registry, so there is no need to re-submit these documents when applying for a *de bonis non* grant. A certified copy of the original will, however, be required.

17–03 The order of priority of persons entitled to apply for a grant of letters of administration intestate is set out in Ord.79, r.5(1) of the 1986 Rules and, on the death of the person to whom such a grant has issued, the person *next* entitled under Ord.79, r.5(1) may apply for a grant of letters of administration intestate *de bonis non*.[4]

Applications for Grants of Letters of Administration with Will Annexed *De Bonis Non*

17–04 The order of priority of persons entitled to apply for a grant of letters of administration with the will annexed is set out in Ord.79, r.5(6) of the 1986 Rules and, on the death of the person to whom such a grant has issued, the person *next* entitled under Ord.79, r.5(6) may apply for a grant of letters of administration with the will annexed *de bonis non*.[5]

Essential Proofs

17–05

1. Form S1 (postal application form) must be lodged with all applications submitted by post;
2. Oath of administrator with will annexed d*e bonis non*;
3. Copy oath of administrator with will annexed d*e bonis non*;
4. Administration bond d*e bonis non*;
5. Revenue Forms A 3(C) (2010 edition) or A3C (Euro version) and D1 (Euro version) where the deceased died before 5 December 2001;
6. Certified copy of will;
7. Affidavit of market value or certificate of market value;
8. Surrender of the grant of letters of administration with will annexed.

---

[4] Albert Keating, *Irish Probate Precedents Service* (Dublin: Round Hall, 2009; See Albert Keating, *Keating on Probate* (4th ed) (Dublin: Round Hall, 2011), Chapter 34.

[5] See Chapter 14 – Applications for Grants of Letters of Administration with Will Annexed; Albert Keating, *Irish Probate Precedents Service* (Dublin: Round Hall, 2009).

Oath of Administrator with Will *De Bonis Non*

A new oath of administrator must be prepared specifying that the grant sought is for the unadministered estate of the deceased only. Where the residuary legatee and devisee extracted the initial grant of letters of administration with the will annexed but died during the course of administering the estate, the person next entitled to apply for a grant must state that the residuary legatee and devisee extracted a grant of letters of administration with the will annexed on a particular date and died leaving part of the estate unadministered, and that he is the person entitled to apply for the *de bonis non* grant. There are also three different oaths of administrator for applications for grants of letters of administration with the will annexed *de bonis non,* and the date of death of the testator will determine the type of oath to be used. Where the testator died prior to 1 June 1959, the oath will be for personal estate only. Where the date of death is between 1 June 1959 and 31 December 1966, the oath must be for both real and personal estate. For deaths occurring on or after 1 January 1967, the oath must also be for real and personal estate. **17–06**

OATH OF ADMINISTRATOR WITH THE WILL DE BONIS NON

THE HIGH COURT
PROBATE

In the estate of [name of deceased] late of [address], deceased.

I, [name of applicant] of [address] aged eighteen years and upwards, make oath and say, that I believe the paper writing hereunto annexed, and marked by me, to contain the true and original last will [or last will with codicils] of late of [address and description], deceased, and that same was made by the said after attaining the age of XX years, and that he did not intermarry with any person after the making of same, and e.g., did therein name as his sole executor [name] who extracted a grant of probate out of the Probate Office (or District Probate Registry) on the day of and died on the day of leaving part of the estate of the said deceased unadministered and that, e.g. I am the residuary legatee and devisee named in the said will and that I will well and faithfully administer the unadministered estate of the said testator, by paying his just debts and the legacies bequeathed by his said will [or will and codicils] and distributing the residue of his estate according to law; and that I will exhibit a true and perfect inventory of the said unadministered estate, and render a true account thereof whenever required by law so to do; and that the testator died at on the day of [where application is made in a District Probate Registry, add: and had at the time of his death a fixed place of abode at within the district of] and that the whole of the unadministered personal estate of the said testator amounts in value to the sum of [the gross personal estate, without any deductions for debts] and that the whole of the unadministered real estate of the said testator which devolves on and vests in his legal personal representative is of the market value of [the amount shown in the affidavit of market value] and no more to the best of my knowledge, information and belief.

Sworn, &c

Administration Bond

17–07 A new administration bond must also be prepared and the word "unadministered" should be inserted wherever there is mention of estate, and the penal figure must be for at least double the gross assets, as specified in the oath of administrator *de bonis non*. The heading of the bond will have to be amended by the addition of the words *de bonis non* and the title of the applicant for the grant may be taken from the oath of administrator *de bonis non*. There are three different administration bonds for applications for grants of letters of administration with the will annexed *de bonis non* and the date of death of the testator will determine the type of bond. Where the testator died prior to 1 June 1959, the bond will be for personal estate only. Where the date of death is between 1 June 1959 and 31 December 1966, the bond will be for both real and personal estate. For deaths occurring on or after 1 January 1967 the bond will also be for real and personal estate. The heading of the bond will have to be amended by the addition of the words *De Bonis Non* and the title of the applicant for the grant may be taken from the oath of administrator *De Bonis Non*.

ADMINISTRATION BOND DE BONIS NON

The High Court

The Probate Office/The District Probate Registry at

I [Insert name address and description of applicant and surety/sureties if applicable] am liable in full to pay to the President of the High Court the sum of [insert penal sum twice gross assets of estate reflecting current market value of immovable property] for which payment I bind myself and my executors, administrators and successors and seal with my seal and dated the [insert day of signing bond] day of [insert month and year of signing bond]. The condition of this obligation is that, if the above-named [insert name of applicant], *the residuary legatee and devisee in the will* of [insert name, address and description of deceased] deceased, and the intended administrator/administratix of the unadministered estate of the said deceased, do, when lawfully called on in that behalf, make or cause to be made a true inventory of the said unadministered estate which has or shall come into his/her hands, possession or knowledge, or into the hands, possession or control of any other person for him/her;

do exhibit the said inventory or cause it to be exhibited in the Probate Office [or in the District Probate Registry at] whenever required by law to do so; do well and truly administer the said unadministered estate according to law, paying all the debts owed by the deceased at the time of his death, all death duties payable in respect of the unadministered estate of the deceased for which the personal representative is accountable and all income tax and surtax payable out of the unadministered estate,

distributing all shares in the unadministered estate to those entitled by law thereto and as the law requires him/her; and further, do make or cause to be made a true account of the said administration whenever required by law to do so;

then this obligation shall be void and no effect, but shall otherwise remain in full force and effect.

Signed, sealed and delivered by the within-named	Applicant(s) signature and seal
Name of applicant and surety/sureties if applicable	Surety's/sureties' signature and seal [if applicable]

In the presence of
[insert Commissioner's/Solicitor's name]

Commissioner/Solicitor to sign here
Commissioner/Solicitor

Applicant(s) should execute bond before Commissioner/Solicitor on oath.[6]

Revenue Forms

Inland Revenue form A3C (2010 edition) must be downloaded and completed on screen by the person applying for the *de bonis non* grant. Form A3C (Euro version) should be used where the deceased died before 5 December 2001. Form D1 (Euro version) dealing with the schedule of buildings, land and timber may also be downloaded and completed on screen and should be used only where the deceased died before 5 December 2001. **17–08**

Any copies of vouching documents should not be included, except where any question is answered by stating 'see attached'. A copy of the "attached" document should be lodged. **17–09**

For Deaths on or after 5 December 2001

Use form A3C. Lodge two original, fully-completed sworn form A3Cs. Insert current market values. The downloaded version of A3C must be completed on a computer. The hard copy version must be completed in blue pen. Both copies must be identical. **17–10**

For Deaths before 5 December 2001

Check www.revenue.ie for the relevant forms. These forms must be lodged with the Revenue Commissioners first and a certificate for the High Court must be obtained. **17–11**

[6] See Ord.79, r.29, Rules of the Superior Courts.

Affidavit or Certificate of Market Value

17–12 A new affidavit of market value must be sworn specifying the current value of unadministered real estate. Where, however, the unadministered real estate is non-agricultural and consists of a dwelling on less than half an acre of land, a certificate of value in the form of a letter by the applicant's solicitors will be a sufficient substitution for the affidavit of market value. The affidavit must state the current value of the real estate and will be valid for six months only.

AFFIDAVIT OF MARKET VALUE

THE HIGH COURT
PROBATE

The Probate Office or District Probate Registry at

In the estate of [name of deceased], late of [address of deceased], deceased.

I [valuer, auctioneer, local farmer or surveyor] of [address and occupation] aged 18 years and upwards, make oath and say as follows:

1. I am acquainted with the value of lands in the vicinity of [address of lands valued] in the County of where lands belonging to the aforesaid [name of deceased] deceased are situate.

2. I have inspected the holdings of the aforesaid deceased at [address of lands valued] and, in my opinion, the said holdings would on the date of swearing hereof have been of the value of [amount in words and figures] if then offered for sale on the open market.

Sworn & c.

CERTIFICATE OF MARKET VALUE

Re: Estate of [name of deceased] deceased, late of [address of deceased]

I/We [name of solicitor or firm], as solicitor(s) for the administrator of the estate of the aforementioned deceased, hereby certify that the current market value of the deceased's dwelling house at [address] would not exceed [value in figures and words).

I/We confirm that the said property, while realty, is comprised of a dwelling house only.

Yours &c.

Certified Copy of Original Will

A certified copy of the original will is also necessary, and the certification must be made by the solicitor applying for the *de bonis non* grant on behalf of the person entitled. The probate engrossment of the will may, however, be a sufficient substitute. **17–13**

Surrender of Original Grant

The initial grant of probate must be surrendered to the Probate Office or District Probate Registry and, where the initial grant is lost or mislaid, a certified copy of it may be bespoken in the Probate Office or District Probate Registry, accompanied with an explanation in writing of the circumstances surrounding the loss or mislaying of the initial grant. **17–14**

Applications for Grants of Letters of Administration Intestate *De Bonis Non*

The order of priority of persons entitled to apply for a grant of letters of administration intestate is set out in Ord.79, r.5(1) of the Rules of the Superior Courts and, on the death of the person to whom such a grant has issued, the person *next* entitled under Ord.79, r.5(1) may apply for a grant of letters of administration intestate *de bonis non*.[7] **17–15**

Essential Proofs

17–16

1. Form S1 (postal application form) must be lodged with all applications submitted by post;
2. Oath of administrator intestate d*e bonis non*;
3. Copy oath of administrator intestate d*e bonis non*;
4. Administration bond d*e bonis non*;
5. Revenue Forms A 3(C) (2010 edition) or A3C (Euro version) and D1 (Euro version) where the deceased died before 5 December 2001;
6. Affidavit of market value or certificate of market value;
7. Surrender of the grant of letters of administration intestate.

[7] See Chapter 15 – Applications for Grants of Letters of Administration Intestate; Albert Keating, *Irish Probate Precedents Service* (Dublin: Round Hall, 2009).

OATH OF ADMINISTRATOR DE BONIS NON

THE HIGH COURT
PROBATE

In the estate of late of , deceased

I, of aged eighteen years and upwards, make oath and say that [name of deceased] late of [address and description], deceased, died intestate and that the lawful husband of the said deceased extracted a grant of letters of administration intestate out of the Probate Office on the day of 20 and died on the day of 20 leaving part of the estate unadministered (Insert title of applicant) and that I will well and faithfully administer the unadministered estate of the said deceased by paying his just debts and distributing the residue of said estate according to law, and that I will exhibit a true inventory of the said unadministered estate and render a true account thereof, whenever required by law so to do; that the said deceased died at on the day of [state month and year] [where application is made in a District Probate Registry, add: and that the said deceased had at the time of his death a fixed place of abode at within the district of] and that the whole of the unadministered personal estate of the said deceased amounts in value to the sum of [the gross personal estate without any deductions for debts] and that the whole of the unadministered real estate of the said deceased which devolves on and vests in his legal personal representatives is of the market value of [the amount shown in the affidavit of market value] and no more to the best of my knowledge, information and belief.

Sworn, &c.

ADMINISTRATION BOND

THE HIGH COURT

The Probate Office/The District Probate Registry at

I [insert name, address and description of applicant and surety/sureties if applicable] am liable in full to pay to the President of the High Court the sum of [insert penal sum twice gross assets of estate reflecting current market value of immovable property] for which payment I bind myself and my executors, administrators and successors and sealed with my seal and dated the [insert day of signing bond] day of [insert month and year of signing bond]. The condition of this obligation is that, if the above-named [insert name and title of applicant] of [insert name, address and description of applicant] and the intended administrator/administratix of the unadministered estate of the said deceased, do, when lawfully called on in that behalf, make or cause to be made a true inventory of the said unadministered estate which has or shall come into his/her hands, possession or knowledge, or into the hands, possession or control of any other person for him/her;

do exhibit the said inventory or cause it to be exhibited in the Probate Office [or in the District Probate Registry at] whenever required by law to do so; do well and truly administer the said unadministered estate according to law, paying all the debts owed by the deceased at the time of his death, all death duties payable in respect of the unadministered estate of the deceased for which the personal representative is accountable and all income tax and surtax payable out of the unadministered estate,

distributing all shares in the unadministered estate to those entitled by law thereto and as the law requires him/her; and further, do make or cause to be made a true account of the said administration whenever required by law to do so;

then this obligation shall be void and no effect, but shall otherwise remain in full force and effect.

Signed, sealed and delivered by the within-named	Applicant(s) signature and seal
Name of applicant and surety/sureties if applicable	Surety's/sureties' signature and seal [if applicable]

In the presence of
[insert Commissioner's/Solicitor's name]

Commissioner/Solicitor to sign here
Commissioner/Solicitor

Applicant(s) should execute bond before Commissioner/Solicitor on oath.[8]

AFFIDAVIT OF MARKET VALUE

THE HIGH COURT
PROBATE

The Probate Office or District Probate Registry at

In the estate of [name of deceased], late of [address of deceased], deceased.

I [valuer, auctioneer, local farmer or surveyor] of [address and occupation] aged 18 years and upwards, make oath and say as follows:

1. I am acquainted with the value of lands in the vicinity of [address of lands valued] in the County of where lands belonging to the aforesaid [name of deceased] deceased are situate.

2. I have inspected the holdings of the aforesaid deceased at [address of lands valued] and, in my opinion, the said holdings would on the date of swearing hereof have been of the value of [amount in words and figures] if then offered for sale on the open market.

Sworn & c.

8 See Ord.79, r.29, Rules of the Superior Courts.

CERTIFICATE OF MARKET VALUE

Re: Estate of [name of deceased] deceased, late of [address of deceased]

I/We [name of solicitor or firm], as solicitor(s) for the administrator of the estate of the aforementioned deceased, hereby certify that the current market value of the deceased's dwelling house at [address] would not exceed [value in figures and words).

I/We confirm that the said property, while realty, is comprised of a dwelling house only.

Yours &c.

Surrender of Original Grant

17–17 The initial grant of letters of administration intestate must be surrendered to the Probate Office or District Probate Registry. Where the initial grant is lost or mislaid, a certified copy of it may be bespoken in the Probate Office or District Probate Registry, accompanied with an explanation in writing of the circumstances surrounding the loss or mislaying of the initial grant.

Chapter 18

CAVEATS AND CITATIONS

Introduction

A person with an interest in the deceased's estate may wish to be informed when an application is made for a grant of probate or letters of administration to the deceased's estate and he may ensure this by lodging a caveat in the Probate Office (Rules Office Section) or a District Probate Office.[1] No grant may then issue without the person who entered the caveat, i.e. caveator, first being informed of the application for the grant. Where, however, a caveat is warned, the caveator is obliged then "either to abandon his claim to a grant or to take contentious proceedings in furtherance of his claim". The entering of a caveat may be the first indication that the will of the deceased testator is about to be challenged. But whatever the reason, once a caveat is lodged, no grant may issue until it ceases to have effect or is removed. A caveat may be entered in the Probate Office or a District Probate Registry. Where it is entered in a District Probate Registry the District Probate Registrar must immediately send a copy of it to the Probate Office.[2] The Probate Office is the central repository for all caveats entered in District Probate Registries throughout the country. **18–01**

The citation procedure in the Rules of the Superior Courts 1986 (the "1986 Rules") may be used by a beneficiary under a will who has finally lost patience with an executor's tardiness in applying for a grant of probate. He or she may enter a citation in the Probate Office compelling the executor to accept or refuse probate of the will.[3] Although an executor or person entitled is under no legal obligation to apply for a grant, his or her replacement may be brought about by use of the citation procedure, otherwise the **18–02**

---

1 See s.38 of the Succession Act 1965; Ord. 79, rrs. 41-51 of the Rules of the Superior Courts 1986; Appendix Q of the Rules of the Superior Courts 1986; *In the Estate of O'Connell* [2014] I.E.S.C. 55..

2 See Albert Keating, *Keating on Probate* (4th ed) (Dublin: Round Hall, 2011).

3 See s.17 of the Succession Act 1965; Ord.79, rrs. 52-58 of the Rules of the Superior Courts 1986; Appendix Q of the Rules of the Superior Courts 1986; Albert Keating, *Keating on Probate*, (4th ed) (Dublin: Round Hall, 2011); Albert Keating, *First Supplement to the Fourth Edition of Keating on Probate* (Dublin: Thomson Round Hall, 2013).

administration of estates could be suspended indefinitely. It may be noted that, while a caveat may be entered in the Probate Office or a District Probate Registry, a citation can issue only out of the Probate Office.[4] A citation will not, however, be signed by the probate officer until the citor enters a caveat against any grant being made in respect of the estate of the deceased to which the citation relates. Notice of the same must be sent to the District Probate Registry of the district in which the deceased appears to have resided at the time of his death. Where no appearance is entered to the citation duly served on a person to accept or refuse probate or administration within the time prescribed by Ord.79, r.56 of the 1986 Rules, or within the time for appearance as extended by the court or the probate officer, his or her non-appearance will be taken as a renunciation of his or her right to apply for probate or letters of administration. The citor may then apply for a grant in place of the person cited. The citor's entitlement to apply for a grant is derived from the cited person's failure to enter an appearance.

18–03 A caveat may be may entered for any one or more of the following purposes:

1. To give the caveator time to make enquiries and obtain information to determine whether there are grounds for opposing a grant;
2. To give the caveator an opportunity to raise any question pertinent to the making of a grant by way of motion procedure or otherwise;
3. As a preliminary step before the commencement of a probate action between the caveator and the person warning the caveat.[5]

18–04 Caveats and citations are therefore useful devices for opposing or compelling the issuing of a grant.

CAVEATS

18–05 The rules and forms dealing with the issuing of caveats are found in Ord. 79 rrs.41-51 and Appendix Q of the 1986 Rules. They are as follows:

1. The caveat must be lodged in the Probate Office or a District Probate Registry:

CAVEAT

THE HIGH COURT
PROBATE

Let nothing be done in the estate of A.B., late of [address] deceased, who

[4] Ord. 79, r.52.

[5] See *Re Nevin's Estate* [1997] I.E.H.C. 209; *In the Estate of O'Connell* [2014] I.E.S.C. 55..

died on the day of at [address] unknown to me [E.F. being the solicitor of] C.D., of [address] in the County of having interest.

[Signed) E.F.

[Registered place of business].

or C.D.,
[Address for service]

2. It must be dated on the day on which it is lodged and it remains in force for six months and will cease to have effect after that time unless renewed;
3. It must contain the name and address of the caveator and the registered place of business of the solicitor lodging the same or, where it is lodged personally, the name and address within the jurisdiction of the person lodging it;
4. Where it is shown that a person knowingly lodges a caveat in the name of a fictitious person or gives a false address of a person on whose behalf it purports to be lodged in the Probate Office, this will be viewed as a contempt of court;
5. Upon lodgment of the caveat in the Probate Office, the probate officer will immediately send notice of its lodgment to the District Probate Registry in which it is alleged the deceased resided at the time of his death, or in which he is known to have had a fixed place of abode at the time of his death and *vice versa*;
6. Where, coincidentally, the caveat is lodged on the same day on which a grant is made or on the day on which notice of its lodgment in the Probate Office is sent to a District Probate Registry, the grant will remain unaffected;
7. The response to a caveat is a warning which must be filed in the Probate Office and it must be served by delivery of a copy at the place mentioned in the caveat as the registered place of business of the caveator's solicitors, or at the address for service of the person who lodged the caveat, within 14 days of its date of issue; otherwise the warning will be deemed inoperative unless otherwise ordered by the probate officer.

WARNING TO CAVEAT

THE HIGH COURT
PROBATE

To C.D. [name of caveator] [or E.F.] [name of solicitor], solicitor of C.D. [name of caveator]]

You are hereby warned within fourteen days after the service of this warning upon you, inclusive of the day of such service, to enter an appearance [for

C.D. name of caveator], in the Probate Office, to the caveat entered by you in the estate of [name of deceased] late of [address], deceased, who died at [address] on the [day] day of 20 , and set forth your [or your said client's] interest, and take notice, that in default of your so doing, the said caveat will cease to have any effect.

[Signed]
Probate officer.

Issued at the instance of R.S. [here set forth what interest R.S. has and, if under a will or codicil, set forth the date thereof, if any, and give an address for service.]
[Indorsement to be made after service.]

This warning was served by J.K. [name of server] on [name of person served] at [state where and how the service was effected] on the day of 20XX

[Signed] J.K.[name of server]

8. The probate officer will also send a copy of the warning signed by him to the solicitor or person at his or her registered place of business or at the address of service mentioned in the warning, and will keep a record of such posting.
9. The warning must contain the name and address of the person on whose behalf it is issued and, if such person claims under a will, the date of the will and the registered place of business of the solicitors lodging the warning or, if there is no professional representation, the address for service within the jurisdiction.
10. The caveator must then enter an appearance in the Probate Office within 14 days of the service of the warning, although time for the appearance may be extended until an action in default of appearance is taken.

APPEARANCE TO A WARNING

THE HIGH COURT
PROBATE

In the estate of A.B. [name of deceased], late of [address] I, C.D. [name of caveator], [or E.F. name of solicitor] appearing [for C.D. name of caveator], deceased being the brother and one of the next-of-kin of the said A.B. [name of deceased], deceased

[or any other interest the said C.D. caveator may have].

Dated
[Signed name of solicitor], solicitor for [name of caveator]

[Registered place of business].

or [signed name of caveator] [address for service]

11. Where no appearance has been entered and in order to clear off the caveat, an affidavit of service of the warning and a certificate of non-appearance must be filed in the Probate Office unless the probate officer makes a special order to the contrary.

CONSENT TO SET ASIDE CAVEAT

THE HIGH COURT
PROBATE

In the estate of A.B. [name of deceased] late of [address], deceased

Whereas the above-named A.B. [name of deceased] died on the day of 20

And whereas on the day of 20 , a caveat was entered by C.D. [name of solicitor], solicitor of [solicitor's address] and on behalf of E.F. [name of caveator], the widow of the deceased having interest

And whereas on the day of 20 , a warning to the said caveat was lodged by G.H. [name of executor's solicitors], solicitor of [address] for and on behalf of H.I. [name of executor] the sole executor named in the said will

And whereas on the day of 20 , an appearance to the said warning was entered by the said C.D. [name of caveator's solicitor] for and on behalf of the said [name of caveator]

And whereas no contentious proceedings have been instituted herein

Now it is hereby agreed and consented by, and between, the said EF [name of caveator or caveator's solicitor] and the said HI [name of executor's solicitor], as testified by their signatures [and the signatures of their respective solicitors] hereunto subscribed, that the said caveat, warning and appearance to the said warning be set aside and that this consent be filed in the Probate Office.

Signed by the said E.F.

in the presence of
[name of witness]

Signed by the said H.I. [executor's solicitor]
in the presence of

Citations

18–06 The rules and forms regarding the issuing of citations are found in Ord.79, rrs.52-58 and Appendix Q of the 1986 Rules. They are as follows:

1. Before a citation issues from the Probate Office under the seal of the High Court, an affidavit must be filed in verification of the facts outlined on its face. Only the Probate Office may issue citations.

AFFIDAVIT TO ISSUE CITATION

The High Court
Probate

In the estate of [name of deceased] late of [address] deceased

I, [name of citor] of [address] [description of citor] aged eighteen years and upwards make oath and say as follows:

1. The above-named [name of deceased] late of [address] (description), died on or about the day of having duly executed his last will and testament on the day of . I beg to refer to a copy of the said will, when produced.

2. In his will, the above-named deceased did therein name A.B. [name of executor] of [address] as sole executor [or residuary legatee and devisee] and also in said will [he gave and bequeathed a sum of 20,000 euro (twenty thousand euro) to me].

3. The said A.B. [name of executor] has failed, neglected or refused to extract a grant of probate of the said will, as a consequence of which [my said bequest remains unpaid].

4. By letters dated the day of , my solicitors, [name and address of citor's solicitors] have requested the said A.B. [name of executor] to extract a grant of probate of the said will. I beg to refer to copies of the said letters, when produced. No reply has been received to any of the said letters.

5. I am desirous, therefore, that a citation should issue against the said A.B. [name of executor] to accept or refuse a grant of probate of the said will.

Sworn &c.

2. The citation may then be served on the person cited if he or she resides within the jurisdiction, but not if he or she resides out of jurisdiction, unless he is an Irish citizen. Where the person to be served resides abroad and is not an Irish citizen, notice only of the citation may be served on him or her. The affidavit for a citation to be served out of the jurisdiction must state whether or not the person to be served is an Irish citizen. The citation itself, or notice

of it, must be served personally where possible. Where personal service of the citation is intended, it is unnecessary to seek an order of the Court regarding service. In the event of personal service not being possible, the citor must apply to the Court for directions as to the mode of service;

3. A citation will not be signed by the probate officer until the citor enters a caveat against any grant being made in respect of the estate of the deceased to which the citation relates. Notice of the same must be sent to the District Probate Registry of the district in which the deceased appears to have resided at the time of his death;
4. A citation must be written, typed or printed and a copy must be made by the citor or his or her solicitors and must be taken to the Probate Office. It must be signed and sealed and a copy deposited in the Probate Office. The citation must contain the address of the registered place of business of the solicitors extracting the citation or, if extracted personally, an address for service within the jurisdiction;
5. The person served with the citation is allowed 14 days to enter an appearance but the time for entering an appearance will be extended until such time as an action in default may be taken under Order 79 rule 57 of the Rules of the Superior Courts 1986.

APPEARANCE TO CITATION (EXCEPT ONE TO ACCEPT OR REFUSE)

THE HIGH COURT
PROBATE

In the estate of A.B. [name of deceased], late of [address] I, C.D. [name of citor], [or E.F. name of citor's solicitor appear [for C.D. name of citor], deceased being the brother, and one of the next-of-kin of the said A.B. [name of deceased], deceased [or any other interest the citor may have].

Dated
[Signed] E.F. Solicitor for C.D.

[Registered place of business].

or C.D. caveator [address for service]

APPEARANCE TO CITATION TO ACCEPT OR REFUSE

THE HIGH COURT
PROBATE

In the estate of [name of the deceased], late of [address] deceased.

C.D., by G.H., his solicitor [or in person, as the case may be], appears in this matter [and if C.D. desires to accept probate or administration add] and desires to accept probate [or administration, as the case may be].

[Name and registered place of business of solicitor; or name and address for service of party.]

6. Where no appearance is entered to the citation duly served on a person to accept or refuse probate or administration within the time prescribed by Ord.79 r.56 of the Rules of the Superior Courts, or within the time for appearance as extended by the probate officer, his or her non-appearance will be taken as a renunciation of his or her right to apply for probate or letters of administration. The citor will then be entitled to obtain a side-bar order from the probate officer to that effect. The citor may then apply for a grant in place of the person cited.The citor's entitlement to apply for a grant is derived from the cited person's failure to enter an appearance.

Chapter 19

THE ADMINISTRATION AND DISTRIBUTION OF ESTATES

Introduction

19–01 Once a grant of probate or letters of administration has issued, the personal representatives may commence to administer and distribute the estate of the deceased.[1] During the course of administering the estate, the personal representatives may sell the whole or any part of the estate, not only for the payment of debts to creditors, but also when distributing the estate among the beneficiaries. The personal representatives may also lease land and premises as may be reasonably necessary for the due administration of the estate.[2] They may raise money by way of mortgage or charge for the payment of expenses, debts and liabilities. They may compromise or settle any debt, account or claim relating to the estate.[3] They also have powers of appropriation over the whole estate. Under s.55 of the Succession Act 1965 (the "1965 Act") they may, for instance, appropriate any part of the estate in or towards the satisfaction of any share in the estate. By virtue of s.56 of the 1965 Act, they may be required by the surviving spouse to appropriate the dwelling and household chattels in or towards the satisfaction of that spouse's share in the estate. Under s.57 of the 1965 Act, they will also be trustees where none is appointed for a minor who is entitled to a share in the estate of a deceased person and they will have trustee powers for

[1] See Albert Keating, *The Law and Practice of Personal Representatives* (Dublin: Thomson Round Hall, 2004).

[2] s.60(1)(a) of the 1965 Act; Albert Keating, *Keating on Probate* (4th ed) (Dublin: Round Hall, 2011); Albert Keating, *First Supplement to the Fourth Edition of Keating on Probate* (Dublin: Thomson Round Hall, 2013).

[3] s.60(8) of the 1965 Act.

this purpose under s.58 of the 1965 Act. The testator may even give them additional powers.

19–02 After the debts and liabilities have been discharged, the personal representatives may then distribute the estate among the beneficiaries in accordance with the provisions of the will or, in the case of intestacies, in accordance with the rules of intestacy.[4] In the case of devises, specific or residuary, the personal representatives will also have to assent to a vesting in writing, and the form of assent will depend on whether the land is registered or unregistered. The time for payment of any income or interest on gifts will depend on the testator's direction on the matter but, in the absence of a direction, the general rule is that income and interest will accrue from the time when a gift becomes payable.

19–03 The personal representatives must perform their duties of administering and distributing the estate not only diligently,[5] but also prudently.[6] Where the estate sustains a loss owing to a breach of duty by a personal representative, he may be personally liable to creditors and beneficiaries for what is called a "devastavit", for wasting assets of the estate. Although personal representatives are not entitled to be remunerated for the performance of their duties, other than out-of-pocket expenses and expenses incurred by the estate, the testator may include a charging clause in his will providing for the payment of professional fees for work done for and on behalf of the estate by a personal representative or trustee in a professional capacity.

The Administration of Estates

19–04 The personal representatives must first discharge all debts, funeral and testamentary expenses, liabilities and legal rights owing and due by the estate of the deceased person. After the payment of funeral and testamentary expenses, the next in order of priority for payment are those who are owed preferential debts. Preferential debts are debts owing by the deceased to the State in the form of taxes or social welfare payments, and also debts in the form of wages or salaries owing and due to employees of the deceased. All of these debts occupy an order of equal priority and must be discharged after the payment of funeral and testamentary expenses. The next in line in the order of priority for payment are the secured creditors of the deceased. These creditors may rely on any security given by the deceased during his lifetime for the discharge of a debt that remains unpaid. They are entitled to realise the security and may also claim the deficiency if the realised security does not fully meet the debt owing and due,[7] or alternatively, they

[4] See Albert Keating, "The Interest of a Creditor and Beneficiary in an Estate under Administration" (2004) 9(3) C.P.L.J. 50; Chapter 7 – Intestate Succession.

[5] *Re Tankard* [1942] Ch. 69 at 72-74.

[6] *Re Gunning* [1918] 1 I.R. 221.

[7] *Re MacEntee* [1960] Ir. Jur.Rep.55; *Re Love* (1883) 9 L.R.Ir. 6.

may accept the security in full discharge of the debt, or indeed, surrender the security and prove the debt.[8] They are also given the further option of seeking a valuation of the security and, if that is insufficient to meet the debt, they may enter a claim for the deficiency based on the valuation without first realising the security.[9] Next in line are creditors who are able to prove their debts against the estate in accordance with rules of bankruptcy.[10] Creditors who are owed money before the death of the deceased will have priority over those creditors whose debts become payable after his death. Where, for instance, the deceased was engaged in business as a sole trader, debts which become owing and due before his death will have priority over debts arising after his death, where his business is carried on as a going concern.[11] However, any creditors who assent to the business being carried on as a going concern may lose their priority afterwards.[12] Where the deceased's business is carried on as a going concern by his personal representatives, they may be indemnified out of the estate for the payment of debts incurred in the course of running the deceased's business.[13]

The personal representatives themselves are not precluded from making **19–05** claims against the estate for debts incurred by them while acting as personal representatives in the course of administering the estate. A personal representative cannot sue the estate for the recovery of the debt, but he is entitled to exercise the right of retainer to pay himself in accordance with the order of priority he would have occupied if he had not been a personal representative of the deceased.[14] Section 46(2) of the 1965 Act continues this right of retainer for the benefit of a personal representative in his own right or, indeed, jointly with another person, but this right will not become exercisable where the estate of the deceased is insolvent. The personal representative's right to prefer creditors is also continued by s.46, and by exercising this right among creditors of equal priority, some creditors may be preferred over others for the payment of debts.[15] Where a personal representative applies an asset out of the order set down in Part II of the First Schedule, or the order set down by a testator in his will, or the rules governing intestacy, the person entitled under the will or intestacy will have the right to have the assets marshalled.[16] The general principle governing

[8] See *Ex Parte Robinson* (1886) 15 L.R. Ir. 496; *Cooper v Teahan* (1890) 23 L.R. Ir. 203.

[9] *Re Clenaghan* (1959) 95 I.L.T.R. 89; *Re Greer* (1877) I.R. 11 Eq. 502; *Findlater v Butler* (1880) 5 L.R. Ir. 95.

[10] *Davoren v Woothen* [1900] 1 I.R. 273; see Albert Keating, *The Law and Practice of Personal Representatives* (Dublin: Thomson Round Hall, 2004).

[11] *McAloon v McAloon* [1900] 1 I.R. 367; *Re O'Kelly* [1920] 1 I.R. 200.

[12] *McGinley v Gallagher* [1929] I.R. 307; *Scott v Scott* [1924] 1 I.R. 141; *Kirkwood v Hamilton* (1902) 36 I.L.T.R. 155.

[13] *O'Neill v McGroarty* [1915] 1 I.R. 1; *Moore v McGlynn* [1904] 1 I.R. 334.

[14] *Re Lynch* (1915) 49 I.L.T.R. 78; *Olpherts v Coryton* [1913] 1 I.R. 221; *Olpherts v Coryton (No.2)* [1913] 1 I.R. 381.

[15] s .46(2)(a) and (b) of the 1965 Act.

[16] s.46(5) of the 1965 Act.

the marshalling of assets is that the person relying on the doctrine will be allowed to seek compensation for losing his place in the order of payment by claiming against the assets that ought to have been applied for the payment of his debt.[17]

19–06 Section 47(1) of the 1965 Act provides that:

> "Where a person dies possessed of, or entitled to, or, under a general power of appointment, by his will disposes of, an interest in property, which at the time of his death is charged with the payment of money, whether by way of legal or equitable mortgage or charge or otherwise (including a lien for unpaid purchase money), and the deceased person has not by will, deed or other document signified a contrary intention, the interest so charged shall, as between the different persons claiming through the deceased person, be primarily liable for the payment of the charge; and every part of the said interest, according to its value, shall bear a proportionate part of the charge on the whole thereof."

19–07 Section 47(1) therefore governs circumstances in which a beneficiary, as distinct from a creditor (although a beneficiary may also be a creditor of the estate), is given a gift of an interest in property by will which is specifically charged with the payment of a debt. Such a charge may arise, for instance, where a beneficiary is devised a gift of property subject to a mortgage. Section 47(1) also applies where more than one beneficiary is given an interest in the property subject to a charge. In such an event, the property will continue to be primarily liable for the payment of the charge, but the extent of a beneficiary's liability for payment of the charge will depend on the value of the interest acquired by him in the property in comparison to the others, and it will also be used as a basis for determining the extent of his contribution towards the payment of the charge. Section 47 of the 1965 Act is applicable only to property that is made primarily liable for the payment of a charge.

19–08 Where the estate is solvent, it will be applicable towards the discharge of funeral, testamentary, administration expenses, debts and, liabilities, and any legal right will be in the order set out in Part II of the First Schedule to the 1965 Act as follows:

1. Property of the deceased undisposed of by will, subject to the retention thereout of a fund sufficient to meet any pecuniary legacies;
2. Property of the deceased not specifically devised or bequeathed but included (either by a specific or general description) in a residuary gift, subject to the retention out of such property of a fund sufficient to meet any pecuniary legacies, so far as provided for as aforesaid – for instance, where the residuary gift is expressed

[17] See *McCarthy v McCartie (No.2)* [1904] 1 I.R. 100; *Re Matthews W.T.* [1961] 1 W.L.R. 1415 at 1419.

to include a particular house and premises, or a specific chattel, for instance, a specified suite of furniture;

3. Property of the deceased specifically appropriated, devised or bequeathed (either by a specific or general description) for the payments of debts. It appears, however, that property here excludes property included in a residuary gift either by a specific or general description, as such property is governed by paragraph 2 unless varied by the testator in his will;
4. Property of the deceased charged with, devised or bequeathed (either by a specific or general description) subject to a charge for the payment of debts. The same comment as in paragraph 3 might be made here also, that property included either by a specific or general description in the residuary gift and subject to a charge for the payment of debts will not form the subject matter of this paragraph, but rather paragraph 2;
5. The fund, if any, retained to meet pecuniary legacies;
6. Property specifically devised or bequeathed, rateably according to value;
7. Property appointed by will under a general power, rateably according to value;
8. The following provisions shall also apply:
   (a) The order of application may be varied by the will of the deceased for instance, where a testator directs that all debts owing by his estate are to be paid out of his residuary estate.
   (b) The liability of land to answer the death duty imposed thereon in exoneration of other assets is not affected by this order of application.

Where the estate is insolvent, it must be administered in accordance with the rules set out in Part I of the First Schedule of the 1965 Act. Part I of the First Schedule specifies that debts owing by an insolvent estate must be discharged as follows: **19–09**

1. The funeral, testamentary and administrative expenses have priority;
2. Subject as aforesaid, the same rules shall prevail and be observed as to the respective rights of secured and unsecured creditors and as to debts and liabilities provable and as to the valuation of annuities and future and contingent liabilities respectively, and as to the priorities of debts and liabilities as may be in force for the time being under the law of bankruptcy with respect to the assets of persons adjudged bankrupt;
3. In the application of the said rules, the date of death shall be substituted for the date of adjudication in bankruptcy.

Save with the exception of paragraph 1, the rules for the payments of debts **19–10** of an insolvent estate are governed by the rules of bankruptcy and must be observed accordingly when administering an insolvent estate.

19–11 A petition to administer an insolvent estate in bankruptcy may be presented to the court by a creditor whose debt would have been sufficient to support a bankruptcy petition were it commenced against the deceased during his lifetime.[18] Where, however, the petition is presented after the death of the deceased, notice of it must be served on the personal representatives. Where there is no known personal representative, the court may direct service on such person as it thinks fit or, indeed, dispense with service altogether. Once the personal representatives have been served with notice of the petition, no payment or transfer of land made by them will operate as a discharge between themselves and the official assignee. On presentation of a petition, the court may make an order for administration in bankruptcy unless it appears that there is a "reasonable probability" that the estate will be sufficient for the payment of the deceased's debts. When a creditor presents the petition, he must first prove his debt. If the court decides to make an order for administration in bankruptcy, the deceased's property will vest in the official assignee for realisation and distribution. In the administration that follows, "proper" funeral and testamentary expenses will be payable in priority to all other payments. Thereafter the provisions of the Bankruptcy Act 1988 will govern the order of administration in bankruptcy in the same way that they govern an order of adjudication in bankruptcy, save for the provisions contained ss.50, 57, 58 and 59. Any surplus funds remaining after the administration has been carried out may be paid to the personal representatives. In the case of administration of an insolvent estate in bankruptcy, the right of retainer of a personal representative will not be exercisable, but he is not prevented from proving a debt owing to him.

19–12 Section 49 of the 1965 Act provides that, where the personal representatives have given notices to creditors and others to send in their claims against the estate of the deceased, the personal representatives will, at the expiration of the time mentioned in the notice, be at liberty to distribute the estate of the deceased among the persons entitled to it, having regard to the claims of which they have then notice.[19]

19–13 Under s.48 of the 1965 Act, the personal representatives may sue or be sued in respect of all causes of action which survive for the benefit of, or against, the estate of the deceased, subject to the provisions of the Civil Liability Act 1961 and the Statute of Limitations 1957 or any other such Act.[20]

---

[18] ss. 115-122 of the Bankruptcy Act 1988.

[19] See Chapter 26 – Succession Act Precedents for Statutory Notice to Creditors.

[20] See Chapter 23 – The Limitation of Actions and Striking Out Proceedings; Chapter 21 – Probate and Administration Actions and Costs.

THE DISTRIBUTION OF ESTATES

Once the debts and liabilities have been discharged, the personal representatives may distribute the estate among the beneficiaries in accordance with the provisions of the will or rules of intestacy. They may do this by assenting to the vesting in the beneficiaries of their respective interests or shares in the estate. In *Re King's Will Trusts*[21] Pennycuick J. defined an assent as "the instrument or act whereby a personal representative effectuates a testamentary disposition by transferring the subject-matter of the disposition to the person entitled to it". In the case of devises, specific or residuary, the personal representatives will have to assent in writing, and the form of assent will depend on whether the land is registered or unregistered. In the case of trust estates consisting of land, the personal representatives will also have to assent in writing to the vesting of it in the trustees. Where the personal representatives are also the trustees, an assent affirms the transition from personal representatives to trustees by giving their assent to the vesting of the trust estate in themselves. Where land is concerned, an assent by the personal representatives to the vesting of it in a beneficiary must be in writing. The form of assent will depend on whether the land is registered or unregistered. Where a personal representative is also a beneficiary of registered land, it appears that, under s.54 of the 1965 Act, he must assent to the vesting of the registered land in himself as beneficiary. In the case of unregistered land, ss.52 and 53 of the 1965 Act are the relevant provisions. As a result of *Mohan v Roche*,[22] it appears that a personal representative need not assent to the vesting of unregistered land in himself as beneficiary, as the land is already vested in him in his capacity as personal representative, and it is unnecessary to the chain of title to assent to a vesting in himself as beneficiary also. In *Mohan v Roche,* the intestate died in 1967 and a grant letters of administration intestate was made to his widow in 1968. There were nine children of the marriage and they released and conveyed their interest in a house to their mother. She died in 1989 leaving a will wherein she appointed one of her sons as executor. After obtaining probate of the will, the executor entered into a contract for the sale of the house. The purchaser refused to complete the contract on the grounds that the title to the house was defective as the widow had not executed an assent to the vesting of the house in herself as a beneficiary. The purchaser argued that this defect in title could only be cured by the taking out of a *de bonis non* grant to the estate of the deceased intestate for the purposes of the execution of an assent and the registration of it in the Registry of Deeds. Keane J. held that, as the intestate's property had already vested in his widow as personal representative on the issuing of the grant of letters of administration intestate to his estate, no assent was **19–14**

21 [1964] 1 All E.R. 833 at 836.

22 [1991] I.R. 560; see Albert Keating, *The Law and Practice of Personal Representatives* (Dublin: Thomson Round Hall, 2004); Albert Keating, *Keating on Probate* (4th ed) (Dublin: Round Hall, 2011); Albert Keating, *First Supplement to the Fourth Edition of Keating on Probate* (Dublin: Thomson Round Hall, 2013).

necessary, and therefore, no *de bonis non* grant was required to perfect title. He refused the declaration sought by the purchaser that the executor had not shown a good marketable title to the house in accordance with the terms of the contract of sale.

19–15 The Law Reform Commission in its Report on Land Law and Conveyancing Law 1998 stated that *Mohan v Roche* applied only in limited circumstances. In the case of intestacy, it was limited to where the administrator was beneficially entitled to the entire estate and all the liabilities had been discharged or had become statute-barred. However, the Commission stated that, in the great majority of cases, it would be much more satisfactory if assents were to be completed. In *Mohan v Roche,* Keane J. acknowledged that a personal representative, by executing an assent in his own favour, signalled that he no longer acted as personal representative charged with completion of administration of the estate, and that this would make clear to prospective purchasers and others contemplating entering into dealings with him that he had become the full beneficial owner. In England, a personal representative must assent to the vesting of land in himself as beneficiary. Such a vesting necessarily implies that he is divesting himself of the estate in his original capacity as personal representative.[23]

19–16 In *Dolan v Reynolds*[24] Abbott J. stated that he was not prepared to extend the principle in *Mohan v Roche* to registered land, as that "would constitute an unwarranted usurpation of the powers of the Oireachtas". An assent or transfer must be executed by a personal representative to vest any interest or land in a beneficiary. The form of the assent depends on whether the land is registered or unregistered. In the case of unregistered land, s.53 of the 1965 Act requires that an assent should be in writing and signed by the personal representatives. Section 54 of the 1965 Act provides that an assent or transfer by a personal representative in respect of registered land must be in the form required by s.61 of the Registration of Title Act 1964. Section 52 of the 1965 Act provides that the personal representatives may, at any time after the death of the deceased, execute an assent vesting any such land in the person entitled thereto. A personal representative, if beneficially entitled, may make an assent in his own favour.

19–17 In the case of unregistered land, s.53(1) of the 1965 Act specifies the form that must be used by the personal representatives when assenting to the vesting of the land.[25] The assent was formerly registered in the Registry of Deeds but now it must be registered in accordance with the provisions of the Registration of Deeds and Title Act 2006.[26] Thereafter, any purchaser of unregistered land from the person entitled may treat the assent given by

[23] *Re King's Will Trusts* [1964] 1 All E.R. 833 at 836.
[24] [2011] I.E.H.C. 334.
[25] See Chapter 26 – Succession Act Precedents.
[26] s.53(2) of the 1965 Act; see Registration of Deeds and Title Act 2006, Part 3, Registration of Deeds.

the personal representatives as conclusive evidence of title, but without prejudice to any existing mortgages or incumbrances affecting the land.[27] Where registered land is involved, the form of assent or transfer by personal representatives is prescribed by s.61 of the Registration of Title Act 1964 (though now cited as the Registration of Title Acts 1964 and 2006) as amended by s.54(2) of the 1965 Act.[28] The Registrar of Titles (now the Chief Executive and Registrar of Deeds and Title under the Registration of Deeds and Title Act 2006) is entitled to assume that the personal representatives were acting correctly when giving the assent, and there is no duty on him to seek any further information regarding the correctness of the assent.[29] The assent will authorise the Registrar to register the person mentioned in the assent as full or limited owner of the registered land, as the case may be. Section 61(7) of the Registration of Title Act 1964 permits an applicant who claims entitlement under the probated will of the registered owner, but without the assent of the executor who has since died, to apply to the court for an order dispensing with further representation to the deceased registered owner, and for an order directing the Registrar to register the applicant without a *de bonis non* grant to the estate of the registered owner. The court will only dispense with further representation where it is satisfied that a period of six years has elapsed since the death of the deceased who was full owner of the registered land, and the executor of the owner has died or is out of jurisdiction. An application may be made to the court by notice of motion and supporting affidavit. Otherwise a *de bonis non* grant will become necessary.[30]

The personal representatives may assent to the vesting of land or any **19–18**
interest in land in the person entitled, including a trustee, at any time after the death of the deceased testator, either subject to or free from a charge for the payment of money that the personal representatives are liable to pay.[31] Where, however, an assent is made subject to a charge for monies payable by the personal representatives, their liability to discharge such monies will cease, except for any acts done or contracts entered into before the transfer or assent is made to the person entitled. Land or any interest in land for this purpose also includes land over which the deceased exercised a power of appointment.[32] The expression "person entitled" includes any person, as well as the personal representatives themselves, who by virtue of a devise, bequest, devolution or otherwise are beneficially entitled to land or any

[27] s.53(3) of the 1965 Act.

[28] s.54(1) of the 1965 Act; Registration of Deeds and Title Act 2006, s.1(2) now provides that the Registration of Title Act 1964 and the 2006 Act may be cited together as the Registration of Deeds and Title Acts 1964 and 2006 and are to be construed together as one since the enactment date of the 2006 Act, 5 May 2006.

[29] s.54(2) of the 1965 Act.

[30] See Chapter 17 – Applications for *De Bonis Non* Grants.

[31] s.52(3) of the 1965 Act; Registration of Deeds and Title Act 2006, s.32(1) (the definition of "deed" includes an assent under the Succession Act 1965).

[32] s.52(1)(a) of the 1965 Act.

interest in land comprised in the estate of the deceased and the trustees of any such person.

19–19 As already stated, an assent by the personal representatives to the vesting of land or any interest in land in the beneficiaries must be in writing, but it appears that an oral assent is sufficient for the vesting of personal estate, although it is perhaps advisable to have at least a record of it in writing for future reference. Where, however, the personal representatives fail or refuse to assent in writing on being requested to do so by a beneficiary, the court may make an order vesting the land in the beneficiary. The personal representatives are the only persons entitled to make assents or to transfer the land of the deceased unless the court orders otherwise. Where a trust estate is involved, the assent by the personal representative to the vesting of the trust estate in the trustees will commence their duties to administer and distribute the trust estate.

19–20 The personal representatives may distribute the estate of the deceased as soon after his death as is reasonably practicable, having regard to the nature of the estate and the manner in which it is to be distributed and all other relevant circumstances. No action may be taken against them for their failure to do so before the expiration of one year after the death of the deceased, except by leave of the court.[33]

The Powers of Personal Representatives

19–21 The main statutory power of personal representatives is that of sale and this allows them to sell the whole or any part of the estate, not only for the payment of debts to creditors, but also for the purpose of distributing the estate among the beneficiaries. When the personal representatives decide to exercise the power of sale, they are obliged "as far as practicable" to take into account the wishes of beneficiaries of full age who are entitled to the property proposed to be sold or, in the case of dispute, the majority wishes according to the value of their combined interests.[34] A purchaser from the personal representatives will be entitled to hold the property sold free and discharged from any debts or liabilities of the deceased, except such properties as are charged otherwise than by the will, and from all claims of the beneficiaries.[35] This provision is, however, limited in its application to estates that are administered within a period of 20 years from the death of the deceased. Where property is sold after 20 years from the date of death, a purchaser will be "put on notice to enquire the reason for the sale, and if he fails to make such enquiry is bound with notice of what

[33] s.62(1) of the 1965 Act.
[34] s.50(1) of the 1965 Act.
[35] s.51(1) of the 1965 Act.

he would have discovered".[36] A purchaser is, however, protected by s.25 of the 1965 Act which provides that all conveyances made to a purchaser by the personal representatives are valid, notwithstanding any subsequent variation or revocation of the grant to them. He may also assume that the personal representatives who carry out the sale are acting correctly and within their powers. The requirement that a purchaser must act in good faith may deprive him of the protection of s.51 of the 1965 Act if it is proved that, for instance, he entered into a fraudulent collusion with the personal representatives regarding the amount of consideration paid for the property sold, the inadequacy of the consideration, perhaps, being evidence of fraud. Where, however, a purchaser acts in good faith and gives valuable consideration, he need not be concerned with the user of the purchase money by the personal representatives.[37]

The personal representatives may also be obliged to apportion or convert the estate by law. In the case of rent payable out of the subject matter of a devise, the devisee's entitlement to receive it will commence from the date of death of the testator, but any rent owing and due before the testator's death will form part of the residuary estate.[38] However, rents payable after the testator's death for periods that cover periods before and after the death of the testator will be apportioned between the devisee and the residuary estate. **19–22**

Legacies may also be subject to apportionment, depending on their subject matter. Where, for instance, a legacy consists of a gift of shares in a company and dividends are declared on the shares, a question may arise as to who is entitled to the dividends. All seems to depend on the timing of the declaration of dividends. If the declaration is made before the death of the testator, then the value of the dividends will form part of the residuary estate of the deceased and this will continue to be the case, even though the dividends do not become payable until after the death of the testator.[39] Apportionment may not occur where there is a bequest of a business in the sole ownership of the testator and the profits arising out of the business, or a legacy consisting of a share in a partnership and the profits arising out of the legacy. It appears that the legatee will become entitled to all profits, whether arising before or after the death of the testator.[40] **19–23**

The equitable rules of apportionment may be applied to settlements to ensure a more even spread of the income arising from the funds or property of a settlement. There are three such rules. The first rule in *Howe v Dartmouth*[41] provides that, where there is residuary bequest of personal estate, including **19–24**

[36] *Crowley v Flynn* [1983] I.L.R.M. 513 at 515 *per* Barron J; *Re Molyneux and White* (1885) 15 L.R. Ir. 383.
[37] s.51(1) of the 1965 Act.
[38] *Ellis v Rowbotham* [1900] 1 Q.B. 740; *Foster v Cunningham* [1956] N.I. 29.
[39] See *O'Brien v Fitzgerald* (1851) 1 Ir.Ch.R. 290.
[40] *Re Lynch-White* [1937] 3 All E.R. 551; *Re Robbins* [1941] Ch. 434.
[41] (1802) 7 Ves. 137.

chattels real, to persons in succession, the trustees must realise such parts of the estate as are of a wasting character and invest the proceeds in some authorised securities, unless a contrary intention appears from the will.[42] The rule in *Howe v Dartmouth* applies to will settlements only.[43] The second rule, in *Re Earl of Chesterfield's Trust,*[44] was primarily designed to protect the interests of the life tenant. It provides for the conversion of future or reversionary assets that produce no income, and for the life tenant to be paid income out of the invested capital. The third rule, in *Allhusen v Whittell,*[45] operates on the presumption that the testator intended all his beneficiaries to have an equal share in the income arising from their interests in the will. It provides that, where the residuary estate is settled on beneficiaries in succession, all should be entitled to an equal share in the income arising from it. However, the common practice is for testators to exclude these rules from their wills, as they confer few advantages on beneficiaries. But they are still rules of law and may be applied unless they are expressly excluded by the will.

19–25 Section 55 of the 1965 Act empowers the personal representatives to appropriate any part of the deceased's estate in its actual condition or state of investment at the time of appropriation in or towards satisfaction of any share in the estate, according to the respective rights of the person interested in the estate. The power to appropriate must, however, be exercised so as not to prejudicially affect any specific devise or bequest in a will.

19–26 The requirements set down by s.55 of the 1965 Act for the valid exercise by personal representatives of their power to appropriate are as follows:

(a) The appropriation must not affect prejudicially any specific devise or bequest, except in cases where s.56 of the 1965 Act is applicable.[46]
(b) Notice of the intended appropriation must be served on all parties entitled to a share in the estate, other than persons who may come into existence after the time of appropriation or who, after reasonable enquiry, cannot be found or ascertained at that time.
(c) Where the appropriation is for the benefit of a person absolutely and beneficially entitled in possession, the consent of that person must be sought. Where the appropriation is in respect of any settled share, the personal representative must obtain the consent of either the trustee (not being also the personal representative), or the person who may for the time being be entitled to the income.
(d) The personal representatives, in making the appropriation, must have regard to the rights of any person who may thereafter come

---

[42] *Re Harris's Estate* [1907] 1 I.R. 32 at 35.
[43] See *Re Abbott* [1934] I.R. 189.
[44] (1883) 24 Ch.D. 643.
[45] (1867) L.R. 4 Eq. 295.
[46] s.55(2).

into existence, or who cannot after reasonable enquiry be found or ascertained at the time of appropriation, and of any person whose consent is not required by s.55.

Where personal representatives appropriate property in furtherance of their power to do so under s.55 of the 1965 Act, the appropriated property will be treated as an authorised investment and may be dealt with accordingly.[47] They may also ascertain and fix the values of the respective parts of the estate and the liabilities of the deceased person as they think fit, and they may appoint a duly-qualified valuer to assist them in the valuation.[48] The appropriation undertaken by the personal representatives will bind all persons with an interest in the property of the deceased, and also those whose consent to the appropriation is unnecessary unless the court orders otherwise on foot of an application to it under s.55(3). The personal representatives are, however, obliged to take into account the rights of any person who may come into existence after the appropriation, or who cannot be traced or ascertained at the time of the appropriation.[49] Section 55 applies whether the deceased died testate or intestate and includes property over which the deceased may exercise a power of appointment and annuities.[50] Where an appropriation is made in or towards the satisfaction of a legacy, or a share in the residuary estate, the stamp duty will not be more than that payable on a transfer of personal property for like purpose.[51] The power to appropriate may also be exercised by the personal representatives in favour of themselves.[52] **19–27**

In *H v O*[53] Henchy J. stated that: **19–28**

> "The right of appropriation given by s.55 is an enabling right which may be exercised only by the personal representative. A person entitled to a share is given no right to compel the personal representative to propose an appropriation under s.55."

He described the jurisdiction of the Court as being "essentially supervisory and prohibitive" when an application is made under s.55(3).[54] The Court will intervene to prohibit an appropriation only:

> "(a) when the conditions in the section have not been complied with; or
> (b) when, notwithstanding such compliance, it would not be just or equitable to allow the appropriation to take place, having regard to the rights of all persons who are or will become entitled to an interest in the estate; or
> (c) when, apart from the section, the appropriation would not be legally permissible."

---

47 s.55(9).
48 s.55(10).
49 s.55(12).
50 s.55(16).
51 s.55(17).
52 s.55(18).
53 [1978] I.R. 194 at 204-205.
54 *H v O* [1978] I.R. 194 at 206.

Since s.10(3) of the 1965 Act treats personal representatives as trustees for persons entitled to the estate of a deceased person,

> "the exercise of the statutory discretion to appropriate must be viewed as an incident of the trusteeship, so that it is the court's duty to prohibit the appropriation if it is calculated to operate unjustly or inequitably by unduly benefiting one beneficiary at the expense of another".[55]

19–29 Where the personal representatives have observed all the statutory requirements and have made a *bona fide* decision to appropriate, the court will not interfere unless it would be unjust or inequitable to allow the appropriation to take place, or the appropriation becomes unlawful for some other reason not covered by s.55 of the Act. Where an appropriation is challenged under s.55 on the grounds of inequality, the onus of proof rests on the applicant to show the inequality on the balance of probabilities. In *Messitt v Henry*[56] Finnegan J. applying the principles set out by Henchy J. in *H v O* held that, as a personal representative when exercising the right of appropriation acts as a statutory trustee, it is necessary for him to ensure that the appropriation would not prejudice the interests of the other beneficiaries who had a share in the deceased intestate's estate.

19–30 Murphy J. stated in *Strong v Holmes*[57] that, as the personal representatives hold the estate as trustees for the persons entitled to it by law, the exercise of the statutory discretion to appropriate must be viewed as an instance of the trusteeship. He said:

> "It is the court's function to prohibit the appropriation if it is calculated to operate unjustly or inequitably by unduly benefiting one beneficiary at the expense of another. Where not prohibited by law and where the conditions of the section have been observed and the personal representatives have made a *bona fide* decision to appropriate, the exercise of the discretion to appropriate should not be interfered with."

19–31 Where the personal representatives have observed all the statutory requirements, and have made a *bona fide* decision to appropriate, the court will not interfere unless it would be unjust or inequitable to allow the appropriation to take place, or the appropriation becomes unlawful for some other reason not covered by s.55 of the 1965 Act.[58] Where an appropriation is challenged under s.55 on the grounds of inequality, the onus of proof rests on the applicant to show the inequality on the balance of probabilities.

19–32 The relevant date for evaluating the assets of the estate for the purposes of appropriation is the date of the appropriation, and not the date of death of the

---

55 *ibid* at 206-207.

56 [2001] 3 I.R. 313.

57 [2010] I.E.H.C. 70; see Albert Keating, "The Valuation Day of Appropriation Day by Personal Representatives" (2011) 16(2) C.P.L.J. 22.

58 *Strong v Holmes* [2010] I.E.H.C. 70.

deceased.[59] Once the estate has been evaluated, the personal representatives may make any conveyance that will give effect to the appropriation.[60]

The Payment of Income and Interest on Gifts

The general rule is that a beneficiary will become entitled to income arising from a gift when it becomes payable. Normally a gift becomes payable at the end of the executor's year (i.e. one year from the death of the testator), but there is nothing preventing a testator from directing that income on a gift shall arise at an earlier date. A testator may, for instance, direct that a gift take immediate effect on his death and, where such is the case, the beneficiary will become entitled to income arising from the gift on the date of death of the testator. Where a beneficiary assumes the mantle of a landlord by virtue of a gift having immediate effect, while he or she will be entitled to receive any rent arising out of property, he or she will also inherit the duties and costs of a landlord to maintain and upkeep property, with the sole exception of contracts entered into by the testator prior to his death for the repair of premises. In such cases, the costs will have to be borne by the testator's estate, and not by the beneficiary.[61] Where shares in a company are the subject-matter of a gift, any dividends declared on them will be viewed as income arising from such shares. If the subject-matter is land, then any rents or profits arising out of the land will be treated as income and the beneficiary will become entitled to such income accordingly.[62] **19–33**

The general rule is that interest accrues on gifts from the time they become payable. The type of gifts on which interest accrues are, of course, pecuniary legacies; other types of bequests by virtue of their nature—for instance, a suite of antique furniture—are not capable of bearing interest. The time for the payment of a pecuniary legacy is at the end of the executor's year. A testator may, however, direct in his will that a legacy be payable at an earlier time and such a direction also commences the accrual of interest from that time. He may, for instance, direct that a legacy becomes payable from the date of his death and such a direction also commences the accrual of interest. Certain legacies automatically bear interest from the date of death and do not require a direction by the testator in his will to this effect. If a legacy is given in satisfaction of a debt, it will carry interest from the date of the testator's death and not from the end of the executor's year, unless a contrary intention appears from the will.[63] Legacies given to children of **19–34**

---

[59] *Strong v Holmes* [2010] I.E.H.C. 70; *Re Charteris* [1917] 2 Ch. 379; *Robinson v Collins* [1975] 1 W.L.R. 309; *Re Gollin's Declaration of Trust* [1969] 1 W.L.R. 1858; see Albert Keating, "The Valuation Day of Appropriation Day by Personal Representatives" (2011) 16(2) C.P.L.J. 22.

[60] s.55(10).

[61] See *Re Pearce* [1909] 1 Ch. 819); *Re Day's W.T.* [1962] 1 W.L.R. 1419.

[62] *Re West* [1909] 2 Ch. 180.

[63] *Re Rattenbury* [1906] 1 Ch. 667.

a testator will also carry interest from the date of the testator's death, the underlying presumption being that the interest will be applied towards the maintenance of such children.[64]

The Liability of Personal Representatives

19–35 The personal representatives, when administering and distributing the estate, are obliged to act not only diligently but also prudently.[65] The duty to act in such way endures until the administration and distribution of the estate are completed. Personal representatives must display the two qualities of diligence and prudence when discharging the debts owing by the estate. Uthwatt J. said in *Re Tankard*[66]:

> "Due diligence may, indeed, require that payment should be made before the expiration of the executor's year, and the circumstances affecting the estate and the assets comprised in it may justify non-payment outside the year, but, if debts are not paid within the year, the onus is thrown upon the executors to justify the delay."

19–36 The personal representatives must also act diligently and prudently when distributing the estate among the beneficiaries, bearing in mind that "the ultimate object of administration of an estate is to place the beneficiaries in possession of their interest". While personal representatives are required to act diligently so as to save the estate unnecessary expenditure, they must also act prudently to ensure that the beneficiaries receive their share in the estate. Where, owing to "carelessness", a beneficiary does not receive the share to which he or she is entitled, the personal representatives may be liable accordingly.[67] Where a beneficiary cannot be traced and is missing, the personal representatives may apply to the court for a Benjamin Order presuming his or her death and to allow them to proceed with the distribution of the estate without further delay.[68] The making of such an order will protect the personal representatives from liability for breach of the duties of diligence and prudence. The personal representatives also owe a duty of vigilance when administering and distributing the estate and where, owing to their lack of vigilance, a devastavit or wasting of assets occurs, they may be liable for it to the estate.[69] There is also the danger of personal liability for loss caused to the estate by a devastavit. The creditors or beneficiaries may institute proceedings against the personal representatives in the event of a devastavit. A testator may, however, protect his personal representatives from

---

64 See *Re Bowlby* [1904] 2 Ch. 685; *Re Pollock* [1943] Ch. 338.

65 *Re Tankard* [1942] 2 All E.R. 458; *Re Gunning* [1918] 1 I.R. 221; *Job v Job* (1877) 6 Ch. D. 562; *Hayward v Kinsey* (1701) 12 Mod.Rep. 568.

66 [1942] 2 All E.R. 458.

67 See Chapter 21 – Probate and Administration Actions and Costs.

68 *Re Benjamin* [1902] 1 Ch. 723; *In the Estate of Meith* [1986] I.L.R.M. 175; See Albert Keating, *The Law and Practice of Personal Representatives* (Dublin: Thomson Round Hall, 2004).

69 See Chapter 21 – Probate and Administration Actions and Costs.

personal liability by a clause to that effect in the will, but such protection will not extend to loss caused by wilful breach of duty or dishonesty.

As the office of personal representative is a voluntary one, personal representatives are not entitled to be paid or remunerated for their services as personal representatives of the estate. They are entitled to be indemnified for any expenses and liabilities incurred by them when administering and distributing the estate, but not for carrying out their functions as personal representatives. Where, however, a personal representative also functions in a professional capacity when administering and distributing the estate, he or she may be entitled to claim fees for work done on behalf of the estate in a professional capacity, especially where a testator includes a charging clause in the will allowing payment of such fees. A solicitor who acts on behalf of personal representatives when administering and distributing the estate owes a professional duty of care and may be liable for any loss sustained by the estate as a result of a breach of duty. **19–37**

A testator may wish to protect his personal representative from personal liability for loss not attributable to dishonesty or a wilful breach of duty during the course of administration of the estate. This may be done by including a suitably-worded clause in the will.[70] While such a clause cannot prevent a creditor or beneficiary from claiming a devastavit, it may allow the personal representative to be indemnified by the estate to the extent of his personal liability if it is shown that the loss was not deliberately caused or arose out of acts of dishonesty. Such a clause may take the following form: **19–38**

> "I declare that no executor (and/or trustee) of this my will shall be liable for loss not attributable to the executor's (and/or trustee) own dishonesty or wilful commission by the executor of any act known to be a breach of duty (and/or breach of trust)."

A Solicitor's Duty of Care to Personal Representatives

As the whole estate of a deceased person vests in his personal representative, the personal representative not only holds the estate for the benefit of those entitled to it, but he is also the appropriate person to bring actions for and on behalf of the estate for the benefit of those entitled to it. A solicitor who is instructed by a personal representative to undertake the administration of an estate on behalf of a personal representative must know that, if he fails in his professional duty to do so, the estate will suffer loss.[71] If, for instance, the estate comprises income-bearing assets but, due to the solicitor's delay in applying for a grant of probate, the assets do not bear interest, the personal representative, once probate is taken out, may bring an action against the **19–39**

70 See Chapter 24 – Wills Precedents.

71 See Albert Keating, "A Solicitor's Duty of Care to Intended Beneficiaries and Personal Representatives" (2004) 9(2) C.P.L.J. 30.

solicitor for the loss sustained by the estate. The type of remedy available to a personal representative in such circumstances was considered in *Chappell v Somers & Blake.*[72] In that case, Neuberger J. referred to *White v Jones*[73]and, in particular, the speech of Lord Goff and stated that the extended *Hedley Byrne*[74] principle in *White v Jones* regarding intended beneficiaries should likewise extended to personal representatives in the case of actions against solicitors for loss caused to the estate.

The Accountability of a Solicitor as Executor to Beneficiaries

19–40 Where a solicitor is appointed as executor, he will not only have a duty to administer the estate but will also be rendered accountable to beneficiaries as clients. This is as a result of an interpretation of ss.2 and 8 of the Solicitors (Amendment) Act 1994 by Kearns P. in *Condon v The Law Society of Ireland.*[75] Section 2 of the 1994 Act provides that

> "a client includes the personal representative of a client and any person on whose behalf the person who gave instructions was acting in relation to any matter in which a solicitor or his firm had been instructed; and includes a beneficiary to an estate under a will, intestacy or trust".

Section 8(1) of the 1994 Act provides that, where the Law Society:

> "receives a complaint from a client of a solicitor, or from any person on behalf of such client, alleging that the legal services provided or purported to have been provided by that solicitor in connection with any matter in which he or his firm had been instructed by the client were inadequate in any material respect and were not of the quality that could reasonably be expected of him as a solicitor or a firm of solicitors, then the Society, unless they are satisfied that the complaint is frivolous or vexatious, shall investigate the complaint and shall take all appropriate steps to resolve the matter by agreement between the parties concerned."

Section 8(1) goes on to provide that the Law Society, following investigation of the complaint, may *inter alia*:

> "direct the solicitor to transfer any documents relating to the subject matter of the complaint (but not otherwise) to another solicitor nominated by the client or by the Society with the consent of the client, subject to such terms and conditions as the Society may deem appropriate having regard to the circumstances, including the existence of any right to possession or retention of such documents or any of them vested in the first-mentioned solicitor or in any other person".

---

[72] [2003] 3 All E.R. 1076.
[73] [1995] 2 A.C. 207.
[74] *Hedley Byrne & Co. Ltd. v Heller & Partners Ltd.* [1963] 2 All E.R. 575.
[75] [2010] I.E.H.C. 52.

CHAPTER 20

PROBATE MOTIONS AND SECTION 27(4) APPLICATIONS

INTRODUCTION

All probate applications to the court by way of motion, whether *ex parte* or by notice of motion, must be lodged in the Rules Office Section of the Probate Office. The Rules Office will indicate the next available date for the placing of an application on the probate list and will issue the application for hearing on that date. Motion applications are usually entertained by the presiding probate judge on each Monday at 10.30 a.m. All applications appearing on the probate list are sent to the probate judge on the Wednesday before the Monday on which the listed applications are heard. Any replying or supplemental affidavits should be lodged in the Rules Office no later than close of business on Wednesday. Order 79, r.88 of the Rules of the Superior Courts 1986 (the "1986 Rules") provides that, when depositing the motion paper in the Probate Office, **20–01**

> "the affidavits in support of the motion and a copy of any testamentary paper writing therein referred to and, if required by the Probate Officer, any original documents referred to in such affidavits or referred to on the hearing of the motion shall also be left in the Probate Office".

But apparently it is policy of the Rules Office not to retain original exhibits either before or after the hearing. All orders made by the probate judge are made available on Thursday afternoon of the week on which they are made.

The motion procedure may be used in applications for grants under s.27(4) of the Succession Act 1965 (the "1965 Act"), for instance, by a creditor of the deceased where all attempts made by him to enforce payment of a debt owing to him are frustrated by the behaviour of the person to whom **20–02** a grant was made. He or she may also use the motion procedure for grants *ad colligenda bona* for the sole purpose of gathering in and preserving the estate of the deceased, limited "to collecting in and preserving, but not distributing, the estate of the deceased," or for grants *pendent lite* under s.27(7) of the 1965 Act where any legal proceedings are pending challenging the validity of the will. For the purposes of obtaining, recalling or revoking any grant, the Court may make a grant to an administrator for the duration of the legal proceedings.

Ex Parte Motions

20–03 Order 79, r.87 of the 1986 Rules provides that:

> "On *ex parte* applications in probate causes and matters, a motion paper shall be lodged with the Probate Officer two clear days before the day on which such motion or application shall be moved or made, with an affidavit or affidavits of any facts to be brought under the notice of the Court in support of the same."

20–04 An *ex parte* motion may be used where the applicant is not required to put another party on notice when applying to the court for a ruling. The motion paper must be lodged in the Rules Office and must comply with the special rules for motion papers in Ord.79, r.87 of the 1986 Rules.

20–05 Order 79, r.87 of the 1986 Rules provides that:

1. The motion paper must contain a brief statement of the main facts on which the application is grounded and conclude with the terms on which the application is to be made;
2. The grounding affidavit or affidavits must contain all the facts of the case that require the attention of the court;
3. The statement in the motion paper must contain no facts which are unsupported by the grounding affidavit or affidavits or official documents, and any ruling made by the probate officer on the subject-matter of the application must be mentioned in the motion paper;
4. The motion paper must be lodged in the Rules Office section of the Probate Office two clear days before it is intended to move the application.

Notice of Motion

20–06 Order 79, r.88 of the 1986 Rules provides that:

> "Motion papers in probate causes and matters shall set forth the style and object of, and the names and descriptions of the parties to, the cause or proceeding before the Court, the proceedings already had in the cause, and the dates of the

same, the prayer of the party on whose behalf the motion is made and briefly the circumstances on which it is founded."

In the case of a notice of motion and where a solicitor is on record, two clear days' notice must be given before the date of the hearing. Where there is no solicitor on record, the notice party must be given four clear days' notice before the date of the hearing.

By Ord.79, r.88 of the 1986 Rules: **20–07**

1. The motion paper must contain the names and descriptions of the parties to the motion, the style and object of the cause or proceeding before the court, and must state any proceedings already heard in the cause mentioned in the motion paper. It must also contain the prayer of the party on whose behalf the motion is made and a brief mention of the circumstances on which it is founded;

2. If the motion paper is deficient in relation to any of the matters mentioned in 1 above, it will not be accepted without the permission of the probate officer;

3. The motion paper must be deposited in the Probate Office, together with the grounding affidavit or affidavits and copies of any testamentary papers referred to as exhibits. The probate officer may require any original documents referred to in the grounding affidavit or affidavits and to be used at the hearing of the motion to be lodged in the Probate Office. However, as already stated, it is not the policy of the Rules Office to retain original exhibits either before, or indeed after, the hearing;

4. Any affidavits or documents already filed or deposited in the Probate Office will be sent with the motion to the court.

Under Ord 79, r.89(2), every order of the court will be issued out of the Probate Office.

When issuing an application for the probate list, the following documents **20–08**
must be presented:

(i) Original notice of motion or motion paper or *ex parte* application and copy of same;
(ii) Original affidavits and copies of same; and
(iii) An indexed, bound and paginated booklet of copies of all the foregoing documentation, including copy exhibits. Original exhibits must not be submitted to the Probate Office.

20–09 The Rules Office will indicate the next available date on the probate list and will issue the application in question for such date. For court applications received by post, the copy motion (with a return date entered thereon) will be returned by post, together with stamped copy affidavits (if relevant). All orders made by the probate court are available by close of business on the Tuesday of the week on which they are made. There is a fee payable on collection of court orders. If the application to the court is for liberty to prove a will in terms of a copy, and the court allows the relief sought, the actual copy of the will which is exhibited in the grounding affidavit is the copy which must be exhibited in the oath of executor/administrator with will annexed. On the court making an order, an application for a grant of representation may be made to the Seat Office of the Probate Office or a District Probate Registry. An official copy of the court order must be exhibited in the oath of executor/administrator with will annexed/administrator. Fees are payable on the notice and the affidavits.[1]

Grounding Affidavits

20–10 The grounding affidavit plays an essential role in motion procedure and, accordingly, special attention should be paid to the supportive evidence and exhibits mentioned in it. There is a whole host of procedural rules that must be complied with in the preparation of grounding affidavits. Order 79, r.39 of the 1986 Rules provides that all affidavits filed or used in the Probate Office must comply with the general provisions of Ord. 40 of the 1986 Rules, as amended by S.I No.95 of 2009: Rules of the Superior Courts (Affidavits) 2009.

Section 27(4) Applications

20–11 Under s.27(4) of the 1965 Act, the court may order that a grant of administration be made to such person as it thinks fit where the special circumstances of the case render it necessary or expedient to do so. Accordingly, where the special circumstances of the case render it necessary or expedient, the court may appoint a person administrator other than the person entitled to apply for grant under the 1986 Rules. It may also be mentioned here that, for the purposes of the amended s.27 of the 1965 Act, i.e. s.27A,

> "the deceased shall be presumed, unless the contrary is shown, not to have been survived by any person related to him whose parents have not married each other or by any person whose relationship with the deceased is deduced through a person whose parents have not married each other".[2]

---

[1] Probate Office Update: 14 August 2012.

[2] s.30 of the Status of Children Act 1987, amended by s.27 of the Succession Act 1965 by the insertion of a new s.27A.

Since the Civil Partnership and Certain Rights and Obligation of Cohabitants Act 2010, s.27A must also be read to include:

> "the deceased shall be presumed, unless the contrary is shown, not to have been survived by any person related to him whose parents have not entered into a civil partnership with each other or by any person whose relationship with the deceased is deduced through a person whose parents have not entered a civil partnership with each other".

A creditor of the deceased may make an application under s.27(4) and the Court may allow him to apply for a grant where the special circumstances show that all attempts made by him to enforce payment of the debt owing to him were frustrated by the behaviour of the person to whom a grant was made. In *Bank of Ireland v King*[3] the deceased was the owner of a farm of registered land and died intestate. He was survived by his wife and four children. A grant of letters of administration intestate was made to his widow. The plaintiffs instituted proceedings against her for the payment of a debt owing by the estate and obtained judgment and costs against her. The plaintiffs registered a judgment mortgage against her two-thirds interest in the deceased's farm. As the widow failed to assent to the vesting of her two-thirds interest in the farm in herself as beneficiary, the plaintiffs were unable to realise the judgment order against her. The plaintiffs sought an order under s.27(4) allowing them to administer the estate. Costello J. appointed an administrator under s.27(4) for the purpose of assenting to the vesting of the two-thirds interest in the widow. **20–12**

Section 27(4) may be coupled with s.26 of the 1965 Act for the purposes of removing a current personal representative and appointing some other person as administrator under s.27(4). In *Dunne v Heffernan*[4] Lynch J. stated that: **20–13**

> "An order removing the appellant as executrix (which would be made by virtue of s.26(2) and not s.27(4) of the Succession Act 1965) and appointing some other person as administrator with the will annexed by virtue of s.27(4) is a very serious step to take. It is not justified because one of the beneficiaries appears to have felt frustrated and excluded from what he considered his legitimate concerns. It would require serious misconduct and/or serious special circumstances on the part of the executrix to justify such a drastic step."

As a result of *Bank of Scotland v Gray and Doyle,*[5] where the administrator appointed by the Court under s.27(4) applies for a grant in compliance with the 1986 Rules but institutes proceedings before a grant has actually issued, he or she will be "contingently competent to represent the estate". Alternatively, **20–14**

> "applying the general principles of the doctrine of relation back to the statutory

---

[3] [1991] 1 I.L.R.M. 796.

[4] [1997] 3 I.R. 431; see *Flood v Flood* [1999] 2 I.R. 234.

[5] [2012] I.E.H.C. 545.

> scheme created by s.27(4) of the Succession Act 1965, and the procedures in the Rules of Court."

his title as administrator to defend proceedings making a claim against the estate relates back to the order made by the court.

20–15 Under s.27(5) of the 1965 Act, the administrator appointed by the court must apply for a grant and

> "the fact that an order under the section has been made shall be stated in the oath of the administrator, in the grant of administration and in the administration bond".[6]

The Appointment of an Administrator *Ad Colligenda Bona*

20–16 A grant *ad colligenda bona* may also be made under s.27(4) of the 1965 Act for the sole purpose of gathering in and preserving the estate of the deceased. It will be limited "to collecting in and preserving, but not distributing, the estate of the deceased". Such a grant is usually made where urgent steps are required to preserve the estate of the deceased. Such a grant may be made to a creditor of the deceased limited to collecting in the estate in order to pay debts or to renew leases to property, or it may be made to the nominee of creditors for the purposes of discharging debts. It may also be the only form of grant that the courts will be prepared to make, especially where the person entitled to a full grant is implicated in the murder of the deceased person and where criminal investigations into the murder of the deceased are still pending.[7] Grants *ad colligenda bona* cease to have effect when a general grant is made to the person entitled.

The Appointment of an Administrator *Ad Litem*

20–17 Plaintiffs contemplating proceedings against estates of deceased persons must ensure that the defendant named in the proceedings is the executor to whom probate has issued or the person to whom a grant of letters of administration has been made. Although it is well established that an executor can institute proceedings and maintain an action before probate of the testator's will is obtained, a grant will be necessary before the hearing of the action. This is because an executor derives his legal title from the testator's will, and the grant of probate before the hearing is necessary "because it is the only method recognised by the rules of court by which the executor can prove the fact that he is executor".[8] Administrators cannot

[6] See Ord.79, r.22 of the 1986 Rules (Probate Office); Ord. 80, r.26 of the 1986 Rules (District Probate Registry).

[7] *Re Nevin*, Unreported, High Court, Shanley J., 13 March 1997.

[8] See *Ingall v Moran* [1944] 1 K.B. 160.

function as defendants in actions brought against an estate unless a grant of letters of administration has issued to them, because it is a fundamental principle of law that:

> "the authority of an administrator of the estate of a deceased person derives from the grant of letters of administration and that, until he obtains the grant, the estate of the deceased does not vest in him".[9]

When proceedings are commenced:

> "the person named as defendant must be competent at that time to answer the alleged wrongdoing and meet the remedy sought. If he is not the action is not maintainable. If he subsequently obtains a grant of administration, that will not cure the fundamental defect and render the action maintainable".

A grant of letters of administration made after the commencement of proceedings "will not cure the fundamental defect". Plaintiffs therefore contemplating proceedings against estates of deceased persons must be careful to ensure that a grant has issued to the defendant. Where no grant has issued at the time, they may be well-advised to seek the appointment of an administrator *ad litem* under s.27(4) of the 1965 Act to avoid later complications regarding competent defendants. **20–18**

THE APPOINTMENT OF AN ADMINISTRATOR *PENDENTE LITE*

Where any legal proceedings are pending challenging the validity of the will, or for the purposes of obtaining, recalling or revoking any grant, the Court may make a grant to an administrator for the duration of the legal proceedings and such administrator will have all the rights and powers of a general administrator, other than that of distributing the estate. Where a grant *pendent lite* is made by the Court pursuant to s.27(7) of the 1965 Act, the person to whom it is made will have **20–19**

> "all the rights and powers of a general administrator, other than the right of distributing the estate of the deceased, and every person to whom such administration is granted shall be subject to the immediate control of the court and act under its direction".

An administrator appointed for this purpose may be assigned a reasonable remuneration by the Court. Invariably the person to whom such a grant is made will not be an interested party in the proceedings unless an interested person applies for such a grant with the consent of all the parties to the proceedings.[10] Before granting administration *pendent lite,* the Court must be satisfied that the necessity of the occasion requires the appointment of an administrator and nothing less than a *lis pendens* will suffice. Any **20–20**

---

[9] *Gaffney v Faughnan* [2006] I.L.R.M. 481.

[10] *Whittle v Keats* (1866) 35 L.J.P. & M. 54; *Re Griffin* [1925] P. 38.

preliminary matters arising between parties prior to the issuing of an originating summons—say in the form of a caveat, a warning or the entry of an appearance to a warning after the issuing of a caveat—will not constitute a *lis pendens*.[11] The administrator's appointment commences from the date the grant is made and ends only when the proceedings that led to the appointment are concluded, and this includes any appeals arising out of the proceedings. Where the proceedings relate to the validity of the will, and if a decree is pronounced in favour of it, the need for an administrator ceases and the person entitled may thereafter apply for a grant.

---

[11] *In the Goods of Gordon* (1867) I.R. 1 Eq. 79; *Re Leary* (1897) 31 I.L.T.R. 55.

CHAPTER 21

PROBATE AND ADMINISTRATION ACTIONS AND COSTS

INTRODUCTION

21–01 A probate action may be instituted for the purposes of challenging the validity of a will on the grounds that it was not executed in compliance with the statutory rules in s.78 of the Succession Act 1965 (the "1965 Act"),[1] or the testator did not know and approve the will,[2] or the testator was of unsound mind at the time he made the will and so lacked the necessary testamentary capacity required by s.77 of the 1965 Act,[3] or the testator was unduly influenced when he made his will.[4] A probate action may be commenced by the issuing of an originating plenary summons. An administration action may be commenced against personal representatives for breach of duty towards creditors or beneficiaries or for the abuse of powers in administering or distributing the estate of the deceased by issuing an originating special summons.[5]

21–02 Order 99, r.1(1) of the Rules of the Superior Courts 1986 (the "1986 Rules") provides that the costs of and incidental to every proceeding in the Superior Courts shall be in the discretion of those courts. Under Ord. 99, r.1(3) of the 1986 Rules, subject to sub-rule (4A) of S.I. No. 12 of 2008, the costs of an action will follow the event unless the Court otherwise directs.[6] In probate actions, however, as a result of the decision in *Vella v Morelli*,[7] the costs of an unsuccessful party may be awarded out of the estate of a deceased testator where it is shown that there were reasonable grounds for the litigation and

1 See Chapter 2 – The Execution of Wills
2 *ibid.*
3 See Chapter 3 – Testamentary Capacity.
4 See Chapter 10 – The Cessation of Succession and Legal Rights.
5 See Chapter 19 – The Administration and Distribution of Estates.
6 Rules of the Superior Courts (Costs) 2008 (operative from 21 February 2008).
7 [1968] I.R. 11; see also *Fairtlough v Fairtlough* (1839) 1 Milw. 36 at 39; *Kavanagh v Fegan* [1932] I.R. 566; *Murphy v Finlen* [1931] L.J. Ir. 50; *Mulligan v McKeown* [1955] I.R. 112.

that the litigation was conducted in a *bona fide* manner. In *Elliott v Stamp*[8] Kearns J. (as he then was) added that:

> "Thus, while it may be reasonable to commence and bring proceedings, and bring them *bona fide*, a point may arrive where, as a result of a disclosure made by the defence, the further maintenance of the claim can no longer be reasonable. In such circumstances, it seems to me a trial judge should not be fettered in the exercise of his discretion as to costs and should be free both to decline costs from the estate to an unsuccessful litigant or even to award costs against such a litigant from the time of disclosure."[9]

21–03 The practice regarding the award of costs set out in *Vella v Morelli* is confined to probate actions and will not be applied when determining the issue of costs in administration actions. In *O'Connor v Markey*[10] Herbert J., while affirming that *Vella v Morelli* dealt with probate issues regarding the due execution or revocation of wills and the testamentary capacity of a testator, went on to say that it did not apply to administration actions involving issues between beneficiaries in a will. In *Young v Cadell*[11] Laffoy J. stated that:

> "The factors which arise in a probate suit which justify the special rule in relation to costs which was reiterated in *Vella v Morelli*, the importance of ensuring that what are presented as testamentary documents are above suspicion and that legal costs are not a deterrent to pursuing *bona fide* beliefs or suspicions as to the validity of such documents, do not arise in administration suits, which, in the case of a death testate, proceed on the assumption that the testamentary document is valid, as was the case here."

21–04 The special practice regarding the award of costs in probate actions is not applicable to intestacies. In *Rennick v Rennick*[12] the deceased died intestate and, as the proceedings involved issues between beneficiaries arising out of intestacy, the decisions in *Vella v Morelli* and *Elliott v Stamp* were not relevant to the issues raised.

Probate Actions

21–05 A probate action means "any proceeding commenced by originating summons and seeking the grant or recall of probate, or letters of administration, or similar relief".[13] A probate action may therefore be instituted for the purposes of challenging the validity of a will on the grounds that:

(i) it was not executed in compliance with the statutory rules in s.78 of the Succession Act 1965[14]; or

[8] [2008] 3 I.R. 387.
[9] See *Scally v Rhatigan* [2012] I.E.H.C. 387.
[10] [2007] 2 I.R. 194.
[11] [2006] I.E.H.C. 49.
[12] [2012] I.E.H.C. 559.
[13] Ord.125, r.1 of the 1986 Rules.
[14] See Chapter 2 – The Execution of Wills.

(ii) the testator did not know and approve the will[15]; or
(iii) the testator was of unsound mind at the time he made the will and so lacked the necessary testamentary capacity required by s.77 of the 1965 Act[16]; or
(iv) the testator when making his or her will was unduly influenced.[17]

A probate action may be commenced by the issuing of an originating plenary summons out of the Central Office. It must be headed with the name of the deceased, as well as the names of the parties to the action. The indorsement in the summons must show whether the plaintiff claims as creditor, executor, administrator, residuary legatee, legatee, next-of-kin, heir-at-law, devisee or in any other capacity. On issuing the summons, the plaintiff must, if he has not already done so, enter a caveat in the Probate Office.[18] The summons must be served in the same way as in all other actions commenced by plenary summons. It may also be served out of the jurisdiction, in the same way as in other actions. The court may also allow for a substituted service where it is necessary. An appearance may be entered in the Central Office. The time for the entry of appearance is the same as in all other actions. In probate actions, however, any person not named in the summons may intervene and appear in the action by filing an affidavit in the Central Office showing his interest in the estate of the deceased. The plaintiff and defendant must, within eight days of the entry of appearance, file affidavits as to scripts in the Central Office whether or not they have any scripts relating to the estate of the deceased in their possession. The affidavit as to scripts must exhibit all testamentary papers in the possession of a party to a probate action. Other documents may be sought by way of discovery. Where there is discovery of documents in a probate action, the rules governing the discovery procedure will be the same as in other actions. The defendant must deliver his defence and counterclaim within 28 days from the date of delivery of the statement of claim. Order 19(1) of the 1986 Rules provides that: **21–06**

> "The plaintiff shall, subject to the provisions of Order 20, and at such time and in such manner as therein prescribed, deliver to the defendant a statement of his claim, and of the relief or remedy to which he claims to be entitled. The defendant shall subject to the provisions of Order 21, and at such time and in such manner as therein prescribed, deliver to the plaintiff his defence, set-off, or counter-claim (if any), and the plaintiff shall, subject to the provisions of Order 23, and at such time and in such manner as therein prescribed, deliver his reply (if any) to such defence, set-off, or counter-claim. Such statements shall be as brief as the nature of the case will admit, and the Taxing Master in adjusting the costs of the action shall, at the instance of any party, or may without any request, inquire into any unnecessary prolixity, and order the costs occasioned by such prolixity to be borne by the party chargeable with the same."

---

15 *ibid.*
16 See Chapter 3 – Testamentary Capacity.
17 See Chapter 10 – The Cessation of Succession and Legal Rights.
18 See Chapter 18 – Caveats and Citations.

21–07 Order 19(6) of the 1986 Rules provides that:

> "In probate actions it shall be stated with regard to every claim or defence which is pleaded, what is the substance of the case on which it is intended to rely; and further:
>
> (1) where undue influence is pleaded, the party making such plea shall, before the case is set down for trial, give particulars of the names of the persons against whom the charge of undue influence is preferred, the nature of the conduct alleged to constitute the undue influence and the dates upon which the acts alleged to constitute undue influence were exercised; and
> (2) where it is pleaded that the testator was not of sound disposing mind, the party making such plea shall, before the case is set down for trial, give particulars of any specific instance of delusion or mental incapacity; and
> (3) except by leave of the Court, no evidence shall be given of any other instance of undue influence or delusion or mental incapacity at the trial."

21–08 The defendant may, however, limit his costs by serving notice with his defence that he intends only to cross-examine the witnesses supporting the will. Where a counterclaim is filed, a reply to it will be governed by the same rules applicable to a defence. The will propounded by the plaintiff in the statement of claim may be counterclaimed by the defendant propounding a later will.

Administration Actions

21–09 An administration action may be instituted by special summons for the following purposes:

(i) The administration of the estate of a deceased person by the Court;
(ii) The determination of any question affecting the rights or interests of any person claiming to be a creditor, devisee, legatee or next-of-kin of the deceased;
(iii) The payment into court of any money in the hands of the personal representatives;
(iv) The determination of any question arising in the administration of any estate or the ascertainment of any class of creditors, legatees, devisees, next-of-kin or others.

21–10 The personal representatives and any person claiming to be interested as a creditor, devisee, legatee or next-of-kin of the deceased may institute proceedings by means of special summons for relief of a nature specified in Ord.3, r.1 to r.7 of the 1986 Rules. However, the personal representatives may sue and be sued as representing the estate of the deceased without joining any persons beneficially interested in the estate and will be considered as representing such persons. In an administration action, when an order is made for an account or affecting the rights or interests of persons not parties to the action, the Court may direct that any person interested in the estate be served with notice of the order and they will be bound by it.[19] However, any person served with such notice may within one month of service apply to the court to vary or add to the order.

It is well established that an executor can institute proceedings before probate of the testator's will is obtained, because an executor derives his title from a will. But a grant will become necessary before the hearing of the action because a grant is "the only method recognised by the rules of court by which the executor can prove the fact that he is executor".[20] As an administrator derives his title from a grant of letters of administration, he will not have the necessary representative capacity to institute proceedings on behalf of the estate, or indeed, defend proceedings, before a grant is issued to him. In *Gaffney v Faughnan*[21] Laffoy J. stated: **21–11**

> "It is a fundamental principle of law that the authority of an administrator of the estate of a deceased person derives from the grant of letters of administration and that, until he obtains the grant, the estate of the deceased does not vest in him."

As a result of *Ingall v Moran*[22] a plaintiff or defendant will not be able to maintain an action before a grant of administration is issued to him, and further, a grant subsequently obtained "will not cure the fundamental defect". Laffoy J., applying the rule in *Ingall v Moran,* stated that: **21–12**

> "When a summons is issued the person named as defendant must be competent at that time to answer the alleged wrongdoing and meet the remedy sought. If he is not the action is not maintainable. If he subsequently obtains a grant of administration, that will not cure the fundamental defect and render the action maintainable."

Neither can an administrator rely on the doctrine of relation back because, in order to maintain an action, "he must have a cause of action vested in him at the date of the writ". McKechnie J. in *Finnegan v Richards*[23] was not, however, in favour of applying the rule in *Ingall v Moran*, especially in cases involving the representative capacity of defendants, because of its inherent capacity to inflict an injustice on plaintiffs. **21–13**

In *Gaffney v Faughnan*[24] the plaintiff instituted proceedings against the defendant by plenary summons before a grant of administration to the deceased's intestate's estate issued to him. The defendant accepted service of the plenary summons after the grant of administration had issued to the plaintiff. He later issued a motion in which he sought an order striking **21–14**

19 Ord. 15, r.31 of the 1986 Rules.
20 See *Ingall v Moran* [1944] 1 K.B. 160.
21 [2006] 1 I.L.R.M. 481.
22 [1944] 1 K.B. 160.
23 [2007] 3 I.R. 671.
24 [2006] 1 I.L.R.M. 481.

out the proceedings on the grounds, *inter alia*, that the plaintiff did not have capacity as administrator of the estate of the deceased at the time the proceedings were instituted. During the course of her judgment, Laffoy J. referred to *Ingall v Moran* and *Creed v Creed*[25] and the principles established by them. Although these authorities dealt with a plaintiff's capacity to institute proceedings as an administrator before the issuing of a grant, she thought that the same principles were applicable to the bringing of an action against a defendant in the capacity of an administrator before a grant has issued. She stated that, in the case before her,

> "the person named as defendant had no status as a representative of the deceased or of his estate when the plenary summons issued. The action initiated by the issue of the plenary summons could not have been maintained and is still not maintainable. In the circumstances it must be struck out".

21–15 In *Finnegan v Richards*[26] the testatrix died on 13 May 2004. She was predeceased by her husband who was executor of her will. There was no issue of the marriage. Her niece became the next person entitled to apply for a grant of letters of administration with the will annexed. The niece, however, appointed two attorneys who were the defendants in the proceedings to act in respect of all matters concerning the administration of the estate, and they obtained a grant of letters of administration with the will annexed on 26 June 2006. A plenary summons was issued on 9 May 2006 in which the plaintiff claimed beneficial ownership of the deceased testatrix's dwelling house. The statement of claim was delivered on 27 September 2006. The plaintiff was faced with a time bar, as s.9(2) of the Civil Liability Act 1961 provides that no proceedings are maintainable against a deceased's estate unless, *inter alia*, the proceedings are commenced within two years after his death. Accordingly, the plaintiff had to institute proceedings by 13 May 2004. The defendants issued a notice of motion on 17 November 2006 in which they sought an order striking out the proceedings on the grounds, *inter alia,* that, at the date of instituting the proceedings, no grant had issued to the them. Consequently they lacked both the competence and capacity to be sued in a representative capacity, and accordingly the proceedings were a nullity and could not be maintained. McKechnie J. found that the defendants' solicitors were

> "fully alive to the twin difficulties arising by virtue of s.9 of the Civil Liability Act 1961 and the potential application of what I might call the rule in *Ingall v Moran*".

This was clearly evident from correspondence passing between the parties.

21–16 In *Finnegan v Richards,* McKechnie J. was highly critical of the rule in *Ingall v Moran,* especially in its application to defendants, and stated that

---

[25] [1913] 1 I.R. 48.
[26] [2007] 3 I.R. 671.

Singleton J. in *Finnegan v Cementation Company*[27] was "perfectly" correct in suggesting that this technicality was "a blot in the administration of the law", and that Lord Templeman in *Austin v Hart*[28] was correct in saying that there should be no extension of the rule's application. McKechnie J. preferred an approach based on justice and, where there were no compelling reasons, he would refuse to uphold a rule capable of inflicting an injustice. He also thought that, if *Austin v Hart* had been opened to Laffoy J. in *Gaffney v Faughnan,* in all probability she

> "would have been impressed with the opinion of Lord Templeman and would at least paused before extending the rule, by applying it, apparently without precedent, to a situation where the representative person was not seeking to maintain an action, but rather was being named as a defendant in such action".

It seemed to him that any rule of law, such as espoused in *Ingall v Moran*, which had such a "rejectionist label" attached to it by the English Court of Appeal and Privy Council, should be followed and applied only where either the court was bound to so do, or alternatively where the underlying reasons of justification so demanded. He went on to state **21–17**

> "I cannot identify any particular reason, consistent with the existence of this rule, which persuades me that in the circumstances of this case it is a good rule."

In *Bank of Scotland v Gray and Doyle*[29] Finlay Geoghegan J. pointed out that Laffoy J. in *Gaffney v Faughnan* was not asked to consider a claim against representative defendants in whose favour an order under s.27(4) had been made. There continues to be: **21–18**

> "no authority which considers the position of proceedings making a claim against an estate commenced against representative defendants in whose favour an order pursuant to s. 27(4) of the Succession Act 1965 had already been made, but to whom the grant had not yet issued and to whom a grant subsequently issued."

She concluded that the proceedings issued against the defendants making a claim against the estate in the intervening period should not be considered a nullity and were valid and maintainable. Thus, *Bank of Scotland v Gray and Doyle* is now an authority which considered the position of proceedings making a claim against an estate commenced against representative defendants in whose favour an order pursuant to s.27(4) of the Succession Act 1965 had already been made, but to whom the grant had not yet issued and to whom a grant subsequently issued, and that the proceedings issued against the defendants making a claim against the estate in the intervening period should not be considered a nullity and are valid and maintainable. **21–19**

---

27 [1953] Q.B. 688 at 699.
28 [1983] 2 W.L.R. 866 at 871
29 [2012] I.E.H.C. 545.

Circuit Court Proceedings

21–20 Probate actions are commenced in the Circuit Court by issuing a testamentary civil bill in accordance with the Circuit Court Rules. Order 50(1) of the Circuit Court Rules provides that:

> "(a) Any person desirous of taking proceedings in the Court for the purpose of obtaining a grant, or revocation of a grant, of Probate or Letters of Administration shall issue a Civil Bill in the form prescribed in Form 2G of the Schedule of Forms; such Civil Bill shall be headed with the words 'Testamentary Civil Bill'. Save in relation to proceedings aforementioned, any person desirous of taking proceedings in the Court pursuant to the provisions of the Succession Act, 1965 shall issue a Civil Bill in the form prescribed in Form 2H of the Schedule of Forms; such Civil Bill shall be headed with the words 'Succession Law Civil Bill'. On issuing a Testamentary Civil Bill or a Succession Law Civil Bill the plaintiff shall, if he has not already done so, lodge a caveat in the Probate Office entitled in the estate of the deceased person. Following the issuing of the Testamentary Civil Bill, details of the lodgement of the caveat shall be endorsed thereon by the Probate Office prior to service thereof. Thereafter, the caveat lodged in the matter will continue in force until the Probate Office is satisfied that the proceedings have been completed whether determined, discontinued or otherwise. For the purposes of this Rule, 'the Probate Office' means the Probate Office or the relevant District Probate Registry.
>
> (b) The issue of a Testamentary Civil Bill shall be preceded by the filing of an affidavit made by the plaintiff, or, if more than one plaintiff, then by one of them, verifying the claim, and specifying the names and residences of the next-of-kin, and of such persons as may be entitled under an intestacy to any interest in the assets of the alleged testator or intestate in the said Civil Bill named."

21–21 The plaintiff may be an executor, administrator, creditor, residuary legatee or devisee or next-of-kin.[30] Any person who has entered a caveat against the grant of probate or letters of administration may be made a defendant to the proceedings.[31] Where proceedings are instituted for the revocation of a grant, the person seeking revocation will be the plaintiff and the person to whom the grant was made will be the defendant.[32] Order 50(9) of the Circuit Court Rules provides that:

> "In Probate actions the plaintiff and defendant, within ten days of the entry of an appearance on the part of the defendant, shall respectively file affidavits as to scripts, whether they have or have not any script in their possession. Such affidavits shall be in the form set out at Form 28 in the Schedule of Forms with such variations as circumstances may require."

Order 50(9) of the Circuit Court Rules provides that:

> "The party opposing a will may with his Defence give notice to the party setting up the will that he merely insists upon the will being proved in solemn form of

---

[30] Order 50(2) of the Circuit Court Rules.

[31] Order 50(3) of the Circuit Court Rules.

[32] Order 50(4) of the Circuit Court Rules.

law, and only intends to cross-examine the witnesses produced in support of the will, and he shall thereupon be at liberty to do so, and shall not in any event be liable to pay the costs of the other side unless the Judge shall be of opinion that there was no reasonable ground for opposing the will."

Costs Generally

The general principles regarding the award of costs in any action are set out in Ord. 99 of the Rules of the Superior Courts 1986, as amended by S.I. No. 12 of 2008. Rule 1(1) of Ord. 99 of the Rules of the Superior Courts 1986 provides that the costs of and costs incidental to every proceeding in the Superior Courts shall be in the discretion of those courts. Rule 1(2) of Ord. 99 provides that no party will be entitled to recover any costs of or costs incidental to any proceeding from any other party to such proceeding, except under an order or as provided by the Rules of the Superior Courts. S.I. No 12 of 2008, the Rules of the Superior Courts (Costs) 2008, amended r.1(3) of Ord.99 by providing that: **21–22**

> "Subject to sub-rule (4A), the costs of an action, question or issue tried by a jury shall follow the event unless the court, for special cause, to be mentioned in the order, shall otherwise direct."

S.I. no.12 of 2008 also amended of Ord.99, r.1(4) by providing that:

> "Subject to sub-rule (4A), the costs of every issue of fact or law raised upon a claim or counterclaim shall, unless otherwise ordered, follow the event."

Order 99, r. 1(4A) as a result of the amendment of the Rules of the Superior Courts 1986 by S.I. No.12 of 2008, provides that:

> "The High Court or the Supreme Court, upon determining any interlocutory application, shall make an award of costs save where it is not possible justly to adjudicate upon liability for costs on the basis of the interlocutory application."

S.I. No.12 of 2008 also provides for the insertion of r.1A(1) immediately following r.1 of Ord.99 of the Rules of the Superior Courts 1986. Rule 1A(1) provides that notwithstanding r.1(3) and r.1(4):

> "(a) The Supreme Court, in considering the awarding of the costs of any appeal or any application in respect of an appeal, may, where it considers it just, have regard to the terms of any offer in writing sent by any party to any other party or parties offering to satisfy the whole or part of that other party's (or those other parties') claim or counterclaim the subject of the appeal, or application.
>
> (b) The High Court, in considering the awarding of the costs of any action (other than an action in respect of a claim or counterclaim concerning which a lodgment or tender offer in lieu of lodgment may be made in accordance with Order 22) or any application in such an action, may, where it considers it just, have regard to the terms of any offer in writing sent by any party to

> any other party or parties offering to satisfy the whole or part of that other party's (or those other parties') claim, counterclaim or application."

Rule 1A(2) provides that "an offer in writing" includes any offer made without prejudice save as to the issue of costs.

21–23 In *Cawley v Lillis*[33] Laffoy J. first stated that:

> "the special jurisprudence in relation to payment of costs out of the estate in probate actions, which had developed in this jurisdiction for the reasons set out by Budd J. in *In bonis Morelli*; *Vella v Morelli* [1968] I.R. 11, and was applied by the Supreme Court in *Elliott v Stamp* [2008] 3 I.R. 387, has no application to the circumstances of these proceedings".

21–24 "Apropos of the application of rule 1A" of the Rules of the Superior Courts (Costs) 2008, Laffoy J. stated that the defendant persisted in his contention that, on the death of the deceased, he became solely beneficially entitled to the joint assets until less than one week before the hearing, when his solicitors sent a letter headed "without prejudice save as to costs" to the plaintiffs' solicitors stating that "we confirm that our client is willing in order to settle all matters present and future", but it was too late to avoid the costs of the hearing. The defendant's conduct of his defence also necessitated the joinder of the beneficiary as plaintiff. Laffoy J. found that:

> "In the circumstances, I think the proper course is to accede to the plaintiffs' application. Accordingly, there will be an order that the plaintiffs be paid their costs (including the reserved costs of the application to join the beneficiary as a plaintiff) out of the joint funds before distribution. There will no order in relation to the defendant's costs."

21–25 In *Scally v Rhatigan*[34] (second module), Laffoy J. found that the issue of costs was not about the type identified by Budd J. in *Vella v Morelli*[35] which had arisen in the first module.[36] In the first module, the plaintiff had acted properly in initiating the proceedings to prove the will of the testator in solemn form and was awarded her costs out of the estate of the testator. In the second module, the principal issue was whether one of the reliefs sought by the defendant in her counterclaim, namely a declaration that the plaintiff was not an appropriate person to act as an executrix of the testator's estate, should result in the plaintiff, as the surviving executrix, being refused a grant of probate of the will of the testator. The defendant's case was that the plaintiff was professionally conflicted. Laffoy J. stated that:

> "While one can understand that the plaintiff would like to fulfil the task which the testator reposed in her, I am of the view that it would be impossible for her

[33] [2012] I.E.H.C. 70.

[34] [2012] I.E.H.C. 387; see also Albert Keating, "The Sting in the Counterclaim" (2013) 18(4) C.P.L.J. 82.

[35] [1968] I.R. 11.

[36] *Scally v Rhatigan* [2011] 1 I.R. 639.

> to steer a non-conflicted passage between the beneficiaries of the estate assets, on the one hand, and the interest of the beneficiaries of the non-estate assets, on the other hand, so as to take all of the steps in the administration, including the protection of the assets, of the estate of the testator and of the trusts created by the will that require to be taken by the personal representative."

She went on to say:

> "I have no doubt that the conflicted position of the executrix amounts to 'serious special circumstances' in the sense intended by Lynch J. in *Dunne v Heffernan*[37] and that the welfare of the beneficiaries of the estate assets would not be protected by the estate of the testator being administered by her."

As regards the issue of costs in the second module, the defendant was awarded her costs out of the estate, but no order was made in relation to the costs of the plaintiff.

Costs in Probate Actions

A probate action may be instituted to determine whether a will was executed in accordance with the formalities required by s.78 of the Succession Act 1965, or whether a testator knew and approved of the contents of a will, or whether, at the time of executing a will, a testator was of sound disposing mind and had capacity to make a valid will. The proceedings leading to a probate action may be set in motion by a party with an interest in a deceased's estate entering a caveat opposing the issue of a grant of probate to the executors of the will. The executors may in turn respond by issuing a warning to the caveat. But where the warning is followed by an entry of appearance by the party opposing the grant, the executors may have no other option save to prove the will in solemn form of law, and this may be done by serving a plenary summons on the party opposed to the issuing of the grant.[38] **21–26**

While the general principles set down in Ord. 99 of the Rules of the Superior Courts 1986, as amended by S.I. No.12 of 2008, are applicable to all actions, the court, when considering whether to award costs out of a testator's estate in a probate action, will also take into account the answer to two questions, *viz.* (a) was there reasonable ground for litigation, and (b) was it conducted *bona fide*. In *Vella v Morelli*[39] Budd J. was able to trace this practice going back to the judgment of Dr Radcliff for the Prerogative Court in *Fairtlough v Fairtlough*.[40] He also referred to a number of later Irish decisions on the matter. In *Keogh v Wall*[41] Keating J. allowed costs out of the estate in a probate action to a plaintiff who had pleaded undue **21–27**

---

37 [1997] 3 I.R. 431.

38 See *Scally v Rhatigan* [2012] I.E.H.C. 387.

39 [1968] I.R. 11.

40 (1839) 1 Milw. 36.

41 (1863) 9 Ir. Jur. N.S. 418.

influence, albeit unsuccessfully, on the basis that there were reasonable grounds for suspicion. Warren J. in *O'Reilly v Forde*,[42] in dealing with the matter of costs of an unsuccessful plaintiff, posed the two questions to be considered: (a) "Was there reasonable ground for litigation?" and (b) "Was it conducted *bona fide*?" In *O'Kelly v Browne*[43] Warren J., when dealing with a motion to vary an order for costs in a probate action, further stated:

> "It is the usual practice of this court, without having regard to the amount or the ownership of the property, if the case has been a proper one for litigation, and the litigation has been properly conducted, to order that the general costs shall be paid out of the assets, *i.e.*, out of the personal estate, for the court has no jurisdiction to order them to be paid out of real estate: *Young v Dendy* L.R. 1 P. & D. 344."

21–28 Since the enactment of the 1965 Act, the Court now has jurisdiction to order the payment of costs out of the entire estate whether it consists of real or personal estate or both real and personal estate. Warren J. was also the presiding judge in *Burke v Moore*,[44] a case that involved a question of the due execution of a will, where the unsuccessful plaintiff was awarded costs out of the estate. The practice as stated by Warren J. was also followed by the Chief Baron in *Gillic v Smyth*[45] a case that also involved a question of due execution of a will where an unsuccessful defendant was allowed his costs out of the estate. Budd J. found the old Irish practice "a very fair and reasonable one" and one that also had the result of allaying the reasonable fears of persons when faced with the decision of whether to litigate or not. He went on to reaffirm the Irish practice by emphasising the fact that, before that practice can operate in any particular case, two questions must be answered, *viz.* (a) Was there reasonable ground for litigation? (b) Was it conducted *bona fide*? In the case before him, having decided to follow the Irish practice, he answered the two questions in the affirmative and allowed the plaintiff her costs out of the estate. The payment of costs out of a deceased's estate therefore appears to depend on the answer to these two basic questions. This special practice regarding the award of costs in probate actions was affirmed in *Vella v Morelli*[46] by Budd J. and in *Elliott v Stamp*[47] by Kearns J.

21–29 In *Elliott v Stamp*[48] Kearns J. pointed out in the course of his judgment for the Supreme Court that the case law in relation to costs was developed in this jurisdiction for the reasons expressed by Budd J. in *Vella v Morelli,* but added that any departure from the case-law on the matter required a "reasoned basis" for doing so. He stated that:

---

42 (1871) 5 I.L.T.R. 54.
43 (1874) I.R. 9 Eq. 353.
44 (1875) I.R. 9 Eq. 609.
45 (1914) 49 I.L.T.R. 36.
46 [1968] I.R. 11.
47 [2008] 3 I.R. 387.
48 *ibid.*

> "Thus, while it may be reasonable to commence and bring proceedings, and bring them *bona fide*, a point may arrive where, as a result of a disclosure made by the defence, the further maintenance of the claim can no longer be reasonable. In such circumstances, it seems to me a trial judge should not be fettered in the exercise of his discretion as to costs and should be free both to decline costs from the estate to an unsuccessful litigant or even to award costs against such a litigant from the time of disclosure."[49]

He went on to say that he was not satisfied, based on an objective evaluation of the documentation supplied to the plaintiffs before the trial, that there was sufficient information to meet all of the requirements or concerns that the plaintiffs may reasonably have had. He awarded the plaintiffs their full costs out of the estate, including the costs of the appeal. **21–30**

In *Scally v Rhatigan* (the first module)[50] the question of the testamentary capacity of the testator at the date on which the will was made was the issue which the Court had to determine. The Court concluded that the testator did have testamentary capacity when he made the will and, accordingly, admitted the will to probate in solemn form. Although unsuccessful, the defendant claimed that she was entitled to her costs out of the estate of the testator. In the course of her judgment, Laffoy J. referred to the Supreme Court judgments in *Vella v Morelli* and *Elliott v Stamp* and said she was satisfied **21–31**

> "that both questions which the court has to consider must be answered in the affirmative in this case when considered from the perspective of the defendant's application for costs of the first module out of the estate".

Having regard to all of the evidence adduced at the hearing and, in particular, to the fact that the testator was suffering from motor neurone disease when he made the will and that the disease had advanced to a stage where he was unable to communicate verbally, there were reasonable grounds for the litigation. She was also satisfied that the defendant conducted the defence in a *bona fide* manner. Accordingly, the defendant was entitled to the costs out of the estate of the testator. **21–32**

Costs in Administration Actions

The practice regarding the award of costs as described by Budd J. in *Vella v Morelli* and confirmed by Kearns J. in *Elliott v Stamp*[51] and Laffoy J. in *Scally v Rhatigan*[52] is confined to probate actions only, and has no application to administrative actions. In *O'Connor v Markey*[53] Herbert J. affirmed that the authorities referred to in *Vella v Morelli* dealt with probate issues regarding **21–33**

49 [2008] 3 I.R. 387 at 396.
50 [2011] 1 I.R. 639.
51 [2008] 3 I.R. 387.
52 [2011] 1 I.R. 639.
53 [2007] 2 I.R. 194; see also *Young v Cadell* [2006] I.E.H.C. 49.

the due execution or revocation of wills and the testamentary capacity of a testator, but by contrast,

> "the instant application bore all the hallmarks of contentious litigation between beneficiaries which did not in any way touch upon the capacity of the testator or the state in which he left his testamentary papers".

21–34 So the issue of costs was not governed by *Vella v Morelli*. In *O'Connor v Markey* a dispute arose in the course of the administration of the estate of a testator between the first and second defendants, both beneficiaries under the will. The first defendant, the principal beneficiary, claimed that the payment of several outstanding debts was solely the liability of the estate and that he was not obliged personally to discharge the debts. The claim was counter to the second defendant, whose residuary request would be substantially or entirely consumed by the payment of those debts. The outcome of the substantive action was that the first defendant was obliged personally to indemnify the estate in respect of the whole amount of those debts.

21–35 Herbert J. referred to the judgment of Kekewich J. in *Buckton v Buckton*[54] where the issue of costs in administration actions was considered. Kekewich J. identified three types of administration action for the purposes of determining the issue of costs:

1. In administration actions where the applicants are the personal representatives or trustees seeking the court's direction in ascertaining the interests of the beneficiaries or to have some question determined which has arisen in the administration of the estate, costs of all parties as necessarily incurred for the benefit of the estate will be taxed as between solicitor and client and paid out of the estate;
2. Where the application is made by some of the beneficiaries by reason of some difficulty of construction or administration that would have justified an application by the personal representatives or trustees, they will also be allowed their costs out of the estate;
3. But where a beneficiary

   > "makes a claim adverse to other beneficiaries, and usually takes advantage of the convenient procedure by originating summons to get a question determined which, but for this procedure, would be the subject of an action commenced by writ and would strictly fall within the description of litigation"

and

> "once convinced that I am determining rights between adverse litigants I apply the rule which ought, I think, be rigidly enforced in adverse litigation, and order the unsuccessful party to pay the costs".

---

[54] [1907] 2 Ch. 406 at 414-415.

Kekewich J. went on to state that, whether

> "he ought to be ordered to pay the cost of trustees, who are, of course, Respondents, or not, is sometimes open to question, but with this possible exception the unsuccessful party bears the costs of all whom he has brought before the court".

Adopting the principles formulated by Kekewich J., Herbert J. found that the case before him fell into the third category, even though it was the administrator who made the application as it was made "essentially in a nominal capacity only and does not in any material way alter the situation". He thought that it would be neither fair nor reasonable that the first defendant, having failed in his claim, should be awarded costs out of the estate or exempted from paying the costs of the special administrator and of the successful second named defendant, both of whom he caused to be involved in this litigation. **21–36**

In *Rennick v Rennick*[55] the deceased died intestate and, as the proceedings did not concern the testamentary disposition of property nor execution of testamentary documents, Laffoy J. held that neither the decision in *Vella v Morelli* nor the decision in *Elliott v Stamp* had any relevance to the proceedings before her. In the course of her judgment, Laffoy J. referred to certain of the observations made by Herbert J. in *O'Connor v Markey*[56]and found that the following observation was particularly relevant to the case before her: **21–37**

> "The present application arose in the course of the administration of the estate, was not a probate action, but neither was it an ordinary administration suit. To all intents and purposes it was a hostile *lis inter partes* between two beneficiaries under the will. It related to the conduct of the testator's business by the first defendant while the testator was still alive and to the issue of whether the first defendant was or was not obliged to pay the particular debts as they arose, so that they would not become a burden upon and payable out of the estate on the death of the testator. The special administrator was in reality only a nominal plaintiff to enable the opinion of the court to be obtained by way of a special summons for directions in the course of the administration. The many issues of fact and of law were litigated as a proceeding *inter partes* between the first defendant and the second defendant on their own evidence, and the evidence of witnesses called by each of them."

Applying this observation to the facts of the case Laffoy J. stated that:

> "[i]f Mrs Rennick had not made the concession she had made, would, in reality, have been a *lis inter partes* between the plaintiffs, as personal representatives of the Deceased, on the one hand, and Mrs Rennick, on the other hand, and would have had to go to plenary hearing. That did not happen because Mrs Rennick conceded that the estate of the Deceased should get the monies on joint deposit. It was emphasised by counsel for the defendants that Mrs Rennick still feels that

---

55 [2012] I.E.H.C. 559.

56 [2007] 2 I.R. 194.

> the monies on joint deposit were hers and Mr Rennick's but, despite her strong views, she accepted that on balance she should make the concession".

21–38 When the concession was made, the proceedings were "finalised". Laffoy J. stated that the concession was the "event" for the purposes of the application of Ord. 99 of the Rules of the Superior Courts "which, subject to the overriding discretion of the court, mandates that costs should follow the event".

Chapter 22

THE CONSTRUCTION OF WILLS

Introduction

The primary rule of construction of wills is that the courts must ascertain and give effect to the intention of the testator. This is the one rule that is applied by the courts in general and unqualified terms. The rule will be applied even though it is **22–01**

> "impossible to reconcile the cases on the basis of such a rule but it is impossible to reconcile them on the basis of a rule less generally stated and more in accordance with fundamental principles in the interpretation of wills of endeavouring to ascertain and give effect to the intention of the testator."[1]

The court will ascertain the intention of the testator from the words used by him in the will. The words used by the testator will be viewed as providing evidence of intention, *viz*. intrinsic evidence. But before the court can give effect to the intention of the testator, it must first be ascertained. This is achieved by deriving the meaning of the words used by the testator from the context of the will as a whole. When doing this, the language used by the testator when creating the devise or legacy will be thoroughly parsed by the application of the Lowry Principles,[2] and also extrinsic evidence may be admitted under s.90 of the Succession Act 1965 (the "1965 Act") "to show the intention of the testator and to assist in the construction of, or to **22–02**

1 *Robinson v Moore* [1962/63] Ir. Jur.Rep. 23 at 29; see Albert Keating, *The Construction of Wills* (Dublin: Round Hall *Sweet & Maxwell*, 2001).

2 *Heron v Ulster Bank Ltd* [1974] N.I. 44 at 52-53.

explain any contradiction in the will".[3] It is also important to take note of s.89 of the 1965 Act which provides that:

> "Every will shall, with reference to all estate comprised in the will and every devise or bequest contained in it, be construed to speak and take effect as if it had been executed immediately before the death of the testator, unless a contrary intention appears from the will."

22–03 On a construction, bearing in mind that the testator's intention is the primary concern, the court will first read the will and give an ordinary meaning to the words used by the testator, unless the context of the will suggests a different meaning. A testator may employ technical legal words or terms of legal signification and in such case they will be interpreted in a legal sense unless the context of the will clearly indicates that another meaning was intended.[4] The *falsa demonstratio* rule may also be applied where the words used by the testator in creating a gift adequately describe the substance of it, but subsequent and additional words tend to render the initial description erroneous, the subsequent and additional words may be rejected as a *falsa demonstratio*.[5]

The rule in s.99 of the 1965 Act may be applied:

> "if the purport of a devise or legacy admits of more than one interpretation, then, in case of doubt, the interpretation according to which the devise or bequest will be operative will be preferred."[6]

22–04 The courts appear to be obliged under s.99 to interpret the devise or bequest in a way that will render it operative. But for this to happen a devise or legacy must be capable of more than one interpretation before s.99 becomes applicable.

Where a testator in a devise or bequest of real or personal estate uses words "dying without issue", or "die without leaving issue", or "have no issue", or other words which may import either a want or failure of issue of any person in his lifetime or at the time of his death, or an indefinite failure of issue, such words:

> "shall be construed to mean a want or failure of issue in his lifetime, or at the time of his death, and not an indefinite failure of his issue, unless a contrary intention appears from the will".[7]

22–05 A will may be made subject to the condition of a testator's death occurring

---

[3] *Rowe v Law* [1978] I.R. 55; see also *O'Connell v Bank of Ireland* [1998] 2 I.R. 596.

[4] See Albert Keating, "The Technical Meaning Rule in the Construction of Wills" (2002) 7(4) C.P.L.J. 76.

[5] See Albert Keating, "The Use of the *Falsa Demonstratio* Rule in the Construction of Wills" (2004) 9(4) C.P.L.J. 78.

[6] See Albert Keating, "A Constructive Interpretation of Section 99 of the Succession Act 1965" (2012) C.P.L.J. 2; Albert Keating, "The Testator's Intention and Doubt Principle" (2006) 24 I.L.T. 54.

[7] s.96 of the 1965 Act.

in the specified circumstances. For instance, a testator may make his will conditional on his death occurring during the course of a hazardous journey and should he die while doing so the condition for making the will would have been satisfied, and the will stands as his last will. Such a condition limits the operation of the will to the occurrence of a specified event. But should the testator return safely from the journey, the will then will cease to have effect, as the conditional circumstances on which it was made no longer exist. Where, however, the words used by the testator merely disclose a reason for making a will, as opposed to a condition, the will may be upheld regardless of the circumstances surrounding the testator's death.[8] The Jeune criteria may be applied by the court when deciding whether or not a will is a conditional one.[9]

A gift in a will may also be made subject to a condition. The condition may take the nature of a condition precedent or a condition subsequent, and the nature of the condition may also determine the validity, or invalidity, of the gift. Where a gift is made subject to a condition precedent, it may fail if the terms of the condition are deemed void, as the gift is dependent on the validity of the condition; a gift made subject to a condition subsequent will continue to be valid even if the condition is void, as the gift is not dependent on the validity of the condition.[10] **22–06**

Where the words used by the testator in creating a devise, legacy or bequest in his or her will are uncertain in purport the assistance of the courts may be required to ascertain the intention of the testator. For this purpose, a construction suit may be instituted by means of an originating special summons. The rules of construction may be applied by the courts in their quest to ascertain and give effect to the testator's intention. **22–07**

The Testator's Intention

The primary duty of the courts when construing a will is to ascertain and give effect to the testator's intention. The words used by the testator will the first port of call to discover "what the testator really meant" by the words used. However, it does not mean that the exact words used will be given their literal meaning. In *Dunlop v Greer*[11] Porter M.R. stated that: **22–08**

> "If, having considered the will and the whole will, it is plain that to place a literal meaning upon one clause would defeat the clear intention, it must be necessary to 'do violence' (as an eminent judge once expressed it) to the language used. The thing to be ascertained is what was the man's will."

---

8 *In the Goods of Groarke* [1949] Ir. Jur.Rep. 8.

9 See *In the Goods of Spratt* [1897] P. 28.

10 Albert Keating, "The Construction of Conditions Attaching to Gifts in Wills" (2008) 1 *Judicial Studies Institute Journal* 171.

11 [1899] 1 I.R. 324.

22–09 But there are limits to what the courts may do when construing a will. The major limitation is that they may not go beyond the bounds of testamentary expression. In *Curtin v O'Mahony*[12] O'Flaherty J., when referring to this limitation, stated: "A judge is to tread cautiously so as not to offend against the judicial inheritance which is that one is entitled to construe a will but not to make one". Extrinsic evidence *de hors* the will may also be admitted by the courts, but only "to show the intention of the testator and to assist in the construction of, or to explain any contradiction in the will".[13]

22–10 In *Rowe v Law*[14] Henchy J., when interpreting s.90 of the 1965 Act, stated that extrinsic evidence may only be adduced if it met the double requirement of: "(a) showing the intention of the testator *and* (b) assisting in the construction of, or explaining any contradiction in, a will". Any interpretation involving either (a) *or* (b) would produce illogical and unreasonable consequences which the legislature could not have intended. If the section made (a) sufficient for the admission of extrinsic evidence, then the court could go outside the will and accept such evidence as to the intention of the testator. This interpretation would run counter to s.78 that lays down the formal requirements for making a will and thus encapsulating the testator's intention. It would be "unreasonable and contradictory" for the legislature to prescribe formal requirements for the purposes of encapsulating the testator's intention in a will and then later on in the same Act to allow in extrinsic evidence of the testator's intention without qualification or restriction. If extrinsic evidence were admissible of the testator's intention without restriction or qualification, the door would be open "for fraud, mistake, unfairness and uncertainty". Moreover, since the function of the Court in construing a will or in finding an explanation for a contradiction in it necessarily involves a search for the testator's intention, it would be unnecessary for the section to include requirement (b) if requirement (a) on its own were sufficient to allow the admission of extrinsic evidence. The conjunctive "and" in the section connotes "a duality of purpose as a condition for the admission under the section of extrinsic evidence". Therefore, the necessary conditions for the admission of extrinsic evidence are to show the intention of the testator *and* to assist in the construction of, or to explain a contradiction in, the will. The two conditions must be satisfied before the court can allow the admission of extrinsic evidence.

22–11 Griffin J. in a concurring judgment was of the view that:

> "on the correct construction of s.90, extrinsic evidence is to be admitted only for the stated purpose of assisting in the construction of, or to explain any contradiction in a will, and not for the purposes of replacing the dispositive intention of the

---

[12] [1991] 2 I.R. 562.

[13] See s.90 of the 1965 Act.

[14] [1978] I.R. 55 at 73-74; see Albert Keating, "Pre-Probate Construction of Testamentary Documents and Extrinsic Evidence" (2006) 11(2) C.P.L.J. 36.

testator as expressed in the will, for that would be outside the range of purposes permitted by the section".

He also stated:

> "If extrinsic evidence of the dispositive intention of a testator is to be admitted without qualification, the effect of this would be that a new will could be written for the testator, this will be collected from the statements and declarations of the deceased at the time of, before, or after the making of the will, without compliance with the provisions of the section 78. The effect of this would be to nullify those provisions and to render ineffective the safeguards provided therein."

In *O'Connell v Bank of Ireland*[15] Keane J. considered the extent of the alteration of the law brought about by s.90 of the 1965 Act favoured the construction put on the section by the majority of the Court in *Rowe v Law* that extrinsic evidence of the testator's intention was admissible only where it assisted in the construction of a will or helped to resolve any contradiction in it. He went on to say that: **22–12**

> "Any other construction of s.90, as the judgments of Henchy J. and Griffin J. in *Rowe v Law* made clear, would have led to a radical and far reaching change in the law which it cannot have been the intention of the Oireachtas to bring about by such, at best, opaque and ambiguous language."[16]

The Lowry Principles

The context of a will as whole may itself provide the key for its construction and for the purposes of revealing a testator's true intention. The six principles of construction devised by Lowry C.J. in *Heron v Ulster Bank Ltd.*[17] may be used when attempting to ascertain the intention of a testator from the language used. These principles may be appropriately called the Lowry principles. They are as follows: **22–13**

> "1. Read the immediate relevant portion of the will as a piece of English and decide, if possible, what it means.
> 2. Look at the other material parts of the will and see whether they tend to confirm the apparently plain meaning of the immediately relevant portion or whether they suggest the need for modification in order to make harmonious sense of the whole or, alternatively, whether an ambiguity in the immediately relevant portion can be resolved.
> 3. If ambiguity persists, have regard to the scheme of the will and consider what the testator was trying to do.
> 4. One at this stage must have resort to rules of construction, where applicable, and aids, such as the presumption of early vesting and the presumptions against intestacy and in favour of equality.

---

15 [1998] 2 I.R. 596.

16 See *In Re Burke; Lynch v Burke*, Unreported, High Court, McCracken J., 30 July 1999; see Albert Keating, "The Testator's Intention and Doubt Principle" (2006) 24 I.L.T. 54.

17 [1974] N.I. 44 at 52.

5. Then see whether any rule of law prevents a particular interpretation from being adopted.
6. Finally, and, I suggest, not until the disputed passage has been exhaustively studied, one may get help from the opinions of other courts and judges on similar words, rarely as binding precedents, since it has been well said that 'no will has a twin brother' (per Werner J. in *Matter of King* 200 N.Y. 189, 192 (1910), but more often as examples (sometimes of the highest authority) of how judicial minds nurtured in the same discipline have interpreted words in similar contexts."

22–14 The Lowry principles were applied by Carroll J. in *Howell v Howell*,[18] and also received the approval of the courts in *Corrigan v Corrigan & Anor*,[19] *McGuinness v Sherry & Anor*[20] and *Mullen v Mullen*.[21]

22–15 The Lowry principles may also be coupled to s.90 of the 1965 Act which provides that "extrinsic evidence shall be admissible to show the intention of the testator and to assist in the construction of, or to explain any contradiction in, a will". In *Corrigan v Corrigan*[22] McGovern J., when construing a bequest in a will using the Lowry principles, admitted the notes of the testator's solicitor when taking instructions for the preparation of his will.

The Ordinary Meaning Rule

22–16 The language used by the testator will be viewed as providing the evidence of his intention.[23] The words used by a testator are deemed to have expressed the testamentary wishes but, where there is lack of clarity in expressing those wishes, the courts may have to decide the issue. The courts, when interpreting the words used by a testator, will first read the will and give them their ordinary meaning unless the context of the will suggests otherwise. The testator will not only be viewed as the author of the will, but also its lexicographer. If he uses words meaning something different from their ordinary meaning – and he is free to do this for the purposes of his will – he must provide the dictionary denoting their meaning. In *Re Cook*[24] Harman J. went so far as to state that: "Testators can cause black to mean white if they make their intention sufficiently clear". The question, then, is what the written words mean for the purposes of his will.[25]

22–17 Words with a variety of meanings may, however, be strictly construed by the courts when construing wills. The word "money" is strictly construed

18 [1992] 1 I.R. 290.
19 [2007] I.E.H.C. 367.
20 [2008] I.E.H.C. 134.
21 [2014] I.E.H.C. 407.
22 [2007] I.E.H.C. 367.
23 See Albert Keating, "The Ordinary Meaning Rule in the Construction of Wills" (2002) 7(2) C.P.L.J. 26.
24 [1948] 1 All E.R. 231.
25 *Perrin v Morgan* [1943] A.C. 399; [1943] 1 All E. R. 187.

by the courts to mean cash or cash in a bank, but that meaning may be subjugated to a contextual meaning ascribed to it by the testator in his will.[26] In *Re Jennings*[27] Meredith J. stated that the Court was entitled to consider the "whole tenor of the will", and indeed the surrounding circumstances, to ascertain what the testator meant when using the word "money" in his will. In *In the Goods of Martin*[28] O'Keeffe P. stated that it was well settled that, although the primary meaning of the word "money" is cash, "the word, in a will, may cover much more", and he referred to the decision of Meredith J. in *Re Jennings* for support. The word "property" is another word that has several meanings standing on its own but the meaning intended by the testator may be derived from the context of his will as a whole.[29]

The Technical Meaning Rule

A testator may employ technical words or terms of legal signification, and where he does so, such words will be given their legal meaning unless the context of the will clearly indicates that another meaning was intended.[30] It was stated in *Re Hogg*[31] that: "Where a testator uses technical words, he is presumed to employ them in their legal signification, unless the context clearly indicates to the contrary." In *Re Hogg* O'Byrne J. stated that: **22–18**

> "The expression 'residuary legatee' in a will is properly applicable to personalty only, and should be so construed, unless there is something in the context (including in that term the entire will) that the testator used it in a wider and more general sense."[32]

The technical term used will determine the entitlement to a particular kind of property unless the testator clearly indicates another meaning. It may be gathered from the context of a will that the testator intended his residuary legatee to receive the residue of both his real and personal estate. In this instance, context will prevail over technical terminology and the residuary legatee will become entitled to both types of residuary estate. Where, however, no context is provided by the will, a residuary legatee will be entitled only to residuary personal estate and any residuary real estate will pass on intestacy. Therefore, while it is true to say that the nature of the property disposed of will determine whether a testamentary gift is a "devise" or a "legacy," the use of the words "legatee" or "devisee" in a residuary clause will determine the entitlement to a particular kind of estate unless the context indicates otherwise. **22–19**

---

26 *Re Jennings* [1930] I.R. 196.
27 [1930] I.R. 196.
28 [1968] I.R. 1 at 5-6.
29 *Fetherston v Haugh-Whitney's Estate* [1924] I.R. 153.
30 See Albert Keating, "The Technical Meaning Rule in the Construction of Wills" (2002) 7(4) C.P.L.J. 76.
31 [1944] I.R. 244 at 252-253.
32 See also *Re Atkinson* [1942] I.R. 268.

22–20 Where a testator indicates the fund or a particular part his property out of which a legacy is to be paid or taken—for instance, where a particular bank account out of which payment of the legacy is to be made is indicated, or where shares in a particular company are designated out of which a number of them are to be given to the legatee—the legacy may be construed as a demonstrative legacy because of the words used by the testator when creating it. Where a particular fund or property is indicated for payment or discharge of a demonstrative legacy, it will be general in effect unless the fund indicated for payment is the precise amount mentioned in the legacy or comprises the exact number of shares mentioned in the bequest. Gibson J. stated in *Re Connor*[33] that:

> "If a testator gives a legacy and directs that it is to be paid out of a particular account or out of the proceeds of sale of particular property, the courts have consistently treated the legacy as demonstrative by notionally importing the word 'primarily' into the reference to the fund for payment. But such a conclusion can only follow if a will does not make it clear that the fund in question is to be the sole source of payment. If a will stipulates or provides that a particular fund and it alone is to feed the legacy, that negatives its character as merely demonstrative."

The *Falsa Demonstratio* Rule

22–21 Where the initial words used by the testator in creating a gift adequately describe the substance of it but subsequent and additional words tend to render the initial description erroneous, the subsequent and additional words may be rejected as a *falsa demonstratio*.[34] The rule of construction is *falsa demonstratio non nocet cum de corpora constat,* which means that, if there is an adequate and sufficient description, with convenient certainty of what is to pass, a subsequent erroneous addition will not vitiate it.[35] In *Morrell v Fisher*[36] Alderson B. stated that the "characteristic of cases within the rule is, so far as it is false, applies to no subject at all; and so far as it is true, applies to one only". But additional words that merely restrict the generality of a gift will not be looked upon as a *falsa demonstratio*. The rule of construction applied in the latter instance is *non accipi debent verba in demonstrationem falsam, quae competunt in limitationem veram,* which means that, if it is doubtful whether the words import a false demonstration, or whether they are words of restriction that limit the generality of the former words, the law will never intend an error or falsehood. If, therefore, in a gift, some of the demonstrations are true, but others are partly true and partly false, these latter demonstrations will be construed as limiting or restricting the gift and those parts only which in the circumstances are true will pass as part of the gift.

---

33 [1969] N.I. 159 at 163-164.

34 See Albert Keating, "The Use of the *Falsa Demonstratio* Rule in the Construction of Wills" (2004) 9(4) C.P.L.J. 78.

35 *Morrell v Fisher* (1849) 4 Ex. 591.

36 *ibid.*

When applying the *falsa demonstratio* rule of construction, the essential question to be addressed is not what a testator meant to do, but what the words of the gift mean. The rule is applied to derive a meaning from the words used, and it will not be applied where the words used by the testator according to their ordinary sense have a clear and unambiguous meaning, and that meaning will not be substituted for another by using the rule. Lord Westbury L.C. said in *West v Lawday*[37] that the rule will not be applied if to do so would violate **22–22**

> "a cardinal principle of language, and saying that when words, according to their ordinary and grammatical and obvious and natural sense and meaning, have a clear and unambiguous interpretation, that meaning ought not to be done away with in order to substitute for it another meaning".

The *falsa demonstratio* rule will become applicable only where, for instance, a devise is created by words of description that denote the substance of the gift of land but are followed by words of enumeration that "do not completely enumerate and exhaust particulars which are comprehended and included within the antecedent, universal, or generic denomination". By applying the rule, the entirety of the land that was expressly given by the devise will not be prejudiced by the subsequent inaccurate enumeration of the particulars. Therefore, the first part of the rule, *falsa demonstratio non nocet cum de corpora constat*, will become applicable only where the words of a gift are made unclear and ambiguous by additional words. Such words will be construed so as to prevent a *falsa demonstratio*, but where the additional words render some of the demonstrations in a gift true and others false, the latter will be construed by applying the second part of the rule, *non accipi debent verba in demonstrationem falsam, quae competunt in limitationem veram*. Such words will be treated as words limiting or restricting the effect of a gift to those parts which are true and will pass accordingly. Where, for instance, a testator devises certain property described as being in County Cork to his niece, but a portion only of the property is situated in County Cork, the residue being in County Kerry, by applying the second part of the rule, *non accipi debent,* the gift will be limited to so much of the land as is situated in County Cork, there being no intention expressed of giving property situated outside of County Cork to the testator's niece. The *falsa demonstratio* rule may also be applied to the initial words creating a gift where it is shown that the subject matter of a gift was inaccurately described as a result of a "blundering mistake".[38] Where, for instance, all the property described in a gift is situated in one place, the generality of the description may not be derogated from by an imperfect or mistaken enumeration of the particulars of the property. **22–23**

But where property in a gift is inaccurately described, and it is shown that the inaccuracy resulted from a latent ambiguity and not a "blundering **22–24**

[37] (1865) 11 H.L.C. 375 at 383.

[38] *Moore v Phelan* [1920] 1 I.R. 232.

mistake", the court may look to the will as a whole in an attempt to discover the intention of the testator when making the gift. In *Flood v Flood*[39] the Master of the Rolls stated that, in cases involving inaccurate descriptions of property, no weight could be given to verbal or written statements of intention, but where a testator uses

> "doubtful words in a particular sense is a fact provable by parol evidence, not to contradict but to explain ambiguous or otherwise insensible expressions; and so I think that the previous will, codicil, and draft codicil are admissible for that purpose, though I do not go further than that".

22–25 Where the inaccurate description found in a gift relates to the identity of a beneficiary, the court may also refer to the written instructions for the will for the purpose of ascertaining the testator's knowledge about his family.[40] Where a beneficiary is designated by description other than by family relationship and the description given sufficiently identifies the beneficiary, the gift will pass, even if followed by an incorrect name.[41]

22–26 Where

> "a testator makes a specific bequest of something which he has not at the date of the will, evidence is admissible to show how the mistake arose, and the fact that the thing in question has been exchanged for something else before the date of the will, will not avoid the legacy. In such a case the legatees are entitled to a sum equal in value to the specific legacy at the testator's death."[42]

In such a case, the court may admit evidence identifying the mistake, and of how it arose at the time when instructions were given for the preparation of the will, though it cannot be used to construe the testamentary dispositions. In *Findlater v Lowe*[43] the Master of the Rolls stated:

> "if a testator has had at a time antecedent to the will a certain kind of stock or property, and has parted with it before the date of the will, and by his will purports to dispose of it in a way which if he had retained it would have been a specific legacy, it will be treated by the court as a general legacy of equivalent amount payable out of the general personal estate".

Where it is established in evidence that the testator never owned the property described in the gift, but owned property similar to that described in it, the latter property may be treated as the subject matter of the gift.[44] In *Findlater v Lowe*, a case involving the admission of evidence in a case of latent ambiguity in the form of a mistake, and where the mistake was

---

39 [1902] 1 I.R. 538.

40 *Robertson v Flynn* [1920] 1 I.R. 78; see *Corrigan v Corrigan & Anor* [2007] I.E.H.C. 367; *Howell v Howell* [1992] 1 I.R. 290.

41 *Re Blake's Trusts* [1904] 1 I.R. 98.

42 See *Findlater v Lowe* [1904] 1 I.R. 519.

43 *ibid.*

44 See *Mosse v Cranfield* [1895] 1 I.R. 80.

made by the testator in expressing the amount of a legacy, it was held that evidence may be admitted to show what the mistake was, and how it arose, at the time of giving instructions for the preparation of his will, though it cannot be used to construe his testamentary dispositions.

Section 75 of the Succession Act 1965

Section 75(1) of the 1965 Act provides that any references to the Statutes of Distribution in a will coming into operation after the commencement of the 1965 Act will, unless a contrary intention appears, be construed as references to Part VI of the 1965 Act which deals with the distribution of estates in cases of intestacy.[45] Further, any references to statutory next-of-kin will also, unless a contrary intention appears in a will, be construed as referring to persons who would succeed on intestacy under the provisions of Part VI of the 1965 Act. Section 75(2) of the 1965 Act provides that trusts declared by reference to any Statute of Distribution in a will effective before the commencement of the 1965 Act on 1 January 1967 will, unless the contrary appears, be construed as referring to enactments (other than the Intestates' Estates Act 1954) relating to the distribution of intestate estates which were in force prior to the commencement of the 1965 Act.[46] **22–27**

Section 96 of the Succession Act 1965

Section 96 of the 1965 Act not only provides a meaning for the expression "dying without issue" but also fixes the time in which the expression is to be construed unless a contrary intention appears from the will. It provides that the time for construing the effect of the contingency is either during the lifetime of a devisee or legatee or at the date of his death. If a beneficiary had issue at either of those times, the contingency will be fulfilled. He will be divested only of the gift where he has no issue at either of those times and the gift in default will take effect instead. While the death of the testator will give effect to the gift, the beneficiary having issue during his lifetime or leaving issue at the date of his death will determine the effect of the contingency. Where, for instance, a testator devises land in fee simple to A but, should A "die without issue", then to B, if A has issue at the date of the testator's death, then the contingency will be satisfied, or if he has no issue at that time but leaves issue at his death, then B receives nothing. It also appears, by virtue of s.100 of the 1965 Act, that once "there is living any issue" of A, the gift over in default to B will "become void and incapable of taking effect". Therefore, by virtue of the combined effect of s.96 and s.100, the contingency "dying without issue" will be fulfilled once A has **22–28**

---

45 See Chapter 7 – Intestate Succession.

46 *ibid.*

living issue, and this will confirm the absolute nature of his interest left to him in the will.[47]

22–29 Therefore, where the expression "dying without issue" or "die without leaving issue" or such similar expression is used in a devise of land, for instance, in a limitation to X, but if he dies without issue then to B, three things must occur before the contingency takes effect. First, the death of the testator will give effect to the devise containing the contingency. Secondly, the death of the devisee will give effect to the contingency in the devise, i.e. X must have issue either during his lifetime or at the date of his death.[48] The effect of the contingency will be ascertained at the date of death of the devisee for the purposes of determining whether his estate will continue to benefit from the devise. Where the devisee leaves issue at the date of the testator's death or at the date of his own death, the contingency on which the gift was made will be satisfied. However, the construction of the expression that it will be taken to mean "a want or failure of issue in his lifetime or at the time of his death" may be subject to a contrary intention appearing from the will. Even though it will be construed not to mean an indefinite failure of issue, the court may hold that a contrary intention appearing from the will (meaning that that was precisely what the testator intended) may prevail.[49] Thirdly, while the contingency of leaving issue may be satisfied by X leaving issue surviving him, a question may arise as to whether the children of X are issue for the purposes of the contingency.[50]

Section 99 of the Succession Act 1965

22–30 Section 99 of the 1965 Act provides that:

> "if the purport of a devise or legacy admits of more than one interpretation, then, in case of doubt, the interpretation according to which the devise or bequest will be operative will be preferred".[51]

22–31 The court is obliged under s.99 to interpret the devise or bequest in a way that will render it operative. But for this to happen, a devise or legacy must be capable of more than one interpretation before s.99 becomes applicable. Where a devise or legacy is capable of only a single interpretation, but that leaves the devise or legacy void for uncertainty, then the devise or legacy will fall into residue and, where the residue is not disposed of, it will be distributed on partial intestacy. It may be added that the principle in s.99 is one of last resort, and that brings the court to the limits of its constructive

47 *Mulhern v Brennan*, Unreported, High Court, McCracken J., 26 May 1998.

48 s.96 of the Succession Act 1965.

49 Succession Act 1965, s.96; *Weldon v Weldon* [1911] 1 I.R. 177.

50 *Berry v Fisher* [1903] 1 I. R. 484; *Re Stamp* [1993] I.L.R.M. 383.

51 See Albert Keating, "A Constructive Interpretation of Section 99 of the Succession Act 1965" (2012) C.P.L.J. 2; Albert Keating, "The Testator's Intention and Doubt Principle" (2006) 24 I.L.T. 54.

powers. The English counterpart to the principle in s.99 is the judicially formulated "rule of despair" which becomes applicable to the later of two irreconcilable provisions in a gift, as that provision is the final expression of the testator's intention.[52] Section 99 apparently requires the court to choose an interpretation that will render a gift operative which may or may not be the later of two irreconcilable provisions, as required by the "rule of despair". While the application of s.99 may take account of the "rule of despair", it is not obliged to, and an Irish court is free to render a gift containing irreconcilable provisions operative by choosing a former, rather than a latter, provision of the gift.

Conditional Wills and Jeune Criteria

In *In the Goods of Spratt*[53] Sir F.H. Jeune formulated the following criteria for purposes of determining whether or not a will is conditional: **22–32**

> "First, whether the nature of the disposition made appears to have relation to the time or circumstances of the contingency; and, secondly, where the contingency is connected with a period of danger to the testator, whether it is coincident with that period, because, if it is, there is ground to suppose that the danger was regarded by the testator only as a reason for making a will, but if not, it is difficult to see the object of referring to a particular period unless it be to limit the operation of the will."[54]

Sir F.H. Jeune formulated his criteria by considering the facts and decisions in previous cases on the matter. He first referred to *Parsons v Lanoe*[55] where the testator commenced his will by stating "If I die before my return from my journey to Ireland" and found that the second of his criteria applied to the contingency connected with the period of danger. On reviewing the facts of *Strauss v Schmidt*[56] and the wording of the will which stated "therefore as I may easily die, I think it my duty to inform you have to do with my property in case I should die. . .", Sir F.H. Jeune thought the words used were not conditional as they provided for "an instance of the period of danger being the same as the period of the contingency".[57] **22–33**

Burton v Collingwood[58] contained the philosophy: **22–34**

> "All men are mortal, and no one knows how soon his life will be required of him. Lest I shall die before the next sun, I make this my last will and testament".

The words here were held to be a typical instance of a condition or

[52] See *Re Potter's W.T.* [1944] Ch.70.
[53] [1897] P. 28.
[54] *ibid* at 30; See also *In the Goods of Stuart* (1888) 21 L.R. Ir. 105.
[55] (1748) 1 Ven. Sen. 189.
[56] (1820) 3 Phill.Ecc. R. 209.
[57] *In the Goods of Spratt* [1897] P. 28.
[58] (1832) 4 Hagg.Ecc. 176.

contingency amounting only to a reason for making a will. In *In the Goods of Winn*,[59] a will contained the following words:

> "Being on the eve of embarking for San Francisco, South America or Mexico, I do hereby, in the case of my decease during my absence being fully ascertained and approved . . ."

22–35 These words were held by Sir Cresswell to have made the will conditional. In *Roberts v Roberts*[60] Sir Cresswell also considered the words "I leave in possession two books to my wife... should anything happen to me on my passage to Wales or during my stay . . ." and held that they were conditional following the reasoning in *Parsons v Lanoe*[61]; Jeune agreed with this conclusion. In *In the Goods of Thorne,*[62] the words "I request that in the event of my death while serving in this horrid climate [Gold Coast now Ghana] or any accident happening to me" were held by Lord Penzance to have covered the contingency contemplated by the testator that resulted in his death. Sir F.H. Jeune thought that the whole language of the will in *Thorne* pointed rather to the necessity for making the will, rather than limiting the operation of it. In *In the Goods of Dobson*,[63] another judgment of Lord Penzance, he held that the words "In the case of any fatal accident happening to me, being about to travel by railway" were not sufficient to make the will conditional, as they did not limit the operation of the will to a certain time.[64] In this instance, however, Sir F.H. Jeune thought that the words used satisfied the second of his criteria.[65] In *In the Goods of Hugo*[66] a will was expressed to be operative in the event of the testator and his wife dying at the same time and in the same accident. It was held to be a conditional will.

22–36 In *In the Goods of Spratt*,[67] the testator, who was a military officer on active service, wrote to his sister a letter containing the following words:

> "The chances are in favour of us being killed, and as I may not have another opportunity of saying what I wish to be done with any little money I may possess in case of an accident, I wish to make everything I possess over to you."

22–37 Sir F.H. Jeune applying his criteria thought that the words "in case of accident" showed only a reason why the testator desired to make a will and held that, as the will had not defined any period within which it was to be

---

59 (1861) 2 Sw. & Tr. 147.
60 (1862) 2 Sw. & Tr. 337.
61 (1748) 1 Ves.Sen. 189.
62 (1865) 4 Sw. & Tr. 36.
63 (1866) L.J. 1 P. & M. 88.
64 See also *In the Goods of Martin* (1867) L.R. 1 P. & D. 380.
65 See *In the Goods of Porter* (1869) L.R. 2 P. & D. 22;*In the Goods of Hugo* [1877] 2 P. & D. 73.
66 [1877] 2 P. & D. 73.
67 [1897] P. 28.

operative, the words used were not conditional and it therefore continued in effect as the testator's will.[68] He stated that:

> "There is no expression of any period to be found in the document within which it alone was to be operative; on the contrary, the request that the will should be kept by his sister till he asked for it appears to me to show that the testator had not in his mind any defined period of time at the expiration of which he intended that his will should cease to be effective. Nor is there anything in the disposition of the property which indicates that it was temporary, or that it did not apply to whatever property of which the testator might at any time be possessed. I am of opinion, therefore, that probate should be granted of the document in question."[69]

In *Halford v Halford*[70] the testator and his wife were about to leave Calcutta for England and, on the eve of their departure, the testator wrote a letter to his brother in England stating that: **22–38**

> "If anything happens to us on the way my will has been accidentally packed away in a tin box to which I cannot get access, as I forget which box it has been put into. However, if we both come to grief, I appoint you my executor; if I only, then in conjunction with Nan (his wife)."

Sir F.H. Jeune held that:

> "There was no period defined in which alone the will is to be operative or is such is to be inferred, it can only be the voyage itself – That is, the period of danger. There is nothing in the disposition of the property which points to a limitation of the effect of the will; on the contrary, the letter, by prescribing what is to become of his property after his wife's death if she does not marry again, makes so necessary and natural a provision that it can hardly be supposed it was intended to lapse so soon as the testator set foot in this country. I think, therefore, that the letter must be admitted to probate."

Where the language expressing the condition is unclear, the will may not be deemed subject to a condition.[71] A codicil which is made conditional on the happening of an event which fails to occur may also result in the revival of an earlier will, as will a codicil which is not properly executed.[72] An impossible condition will not limit a will.[73] **22–39**

When dealing with conditional wills, the primary function of the courts will be to ascertain the meaning of the words used by the testator, and if they fail to satisfy the criteria limiting the operation of a will to the occurrence of stated events, the courts will view the words as merely stating a reason for making a will, and not rendering it a conditional will. In *In the Goods of* **22–40**

---

[68] *In the Goods of Spratt* [1897] P. 28 at 35; *Halford v Halford* [1897] P. 36.
[69] *In the Goods of Spratt* [1897] P. 28 at 35.
[70] [1897] P. 36.
[71] See *In the Goods of Mayo* (1880) 6 P.D. 17; *In the Estate of Vines* [1910] P. 147; *Halford v Halford* [1897] P. 36.
[72] See *In the Goods of Mendes Da Silva* (1861) 2 Sw. & Tr. 315.
[73] *Bumbury v Doran* (1875) Ir. R. 9 C.L. 284.

Groarke[74] a will was made by the testator before undergoing an operation and he wrote the words "If it is God's will I should die under this operation" preceding the dispositions in the will, and the Court was asked whether these words made the will conditional. The contemplated operation was never performed and the testator later recovered from his illness. As a result, the Court held that the words used disclosed a reason only for making the will, and that it was not therefore a conditional will.

Conditional Gifts

22–41 The courts, when determining the nature of a condition attached to a gift, must "see from the beginning, precisely and distinctly, upon the happening of what event it was that the preceding vested estate was to determine."[75] The terms of the condition will determine whether the condition is a condition precedent or a condition subsequent. Where a condition purports to suspend the vesting of a gift until the terms specified in the condition have been satisfied, the condition will be classified as a condition precedent. Where, on the other hand, a condition purports to divest a beneficiary of the gift in the event of failure of its terms, the condition will be classified as a condition subsequent. The practical effect of the distinction between a condition precedent and a condition subsequent is that "a gift made subject to a condition precedent fails altogether, as a rule, if the condition is found to be void or inapplicable, but, if a gift is made subject to a condition subsequent which is found to be void or inapplicable, the condition disappears and the gift takes effect independently of the condition".[76] In the case of a condition precedent, futurity is annexed to the substance of the gift and the vesting is suspended until the event occurs.[77] Where, however, there is any doubt as to the nature of the condition, the court will lean

> "towards a construction which will hold it to be a condition subsequent, for that construction will lead to an early vesting of the gift, and there is a presumption in favour of early vesting."[78]

22–42 *Prima facie,* the court will view a condition as a condition subsequent.[79] But where a condition subsequent (or indeed a condition precedent) is clear and certain in its expression and operation, the court will uphold it, even where it results in the forfeiture of the gift.[80] It appears then that the terms of the

---

74 [1949] Ir. Jur.Rep. 8.

75 *Clavering v Ellison* (1859) 7 H.L.C. 707 at 725; *Re McKenna* [1947] I.R. 277; *Re McDonnell* [1965] I.R. 354 at 358; see also *Re Coughlin* [1963] I.R. 246.

76 *Re Burke* [1951] I.R. 216 at 224.

77 *Re Farrelly* [1941] I.R. 261 at 268.

78 *Re Porter* [1975] N.I. 157 at 160 *per* Lowry L.C.J.; see also *Re McDonnell* [1965] I.R. 354.

79 *Re McDonnell* [1965] I.R. 354 at 358; *Mackessy v Fitzgibbon* [1993] 1 I.R. 520 at 522; *McGowan v Kelly* [2007] I.E.H.C. 228.

80 See *Fitzsimons v Fitzsimons* [1993] I.L.R.M. 478.

condition will determine the nature of the condition, and the nature of the condition will determine the efficacy of the gift.

Gavin Duffy J. stated in *Re McKenna*[81] that the test for a valid condition subsequent **22–43**

> "has never been more tersely and more simply formulated than it was in the words of that master of Equity, the late Lord Parker, in *In Re Sandbrook, Noel v Sandbrook* [1912] 2 Ch. 471 at 477: 'conditions subsequent,' he said, 'in order to defeat vested estates, or cause forfeiture, must be such that from the moment of their creation the court can say with reasonable certainty in what events the forfeiture will occur'; the fatal event or events must be described in clear language; so much the law exacts, but it lays down no requirements as to facility of proof, if forfeiture is alleged to have been incurred".

Conditions of this kind will therefore be construed

> "with strictness and before an interest which has become vested will be defeated it is essential that it be proved that the condition upon which defeasance is to occur has come into operation".[82]

There is also a presumption in favour of early vesting, and, where doubt persists as to whether a condition is a condition precedent or subsequent, the Court will *prima facie* treat it as a condition subsequent.[83] In *Re McDonnell*[84] the testator left all his property to his executors and trustees in trust for his wife for life with remainder to his son, provided that he behaved himself to the satisfaction of the testator's executors. The testator went on to direct that his property be held in trust for another son in the event of the beneficiary failing to behave himself. The son died without any decision as to his behaviour by the executors. He made a will devising the property left to him by his father to the plaintiff. It was held by Budd J. that the condition relating to the behaviour of the testator's son was a condition subsequent and, on the death of the testator, the son had acquired a vested interest in the remainder. As he had not been divested by the operation of the condition, he became entitled to an absolute interest at the date of his death. In *Mackessy v Fitzgibbon*[85] the testator devised his farm to his grandnephew "provided he lives and works on the land" but, if he did not, then to his niece absolutely. Carroll J. stated that where there was a doubt about whether a condition was a condition precedent or a condition subsequent, the Court *prima facie* treated it as subsequent. As a result, she was satisfied that the condition requiring the grandnephew to live and work on the land was a condition subsequent. **22–44**

[81] [1947] I.R. 277 at 284–285; see also *Clavering v Ellison* (1859) 7 H.L.C. 707.

[82] *Re McDonnell* [1965] I.R. 354 at 358; see also Albert Keating, *The Construction of Wills* (Dublin: Round Hall *Sweet & Maxwell*, 2001).

[83] *Mackessy v Fitzgibbon* [1993] 1 I.R. 520; *McGowan v Kelly* [2007] I.E.H.C. 228; see also Succession Act 1965, s.99.

[84] [1965] I.R. 354; see also *In re Hennessy* (1963) 98 I.L.T.R. 39 at 45.

[85] [1993] 1 I.R. 520.

22–45 A pre-probate question of construction may arise concerning the document that constitutes the last will of the testator. The *Jeune criteria* may be applied by the courts when determining whether or not a will is a conditional will. Under the criteria, a will may be conditional where its operation is limited to the occurrence of a specified event. Where the words used by the testator merely express a reason only for making a will, it will not be viewed as a conditional will, and will take effect regardless of the circumstances surrounding his eventual death.

22–46 A post-probate question of construction may arise concerning the conditional nature of a gift in a will already admitted to probate. The terms of the condition will determine whether it is a condition precedent or a condition subsequent. Where the condition is classified as a condition precedent, and the terms of the condition are found to be void, the gift will also fail. Where the condition is classified as a condition subsequent, and the terms of the condition are void, the gift may yet be deemed valid, as the efficacy of a gift is not dependent on the success or failure of such a condition. Where, however, there is some doubt about the classification of a condition as precedent or subsequent, the courts will lean "towards a construction which will hold it to be a condition subsequent, for that construction will lead to an early vesting of the gift, and there is a presumption in favour of early vesting".[86] While the courts may construe a condition precedent or a condition subsequent with "strictness", it may still be upheld if it is "certain in its expression and in its operation". But where the condition is found to be void for uncertainty, and the condition is a condition precedent, the gift to which it is attached will fail, though where the condition is a condition subsequent, the gift to which it is attached will take effect independently of the condition.

22–47 When construing conditional wills or gifts, the Court will, as in all cases of construction, first attempt to ascertain and give effect to the intention of the testator. The Lowry principles may be applied to the wording of a condition attaching to gifts to ascertain the intention of the testator.[87] The courts may also allow the admission of extrinsic evidence in accordance with the provisions of s.90 of the 1965 Act "to show the intention of the testator and to assist in the construction of, or to explain any contradiction in the will". Section 99 of the 1965 Act may also be of relevance and, where a condition "admits" of more than one interpretation , in such event and "in case of doubt" the interpretation according to which the devise or bequest will be operative will be preferred.[88] The basic presumption against intestacy will always be taken into account by the courts when the validity of a will, or indeed, a gift in a will, is challenged.[89]

---

[86] *Re Porter* [1975] N.I. 157 at 160; see also *Re McDonnell* [1965] I.R. 354 at 357.

[87] See *Keating on Probate* (4th ed) (Dublin: Round Hall, 2011), Chapter 27.

[88] *ibid* Chapter 33.

[89] *Re McDonnell* [1965] I.R. 354 at 357; *Mackessy v Fitzgibbon* [1993] 1 I.R. 520; *McGowan v Kelly* [2007] I.E.H.C. 228.

An Exercise in Construction of a Will

An excellent example of a case involving the construction of a will and the application of the rules of construction is found in *Thornton v Timlin*.[90] In that case the plaintiff, who was a personal representative of the testator, sought orders from the Court determining the true construction of a provision in the will of the testator. The testator died on 27 June 2006 at the age of 82, having never married. He died without issue. He made his last will and testament on 10 August 1983. Probate of the will was granted on 16 November 2009 to the plaintiff, the surviving executor named therein. The testator made the following bequests in his will: **22–48**

(a) Bequest of certain shares to the trustees of Bonniconlon GAA Club "to be used for the benefit of the Club";
(b) Sum of IR£500 to the committee in charge of Killaser Community Centre to be used for charitable purposes;
(c) Sum of IR£500 "to Mayo County Council (Ballina area) workers", being the bequest which gave rise to these proceedings;
(d) Sum of IR£500 to "the Association for the Blind, Hatch Street Dublin", to which bequest there was added the rider: "I forget the precise name of the organisation";
(e) Sum of IR£200 to the Wireless for the Blind Association;
(f) Sum of IR£500 to Divine Word Missionaries for charitable purposes;
(g) Sum of IR£500 to the parish priest for the time being in Knock for charitable purposes;
(h) Sum of IR£500 to the parish priest for the time being in charge of the church on Croke (*sic*) Patrick for charitable purposes;
(i) Sum of IR£1,000 to the bursar in St. Murdach's (*sic*) College Ballina "for a trust to be used to help a pupil most in need of financial help and assistance";
(j) Sum of IR£1,000 to the Vocational Educational Committee for County Mayo on trust to help a pupil in Ballina Vocational School in need of financial help and assistance; and
(k) Sum of IR£500 to "the Boy Scouts Organisation in Ballina".

The residuary clause in the will was in the following terms:

> "All the rest residue and remainder of assets are to be realised and invested in Prize Bonds and all of the beneficiaries in my Will are to benefit equally from them."

Laffoy J. outlined the relevant provisions of the 1965 Act and legal principles which govern the approach the Court must adopt to construction of the provision in the testator's will which the Court had been asked to construe and the consequences of a particular construction and relevant legal principles. **22–49**

[90] [2012] I.E.H.C. 239.

22–50 Section 89 of the 1965 Act provides:

> "Every will shall, with reference to all estate comprised in the will and every devise or bequest contained in it, be construed to speak and take effect as if it had been executed immediately before the death of the testator, unless a contrary intention appears from the will."

Section 90 of the 1965 Act provides:

> "Extrinsic evidence shall be admissible to show the intention of the testator and to assist in the construction of, or to explain any contradiction in, a will."

22–51 The main focus of both counsel for the plaintiff and counsel for the defendant in their written and oral submissions was on s.90. The basis on which the court can admit extrinsic evidence under s.90 was succinctly summarised in the following passage from the judgment of Keane J., as he then was, with whom the other judges of the Supreme Court concurred, in *O'Connell v Bank of Ireland*[91]:

> "There are thus two conditions which must be met before such evidence is admissible: it must assist in the construction of the will or resolve a contradiction and it must, in either event, show what the intention, in the particular context, of the testator was."

Section 91 of the 1965 Act provides:

> "Unless a contrary intention appears from the will, any estate comprised or intended to be comprised in any devise or bequest contained in the will which fails or is void by reason of the fact that the devisee or legatee did not survive the testator, or by reason of the devise or bequest being contrary to law or otherwise incapable of taking effect, shall be included in any residuary devise or bequest, as the case may be, contained in the will."

Section 99 of the 1965 Act provides:

> "If the purport of a devise or bequest admits of more than one interpretation, then, in case of doubt, the interpretation according to which the devise or bequest will be operative shall be preferred."

22–52 The primary duty of the court in construing a will is to ascertain and give effect to the intention of the testator. In recent years the High Court in this jurisdiction has adopted the guidance on the construction of wills generally given by Lowry LCJ in *Heron v Ulster Bank Ltd.*,[92] as appears from *Howell v Howell*,[93] *Corrigan v Corrigan*[94] and, most recently, *O'Donohue v O'Donohue*.[95] Lowry LCJ stated:

---

[91] [1998] 2 I.R. 596 at 611.
[92] [1974] N.I. 44.
[93] [1992] 1 I.R. 290.
[94] [2007] I.E.H.C. 367.
[95] [2011] I.E.H.C. 511.

"I consider that, having read the whole will, one may with advantage adopt the following procedure:

1. Read the immediately relevant portion of the will as a piece of English and decide, if possible, what it means.
2. Look at the other material parts of the will and see whether they tend to confirm the apparently plain meaning of the immediately relevant portion or whether they suggest the need for modification in order to make harmonious sense of the whole, or, alternatively, whether an ambiguity in the immediately relevant portion can be resolved.
3. If the ambiguity persists, have regard to the scheme of the will and consider what the testator was trying to do.
4. One may at this stage have resort to rules of construction, where applicable, and aids, such as the presumption of early vesting and the presumption against intestacy and in favour of equality.
5. Then see whether any rule of law prevents a particular interpretation from being adopted.
6. Finally, and, I suggest, not until the disputed passage has been exhaustively studied, one may get help from the opinions of other courts and judges on similar words, rarely as binding precedents since it has been well said that 'no will has a twin brother' ...."

The problem which the Court had to address was who the testator intended to benefit from the bequest "to Mayo County Council (Ballina area) workers", or who were the objects of that bequest and what, if any, entitlement did the objects have to benefit under the residuary clause in the will.

Laffoy J. thought that the starting point in addressing that problem was that, on a plain reading of the bequest in issue, whether on its own or in the context of the will as a whole, no intention contrary to the application of s.89 of the 1965 Act was discernible. Therefore, s.89 applied. Accordingly, the will spoke from the death of the testator as to identifying the beneficiary or beneficiaries. Therefore, the question for the court was whether it was possible to identify who or what constituted "Mayo County Council (Ballina area) workers" as intended by the testator. All of the other bequests in the will were made to organisations, associations, office holders and, in one case to a public body, and they were all given for charitable purposes, or otherwise benevolent purposes. **22–53**

She stated that: **22–54**

"It is clear on the evidence that the term 'Mayo County Council (Ballina area) workers' is not a term which is used by Mayo County Council. There is no evidence that there was any organisation or association or other body of such workers. Therefore, it is necessary to consider whether it is possible to identify a cadre or class of, or individual, workers whom the Testator intended to benefit."

She found, however, that it was not possible to identify the workers whom the testator intended to benefit, either from the plain meaning of the bequest on its own or in the context of the will as a whole. The problem was one of lack of clarity, rather than ambiguity. In her view, s.90 of the 1965 Act did not assist because there was no admissible extrinsic evidence as to whom the testator intended to benefit. There was evidence as to the identity of the Mayo County Council workers who were working in the Ballina area on 27 June 2006. However, she thought that it would be proper to conclude that it was the intention of the testator that the 70-plus workers employed by Mayo County Council on, or in connection with, outdoor work in the Ballina area 16 years after his retirement should benefit under the bequest or under the residuary clause in the will. The only other evidence before the Court was evidence as to the identity of co-workers who were particularly friendly with the testator during his lifetime. However, in her view, that evidence was not admissible under s.90 to inform the Court in determining who should benefit under the clause in issue. In her view, it did not fulfil the second condition laid down by the Supreme Court in *O'Connell v Bank of Ireland*, in that it did not show what the intention of the testator was in the particular context. It merely reflected the opinion and belief of the witnesses. Apart from that, there was nothing in the bequest on its own, or in the context of the will as a whole, to indicate that what the testator intended was that work colleagues with whom he was friendly and who were kind and generous to him should benefit under the bequest. To construe the will on that basis would, in effect, be rewriting the will.

22–55 She concluded that the bequest was void for uncertainty. The pecuniary bequest of IR£500 "to Mayo County Council (Ballina area) workers" did not admit of any interpretation which would preserve it by virtue of the operation of s. 99 of the 1965 Act. Therefore, by virtue of the operation of s. 91 of the Act of 1965,

> "that bequest is included in the residuary clause in the will. It follows from the conclusion that the pecuniary bequest is void for uncertainty that the beneficiaries of the residuary estate do not include 'Mayo County Council (Ballina area) workers' as named in the pecuniary bequest".

CHAPTER 23

THE LIMITATION OF ACTIONS AND STRIKING OUT OF PROCEEDINGS

INTRODUCTION

The statutory provisions dealing with limitation of actions in respect of claims brought by beneficiaries, and the legal right of surviving spouses and civil partners, concerning the estate of a deceased person are contained in s.126(1) of the Succession Act 1965 (the "1965 Act"). Section 126(1) of the 1965 Act provides that no action in respect of any claim to the estate of a deceased person, or to any share or interest in such estate, whether under a will, on intestacy or under s.111 of the of the 1965 Act, may be brought after the expiration of six years from the date when the right to receive the share or interest accrued. As s.126(1) does not, however, provide for actions taken by personal representatives on behalf of the estate, they may resort to the general provisions in s.13(2)(a) of the Statute of Limitations 1957 (the 1957 Act), which prescribes a 12-year period of limitation for the recovery of land belonging to the estate of the deceased person.[1] Where actions are brought by third parties against the estate, s.8(1) of the Civil Liability Act 1961 (the 1961 Act) provides that, on the death of a person on or after the date of the passing of the 1961 Act, all causes of action subsisting against him shall survive against his estate. Section 9(2) of the 1961 Act goes on to provide that no proceedings 23–01

> "shall be maintainable in respect of any cause of action whatsoever which has survived against the estate of a deceased person unless either – (a) proceedings against him in respect of that cause of action were commenced within the relevant period and were pending at the date of death, or (b) proceedings are commenced in respect of that cause of action within the relevant period or within the period of two years after his death, whichever period first expires".

[1] See Albert Keating, "Time Limits for a Beneficiary or a Personal Representative to Commence Proceedings" (2004) 9(1) C.P.L.J. 2.

23–02 The relevant period mentioned in s.9(2) means the period of limitation prescribed by the 1957 Act or any other limitation enactment.[2] Thus, in relation to causes of action commenced and pending prior to the death of the deceased, the period of limitation prescribed by the 1957 Act (or amendments thereto) will continue to apply after the death of the deceased. But in relation to actions instituted after the death of the deceased, the relevant period of limitation will be that prescribed by the 1957 Act or two years after the death of the deceased, whichever period first expires.[3]

23–03 Section 13(1)(a) of the 1957 Act provides that:

> "Subject to paragraphs (b) and (c) of this subsection, no action shall be brought by a State authority to recover any land after the expiration of thirty years from the date on which the right of action accrued to a State authority or, if it first accrued to some person through whom a State authority claims, to that person."

Section 13(2) of the 1957 Act provides that:

> "The following provisions shall apply to an action by a person (other than a State authority) to recover land – (a) subject to paragraph (b) of this subsection, no such action shall be brought after the expiration of twelve years from the date on which the right of action accrued to the person bringing it or, if it first accrued to some person through whom he claims, to that person; (b) if the right of action first accrued to a State authority, the action may be brought at any time before the expiration of the period during which the action could have been brought by a State authority, or of twelve years from the date on which the right of action accrued to some person other than a State authority, whichever period first expires."

23–04 There are five State authorities recognised by s.2(1) of the 1957 Act: a Minister of State, the Commissioners of Public Works in Ireland, the Irish Land Commission, the Revenue Commissioners and the Attorney General. The Chief State Solicitor may institute proceedings on behalf of the State for the recovery of the estate from persons in adverse possession of it under s.65(1) of the 1965 Act.

23–05 The doctrine of relation back may also be relevant to a case involving the limitation of actions. It provides that, when a grant of representation issues, the title of the personal representative to the estate of the deceased relates back to the date of the deceased's death. By reliance on the doctrine, a personal representative may institute proceedings for any wrongdoing to the estate during the interval of time that existed between the date of death of the deceased and the issuing of the grant.[4]

23–06 Where the plaintiff's delay in instituting proceedings is inordinate and inexcusable, the Court may look to the facts and prevailing circumstances

---

[2] See s.9(1) of the 1961 Act.

[3] See Albert Keating, "The Representative Capacity of Administrators and Section 9(2) of the Civil Liability Act 1961" (2013) 2(1) I.P.L.J.

[4] See *O'Hagan v Grogan* [2012] I.E.S.C. 8.

of the case when deciding whether or not to strike out the proceedings. In *Toal v Duignan*[5] Finlay C.J. stated that

> "where there is a clear and patent unfairness in asking a defendant to defend a case after a very long lapse of time between the acts complained of and the trial, then if that defendant has not himself contributed to the delay, irrespective of whether the plaintiff has contributed to it or not, the court may as a matter of justice have to dismiss the action".

The principles regarding inordinate and inexcusable delay in instituting proceedings are applicable to all actions, including those involving wills or actions arising out of wills.

The Periods of Limitation

Section 126(1) of the 1965 Act provides that no action in respect of any claim to the estate of a deceased person or to any share or interest in such estate, whether under a will, on intestacy or under s.111 of the of the 1965 Act, may be brought after the expiration of six years from the date when the right to receive the share or interest accrued. Section 126(1) of the 1965 Act was amended by s.89 of the Civil Partnership and Certain Rights and Obligations of Cohabitants Act 2010 (the 2010 Act) by inserting "or section 111A" after "section 111". The new s.111A of the 1965 Act as inserted by s.89 of the 2010 Act deals with the legal right of a civil partner. The limitation period for the purposes of s.126(1) will commence to run from the date when a beneficiary's right to receive a share or interest accrues. It is also worth noting that s.62(1) of the 1965 Act provides that no action may be brought against the personal representatives in respect of their failure to distribute an estate before the expiration of one year from the date of death of the deceased, i.e. the executor's year. Section 127 of the 1965 Act provides that: **23–07**

> "Section 49 of the Statute of Limitations, 1957, which extends the periods of limitation fixed by that Act where the person to whom a right of action accrued was under a disability, shall have effect in relation to an action in respect of a claim to the estate of a deceased person or to any share in such estate, whether under a will, on intestacy or as a legal right, as if the period of three years were substituted for the period of six years mentioned in subsection (1) of that section."

The provisions of s.126 do not include applications by the children of testators under s.117 of the 1965 Act. The limitation period for such applications is found in s.117(6) which provides that an application under s.117 must be brought within six months from the first taking out of representation.[6] The provisions of s.127 of the 1965 Act also do not include applications under s.117(1) in its provisions. In *MPD v MD*[7] Carroll J. considered whether **23–08**

[5] [1991] I.L.R.M. 135 at 139.

[6] See s.117(6) of the 1965 Act as amended by the Family Law (Divorce) Act 1996, s.46; Chapter 9 – The Moral Duty of Testators.

[7] [1981] I.L.R.M. 179.

s.127 of the 1965 Act applied to an application under s.117 and found that it did not. She stated that:

> "If there is no extension of time under s.127 for the infant children, they are deprived of their remedy under s. 117. I am sure that there are many other examples which would show that there are compelling reasons why a time limit of twelve months set out in s. 117(6) should be mitigated by the application of s.49 of the Statute of Limitations as amended by s. 127 of the Succession Act 1965, or in some other way. Equally there are reasons why the administration of estates should not be delayed beyond reasonable time. This was adverted to by the Supreme Court in *Moynihan v Greensmyth* [1977] I.R. 55 at 72."[8]

23–09 In *S. 1 and S. 2 v P.R. 1 and P.R. 2*[9] Laffoy J. agreed with the views expressed by Carroll J. in *MPD v MD* regarding s.127. However, as S. 1 and S. 2 were of full age, the issue of the application or otherwise of s.127 to an application under s. 117 was immaterial.

23–10 Section 71 of the 1957 Act postpones the date of the accrual of the cause of action in cases involving fraud to the date when the fraud was, or could with reasonable diligence have been, discovered. Section 72(1) of the 1957 Act postpones the date of the accrual of the cause of action in cases of mistakes and provides that:

> "Where, in the case of any action for which a period of limitation is fixed by this Act, the action is for relief from the consequences of mistake, the period of limitation shall not begin to run until the plaintiff has discovered the mistake or could with reasonable diligence have discovered it."

23–11 As s.126(1) of the 1965 Act does not cover actions taken by personal representatives on behalf of the estate, they are entitled to rely on the general provisions in s.13(2)(a) of the 1957 Act which prescribes a 12-year period of limitation. It was confirmed in *Drohan v Drohan*[10] that s.13(2)(a) of the 1957 Act provides the time limit for actions brought by personal representatives on behalf of the estate of a deceased person. Section 13(2)(a) provides that no action may brought after the expiration of 12 years from the date on which the right of action accrued to the person entitled to bring it or, if it first accrued to some other person through whom he claims, then from the time that person was entitled to bring it. Therefore, the time limit for the personal representative to bring actions on behalf of the estate is 12 years from the date the right of action first accrued by virtue of s.13(2)(a) of the 1957 Act.

23–12 Sections 8 and 9 of the 1961 Act are applicable to all causes of action in common law and equity, regardless of whether or not there is a "relevant period" prescribed by the 1957 Act (or amendments thereto). As was

---

8 *ibid* at 183.
9 [2013] I.E.H.C. 407.
10 [1984] I.L.R.M. 179.

stated by Fennelly J. in *Corrigan v Martin*,[11] when referring to s.8(1), the Oireachtas intended that provision to apply to "all causes of action" coming into existence right up to the point of death itself and, when referring to s.9(2)(a) and (b), an action

> "cannot be maintained unless the plaintiff can bring himself within one of the two subparagraphs, in this case subparagraph (b). This is not affected by the fact that there is no 'relevant period' for the purposes of the 1957 Act. The applicable period is the one that which 'first expires'. That may or may not be the two-year period. If the 'relevant period' expired within two years of death, the claim is barred. If there is no such period, it is barred after two years. I believe this interpretation is in accordance with common sense and the clear intention of the legislature."

In *Corrigan*, the plaintiff, a nephew of the deceased, was injured while working on the deceased's farm. The deceased was not insured and, in consideration of the plaintiff forbearing to issue proceedings for the injury sustained, agreed to transfer or devise his lands to the plaintiff. The plaintiff sought specific performance of the agreement outside of the limitation period prescribed by s.9(2)(b) of the 1961 Act. There is no "relevant period" in the 1957 Act limiting the time within a specific performance suit must be instituted. Nevertheless, Fennelly J. categorised the plaintiff's cause of action as one falling within s.8 of the 1961 Act. He was satisfied that **23–13**

> "the correct interpretation of the plaintiff's cause of action in the light of the section is that the obligation of the deceased was to perform the contract during his lifetime and not at the moment of his death. Hence, the cause of action was complete immediately before his death. It is unnecessary to decide how long before his death".

He was further satisfied that

> "the Oireachtas intended by the strong and clear language of section 9(2) to apply a maximum two year limitation period to all claims against the estates of deceased persons."

He went on to say that it was

> "unreal and almost metaphysical to distinguish between causes of action existing immediately prior to the death and those which matured on the death itself. I do not believe that the Oireachtas can have intended to make such fine distinction. It would serve no useful purpose which has been identified in this case".

The courts favour the early vesting of estates, and that:

> "those charged as executors or administrators of estates of deceased persons are entitled and, indeed, bound to carry out their tasks with reasonable expedition and that creditors of the estate and, ultimately, the beneficiaries are entitled to have the estate administered within a reasonable time. I believe the Oireachtas

[11] Unreported, High Court, Fennelly J., 13 March 2006.

deliberately chose to impose a short but fair time limit on claims so that these desirable objectives would be achieved".[12]

23–14 In *S.1 and S.2 v P.R.1 and P.R.2*[13] the Court also had to consider whether the first plaintiff was statute-barred by virtue of the provisions of s.9(2)(b) of the 1961 Act, as the proceedings were issued more than two years after the date of the death of the deceased testator. Section 9(2)(b) of the 1961 Act provides that no proceedings shall be maintainable unless they are commenced within the "relevant period or within the period of two years after his death," whichever period first expires. Thus, while an action may be commenced within the relevant period prescribed by the 1957 Act, because it is commenced against the estate of a deceased after his death, it will become statute-barred two years from the date of death, even though a greater period may be allowed by the 1957 Act for the action, as s.9(2)(b) provides "whichever period first expires" will govern the matter.[14] Where the 1957 Act prescribes no limitation period for a particular cause of action, the relevant period for instituting proceedings is two years after the death of the deceased. In *S.1 and S.2 v P.R.1 and P.R.2,* the defendants contended that the plaintiff S.1's claim against the estate of the testator was statute-barred by s.9(2) of the 1961 Act because the plenary proceedings instituted by him were not commenced within two years after the death of the testator. During the course of her judgment, Laffoy J., when construing s.9(2) of the 1961 Act, referred with approval to the judgment of Fennelly J. in *Corrigan v Martin.*[15]

23–15 In *Prendergast v McLaughlin*[16] O'Keeffe J. also found that the plaintiff's claim came within s. 9(2)(b) of the Act of 1961 and that, as the proceedings had not been issued within two years of the death of the deceased, the plaintiff's claim, whether arising in contract, quasi-contract or in equity, was statute-barred. In *S.1 and S.2 v P.R.1 and P.R.2,* Laffoy J. agreed "with the analysis of the law set out in the judgments of Fennelly J. and O'Keeffe J". She held that S.1 was statute-barred under and by virtue of s.9(2) of the 1961 Act.

23–16 In *FDC v AC, JO'D and P.O'R*[17] Herbert J. also referred with approval to the decision of Fennelly J. in *Corrigan v Martin* and stated that:

> "the obligation of the deceased was to perform the contract during his lifetime and not at the moment of his death.Hence the cause of action was completed

---

12 See *Moynihan v Greensmyth* [1977] I.R. 55.
13 [2013] I.E.H.C. 407.
14 See Albert Keating, "The Application of s.9(2) of the Civil Liability Act 1961 to Equitable Causes of Action Against Estates of Deceased Persons" (2010) 15(2) C.P.L.J. 37.
15 Unreported, High Court, Fennelly J., 13 March 2006.
16 [2011] 1 I.R. 102; see *Cavey v Cavey* [2014] I.E.S.C. 16.
17 [2012] I.E.H.C. 537.

> immediately before his death ... the cause of action, therefore subsisted at the moment of death and survived against his estate by virtue of section 8(1)".

Furthermore, he preferred the reasoning of Fennelly J. in *Corrigan v Martin* to that of Barron J. in Reidy's case. In the *Corrigan* case, Fennelly J. analysed in detail the interplay between ss. 8 and 9 of the Act. There is no such analysis or examination of the two sections in the *Reidy* case. In referring to s. 8(1) which applies to "all causes of action (other than excepted causes of action) subsisting against him", Fennelly J. stated: **23–17**

> "The Oireachtas intended that provision to apply to all causes of action coming into existence right up to the point of death itself. It is unreal and almost metaphysical to distinguish between causes of action existing immediately prior to death and those which matured on the death itself. I do not believe the Oireachtas can have intended to make such a fine distinction. It would serve no useful purpose which has been identified in this case."

The Recovery of Estates by a State Authority

Section 13(1)(a) of the 1957 Act provides that: **23–18**

> "Subject to paragraphs (b) and (c) of this subsection no action shall be brought by a State authority to recover any land after the expiration of thirty years from the date on which the right of action accrued to a State authority or, if it first accrued to some person through whom a State authority claims, to that person."

There are five State authorities listed in s.2(1) of the 1957 Act: a Minister of State, the Commissioners of Public Works in Ireland, the Irish Land Commission, the Revenue Commissioners and the Attorney General, and the list appears to be exhaustive. Section 3 of the statute provides that the statute will apply to proceedings by or against a State authority "in like manner as if that State authority were a private individual." In *O'Hagan v Grogan*[18] Macken J., referring to the Attorney General as a State authority, stated that: **23–19**

> "The Attorney General is the legal representative of the State in all legal proceedings. The State does not, in general, act in its own name, independently of its Ministers or others officers, although it may, of course, do so. It acts through Ministers, including the Minister for Finance. The Attorney General falls into a different category to Ministers of State and those other parties mentioned expressly in s.2(1) of the Statute of Limitations. The Attorney General may hold property, qua Attorney General, although I do not know in what circumstances this occurs, but undoubtedly is also entitled to deal with the State's own property and in property to which it may become entitled, such as on an intestacy, by virtue of the unique position of the Attorney General as such legal representative. No limitation is placed on the scope of the Attorney General's role as a 'State authority' in s.2(1), and he/she may act in more than one capacity, although always for and on behalf of the State, or on behalf of a Minister of State. The State itself is not separately represented in the list, although it must be accepted as a given, and, in the course of argument was accepted by counsel for the defendant, that it would be entitled

[18] [2012] I.E.S.C. 8.

> to raise representation to the estate of Mrs. Dolan. But if it did so decide, it would act through the Attorney General, or the Chief State Solicitor. In circumstances where the State is the ultimate intestate successor to an intestate estate, as here, the Attorney General may act as a 'State authority', and, as such, clearly is within the ambit of s.2(1) of the Statute."

23–20 The Chief State Solicitor, under s.65 of the 1965 Act, may institute proceedings for the recovery of the estate against persons who may be in adverse possession of it. But is he a State authority for the purposes of s.13 of the 1957 Act? Section 13(1)(a) of the 1957 Act provides that:

> "Subject to paragraphs (b) and (c) of this subsection, no action shall be brought by a State authority to recover any land after the expiration of thirty years from the date on which the right of action accrued to a State authority or, if it first accrued to some person through whom a State authority claims, to that person."

23–21 In *O'Hagan v Grogan*[19] the Chief State Solicitor based his case as a State authority on the Ministers and Secretaries Act 1924, s.6(1) which provided that there shall be vested in the Attorney General the "business, powers, authorities, duties and functions" formerly vested or exercised by the Attorney-General for Ireland and Solicitor-General and any or all of them respectively, and the administration and control of the business, powers, authorities, duties and functions of the branches and officers of the public services specified in the Ninth Part of the schedule to the 1924 Act. The Ninth Part of the Schedule includes the Chief State Solicitor's department and all local State Solicitors. However, Macken J. stated that:

> "even if the plaintiff, or any predecessor to him is – pursuant to the provisions of the Act of 1924 – under the control of the Attorney General, he is not himself, a 'State authority' within s.2(1)".

23–22 As a result, the Chief State Solicitor was unable to claim a 30-year limitation period for the recovery of the land from the defendant. The Attorney General is one of the State authorities mentioned in s.2(1) of the 1957 Act and, as such, is entitled to institute proceedings for the recovery of State property, including property to which the State may become entitled as ultimate intestate successor under s.73(1) of the 1965 Act. Although s.65 of the 1965 Act expressly recognises the Chief State Solicitor as an appropriate person to apply for and be granted letters of administration intestate on behalf of the State, and a person who may institute proceedings for the recovery of estate, he is not a State authority, and may not rely on the 30-year limitation period for the recovery of the estate against a person in adverse possession of it.[20]

---

[19] *ibid.*

[20] *ibid.*

The Doctrine of Relation Back

Under the doctrine of relation back, once a grant issues, the title of the personal representative to the estate of the deceased relates back to the date of the deceased's death. By reliance on the doctrine of relation back, he may institute proceedings for any wrongdoing to the estate during the interval of time that existed between the date of death of the deceased and the issuing of the grant. Section 23 of the 1957 Act provides that an administrator of the estate "shall be deemed to claim as if there had been no interval of time between the date of the death of the deceased and the grant of letters of administration".[21] Otherwise, under s.24 of the 1957 Statute, at the expiration of the limitation period for any person to bring an action, "the title of that person shall be extinguished". In *O'Hagan v Grogan*[22] Macken J., when considering the effect of s.23 of the 1957 Act and the recovery of land by the Chief State Solicitor as administrator of the estate, stated that: **23–23**

> "[I]f in the interval between the death of an intestate and the appointment of an administrator, a party has procured a lawful interest in lands the subject of the administration, that interest may be sufficient to bar its recovery by the administrator, when appointed, acting in the interests of those who, but for such event would have been entitled to the lands."

Referring to the facts of the case, she stated:

> "In the result, time commenced to run against the estate for the purposes of adverse possession from either the date of death of Mrs Dolan, or the date of possession by the defendant. In either event, in this case, well more than 12 years passed before July, 2000. It does not follow, however, in the present case, that by reason of this interpretation of s.23 of the Statute of Limitations, the claim of the defendant to adverse possession is thereby determined. That issue at all times depends on the appropriate limitation period."

When referring to s.24 of the 1957 Act, Macken J. stated that:

> "The estate itself in the land is not extinguished, but title to that estate may well be, if a party has successfully established that he has adversely possessed the property for the relevant period."

Thus, if during the interval of time between the date of death of the deceased and the issuing of a grant to the administrator, the period of limitation fixed by the 1957 Act expires, the title of the administrator to the land will be extinguished against a person who has been in adverse possession for the period of limitation set out in the 1957 Act. **23–24**

21 *ibid.*
22 *ibid.*

Striking Out Proceedings

23–25 Where the plaintiff's delay in instituting proceedings is inordinate and inexcusable, the court will look to the facts and prevailing circumstances of the case when deciding whether or not to strike out the proceedings. The principles regarding inordinate and inexcusable delay in instituting proceedings are applicable to all actions, including those involving wills or actions arising out of wills. In *McHugh v McHugh*[23] Murphy J. had to consider whether there was inordinate and inexcusable delay by the plaintiff in instituting an action involving the transfer of land to the defendants by the deceased testatrix during her lifetime, which formed the subject matter of a gift to them in her will. In that case, the plaintiff sought an order of the Court setting aside a transfer of certain lands on 5 February 1990 between the deceased and the defendants. The deceased made a will on 9 July 1987 leaving those lands to the plaintiff and appointing him executor. On 19 February 1991, the defendants became the registered owners of the subject lands. The deceased died on 12 January 1998. The plaintiff instituted proceedings on 4 March 2004. A grant of probate of the will was extracted by the plaintiff in October 2011, 13 years after the death of the deceased and seven years after the issue of proceedings. The defendants, in their turn, sought an order of the Court dismissing the plaintiff's action save to the extent that it comprised a claim to prove the purported last will and testament of the deceased dated 9 July 1987. They claimed that the plaintiff's inordinate and inexcusable delay in instituting, prosecuting and maintaining the claims also constituted an abuse of process. Murphy J. found that, at the time of initiation of the action in 2004, the plaintiff was not the legal personal representative of the deceased and did

> "not have *locus standi* and that the purported claims are not maintainable by reason of the effluxion of time and the statutory period of time for the bringing of same".

23–26 He stated that it was clear from the provisions of s.9(2)(b) of the 1961 Act that the relevant limitation period was that which first expired, the period of two years after date of death, or, at most, a 12-year period from 5 February 1990, the date of the transfer of the lands of the deceased to the defendants. He was satisfied that s.9(2) of the 1961 Act precluded the plaintiff from making a claim after two years from the date of the death of the deceased. The question whether such an inordinate delay is excusable had to be further considered in the light of the circumstances of the plaintiff remaining for some time on the land after the deceased's death on 12 January 1998. Six years passed from that date until proceedings commenced. Murphy J was satisfied that such a delay was, in the circumstances, also inexcusable. While the plaintiff submitted that he was not aware of the transfer until the defendants sought possession after the deceased's death, no action was taken by the plaintiff for a further six years. Accordingly, he dismissed the plaintiff's claim.

[23] [2012] I.E.H.C. 537.

The courts may also strike out proceedings which are frivolous and vexatious, or which are an abuse of process. In *Barry v Buckley*[24] Costello J. was of the view that the courts were entitled to ensure that access to the courts would only be used for the resolution of genuine disputes and not as a forum for lost causes which, no matter how strongly the party concerned might feel about them, nevertheless had no basis for a complaint in law. The second and equally important purpose of the jurisdiction is to ensure that litigants will not be subjected to the time consuming, expensive and worrying process of being asked to defend a claim which cannot succeed. In *Sun Fat Chan v Osseous*[25] McCarthy J. approved of the decision of Costello J. in *Barry v Buckley* and found that the courts had inherent jurisdiction to dismiss an action on the basis that, on admitted facts, it could not succeed. But he also said that the courts should be slow to entertain an application of that kind and grant the relief sought. In *Loughrey v Dolan*[26] Laffoy J. explained the jurisdiction and the manner in which the court should exercise it in relation to vexatious proceedings and abuse of process by referring to a passage from the judgment of Irvine J. in *Behan v McGinley*[27]: 23–27

> "For the purpose of the court's adjudication as to whether or not proceedings are vexatious within the meaning of O. 19, r. 28 of the Rules . . . or, indeed, for the purpose of the court's consideration as to whether it will exercise its inherent jurisdiction to stay or dismiss proceedings, the court must consider whether the proceedings have been brought without any reasonable grounds. The High Court (Ó Caoimh J.), in *Riordan v Ireland* (No. 5) [2001] 4 I.R. 463, has referred to a helpful decision of the Ontario High Court in *Re Lang, Michener and Fabian* (1987) 37 D.L.R. (4th) 685 at p. 691, where the following matters were held to be indicators of proceedings which were potentially vexatious, namely:-
>
> (a) the bringing up on one or more actions to determine an issue which has already been determined by a court of competent jurisdiction;
> (b) where it is obvious that an action cannot succeed, or if the action would lead to no possible good, or if no reasonable person can reasonably expect to obtain relief;
> (c) where the action is brought for an improper purpose, including the harassment and oppression of other parties by multifarious proceedings brought for purposes other than the assertion of legitimate rights;
> (d) where issues tend to be rolled forward into subsequent actions and repeated and supplemented, often with actions brought against the lawyers who have acted for or against the litigant in earlier proceedings;
> (e) where the person instituting the proceedings has failed to pay the costs of unsuccessful proceedings;
> (f) where the respondent persistently takes unsuccessful appeals from judicial decisions."

As well as seeking an order to strike out proceedings, an "Isaac Wunder order" may be sought to restrain a person from instituting any other proceedings 23–28

[24] [1981] I.R. 306 at 308.
[25] [1992] 1 I.R. 425.
[26] [2012] I.E.H.C. 578.
[27] [2011] 1 I.R. 47 at 66.

against parties to earlier proceedings without first obtaining the leave of the court. In *Gunning v Sherry*[28] Hogan J. found that the inherent jurisdiction of the courts to make such an Isaac Wunder order was well established. He referred to the judgment of Irvine J. in *Burke v Judge Fulham*[29] where she explained that the purpose of the *Isaac Wunder* jurisdiction is to regulate the constitutional right of access to the courts, albeit in a manner which is proportionate and strictly necessary to protect the proper administration of justice and the rights of third parties who might otherwise be oppressed by abusive litigation.

[28] [2012] I.E.H.C. 88.
[29] [2010] I.E.H.C. 448.

CHAPTER 24

WILLS PRECEDENTS

INTRODUCTION

The instructions sheet provides the blueprint for the preparation of a will, and all necessary data concerning a testator's status and family. His assets and his beneficiaries will also be recorded there. The instructions sheet takes the form of a questionnaire. The data recorded in the instructions sheet will thereafter be couched in the testamentary language of wills for due execution by the testator. Where a will cannot be prepared at the time of taking instructions, the instructions sheet should be signed and witnessed, and further, it should contain a revocation clause, thereby allowing it to stand as the last will and testament until a formal will is prepared and executed.[1] In the absence of a revocation clause in the instructions sheet, and in the event of the client's death before the execution of a formal will by him or her, an application to the courts may be necessary to determine what testamentary paper or papers constitute the last will of the testator.[2] It is also important since the enactment of the Civil Partnership and Certain Rights and Obligations of Cohabitants Act 2010 that an instructions sheet takes account of the provisions introduced by that Act relating to civil partners and qualified cohabitants, and the children of such relationships **24–01**

Once the testator's instructions are taken and recorded in the instructions sheet, his or her will may then be prepared. The preparation of a will involves the translation of the testator's wishes into the testamentary language found in the relevant wills precedents. Wills precedents lend legal precision and clarity to the testator's wishes when disposing of his property to beneficiaries. After a will is prepared, a testator must be given the opportunity to read his **24–02**

---

1 See Chapter 4 – The Revocation and Revival of Wills.

2 See Albert Keating, *Irish Wills Precedents Service* (Dublin: Round Hall, 2009; Albert Keating, *Keating on Probate* (4th ed) (Dublin: Round Hall, 2011); Albert Keating, *Keating on Probate* (4th ed) (Dublin: Round Hall, 2011); Albert Keating, *First Supplement to the Fourth Edition of Keating on Probate* (Dublin: Thomson Round Hall, 2013).

will for the purposes of approving of its contents. This will also provide the occasion for explaining (or translating) the testamentary language used in the disposition of his property. After the testator has indicated his approval, the will may then be executed in compliance with the provisions of s.78 of the Succession Act 1965 as reflected in the relevant *testimonium* and attestation clauses in the will.

24–03 Wills, prepared on single pages with writing on one side only, should be bound by ribbon or tape or fastened together by brass eyelets and, where there is any stapling of pages, the staples must be covered by adhesive materials. Where a will consists of a number of pages with writing on one side, each written page should be numbered page one of the total number of pages, e.g. page 1 of 5, 2 of 5, and so on. The attestation clause should mention that the will is written on the front side only of a page and the number of pages as follows: "Signed by the testator in the presence of us and signed by us in the presence of the testator, this will having been printed on the front side only of the foregoing 5 sheets of A4 paper."

Specimen Instructions Sheet

24–04 Testator's name:
(known by any other name?):
Current address:
Telephone: (home) (mobile):
Email:
Occupation:
PPS number:
Date of birth:
Nationality:
Domicile:
Does the testator intend to marry or enter into a civil partnership?
Has the testator married or entered into a civil partnership before?
Is the testator separated?
Is the testator divorced or is a civil partnership dissolved?
Is the testator a cohabitant?

Spouse or civil partner or cohabitant of testator

Name:
(Known by any other name):
Current address:
Date of birth:
Nationality:
Domicile:
Date and place of marriage or civil partnership:
Any ante-nuptial or ante-civil partnership agreement/ renunciation of legal right of spouse or civil partner?

Any cohabitants' agreement?

Children (marital and non-marital)

Name:
Date and place of birth:
Nationality:
Domicile:

Other financially dependent relatives

Name:
Address:
Relationship to testator:

Property

Family home
Address:
Freehold/leasehold:
Details of mortgage (if any):
Sole/joint ownership:
If jointly, name of joint owner:

Other Properties

Address:
Freehold/leasehold:
Value:
Details of any mortgage:
Sole/joint ownership:
If jointly, name of joint owner:

Business

Name of business:
Address:
Nature of business:
Does business trade?
Does business hold investment assets?
How is business organised? Sole trader/company?
How tuch of the company is owned by the testator?
Details of shares and number nheld by testator or testator's spouse or civil partner or cohabitant (if any):
Partnership:
How organised?
How many partners?

Details of testator's partnership interest and that of testator's spouse or civil partner or cohabitant (if any):

Bank/building society/credit union/post office accounts

Name of bank/building society/credit union:
Address of branch:
Account number:
Value:
Joint account? If yes, provide name of joint account holder:
Who provided the funds and in what shares?

Life assurance and pension policies

Details of life assurance policy:
Life assured:
Value:
Details of pension policy:
Value:

Investments

Nature of investments:
Sole name/joint names with spouse or civil partner or cohabitant:
Assets outside Ireland?
Type of assets:
Where situated:
Value:

Trust interests

Type of trust?
Life/maintenance/discretionary:
Date of trust:
Date of death of settlor/testator:
Value of trust assets:
Powers of appointment:

Other wills

Details of existing wills (including wills dealing only with foreign assets):
Where are original wills located:

Funeral wishes

Does testator wish his body to be:

Used for organ donation
Used for medical research
Buried
Cremated

Executors

Name and address of executor 1:
Name and address of executor 2:

Guardians (for children under 18 years)

Name and address of guardian 1:
Name and address of guardian 2:

Beneficiaries

Pecuniary legacies and bequests
Name and address of legatee:
Value of legacy or bequest:
Property (including business) gifts
Name and address of beneficiary:
Where property situated:
Personal belongings (e.g. jewellery etc.)
Name and address of beneficiary:
Item:

Charitable gifts

Name of charity:
Address:
Value of gift:

Trust provisions for children

Names and addresses of children:
Income at (age 18/21/25):
Capital at (age 18/21/25):
Powers of trustees:
Professional charge clause:
Indemnity clause:

Gift of residue (e.g. to spouse, civil partner or cohabitant, children or grandchildren)

Name and address of beneficiary:
Share of residue:

Powers of attorney

Name and address of attorney:
Degree of relationship to testator:
Where original power is located:

Living will

Does testator have a living will?
If yes, where located:
Original will to be held by:
Costs:

Date:
Place (if not solicitor's office):
Signed by the testator:
Witness: 1
Witness: 2

24–05 Advise on the following:

- The legal right of a surviving spouse or civil partner[3];
- Where relevant, s.194 of the Civil Partnership and Certain Rights and Obligations of Cohabitants Act 2010 regarding court applications by surviving cohabitants for provision to be made out of the net estate[4];
- Moral duty of a testator under s.117 Succession Act 1965[5];
- Provisions of the Status of Children Act (where relevant)[6];
- Lifetime advancements to children and s.63 Succession Act 1965[7];
- Lapse of gifts vis-à-vis issue of testator under s.98 Succession Act 1965[8];
- The effect of separation, judicial separation and divorce (where relevant)[9];
- Relevant inheritance taxation issues.

3 See Chapter 8 – The Legal Right of Spouses and Civil Partners and Applications by Qualified Cohabitants.

4 *ibid.*

5 See Chapter 9 – The Moral Duty of Testators.

6 *ibid.*

7 See Chapter 11 – *Donationes Mortis Causa*, Joint Bank Accounts and Advancements.

8 See Chapter 6 – The Ademption, Lapse and Modification of Gifts.

9 See Chapter 8 – The Legal Right of Spouses and Civil Partners and Applications by Qualified Cohabitants.

Precedents Appointing Executors, Trustees and Guardians[10]

1. Appointment of two Executors 24–06

I appoint (name and address) and (name and address) to be executors of this my will.

2. Appointment of Executors with a Substitute Executor

I appoint (name of executor) of (address) and (name of executor) of (address) to be executors of this my will, but if either or both of my executors shall predecease me or is unwilling to act as executor or renounces, I appoint (name of executor) of (address) as executor in substitution.

3. Appointment of Two Executors and Trustees

I appoint AB of (address) and CD of (address) (hereinafter called "my trustees") to be executors and trustees of this my will and appoint them trustees for the purposes of the Land and Conveyancing Law Reform Act 2009, the Conveyancing Acts and Section 57 of the Succession Act 1965.

4. Appointment of an Executor and a Trust Corporation to Act as Executors and Trustees

I appoint (name and address of executor) and (name and registered offices of trust corporation) Trust Corporation to be the executors and trustees (hereinafter called "my trustees") of this my will and for the purposes of the Land and Conveyancing Law Reform Act 2009, the Conveyancing Acts and Section 57 of the Succession Act 1965.

5. Appointment of Trustees as Guardians

I appoint my trustees as guardians of my infant son/daughter.

Or

I appoint my trustees to be the guardians of my infant children. Such appointment shall take effect on the death of the survivor of my wife and myself (or my civil partner and myself). I revoke all previous appointments of guardians of my infant children made by me before the date of my will.

Testimonium and Attestation Precedents[11]

1. Standard Testimonium and Attestation Clause 24–07

In witness whereof, I have hereunto signed my name the day of 20 .

[10] See Chapter 13 – Applications for Grants of Probate.

[11] See Chapter 2 – The Execution of Wills.

SIGNED by the said (testator's name) as and for his/her last will and testament in the presence of us who, at his/her request and in his presence and in the presence of each other (all three being present at the same time), have hereunto subscribed our names as witnesses.

Witness 1 (name and address)

Witness 2 (name and address)

Or briefly,

In witness whereof I have hereunto signed my name the day of 20 .

SIGNED by the testator in our presence and signed by us in the presence of him and of each other.

Witness 1 (name and address)

Witness 2 (name and address)

2. Testimonium and Attestation Clause of a Testator Who Signs His Initials Due to a Physical Injury Sustained to His Writing Hand

In witness whereof I have hereunto signed my name the day of 20 .

SIGNED by the said testator by using his initials as and for his last will and testament, being unable to write due to a physical injury to his writing hand, in the presence of us both present at the same time who, in his presence and at his request and in the presence of each other, have hereunto subscribed our names as witnesses.

Witness 1 (name and address)

Witness 2 (name and address)

3. Testimonium and Attestation Clause of a Testator who Signs by Making a Mark Due to a Physical Injury Sustained to His Writing Hand

In witness whereof I have hereunto signed my name the day of 20 .

SIGNED by the said testator by making his mark as and for his last will and testament, being unable to write due to a physical injury to his writing hand, in the presence of us both present at the same time who, in his presence and at his request and in the presence of each other, have hereunto subscribed our names as witnesses.

Witness 1 (name and address)

Witness 2 (name and address)

4. Testimonium and Attestation Clause of a Blind Testator

In witness whereof I have hereunto signed my name the day of 20 .

SIGNED by the said testator (or by making his mark) as and for his last will and testament after the same had been first read over to the said testator because of his being blind by (name of person who read over the will) in our presence, and it appeared to be perfectly understood and approved by him, in the presence of us both present at the same time who, in his presence and at his request and in the presence of each other, have hereunto subscribed our names as witnesses.

Witness 1 (name and address)

Witness 2 (name and address)

REVOCATION PRECEDENTS[12]

1. Standard Revocation Clause 24–08

I (name and address of testator) make this as and for my last will and testament and hereby revoke all former wills and other testamentary dispositions heretofore made by me.

2. Partial Revocation by Codicil

I, (name of testator/testatrix) of (address) declare this to be a codicil to my will dated the day of 20 .

Whereas by my said will I bequeathed the sum of to (name of legatee), now I hereby revoke the said bequest and in lieu thereof I give and bequeath the sum of to the said (name of legatee).

In all other respects I confirm my said will dated the day of 20 .

In witness whereof I have hereunto set my hand this day of 20 .

Signed by the said testator as a codicil to his will dated the day of 20 in our presence and signed by us in the presence of him and each other.

Witness 1 (name and address)

Witness 2 (name and address)

3. Revocation Conditional on Marriage

I, (name of testator) of (address) declare that this, my last will and testament, is made in contemplation of my marriage to (name and address of the person the testator intends to marry) and is conditional on the marriage being solemnised. I further declare that all former wills and testamentary dispositions heretofore made

[12] See Chapter 4 – The Revocation and Revival of Wills.

by me shall not be revoked until the solemnisation of my marriage (or entering into my civil partnership) to the said (name of the person the testator intends to marry).

Legacies, Devises and Trusts Precedents[13]

24–09 ***1. Specific Legacies and Bequests***

I give and bequeath my deposit account in (name and address of bank) to (name of beneficiary) absolutely.

I give and bequeath my yacht called (name of yacht) to (name of beneficiary) absolutely.

I give and bequeath my motor car to (name of beneficiary) absolutely.

I give and bequeath my stamp collection to (name of beneficiary) absolutely.

I give and bequeath my first edition copy of James Joyce's Ulysses to (name of beneficiary) absolutely.

2. A General Pecuniary Legacy

I give and bequeath €100,000 (one hundred thousand euro) to (name of beneficiary) absolutely.

3. A Gift of Shares in a Company

I give and bequeath to (name of beneficiary) absolutely all my ordinary shares in (name of company) now standing in my name and declare that, if at my death, those shares shall by virtue of any amalgamation, reconstruction or rearrangement of capital of the company or sale of the company's business be represented by a different capital holding, whether in the same company or in any other company to which at my death I am entitled, then this gift shall take effect as if it has been a gift of the capital holding or capital holdings resulting from such amalgamation, reconstruction or rearrangement of capital or sale, and I declare that the said legacy shall exclude the cash proceeds of sale (or the money, investments and property from time to time representing the same) of my capital holdings and interests if sold before my death.

4. Demonstrative Pecuniary Legacies

I give and bequeath €100,000 (one hundred thousand euro) out of my deposit account in (name and address of bank) to (name of beneficiary) absolutely.

I give and bequeath €100,000 (one hundred thousand euro) out of my deposit account in (post office and address) to (names of beneficiaries) in equal shares absolutely.

I give and bequeath €100,000 (one hundred thousand euro) out of my deposit account in (name and address of credit union) to (names of beneficiaries) jointly.

---

[13] See Chapter 5 – Testamentary Gifts and Trusts.

5. A Pecuniary Legacy to a Minor

I give and bequeath the sum of €100,000 (one hundred thousand euro) to my nephew (name of nephew) and, in the event that my said nephew has not attained the age of 18 years at the date of my death, then the said legacy shall be paid to the father or mother or guardian of the said nephew, and the receipt of such father, mother or guardian to my executors shall be in full discharge of the said legacy.

6. Gift of All Real Estate to One Beneficiary

I give and devise all my real estate of whatsoever nature and wheresoever situate to (name of beneficiary) absolutely.

7. Gift of the Whole Estate to One Beneficiary

I give, devise and bequeath all my real and personal estate of whatsoever nature and wheresoever situate to (name of beneficiary) absolutely.

8. Gift of Residuary Estate to One Beneficiary

I give, devise and bequeath all the rest, residue and remainder of my real and personal estate of whatsoever nature and wheresoever situate to (name of beneficiary) absolutely.

9. Trust by Husband/Civil Partner/Cohabitant For Wife/Civil Partner/ Cohabitant with Substitutive Provisions for Son/Daughter[14]

I (name of testator) of (address) make this as and for my last will and testament and hereby revoke all former wills and testamentary dispositions heretofore made by me.

1. If my wife/husband/civil partner/cohabitant (name) survives me by 30 days, I give, devise and bequeath the whole of my estate to him/her and appoint him/her my executor/executrix. If my wife/husband/civil partner/cohabitant does not survive me by 30 days, the following provisions shall apply:
2. I appoint AB of (address) and CD of (address) (hereinafter called "my trustees") to be executors and trustees, and appoint them trustees for the purposes of the Land Conveyancing Reform Act 2009 Act and for the purposes of the Conveyancing Acts and for the purposes of s.57 of the Succession Act 1965.
3. I appoint my trustees guardians of my infant sons/daughters.
4. I give, devise and bequeath to my trustees the whole of my estate on trust to sell the same (with power to postpone such sale in whole or in part for such time or times as they shall think fit) and to hold the same or the proceeds of sale thereof on the following trusts:
   (a) To pay my debts, funeral and testamentary expenses;
   (b) (Provision for legacies, house and/or contents to (name) etc., if intended)
   (c) To hold the residue (hereinafter called "my residuary estate") in trust for my son/daughter until he/she attains the age of 21 years (or 18), BUT if my son/daughter should die before me or before attaining a vested interest leaving a child or children, then such

---

[14] See Chapter 5 – Testamentary Gifts and Trusts.

child or children shall, on reaching the age of 21 years (or 18 years), take the share my son/daughter would otherwise have taken and, if more than one, in equal shares absolutely, AND I DECLARE that no advancement within the meaning of Section 63 of the Succession Act 1965 shall be brought into account in the distribution of my estate;

(d) To pay to my son/daughter on reaching the age of 18 years the annual income of his/her share of my residuary estate until he/she reaches the age of 21 years.

10. Discretionary Trust[15]

I (name of testator) of (address) make this as and for my last will and testament and hereby revoke all former wills and testamentary dispositions heretofore made by me.

1. I appoint AB of and CD of (hereinafter called "my trustees") to be executors and trustees of this my last will and I direct them to discharge all my just debts, funeral and testamentary expenses.
2. I appoint my trustees to be trustees for all the purposes of the Land and Conveyancing Law Reform Act 2009, for all the purposes of the Conveyancing Acts 1881 and 1911, and for the purposes of Sections 57 and 58 of the Succession Act 1965.
3. In this my will, the following terms shall, where the context so admits or requires, have the following meanings:
   (a) "my trustees" shall mean the trustee or trustees for the time being appointed in accordance with the terms hereof;
   (b) "the vesting day" shall mean the day on which shall expire the period of 20 years after the date of my death;
   (c) "the beneficiaries" shall mean:
      (i) my wife (or civil partner);
      (ii) my children.
4. I give and bequeath to my wife (or civil partner) (name) such furnishings and contents in my residence as are my property for her own use and benefit absolutely.
5. All the rest residue and remainder of my property whatsoever and wheresoever situate, including property over which I may have a general power of appointment, I give, devise and bequeath the same (hereinafter called "the Trust Fund") to my trustees on trust for the benefit of the beneficiaries or any one or more of them exclusive of the others or other of them, in such shares and proportions and subject to such trusts, powers, terms, limitations and provisions as my trustees shall from time to time and at any time by deed or deeds revocable or irrevocable or by will executed before the vesting day appoint, and failing such appointment on trust subject to the provisions hereinafter contained as to advancement and insofar as assets may remain in settlement at the vesting day for such of the beneficiaries as shall be living on the vesting day, if more than one in equal shares.
6. (a) My trustees shall have power in their absolute discretion to sell, call in or convert into money at such time or times and in such manner as they shall think fit so much of the Trust Fund as shall not be in money form, nevertheless to postpone such sale, conversion or calling in indefinitely without being liable for any loss, and further my trustees shall have power in their absolute discretion

[15] See Chapter 5 – Testamentary Gifts and Trusts.

and without restriction of any kind to borrow any amount of money on the security of all or any assets comprised in the Trust Fund or without security and generally on such terms as they shall decide without limitation of any kind.

(b) My trustees shall have power at any time or times until the vesting day in their absolute discretion to pay, apply or transfer (in *specie* or otherwise) any part or parts of the capital and income of the Trust Fund to or for the maintenance, benefit, education or advancement of all or any one or more of the beneficiaries in such shares and manner as they shall think fit, notwithstanding that the Trust Fund may be thereby exhausted.

(c) My trustees shall not be obliged to invest in trustee securities and may retain any part of my estate in the form of investment in which it may be at the time of my death and may sell, vary or transpose such investment and may invest in any form of security whether of a wasting nature or not in their absolute discretion in all respects as if they were the beneficial owners thereof, and shall not be liable for any involuntary loss.

(d) My trustees shall be empowered to buy, sell, lease for any term, borrow on the security of, mortgage, charge and deal generally with land and property of every description (including residential property and apartments) as if they were beneficial owners thereof and without restriction whatsoever and whether or not such property may be utilised by a beneficiary hereunder as a residence or otherwise.

7. I DIRECT that the power of appointing a new trustee or trustees of this my will, whether additional or substitutive, shall be vested in my trustees for the time being or in the survivor or survivors of them or in the personal representative of the last survivor.

8. I DECLARE that no trustee of the Trust Fund shall be liable for any loss not attributable to the trustee's own dishonesty or to the wilful commission by the trustees or trustee of any act known to be a breach of trust.

9. I DIRECT that any trustee for the time being hereof being a person engaged in any profession or business shall be entitled to charge and be paid all usual professional fees and charges.

IN WITNESS whereof I have hereunto set my hand this day of 20 .

SIGNED, PUBLISHED AND DECLARED by the said testator as and for his last will and testament in the presence of us both who, at his request in his presence and in the presence of each other, have subscribed our names as witnesses.

Witness 1 (name and address)

Witness 2 (name and address)

Codicil Precedents[16]

24–10 ### *1. Codicil Revoking A Legacy in the Will*

This is a codicil to my last will dated the day of 20

Whereas by the said will I gave €20,000 (twenty thousand euro) to X, I hereby revoke the said legacy given to X in my will.

In all other respects, I confirm my said will.

Signed by the testator as and for his codicil to his/her last will and testament dated the day of 20 in the presence of us, both being present at the same time and signed by us in his/her presence.

Witness 1 (name and address)

Witness 2 (name and address)

2. Codicil Revoking and Increasing (Or Decreasing) A Legacy in the Will

This is a codicil to my last will dated the day of 20

Whereas by the said will I gave €20,000 (twenty thousand euro) to X, I hereby revoke the said legacy given to X and instead I give €40,000 (forty thousand euro) to the said X.

In all other respects, I confirm my said will.

Signed by the testator as and for his codicil to his last will and testament dated the day of 20 in the presence of us, both being present at the same time and signed by us in his presence.

Witness 1 (name and address)

Witness 2 (name and address)

3. Codicil Replacing A Sole Executor Appointed by the Will

This is a codicil to my last will dated the day of 20

Whereas by the said will, X of (address) was appointed executor, I hereby revoke the appointment of X as sole executor and instead I appoint Y of (address) and Z of (address) to be my executors.

In all other respects, I confirm my said will.

Signed by the testator as and for his codicil to his last will and testament dated the

[16] See Chapter 2 – The Execution of Wills.

day of 20 in the presence of us, both being present at the same time and signed by us in his presence.

Witness 1 (name and address)

Witness 2 (name and address)

4. Codicil Revoking A Devise in the Will

This is a (second) codicil to my last will dated the day of 20

Whereas by the said will I gave and devised my house situate at (address) to X and I hereby revoke the said devise and instead I give and devise the said house to Y of (address).

In all other respects I confirm my said will.

Signed by the testator as and for his (second) codicil to his/her last will and testament dated the day of 20 in the presence of us, both being present at the same time and signed by us in his presence.

Witness 1 (name and address)

Witness 2 (name and address)

Chapter 25

PROBATE PRECEDENTS

Introduction

The bundle of proofs used in applying for a grant will depend on whether the deceased has died leaving a will appointing executors, or left a will without appointing executors or the executors have predeceased him or have renounced, or the deceased has left no will and died intestate. Where the testator has appointed executors, they may apply for a grant of probate.[1] Where, however, the executors have renounced or predeceased the testator, a grant of letters of administration with the will annexed may be sought by the person entitled to apply for such grants in accordance with Ord. 79, r.6 of the Rules of the Superior Courts 1986 (the "1986 Rules"). Where a person dies intestate, a grant of letters of administration intestate may be sought by the person entitled to do so in accordance with Ord. 79, r.1 of the 1986 Rules. In the case of applications for grants of probate, the title of the executor must be expressly stated in the oath of executor. In the case of applications for grants of letters of administration with the will annexed or **25–01**

[1] See Chapter 13 – Applications for Grants of Probate; Chapter 14 – Applications for Grants of Letters of Administration with Will Annexed; Chapter 15 – Applications for Grants of Letters of Administration Intestate.

intestate, the title of the person in accordance with Ord. 79, r.1 and Ord. 79, r.5 must be expressly stated in the oath of administrator and administration bond. The precedents for the oath of executor, oath of administrator with the will annexed and oath of administrator intestate are found in Appendix Q of the 1986 Rules. The title of the person entitled to apply for a grant—whether for a grant of probate, letters of administration with the will annexed or intestate —must appear in the relevant oath, and also in the case of letters of administration in the relevant administration bond.

25–02 After the death of the testator, an executor must decide whether to accept the office of executor or to renounce it. An executor, of course, may accept the office by applying for a grant of probate but, where he renounces, he must do so in writing. The renunciation must be exhibited by another executor in the oath of executor and included among the proofs submitted for a grant of probate by another executor. Once an executor renounces, his right to probate will wholly cease.[2] Where a sole executor renounces, the person next entitled by virtue of the Ord. 79, r.5(6) of the Rules of the Superior Courts 1986 (the "1986 Rules") may apply for a grant of letters of administration with the will annexed, but not probate. The renunciation of the executor must be exhibited in the oath of administrator with the will annexed and included among the proofs submitted for the grant. Where there is no executor named in the will and the person entitled to apply for a grant of letters of administration with the will annexed renounces, the person next entitled may apply, and the renunciation by the person with prior title must be exhibited in the oath of administrator intestate and included among the proofs submitted for the grant. Where the deceased dies intestate and the person next entitled to apply for a grant of letters of administration intestate under Ord. 79, r.5(1) of the 1986 Rules renounces, the person next entitled may apply. The renunciation by the person with prior title must be exhibited in the oath of administrator intestate and included among the proofs submitted for the grant. Once a person entitled to apply for a grant of letters of administration with the will or intestate renounces his rights, he will not be given representation in another character unless by order of the Court.[3] Furthermore, where an executor or administrator to whom a grant issued dies leaving part of the estate unadministered, a *de bonis non* grant will become necessary. Again, where the person entitled to apply for such a grant renounces, the person next entitled under Ord. 79, r.5(1) or (6) of the 1986 Rules may apply for one and the renunciation must be included among the papers submitted for such a grant.[4]

---

[2] See s.17 and s.18 of the Succession Act 1965; see also Albert Keating, "Renunciations and Disclaimers" (2009) 27 I.L.T. 285; Albert Keating, *Irish Probate Precedents Service* (Dublin: Round Hall, 2009); Albert Keating, *Keating on Probate* (4th ed) (Dublin: Round Hall, 2011); Albert Keating, *First Supplement to the Fourth Edition of Keating on Probate* (Dublin: Thomson Round Hall, 2013).

[3] See Ord. 79, r.38 of the Rules of the Superior Courts 1986.

[4] See Chapter 17 – Applications for *De Bonis Non* Grants.

A grant of letters of administration with the will annexed or intestate may be made to the guardian of a minor, and the guardian will remain the personal representative of the estate of the deceased person until the minor attains the age of majority and applies for a grant himself.[5] A person of unsound mind is also incapable of applying for a grant and, in such cases, the committee appointed by the probate officer may apply for a grant of letters of administration with the will annexed or intestate on behalf of the person entitled to apply for a grant.[6] Where the executor appointed by the will, or the person entitled to apply for a grant of letters of administration with the will annexed or intestate under Ord.79 of the 1986 Rules, is residing outside the jurisdiction, a grant may be made to his or her attorney until he or she returns to the jurisdiction.[7] **25–03**

Application for a Grant of Probate by a Sole Executor[8]

Essential Proofs

1. Form S1 (postal application form) must be lodged with all applications submitted by post; **25–04**
2. The original will (and codicils, if any);
3. Certified copy of will (and codicils, if any);
4. Oath of executor;
5. Copy oath of executor;
6. Inland Revenue Affidavit (CA 24 (2010 edition) for deaths after 5 December 2001 and CA24 (2000 edition) where the deceased died before 5 December 2001);
7. Death certificate of the testator;
8. Charitable bequest form (form PAS3 is required where there are charitable bequests in the will relating to Irish charities).

OATH OF EXECUTOR

The High Court
Probate

The Probate Office/The District Probate Registry at

[5] See Chapter 16 – Applications for Grants by Guardians, Committees and Attorneys; Albert Keating, "Beneficial Grants of Representation" (2008) 13(4) C.P.L.J. 85.

[6] See Chapter 16 – Applications for Grants by Guardians, Committees and Attorneys; Albert Keating, "Beneficial Grants of Representation" (2008) 13(4) C.P.L.J. 85.

[7] See Chapter 16 – Applications for Grants by Guardians, Committees and Attorneys; Albert Keating, "Beneficial Grants of Representation" (2008) 13(4) C.P.L.J. 85; Albert Keating, *Keating on Probate* (4th ed) (Dublin: Round Hall, 2011); Albert Keating, *First Supplement to the Fourth Edition of Keating on Probate* (Dublin: Thomson Round Hall, 2013).

[8] See Chapter 13 – Applications for Grants of Probate.

In the estate of (name of testator) late of (address) deceased.

I, (name of executor) of (address) aged 18 years and upwards, make oath and say that I believe the paper writing hereto annexed, and marked by me, to contain the true and original last will [*or* last will with codicils] of (name of testator) late of [*address and description*] deceased; that same was made by the said after attaining the age of 18 years, and that he did not intermarry with any person after the making of same; that I am the [*state relationship, if not a blood relation insert 'stranger in blood'*] of the said (name of testator) and the *sole executor named in the said will*; that I will faithfully administer the estate of the said testator, by paying his just debts and the legacies bequeathed by his said will [*or* will and codicils], so far as the same shall thereto extend and the law bind me; that I will exhibit a true inventory of the said estate, and render a true account thereof, whenever required by law so to do; that the testator died at on the day of [*where application is made in District Probate Registry add* and that the testator has at the time of his death a fixed place of abode at within the district of] and that the whole of the estate which devolves on and vests in his legal personal representative amounts in value to [*the gross assets, without any deductions for debts*] and no more, to the best of my knowledge, information and belief.

Sworn, &c.

Application for a Grant of Letters of Administration with Will Annexed by a Residuary Legatee where Executor Predeceased the Testator[9]

Essential Proofs

25–05

1. Form S1 (postal application form) must be lodged with all applications submitted by post;
2. The original will (and codicils, if any);
3. A certified copy of the will;
4. Oath of administrator with will;
5. Copy oath of administrator with will;
6. Administration bond;
7. Inland Revenue Affidavit (CA 24(2010 edition) for deaths after 5 December 2001 and CA24 (2000 edition) where the deceased died before 5 December 2001);
8. Affidavit of market value or certificate of market value;
9. Death certificate of the testator;
10. Charitable bequest form (form PAS3 is required where there are charitable bequests in the will relating to Irish charities).

[9] See Chapter 14–Applications for Grants of Letters of Administration with Will Annexed.

OATH OF ADMINISTRATOR WITH THE WILL

THE HIGH COURT
PROBATE

The Probate Office/The District Probate Registry at

In the estate of (name of testator) late of (address) deceased.

I, (name of applicant) of (address) aged 18 years and upwards, make oath and say that I believe the paper writing hereunto annexed, and marked by me, to contain the true and original last will [*or* last will with codicils] of late of [*address and description*], deceased, and that same was made by the said after attaining the age of [age] years, and that he did not intermarry with any person after the making of same, *and that he did therein name AB sole executor who predeceased the deceased and that I am the residuary legatee and devisee named in said will* and that I will well and faithfully administer the estate of the said testator, by paying his just debts and the legacies bequeathed by his said will [*or* will and codicils] and distributing the residue of his estate according to law; and that I will exhibit a true and perfect inventory of the said estate, and render a true account thereof whenever required by law so to do; and that the testator died at on the day of [*where application is made in a District Probate Registry, add*: and had at the time of his death a fixed place of abode at within the district of] and that the whole of the personal estate of the said testator amounts in value to the sum of [*the gross personal estate, without any deductions for debts*] and that the whole of the real estate of the said testator which devolves on and vests in his legal personal representative is of the market value of [*the amount shown in the affidavit of market value*] and no more, to the best of my knowledge, information and belief.

Sworn, &c.

ADMINISTRATION BOND

THE HIGH COURT

The Probate Office/The District Probate Registry at

I (Insert name, address and description of applicant and surety/sureties if applicable) am liable in full to pay to the President of the High Court the sum of (insert penal sum twice gross assets of estate reflecting current market value of immovable property) for which payment I bind myself and my executors, administrators and successors and sealed with my seal and dated the (insert day of signing bond) day of (insert month and year of signing bond). The condition of this obligation is that, if the above-named (insert name of applicant) *the residuary legatee and devisee named in the will* of (insert name, address and description of deceased) deceased, and the intended administrator/administratix of the estate of the said deceased, do, when lawfully called on in that behalf, make or cause to be made a true inventory of the said estate which has or shall come into his/her hands, possession or knowledge, or into the hands, possession or control of any other person for him/her;

do exhibit the said inventory or cause it to be exhibited in the Probate Office (or in the District Probate Registry at) whenever required by law to do so; do well and truly administer the said estate according to law, paying all the debts owed by the deceased at the time of his death, all death duties payable in respect of the estate of the deceased for which the personal representative is accountable and all income tax and surtax payable out of the estate,

distributing all shares in the estate to those entitled by law thereto and as the law requires him/her; and further, do make or cause to be made a true account of the said administration whenever required by law to do so;

then this obligation shall be void and no effect, but shall otherwise remain in full force and effect.

Signed, sealed and delivered by the within-named	Applicant(s) signature and seal
Name of applicant and surety/sureties if applicable	Surety's/sureties' signature and seal [if applicable]

In the presence of
(insert Commissioner's/Solicitor's name)

Commissioner/Solicitor to sign here
Commissioner/Solicitor

Applicant(s) should execute bond before Commissioner/Solicitor on oath.[10]

AFFIDAVIT OF MARKET VALUE

THE HIGH COURT
PROBATE

The Probate Office or District Probate Registry at

In the estate of (name of deceased), late of (address) deceased.

I (name of valuer, auctioneer or surveyor) of (address), (state occupation), aged 18 years and upwards, make oath and say as follows:

1. I am acquainted with the value of lands in the vicinity of (address of lands valued) in the County of , where lands belonging to the aforesaid (name of deceased) deceased are situate.

I have inspected the holdings of the aforesaid deceased at (address of lands valued) and, in my opinion, the said holdings would, on the date of swearing hereof, have been of the value of (amount in words and figures) if then offered for sale on the open market.

Sworn &c.

[10] See Ord 79, r.29, Rules of the Superior Courts 1986.

CERTIFICATE OF MARKET VALUE

Re: Estate of (name of deceased), deceased, late of (address of deceased)

I/We (name of solicitor or firm), as solicitor(s) for the administrator of the estate of the aforementioned deceased, hereby certify that the current market value of the deceased's dwelling house at (address) would not exceed (value in figures and words).

I/We confirm that the said property, while realty, comprises a dwelling house only.

Yours &c.

Application for a Grant of Letters of Administration Intestate by a Husband[11]

Essential Proofs

1. Form S1 (postal application form) must be lodged with all applications submitted by post; **25–06**
2. Oath of administrator;
3. Copy oath of administrator;
4. Administration bond;
5. Inland Revenue Affidavit (CA 24 (2010 edition) for deaths after 5 December 2001 and CA24 (2000 edition) where the deceased died before 5 December 2001);
6. Death certificate;
7. Affidavit of market value or certificate of market value.

OATH OF ADMINISTRATOR

The High Court
Probate

In the estate of (name of intestate), late of (address) deceased.

I, (name of applicant) of (address), aged 18 years and upwards, make oath and say that late of [*address and description*], deceased, died intestate and that *I am the lawful husband of said deceased* and that I will well and faithfully administer the estate of the said deceased by paying his just debts and distributing the residue of said estate according to law, and that I will exhibit a true inventory of the said estate and render a true account thereof, whenever required by law so to do; that the said deceased died at on the day of [*where application is made in a District Probate Registry, add:* and that the said deceased had at the time of his death a fixed place of abode at within the district of] and that the whole of the personal estate of the said deceased amounts in value to the sum of [*the gross personal estate without any deductions for debts*] and that the whole of the real estate of the

[11] See Chapter 15 – Applications for Grants of Letters of Administration Intestate.

said deceased which devolves on and vests in his legal personal representatives is of the market value of [*the amount shown in the affidavit of market value*] and no more, to the best of my knowledge, information and belief.

Sworn, &c.

ADMINISTRATION BOND

THE HIGH COURT

The Probate Office/The District Probate Registry at

I (insert name address and description of applicant and surety/sureties if applicable) am liable in full to pay to the President of the High Court the sum of (insert penal sum twice gross assets of estate reflecting current market value of immovable property) for which payment I bind myself and my executors, administrators and successors and sealed with my seal and dated the (insert day of signing bond) day of (insert month and year of signing bond). The condition of this obligation is that, if the above-named (insert name of applicant) *the lawful husband* of (insert name address and description of deceased) deceased, and the intended administrator of the estate of the said deceased, do, when lawfully called on in that behalf, make or cause to be made a true inventory of the said estate which has or shall come into his hands, possession or knowledge, or into the hands, possession or control of any other person for him/her;

do exhibit the said inventory or cause it to be exhibited in the Probate Office (or in the District Probate Registry at) whenever required by law to do so; do well and truly administer the said estate according to law, paying all the debts owed by the deceased at the time of his death, all death duties payable in respect of the estate of the deceased for which the personal representative is accountable and all income tax and surtax payable out of the estate,

distributing all shares in the estate to those entitled by law thereto and as the law requires him/her; and further, do make or cause to be made a true account of the said administration whenever required by law to do so;

and further do, if so required, render and deliver up the letters of administration in the High Court if it shall hereafter appear that any will was made by the deceased which is exhibited in the said Court, with a request that it be allowed and approved accordingly;

then this obligation shall be void and no effect, but shall otherwise remain in full force and effect.

Signed, sealed and delivered by the within-named	Applicant(s) signature and seal
Name of applicant and surety/sureties if applicable	Surety's/sureties' signature and seal [if applicable]

In the presence of
(insert Commissioner's/Solicitor's name)

Commissioner/Solicitor to sign here
Commissioner/Solicitor

Applicant(s) should execute bond before Commissioner/Solicitor on oath.[12]

AFFIDAVIT OF MARKET VALUE

THE HIGH COURT
PROBATE

The Probate Office or District Probate Registry at

In the estate of (name of deceased intestate), late of (address of deceased), deceased.

I (name of valuer, auctioneer or surveyor) of (address), (state occupation), aged 18 years and upwards, make oath and say as follows:

1. I am acquainted with the value of lands in the vicinity of (address of lands valued) in the County of , where lands belonging to the aforesaid (name of deceased), deceased, are situate.

I have inspected the holdings of the aforesaid deceased at (address of lands valued) and, in my opinion, the said holdings would, on the date of swearing hereof, have been of the value of (amount in words and figures), if then offered for sale on the open market.

Sworn & c.

CERTIFICATE OF MARKET VALUE

Re: Estate of (name of deceased intestate), deceased, late of (address)

I/We (name of solicitor or firm), as solicitor(s) for the administrator of the estate of the aforementioned deceased, hereby certify that the current market value of the deceased's dwelling house at (address) would not exceed (value in figures and words).

I/We confirm that the said property, while realty, comprises a dwelling house only.

Yours &c.

---

[12] See Ord. 79, r.29, Rules of the Superior Courts 1986.

Application for a Grant of Letters of Administration Intestate by a Surviving Civil Partner[13]

Essential Proofs

25–07 1. Form S1 (postal application form) must be lodged with all applications submitted by post;
2. Oath of administrator;
3. Copy oath of administrator;
4. Administration bond;
5. Inland Revenue Affidavit (CA 24 (2010 edition) for deaths after 5 December 2001 and CA24 (2000 edition) where the deceased died before 5 December 2001);
6. Death certificate;
7. Affidavit of market value/certificate of market value.

OATH OF ADMINISTRATOR

THE HIGH COURT
PROBATE

In the estate of (name of intestate), late of (address), deceased.

I, (name of applicant) of (address), aged 18 years and upwards, make oath and say that late of [*address and description*], deceased, died intestate and that *I am the lawful civil partner of said deceased* and that I will well and faithfully administer the estate of the said deceased by paying his just debts and distributing the residue of said estate according to law, and that I will exhibit a true inventory of the said estate and render a true account thereof, whenever required by law so to do; that the said deceased died at on the day of [*where application is made in a District Probate Registry, add:* and that the said deceased had at the time of his death a fixed place of abode at within the district of] and that the whole of the personal estate of the said deceased amounts in value to the sum of [*the gross personal estate without any deductions for debts*] and that the whole of the real estate of the said deceased which devolves on and vests in his legal personal representatives is of the market value of [*the amount shown in the affidavit of market value*] and no more, to the best of my knowledge, information and belief.

Sworn, &c.

ADMINISTRATION BOND

THE HIGH COURT

The Probate Office/The District Probate Registry at

[13] See Chapter 15 – Applications for Grants of Letters of Administration Intestate.

I (insert name, address and description of applicant and surety/sureties if applicable) am liable in full to pay to the President of the High Court the sum of (insert penal sum twice gross assets of estate reflecting current market value of immovable property) for which payment I bind myself and my executors, administrators and successors and sealed with my seal and dated the (insert day of signing bond) day of (insert month and year of signing bond). The condition of this obligation is that, if the above-named (insert name of applicant) *the lawful civil partner* of (insert name, address and description of deceased) deceased, and the intended administrator of the estate of the said deceased, do, when lawfully called on in that behalf, make or cause to be made a true inventory of the said estate which has or shall come into his/her hands, possession or knowledge, or into the hands, possession or control of any other person for him/her;

do exhibit the said inventory or cause it to be exhibited in the Probate Office (or in the District Probate Registry at) whenever required by law to do so; do well and truly administer the said estate according to law, paying all the debts owed by the deceased at the time of his death, all death duties payable in respect of the estate of the deceased for which the personal representative is accountable and all income tax and surtax payable out of the estate,

distributing all shares in the estate to those entitled by law thereto and as the law requires him/her; and further, do make or cause to be made a true account of the said administration whenever required by law to do so;

and further do, if so required, render and deliver up the letters of administration in the High Court if it shall hereafter appear that any will was made by the deceased which is exhibited in the said Court, with a request that it be allowed and approved accordingly;

then this obligation shall be void and no effect, but shall otherwise remain in full force and effect.

Signed, sealed and delivered by the within-named	Applicant(s) signature and seal
Name of applicant and surety/sureties if applicable	Surety's/sureties' signature and seal [if applicable]

In the presence of
(insert Commissioner's/Solicitor's name)

Commissioner/Solicitor to sign here
Commissioner/Solicitor

Applicant(s) should execute bond before Commissioner/Solicitor on oath.[14]

[14] See Ord.79, r.29, Rules of the Superior Courts 1986.

AFFIDAVIT OF MARKET VALUE

THE HIGH COURT
PROBATE

The Probate Office or District Probate Registry at

In the estate of (name of deceased intestate), late of (address of deceased), deceased.

I (name of valuer, auctioneer or surveyor) of (address), (state occupation), aged 18 years and upwards, make oath and say as follows:

1. I am acquainted with the value of lands in the vicinity of (address of lands valued) in the County of , where lands belonging to the aforesaid (name of deceased), deceased, are situate.

I have inspected the holdings of the aforesaid deceased at (address of lands valued) and, in my opinion, the said holdings would, on the date of swearing hereof, have been of the value of (amount in words and figures) if then offered for sale on the open market.

Sworn &c.

CERTIFICATE OF MARKET VALUE

Re: Estate of (name of deceased intestate), deceased, late of (address)

I/We (name of solicitor or firm), as solicitor(s) for the administrator of the estate of the aforementioned deceased, hereby certify that the current market value of the deceased's dwelling house at (address) would not exceed (value in figures and words).

I/We confirm that the said property, while realty, comprises a dwelling house only.

Yours &c.

Application for a Grant of Probate Where One of Two Executors Renounces

Essential Proofs

25–08

1. Form S1 (postal application form) must be lodged with all applications submitted by post;
2. The original will (and codicils, if any);
3. Certified copy of will (and codicils, if any);
4. Oath of executor;
5. Copy oath of executor;
6. Inland Revenue Affidavit (CA 24 (2010 edition) for deaths after

5 December 2001 and CA24 (2000 edition) where the deceased died before 5 December 2001);
7. Death certificate of the testator;
8. Charitable bequest form (form PAS3 is required where there are charitable bequests in the will relating to Irish charities);
9. Renunciation of probate by executor.

OATH OF EXECUTOR

THE HIGH COURT
PROBATE

The Probate Office/The District Probate Registry at

In the estate of (name of deceased), late of (address), deceased.

I, (name of executor) of (address), aged 18 years and upwards, make oath and say that I believe the paper writing hereto annexed, and marked by me, to contain the true and original last will [*or* last will with codicils] of late of [*address and description*] deceased; that same was made by the said after attaining the age of years, and that he did not intermarry with any person after the making of same; *and that I am one of the executors named in the will, the other executor [name and address] having duly renounced his/her rights herein dated the [day] day of [month and year] on which renunciation I have signed my name and marked the letter 'A' prior to the swearing hereof,* and that I will faithfully administer the estate of the said testator, by paying his just debts and the legacies bequeathed by his said will [*or* will and codicils], so far as the same shall thereto extend and the law bind me; that I will exhibit a true inventory of the said estate, and render a true account thereof, whenever required by law so to do; that the testator died at on the day of [*where application is made in District Probate Registry add* and that the testator has at the time of his death a fixed place of abode at within the district of] and that the whole of the estate which devolves on and vests in his legal personal representative amounts in value to [*the gross assets, without any deductions for debts*] and no more, to the best of my knowledge, information and belief.

Sworn, &c.

RENUNCIATION OF PROBATE

THE HIGH COURT
PROBATE

In the estate of (name of deceased)
Whereas (name of deceased), late of (address), deceased, died on the day of 20 , at
[*where application is made in a District Probate Registry, add* having at the time of his death a fixed place of abode at within the district of] and whereas he made and duly executed his last will [*or* will and codicils] bearing date the day of 20 , and thereof appointed X and Y executors.

Now I, the said Y aged eighteen years and upwards, do declare that I have not intermeddled with the estate of the said deceased, and will not hereafter intermeddle therein with the intent to defraud creditors, and I do hereby expressly renounce my right to probate of the said will of the estate of the said deceased.

Dated
(Signed)

Witness

Application for a Grant of Letters of Administration with Will Annexed by the Residuary Legatee and Devisee Where a Sole or Surviving Executor Renounces Probate

Essential Proofs

25–09
1. Form S1 (postal application form) must be lodged with all applications submitted by post;
2. The original will (and codicils, if any);
3. A certified copy of the will;
4. Oath of administrator with will;
5. Copy oath of administrator with will;
6. Administration bond;
7. Inland Revenue Affidavit (CA 24 (2010 edition) for deaths after 5 December 2001 and CA24 (2000 edition) where the deceased died before 5 December 2001);
8. Affidavit of market value or certificate of market value;
9. Death certificate of the testator;
10. Charitable bequest form (form PAS3 is required where there are charitable bequests in the will relating to Irish charities);
11. Renunciation by executor.

OATH OF ADMINISTRATOR WITH THE WILL

THE HIGH COURT
PROBATE

The Probate Office/The District Probate Registry at

In the estate of (name of deceased), late of (address), deceased.

I, (name of applicant) of (address), aged 18 years and upwards, make oath and say that I believe the paper writing hereunto annexed, and marked by me, to contain the true and original last will [*or* last will with codicils] of late of [*address and description*], deceased, and that same was made by the said [name of deceased] after attaining the age of years, and that he did not intermarry with any person after the making of same, and *that he did therein name AB sole executor and that the said AB duly renounced his rights, on which renunciation dated the day of 20 I have signed my name and marked the letter 'A' prior to the swearing hereof and that I am the residuary legatee and devisee named in the said will* and that I will well and faithfully administer the estate of the said testator, by paying his just debts and the legacies bequeathed by his said will [*or* will and codicils] and distributing the residue of his estate according to law; and that I will exhibit a true and perfect inventory of the said estate, and render a true account thereof whenever required by law so to do; and that the testator died at on the day of [*where application is made in a District Probate Registry, add*: and had at the time of his death a fixed place of abode at within the district of] and that the whole of the personal estate of the said testator amounts in value to the sum of [*the gross personal estate, without any deductions for debts*] and that the whole of the real estate of the said testator which devolves on and vests in his legal personal representative is of the market value of [*the amount shown in the affidavit of market value*] and no more, to the best of my knowledge, information and belief.

Sworn, &c.

RENUNCIATION OF PROBATE

THE HIGH COURT
PROBATE

In the estate of (name of deceased)
Whereas (name of deceased), late of (address)
deceased, died on the day of 20 , at [*where application is made in a District Probate Registry, add* having at the time of his death a fixed place of abode at within the district of] and whereas he made and duly executed his last will [*or* will and codicils] bearing date the day of 20 , and thereof named AB sole executor.

Now I, the said AB, aged 18 years and upwards, do declare that I have not intermeddled with the estate of the said deceased, and will not hereafter intermeddle therein with the intent to defraud creditors, and I do hereby expressly renounce my right to probate of the said will and of the estate of the said deceased.

Dated
(Signed)

Witness

ADMINISTRATION BOND

THE HIGH COURT

The Probate Office/The District Probate Registry at

I (insert name address and description of applicant and surety/sureties if applicable) am liable in full to pay to the President of the High Court the sum of (insert penal sum twice gross assets of estate reflecting current market value of immovable property) for which payment I bind myself and my executors, administrators and successors and sealed with my seal and dated the (insert day of signing bond) day of (insert month and year of signing bond). The condition of this obligation is that, if the above-named (insert name of applicant) *the residuary legatee and devisee named in the will* of (insert name, address and description of deceased), deceased, and the intended administrator/administratix of the estate of the said deceased, do, when lawfully called on in that behalf, make or cause to be made a true inventory of the said estate which has or shall come into his/her hands, possession or knowledge, or into the hands, possession or control of any other person for him/her;

do exhibit the said inventory or cause it to be exhibited in the Probate Office (or in the District Probate Registry at) whenever required by law to do so; do well and truly administer the said estate according to law, paying all the debts owed by the deceased at the time of his death, all death duties payable in respect of the estate of the deceased for which the personal representative is accountable and all income tax and surtax payable out of the estate,

distributing all shares in the estate to those entitled by law thereto and as the law requires him/her; and further, do make or cause to be made a true account of the said administration whenever required by law to do so;

then this obligation shall be void and no effect, but shall otherwise remain in full force and effect.

Signed, sealed and delivered by the within-named	Applicant(s) signature and seal
Name of applicant and surety/sureties if applicable	Surety's/sureties' signature and seal [if applicable]

In the presence of
(insert Commissioner's/Solicitor's name)

Commissioner/Solicitor to sign here
Commissioner/Solicitor

Applicant(s) should execute bond before Commissioner/Solicitor on oath.[15]

AFFIDAVIT OF MARKET VALUE

THE HIGH COURT
PROBATE

The Probate Office or District Probate Registry at

In the estate of (name of deceased), late of (address), deceased.

I (name of valuer, auctioneer or surveyor) of (address), (state occupation), aged 18 years and upwards, make oath and say as follows:

---

[15] See Ord.79, r.29, Rules of the Superior Courts 1986.

1. I am acquainted with the value of lands in the vicinity of (address of lands valued) in the County of , where lands belonging to the aforesaid (name of deceased), deceased, are situate.

I have inspected the holdings of the aforesaid deceased at (address of lands valued) and, in my opinion, the said holdings would, on the date of swearing hereof, have been of the value of (amount in words and figures) if then offered for sale on the open market.

Sworn &c.

CERTIFICATE OF MARKET VALUE

Re: Estate of (name of deceased) deceased late of (address of deceased)

I/We (name of solicitor or firm), as solicitor(s) for the administrator of the estate of the aforementioned deceased, hereby certify that the current market value of the deceased's dwelling house at (address) would not exceed (value in figures and words).

I/We confirm that the said property, while realty, comprises a dwelling house only.

Yours &c.

Renunciation by the Person Entitled to Apply for a Grant of Letters of Administration with Will Annexed

Where the person entitled to apply for a grant of letters of administration with the will annexed renounces, the person next entitled may apply and the renunciation by the person with prior title must be exhibited in the oath of administrator with will annexed and included among the proofs submitted for the grant. **25–10**

Essential Proofs

1. Form S1 (postal application form) must be lodged with all applications submitted by post; **25–11**
2. The original will (and codicils, if any);
3. A certified copy of the will;
4. Oath of administrator with will;
5. Copy oath of administrator with will;
6. Administration bond;
7. Inland Revenue Affidavit (CA 24 (2010 edition) for deaths after 5 December 2001 and CA24 (2000 edition) where the deceased died before 5 December 2001);
8. Affidavit of market value or certificate of market value;
9. Death certificate of the testator;

10. Charitable bequest form (form PAS3 is required where there are charitable bequests in the will relating to Irish charities);
11. Renunciation of administration with the will annexed by person first entitled to a grant.

OATH OF ADMINISTRATOR WITH THE WILL

THE HIGH COURT
PROBATE

The Probate Office/The District Probate Registry at

In the estate of (name of deceased), late of (address), deceased.

I, (name of applicant) of (address), aged 18 years and upwards, make oath and say that I believe the paper writing hereunto annexed, and marked by me, to contain the true and original last will [*or* last will with codicils] of late of [*address and description*], deceased, and that same was made by the said [name of deceased] after attaining the age of years, and that he did not intermarry with any person after the making of same, and *that he did therein name CD residuary legatee and devisee and that the said CD duly renounced his rights,on which renunciation dated the day of 20 I have signed my name and marked the letter 'A' prior to the searing thereof, and that I am the lawful widow of the said deceased,* that I will well and faithfully administer the estate of the said testator, by paying his just debts and the legacies bequeathed by his said will [*or* will and codicils] and distributing the residue of his estate according to law; and that I will exhibit a true and perfect inventory of the said estate, and render a true account thereof whenever required by law so to do; and that the testator died at [address] on the day of [*where application is made in a District Probate Registry, add*: and had at the time of his death a fixed place of abode at within the district of] and that the whole of the personal estate of the said testator amounts in value to the sum of [*the gross personal estate, without any deductions for debts*] and that the whole of the real estate of the said testator which devolves on and vests in his legal personal representative is of the market value of [*the amount shown in the affidavit of market value*] and no more to the best of my knowledge, information and belief.

Sworn, &c.

RENUNCIATION OF ADMINISTRATION WITH THE WILL ANNEXED

THE HIGH COURT
PROBATE

In the estate of (name of deceased)

Whereas (name of deceased) late of (address), deceased, died on the day of 20 , at [address]

[*where application is made in a District Probate Registry, add* having at the time of his death a fixed place of abode at within the district of] and whereas he made and duly executed his last will [*or* will and codicils] bearing date the day of 20 , and thereof named CD residuary legatee and devisee [*or as the case may be*].

Now I, the said CD aged 18 years and upwards, do declare that I have not intermeddled with the estate of the said deceased, and will not hereafter intermeddle therein with the intent to defraud creditors, and I do hereby expressly renounce my right to letters of administration with the said will of the estate of the said deceased.

Dated

(Signed)

Witness

ADMINISTRATION BOND

THE HIGH COURT

The Probate Office/The District Probate Registry at

I (insert name address and description of applicant and surety/sureties if applicable) am liable in full to pay to the President of the High Court the sum of (insert penal sum twice gross assets of estate reflecting current market value of immovable property) for which payment I bind myself and my executors, administrators and successors and sealed with my seal and dated the (insert day of signing bond) day of (insert month and year of signing bond). The condition of this obligation is that, if the above-named (insert name of applicant) *the lawful widow* of (insert name, address and description of deceased), deceased, and the intended administratix of the estate of the said deceased, do, when lawfully called on in that behalf, make or cause to be made a true inventory of the said estate which has or shall come into his/her hands, possession or knowledge, or into the hands, possession or control of any other person for him/her;

do exhibit the said inventory or cause it to be exhibited in the Probate Office (or in the District Probate Registry at) whenever required by law to do so; do well and truly administer the said estate according to law, paying all the debts owed by the deceased at the time of his death, all death duties payable in respect of the estate of the deceased for which the personal representative is accountable and all income tax and surtax payable out of the estate,

distributing all shares in the estate to those entitled by law thereto and as the law requires him/her; and further, do make or cause to be made a true account of the said administration whenever required by law to do so;

then this obligation shall be void and no effect, but shall otherwise remain in full force and effect.

Signed, sealed and delivered by the within named   Applicant(s) signature and seal

Name of applicant and surety/sureties if applicable	Surety's/sureties' signature and seal [if applicable]

In the presence of
(insert Commissioner's/Solicitor's name)

Commissioner/Solicitor to sign here
Commissioner/Solicitor

Applicant(s) should execute bond before Commissioner/Solicitor on oath[16]

AFFIDAVIT OF MARKET VALUE

THE HIGH COURT
PROBATE

The Probate Office or District Probate Registry at

In the estate of (name of deceased), late of (address), deceased.

I (name of valuer, auctioneer or surveyor) of (address), (state occupation), aged 18 years and upwards, make oath and say as follows:

1. I am acquainted with the value of lands in the vicinity of (address of lands valued) in the County of , where lands belonging to the aforesaid (name of deceased), deceased, are situate.

I have inspected the holdings of the aforesaid deceased at (address of lands valued) and, in my opinion, the said holdings would, on the date of swearing hereof, have been of the value of (amount in words and figures) if then offered for sale on the open market.

Sworn &c.

CERTIFICATE OF MARKET VALUE

Re: Estate of (name of deceased), deceased, late of (address of deceased)

I/We (name of solicitor or firm), as solicitor(s) for the administrator of the estate of the aforementioned deceased, hereby certify that the current market value of the deceased's dwelling house at (address) would not exceed (value in figures and words).

I/We confirm that the said property, while realty, comprises a dwelling house only.

Yours &c.

[16] See Ord.79, r.29, Rules of the Superior Courts 1986.

Application for a Grant of Letters of Administration Intestate by a Son or Daughter Where the Surviving Spouse of the Deceased Renounces

Essential Proofs

1. Form S1 (postal application form) must be lodged with all applications submitted by post; **25–12**
2. Oath of administrator;
3. Copy oath of administrator;
4. Administration bond;
5. Inland Revenue Affidavit (CA 24 (2010 edition) for deaths after 5 December 2001 and CA24 (2000 edition) where the deceased died before 5 December 2001);
6. Death certificate;
7. Affidavit of market value or certificate of market value;
8. Renunciation of administration by surviving spouse.

OATH OF ADMINISTRATOR

The High Court
Probate

In the estate of (name of deceased) late of (address), deceased.

I, (name of applicant) of (address), aged 18 years and upwards, make oath and say that [name of deceased], late of [*address and description*], deceased, died intestate *leaving AB his lawful widow him surviving and that the said AB duly renounced her rights dated the day of 20 on which I have signed my name and marked the letter 'A' prior to the swearing hereof and that I am the lawful son/daughter of the said deceased,* that I will well and faithfully administer the estate of the said deceased by paying his just debts and distributing the residue of the said estate according to law, and that I will exhibit a true inventory of the said estate and render a true account thereof, whenever required by law so to do; that the said deceased died at on the day of [*where application is made in a District Probate Registry, add:* and that the said deceased had at the time of his death a fixed place of abode at within the district of] and that the whole of the personal estate of the said deceased amounts in value to the sum of [*the gross personal estate without any deductions for debts*] and that the whole of the real estate of the said deceased which devolves on and vests in his legal personal representatives is of the market value of [*the amount shown in the affidavit of market value*] and no more, to the best of my knowledge, information and belief.

Sworn, &c.

RENUNCIATION OF ADMINISTRATION

THE HIGH COURT
PROBATE

In the estate of (name of deceased)
Whereas (name of deceased) late of (address), deceased,
died
on the day of 20 , at [*where application is made to a District Probate Registry, add* having at the time of his death a fixed place of abode at within the district of].

And whereas, I AB of (address) am his lawful widow.

Now I, the said AB, aged 18 years and upwards, do hereby renounce all my right to letters of administration of the estate of the said deceased.

Dated
(Signed)

Witness

ADMINISTRATION BOND

THE HIGH COURT

The Probate Office/The District Probate Registry at

I (insert name address and description of applicant and surety/sureties if applicable) am liable in full to pay to the President of the High Court the sum of (insert penal sum twice gross assets of estate reflecting current market value of immovable property) for which payment I bind myself and my executors, administrators and successors and sealed with my seal and dated the (insert day of signing bond) day of (insert month and year of signing bond). The condition of this obligation is that, if the above-named (insert name of applicant) *the lawful son/daughter* of (insert name address and description of deceased) deceased, and the intended administrator/administratix of the estate of the said deceased, do, when lawfully called on in that behalf, make or cause to be made a true inventory of the said estate which has or shall come into his/her hands, possession or knowledge, or into the hands, possession or control of any other person for him/her;

do exhibit the said inventory or cause it to be exhibited in the Probate Office (or in the District Probate Registry at) whenever required by law to do so; do well and truly administer the said estate according to law, paying all the debts owed by the deceased at the time of his death, all death duties payable in respect of the estate of the deceased for which the personal representative is accountable and all income tax and surtax payable out of the estate,

distributing all shares in the estate to those entitled by law thereto and as the law requires him/her; and further, do make or cause to be made a true account of the said administration whenever required by law to do so;

and further do, if so required, render and deliver up the letters of administration in the High Court if it shall hereafter appear that any will was made by the deceased which is exhibited in the said Court, with a request that it be allowed and approved accordingly;

then this obligation shall be void and no effect, but shall otherwise remain in full force and effect.

Signed, sealed and delivered by the within-named	Applicant(s) signature and seal
Name of applicant and surety/sureties if applicable	Surety's/sureties' signature and seal [if applicable]

In the presence of
(insert Commissioner's/Solicitor's name)

Commissioner/Solicitor to sign here
Commissioner/Solicitor

Applicant(s) should execute bond before Commissioner/Solicitor on oath.[17]

AFFIDAVIT OF MARKET VALUE

THE HIGH COURT
PROBATE

The Probate Office or District Probate Registry at

In the estate of (name of deceased intestate), late of (address of deceased), deceased.

I (name of valuer, auctioneer or surveyor) of (address), (state occupation), aged 18 years and upwards, make oath and say as follows:

1. I am acquainted with the value of lands in the vicinity of (address of lands valued) in the County of , where lands belonging to the aforesaid (name of deceased), deceased, are situate.

I have inspected the holdings of the aforesaid deceased at (address of lands valued) and, in my opinion, the said holdings would, on the date of swearing hereof, have been of the value of (amount in words and figures) if then offered for sale on the open market.

Sworn &c.

[17] See Ord. 79, r.29, Rules of the Superior Courts 1986.

CERTIFICATE OF MARKET VALUE

Re: Estate of (name of deceased intestate) deceased, late of (address)

I/We (name of solicitor or firm), as solicitor(s) for the administrator of the estate of the aforementioned deceased, hereby certify that the current market value of the deceased's dwelling house at (address) would not exceed (value in figures and words).

I/We confirm that the said property, while realty, comprises a dwelling house only.

Yours &c.

Rival Applicants[18]

25–13 Order 79, r. 5(3) of the 1986 Rules provides that, where there are conflicting claims for a grant between members of a class with equal entitlement to apply, the grant will be made to such of the claimants as the probate officer may select, having given not less than 21 days' notice to all rival claimants. If any objection is made to the probate officer's selection within that period, the Court may make the selection. The suitability of a person for the office of administrator and the one who best serves the interests of the estate are the main criteria used when making a selection among rival claimants.

25–14 When the probate officer is called upon to exercise his or her discretion under the relevant rule, the probate officer may make an order allowing one applicant to proceed, but only where there are no objections received. If objections are received, then a court application will be necessary.

25–15 Proofs required (to be lodged in the Probate Office):

1. Affidavit from the solicitor for the moving party (setting out the facts, the right of the applicant and details of the rival application and requesting a 21 day order);
2. Fees.

25–16 If the application is in order, the probate officer will make a 21-day order which must then be served on the rival applicant. It can be served personally, but is usually served by registered post. Where, however, objections are received within the 21-day period, the applicant must apply to the Court to resolve the issue. Where no objections are received within the 21-day period, the probate officer will make a further order allowing the applicant to proceed. In order to obtain this order, an affidavit of service must be filed in the first instance.

---

[18] See Chapter 15 – Applications for Grants of Letters of Administration Intestate.

Relevant Legislation/Rules

Order 79, r. 5(3)[19] **25–17**

AFFIDAVIT OF APPLICANT REQUESTING THE PROBATE OFFICER TO SERVE A TWENTY ONE DAY NOTICE ON A RIVAL APPLICANT

THE HIGH COURT
PROBATE

In the estate of (name of deceased intestate) of (address), deceased

I, (name, address and description of applicant), aged 18 years and upwards, make oath and say as follows:

1. The above-named deceased died intestate on the day of 20 and I beg to refer to his death certificate on which, marked with the letter 'A', I have endorsed my name prior to the swearing hereof.

2. The deceased died a bachelor without parent, leaving him surviving this deponent his lawful and only brother and (name and address of rival applicant), his lawful and only sister. He left no nephew or niece, the issue of a predeceased brother or sister.

3. On the day of 20 , (name and business address of applicant's solicitors) lodged on my behalf in the Probate Office an application for a grant of letters of administration intestate of the estate of the said deceased.

4. On the day of 20 , my solicitors were informed by the probate officer that a rival application had been lodged in the Probate Office by (name and business address of rival applicant's solicitors) on behalf of (name of rival applicant).

5. On the day of 20 , my solicitors wrote to (name of rival applicant's solicitors) informing them of my application and requesting them to withdraw the application on behalf of the said (name of rival applicant). I beg to refer to a copy of the said letter marked 'B', on which I have endorsed my name.

6. I am informed that, up to the date of swearing hereof, the application has not been withdrawn.

7. I therefore request the probate officer to issue the 21-day notice pursuant to Order 79 Rule 5(3) of the Rules of the Superior Courts, and direct the same to the said (name of rival applicant).

Sworn, &c.

[19] Probate Office Update: 13 August 2012.

NOTICE TO RIVAL APPLICANTS BY PROBATE OFFICER

The High Court
Probate

In the estate of (name of deceased intestate) of (address), deceased

An application has been made to me on behalf of (name and address of applicant) for an order pursuant to Order 79 Rule 5(3) of the Rules of the Superior Courts giving him liberty to extract a grant of letters of administration intestate in the estate of the above-named deceased.

Any objections that you might have to the granting of such an order to the said applicant should be made in writing to me within 21 days of the date of service on you of this notice.

TAKE NOTICE that, in default of the submission of such objections within the aforesaid period, the order will be given to the said applicant as sought.

DATED the day of 20

Signed: (by the probate officer)

Chapter 26

SUCCESSION ACT PRECEDENTS

Introduction

26–01 The legal right of a spouse may be renounced in an ante-nuptial contract made in writing between the parties to an intended marriage or may be renounced in writing by the spouse after marriage and during the lifetime of the testator.[1] Since the enactment of the Civil Partnership and Certain Rights and Obligations of Cohabitants Act 2010, the legal right may also be renounced by an ante-civil partnership contract made in writing between the parties to an intended civil partnership or may be renounced in writing by the civil partner after the civil partnership was entered into and during the lifetime of the testator.[2] During the course of administering and distributing the estate, the personal representatives may have to give notices and assents in furtherance of certain provisions of the Succession Act 1965 (the "1965 Act"). The personal representatives may have to give statutory notices to creditors under s.49 of the 1965 Act,[3] and notices to the surviving spouse or civil partner of the deceased regarding his or her right of election in pursuance of s.115 of the 1965 Act.[4] As the whole estate of a deceased person vests in the personal representatives, they will have to assent to the vesting of property in beneficiaries. Where land is concerned, the assent must be in writing, and further where registered land is involved, the correct form to

---

1 s.113 of the Succession Act 1965; see Chapter 8 – The Legal Right of Spouses and Civil Partners and Applications by Qualified Cohabitants; Chapter 10 – The Cessation of Succession and Legal Rights.

2 s.113 of the 1965 Act.

3 See Chapter 21 – The Administration and Distribution of Estates.

4 See Chapter 8 – The Legal Right of Spouses and Civil Partners and Applications by Qualified Cohabitants.

be used is that as prescribed by the Registration of Title Act 1964, s.61, and since 7 May 2006, the Registration of Title Act 1964 and 2006 by virtue of s.1(2) of the Registration of Deeds and Title Act 2006.[5] The following are specimens of such renunciations, notices and assents.[6]

Renunciation of the Legal Right by a Spouse[7]

26–02 TO ALL WHOM IT MAY CONCERN

I, (name of spouse renouncing) of (address of spouse), the wife/husband of (name of other spouse) of (address) hereby revoke all and any rights or claims to which I may be or may become entitled to any share or interest in the estate of the said (name of spouse) under and by virtue of the provisions of the Succession Act 1965, and particularly under and by virtue of Part IX of the said Act on the death of the said (name of other spouse). I hereby declare that the nature and extent of the said rights referred to above have been explained to me prior to the execution of this renunciation and I am aware of and understand the nature and effect of this renunciation and have executed this renunciation for good and sufficient reasons.

Dated the day of 20 .

Signed by the said (name of spouse renouncing)
in the presence of (name of witness)

A Spouse's Right of Election[8]

26–03 NOTICE WHERE WILL DISPOSES OF ALL THE DECEASED'S PROPERTY

In the estate of (name of deceased), deceased

1. We, (names of personal representatives), being the personal representatives of the aforesaid deceased, late of (address of deceased) who died on the day of 20 hereby give notice to you, being the surviving spouse of the aforesaid deceased, in pursuance of s.115 of the Succession Act 1965.

2. Under and by virtue of his will dated the day of 20 , the aforesaid deceased devised and bequeathed in clause of his will, attached hereto.

---

5 See Chapter 21 – The Administration and Distribution of Estates.

6 See Albert Keating, *Irish Wills Precedents Service* (Dublin: Round Hall, 2009; Albert Keating, *Keating on Probate* (4th ed) (Dublin: Round Hall, 2011); Albert Keating, *First Supplement to the Fourth Edition of Keating on Probate* (Dublin: Thomson Round Hall, 2013).

7 See Chapter 8 –The Legal Rights of Spouses and Civil Partners and Applications by Qualified Cohabitants.

8 *ibid.*

3. You are hereby notified that you may elect to take the devise and bequest given to you in clause of the will attached hereto or your legal right share in pursuance of s.111 of the said Act, as the said devise and bequest was expressed not to be in addition to the said legal right share.

4. You are hereby further notified that, in default of election by you to take either the said devise or bequest in the will attached hereto or the said legal right share, you shall become entitled only to take the said devise and bequest in the will.

5. This right of election given to you in pursuance of s.115 of the said Act shall not be exercisable by you after the expiration of six months from the date of receipt hereof or one year from the day of 20 , being the date when the grant of probate of the deceased's will was first made to us, whichever is the later.

Dated the day of 20

Signed (by the personal representatives)

NOTICE WHERE THE DECEASED LEAVES A WILL AND IS PARTIALLY INTESTATE

In the estate of (name of deceased), deceased

1. We, (names of personal representatives), being the personal representatives of the aforesaid deceased late of (address of deceased) who died on the day of 20 , hereby give notice to you, being the surviving spouse of the aforesaid deceased in pursuance of s.115 of the Succession Act 1965.

2. Under and by virtue of his will dated the day of 20 , the aforesaid deceased devised and bequeathed in clause of his will attached hereto.

3. The aforesaid deceased died intestate in respect of the following property: (The property and value thereof subject to the intestacy should be stated here, and the share the surviving spouse is entitled to, depending on whether or not there are children surviving)

4. You are entitled as spouse to elect to take under and by virtue of the provisions of s.115 of the Succession Act 1965 either:
   (i) Your legal right share under the Act; or
   (ii) Your intestate share in respect of the property not disposed of by the deceased in his will and the devise and bequest given to you in his will.

4. In default of electing between (i) and (ii) of paragraph 4 above, you will be entitled only to your intestate share in respect of the property not disposed of by the deceased in his will and the devise and bequest given to you in his will.

5. This right of election given to you in pursuance of s.115 of the said Act shall not be exercisable by you after the expiration of six months from the date of

receipt hereof or one year from the day of 20 , being the date when the grant of probate of the deceased's will was first made to us, whichever is the later.

Dated the day of 20

Signed (by the personal representatives)

A Spouse's Right of Appropriation[9]

26–04

NOTICE OF RIGHT OF APPROPRIATION OF DWELLING AND HOUSEHOLD CHATTELS

In the estate of (name of deceased), deceased

1. We, (names of personal representatives), being the personal representatives of the aforementioned deceased late of (address of deceased) who died on the day of 20 , hereby give you notice, being the surviving spouse of the aforementioned deceased, pursuant to s.56 of the Succession Act 1965, that you are entitled to require us to appropriate to you the dwelling in which you were ordinarily resident at the time of the death of the deceased and also any household chattels in or towards satisfaction of any share of the estate to which you are entitled in pursuance of s.55 of the said Act.

2. The right of appropriation given to you by s.56 of the said Act may also be exercised by you in relation to the share of any infant for whom you are trustee under s.57 of the said Act or otherwise, if your aforesaid share is insufficient to enable the aforesaid appropriation to be made.

3. Further take notice that, if you fail, neglect or refuse to exercise the aforesaid right of appropriation before the expiration of six months from the receipt of the notice hereof or one year from day of 20 , being the date of the grant of probate of the deceased's will first made to us, the aforesaid right shall not be exercisable thereafter.

4. Confirmation of your intention to exercise the aforesaid right must be notified to us in writing before the expiration of the aforesaid dates.

Dated and signed (by the personal representatives)

[9] See Chapter 8 – The Legal Right of Spouses and Civil Partners and Applications by Qualified Cohabitants.

RENUNCIATION OF THE LEGAL RIGHT BY A CIVIL PARTNER[10]

TO ALL WHOM IT MAY CONCERN **26–05**

I, (name of civil partner renouncing) of (address of civil partner), civil partner of (name of other civil partner) of same address hereby revoke all and any rights or claims to which I may be or may become entitled to any share or interest in the estate of the said (name of civil partner) under and by virtue of the provisions of the Succession Act 1965, and particularly under and by virtue of Part IX of the said Act on the death of the said (name of other civil partner). I hereby declare that the nature and extent of the said rights referred to above have been explained to me prior to the execution of this renunciation and I am aware of and understand the nature and effect of this renunciation and have executed this renunciation for good and sufficient reasons.

Dated the day of 20

Signed by the said (name of civil partner renouncing)
in the presence of (name of witness)

A CIVIL PARTNER'S RIGHT OF ELECTION[11]

NOTICE WHERE WILL DISPOSES OF ALL
THE DECEASED'S PROPERTY **26–06**

In the estate of (name of deceased), deceased

1. We, (names of personal representatives), being the personal representatives of the aforesaid deceased late of (address of deceased), who died on the day of 20 , hereby give notice to you, being the surviving civil partner of the aforesaid deceased, in pursuance of s.115 of the Succession Act 1965.

2. Under and by virtue of his will dated the day of 20 , the aforesaid deceased devised and bequeathed in clause of his will attached hereto.

3. You are hereby notified that you may elect to take the devise and bequest given to you in clause of the will attached hereto or your legal right share in pursuance of s.111 of the said Act, as the said devise and bequest was expressed not to be in addition to the said legal right share.

4. You are hereby further notified that, in default of election by you to take either the said devise or bequest in the will attached hereto or the said legal right share, you shall become entitled only to take the said devise and bequest in the will.

5. This right of election given to you in pursuance of s.115 of the said Act shall

[10] *ibid.*

[11] See Chapter 8 – The Legal Right of Spouses and Civil Partners and Applications by Qualified Cohabitants.

not be exercisable by you after the expiration of six months from the date of receipt hereof or one year from the day of 20 , being the date when the grant of probate of the deceased's will was first made to us, whichever is the later.

Dated the day of 20

Signed (by the personal representatives)

NOTICE WHERE THE DECEASED LEAVES A WILL AND IS PARTIALLY INTESTATE

In the estate of (name of deceased), deceased

1. We, (names of personal representatives), being the personal representatives of the aforesaid deceased late of (address of deceased) who died on the day of 20 , hereby give notice to you being the surviving civil partner of the aforesaid deceased in pursuance of s.115 of the Succession Act 1965.

2. Under and by virtue of his will dated the day of 20 , the aforesaid deceased devised and bequeathed of his will attached hereto.

3. The aforesaid deceased died intestate in respect of the following property: (The property and value thereof subject to the intestacy should be stated here and the share the surviving civil partner is entitled to, depending on whether or not there are children surviving)

4. You are entitled as civil partner to elect to take under and by virtue of the provisions of s.115 of the Succession Act 1965 either:
   (i) Your legal right share under the Act; or
   (ii) Your intestate share in respect of the property not disposed of by the deceased in his will and the devise and bequest given to you in his will.

5. In default of electing between (i) and (ii) of paragraph 4 above, you will be entitled only to your intestate share in respect of the property not disposed of by the deceased in his will and the devise and bequest given to you in his will.

6. This right of election given to you in pursuance of s.115 of the said Act shall not be exercisable by you after the expiration of six months from the date of receipt hereof or one year from the day of 20 , being the date when the grant of probate of the deceased's will was first made to us, whichever is the later.

Dated the day of 20 .

Signed (by the personal representatives)

A Civil Partner's Right of Appropriation[12]

NOTICE OF RIGHT OF APPROPRIATION OF DWELLING AND HOUSEHOLD CHATTELS **26–07**

In the estate of (name of deceased), deceased

1. We, (names of personal representatives), being the personal representatives of the aforementioned deceased late of (address of deceased) who died on the day of 20 , hereby give you notice being the surviving civil partner of the aforementioned deceased, pursuant to s.56 of the Succession Act 1965, that you are entitled to require us to appropriate to you the dwelling in which you were ordinarily resident at the time of the death of the deceased and also any household chattels in or towards satisfaction of any share of the estate to which you are entitled in pursuance of s.55 of the said Act.

2. The right of appropriation given to you by s.56 of the said Act may also be exercised by you in relation to the share of any infant for whom you are trustee under s.57 of the said Act or otherwise, if your aforesaid share is insufficient to enable the aforesaid appropriation to be made.

3. Further take notice that, if you fail, neglect or refuse to exercise the aforesaid right of appropriation before he expiration of six months from the receipt of the notice hereof or one year from day of 20 , being the date of the grant of probate of the deceased's will first made to us, the aforesaid right shall not be exercisable thereafter.

4. Confirmation of your intention to exercise the aforesaid right must be notified to us in writing before the expiration of the aforesaid dates.

Dated and signed (by the personal representatives)

Specimen Statutory Notice to Creditors under Section 49 of the Succession Act 1965[13]

STATUTORY NOTICE TO CREDITORS **26–08**

In the estate of (name of testator/intestate), late of (address of testator/intestate)

Notice is hereby given, pursuant to s.49 of the Succession Act 1965, that particulars in writing of all claims against the estate of the above-named deceased who died on the day of 20 (probate/letter of administration of his estate was granted to the executors/administrator on the day of 20) should be furnished to the undersigned solicitors for the executors/administrator on or before the day of 20 , after which date the assets will be distributed having regard only to the claims furnished.

[12] See Chapter 8 – The Legal Right of Spouses and Civil Partners and Applications by Qualified Cohabitants.

[13] See Chapter 21 – The Administration and Distribution of Estates.

Dated this day of 20

Name and address of Solicitors

Assent by Personal Representatives to Unregistered Land[14]

26–09 We, (names of personal representatives), the personal representatives of (name of deceased) late of (address of deceased), deceased, hereby assent to the vesting in (name of beneficiary) of ALL THAT AND THOSE the land and premises situate at (state where) for all the estate and interest of the aforesaid (deceased's name) therein at the time of his death.

In witness whereof we have hereunto set our hands this day of 20

This form is sufficient to assent and convey the interest to which the beneficiary is entitled to in the will and it may be registered in accordance with the Registration of Deeds and Title Act 2006, and formerly in compliance with the Registration of Deeds Act 1707.[15] This form may be extended to include other matters like, for example, a reference to the will of the deceased and the grant of probate made in relation to it. However, the above specimen will be sufficient to satisfy the provisions of s.53 of the 1965 Act. An assent by the personal representatives to registered land must be done in accordance with s.61 of the Registration of Title Act 1964 and in the form required by the Land Registration Rules 2012.[16] There is no discretion as regards the form the documents should take in assenting to registered land; they must be drafted in compliance with the rules and forms prescribed by the 2012 Rules.

[14] *ibid.*

[15] See Registration of Deeds and Title Act 2006. Part 3 repealed the whole of the Registration of Deeds Act 1707.

[16] See Registration of Deeds and Title Act 2006, Part 3 (Registration of Deeds) and Part 4 (Other Amendments to Registration of Title Act 1964).

INDEX